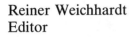
Reiner Weichhardt
Editor

Assistant Director
NATO Economics Directorate

NATO

The Soviet Economy: A New Course?

Colloquium

1-3 April 1987

Brussels

OTAN

L'économie soviétique à un tournant?

Colloque

1-3 avril 1987

Bruxelles

First edition 1988
ISBN-92-845-0038-9

This is the latest in a series bringing together papers presented at the NATO
Colloquia organised by the NATO Economics and Information Directorates
on economic issues in the Communist World. For further information please
write to the Director, Information Directorate, NATO, 1110 Brussels,
Belgium.

The articles contained in this volume represent the views of the authors and do
not necessarily reflect the official opinions or policies of individual member
countries of NATO.

Printed in Belgium by Imprimerie Malvaux s.a., rue Delaunoy, 69 -
1080 Bruxelles.

4

1002745128

The Soviet Economy at a New Course?

L'économie soviétique à un tournant?

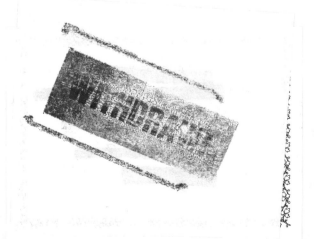

Contents

Opening Speech by the Acting Secretary General of NATO Ambassador Marcello Guidi

Permettez-moi tout d'abord de vous souhaiter la bienvenue au nom de l'OTAN. Nous sommes bien conscients que le succès de ce genre de colloque dépend, dans une large mesure, des efforts que vous autres, participants, déployez avant l'ouverture des travaux — en préparant vos communications — puis en séance même. Nous sommes persuadés que vos contributions nous permettront, sinon d'apporter des réponses définitives aux questions évoquées, du moins de progresser dans l'évaluation de la situation actuelle de l'économie soviétique. J'espère qu'en échange, vous ne repartirez pas avec un sentiment de frustration et que votre participation vous aura paru enrichissante.

Je constate, à en juger par la qualité des personnes présentes à ce seizième colloque économique de l'OTAN, que nous pouvons compter sur une somme d'expérience et de connaissance particulièrement élevée. Comme vous le savez, nous essayons toujours de faire appel à des compétences que nous considérons complémentaires en choisissant les orateurs dans les milieux de la recherche, aussi bien que dans le monde des affaires. Je crois que nous avons cette fois composé une tribune aussi brillante que l'exigeait le thème du colloque.

When we looked at the impact of new technologies on the Soviet economy, during the NATO Economics Colloquium in April 1985, the Gorbachev era was barely a few weeks old. At that time, it was too early to say whether Mr. Gorbachev would bring anything new and different to the Soviet economy. Now, after two years, we have a better basis for examining this question.

During your deliberations you will look behind the numerous Soviet announcements since 1985 to see to what degree the changes are reflected in reality. You will also be called on to gaze into the crystal ball and try to forecast future developments, particularly through the period of the 1986-1990 Five-Year Plan. Since Gorbachev's approach may look different for various economic sectors, we are particularly interested in the performance of the energy, agriculture, industry and defence areas. As always, it is worthwhile to have a close look at Soviet plans for foreign economic relations, even more so at a time when Soviet leaders are talking of new trade and cooperation policies, such as joint ventures with Western firms in the USSR.

I look forward to your deliberations on a fascinating subject. It is readily apparent that we must comprehend Mr. Gorbachev's economic strategy, and the chance of its success, if we are to understand today's Soviet Union. We all owe you a great debt for your contribution to that understanding. I thank you again and wish you an enjoyable and interesting stay in Brussels.

Observations liminaires

de M. Jean-Claude Renaud,
Directeur des Affaires économiques, OTAN

L'OTAN est une organisation de caractère essentiellement politique et militaire, dans laquelle l'économie ne joue qu'un rôle de support, limité, mais essentiel à nos yeux, aussi bien pour ce qui concerne l'examen des problèmes économiques qui affectent les Alliés que pour ceux qui caractérisent les systèmes en vigueur au sein du Pacte de Varsovie. C'est dans cette seconde perspective que se situe le présent colloque.

Certains ont tendance à croire que, contrairement aux choses de la politique, les données économiques relèvent d'un jugement objectif et infaillible, à l'image des données scientifiques. Les discussions que nous allons avoir démontreront que tel n'est pas le cas. Nous n'aurons pas à nous prononcer sur le point de savoir si l'URSS est en voie de démocratisation, mais à déterminer si elle est en voie de modernisation, comme le souhaite Monsieur Gorbatchev : tel est le « tournant » auquel se réfère le titre de ce colloque. Et il apparaîtra vite que, sur l'ampleur de ce tournant, sur son existence même, les avis divergeront, d'autant plus que nous vous demanderons de vous attacher, davantage qu'aux textes et aux discours quasi quotidiens du Secrétaire Général, aux réalités pratiques de la Russie d'aujourd'hui.

In this respect and since such a debate would have been of great interest for him, let me evoke the memory of our Norwegian friend, Thorolf Rafto, who died a few months ago after a long illness. All those who knew him will remember his passionate interventions, his warmth and his sympathy. We shall miss him this year, as we missed him last year, when we were still hoping to see him again.

9

The Soviet Twelfth Five-Year Plan

Philip Hanson

Introduction

Mikhail Gorbachev, like Peter the Great and Stalin, is an energetic leader who wants to modernise Russia. He has come to power at what can plausibly be represented as a turning-point in Soviet history. If the trends of the recent past in Soviet economic performance are not reversed, the USSR will slide down the economic league-table of nations. The Soviet official annual handbook of statistics has shown no further « catching-up » on the US economy for the past decade; in other words, the ratio of Soviet to US net material product, on Soviet official measures, has not changed since the mid-1970s[1]. That is one measure of Gorbachev's problem. When he refers to the future of socialism in the world depending on its economic performance, and when he says that the recent (official) growth rate of around 3 percent is inadequate and « at least 4 » is needed[2], he is defining what he apparently sees as his historic mission. There are times, indeed, when the naive observer wonders if Gorbachev is not pursuing modernization and economic acceleration at the expense of his own security of tenure as leader. At all events, economic acceleration and technological modernization are virtually the sum of his agenda. The plan for 1986-90 is a crucial stage in his pursuit of the strategy of *uskorenie* - acceleration.

It is not surprising, therefore, that the plan is more ambitious than other recent Soviet five-year plans. Nor is it surprising that it contains some sharp changes of priorities. What is not so clear is whether this is a perilously over-ambitious or merely a routinely over-ambitious plan; whether it calls for priority changes that are a source of serious internal political conflict; and whether it is at odds with the restructuring of economic organization that Gorbachev also claims to be pursuing. Those are the most basic questions to be addressed in this paper.

The Main Features of the Plan

Table 1 illustrates the slowdown of the Soviet economy during the Brezhnev era. That slowdown did not end with Brezhnev's death. Nor, for that matter, did it appear to end with Gorbachev's assumption of the party leadership. Indeed growth between 1984 and 1985 was exceptionally slow. (The most widely-used Soviet official measures of national income, given in Table 1, do not show this, but other Soviet official measures of national income growth — in current prices and in 1973 prices — do.) However, there are some grounds for thinking that there

10

was an underlying improvement in 1985-86. This was masked by unusually unfavourable weather in 1985 and by the impact of the anti-alcohol campaign, with little or no provision of extra consumer-goods to offset the effect of the enforced cut in alcohol sales[3]. Thus, despite appearances, there is something to be said for the view that Gorbachev's personnel changes and general new-broom effect had begun to raise the tempo of production growth before the start of the plan.

The Brezhnevian slowdown had several causes. One that is generally agreed to have been important was a slowdown of the growth of the labour-force. Another generally accepted reason for the slowdown is the increasing real cost of natural resource exploitation as the more easily accessible reserves of fuels and minerals become depleted. The leadership might have tried to offset these tendencies by raising or even maintaining the growth rate of the capital stock. This however would have meant raising the share of investment in national income, at the expense of consumption or defence or both. The view is now widely held by both Western and Soviet economists that the Brezhnev leadership indeed compounded the problem by deliberately slowing the growth of investment and by pursuing a branch pattern of investment which created capacity bottlenecks, particularly in extractive industries. (The timing, scale and sometimes even the direction of recent Soviet priority shifts between investment, consumption and defence, however, are very difficult to assess[4].)

There are other considerations whose bearing on the Soviet slowdown is less clear. One is the inertia and drift that seemed to become more pervasive in Soviet life after the early 1970s. It is obvious that the Soviet economic system, with its lack of competitive pressure and its incentives for production units to hoard, not economise on, resources will generally operate with a large margin of operational slack or « X-inefficiency ». What is not clear is whether that margin was tending to increase in the 1970s and early 1980s. If it was, a policy of creative beastliness — sacking elderly office-holders, breaking up cosy little mutual-protection circles among the officials, imposing high targets and raising anxiety levels all round — might have quite a substantial pay-off. That is to say, it would do nothing for peace and tranquillity but it might do a surprising amount for the production statistics. If, however, the economy had never been very far from its (system-constrained) production-possibility frontier, tauter plans and tougher personnel policies might only make things worse.

The second problematic consideration is technological performance. Nobody any longer doubts that the traditional Soviet economic system is worse than modern capitalism at introducing and diffusing new products and processes across a wide range of technologies. This impedes the

11

growth of Soviet productivity and average levels of material prosperity. The practical question for the Soviet authorities is what they can do about it.

Is there a politically acceptable economic reform which could significantly improve innovation? If there is, it would presumably entail substantial institutional changes giving greater independence to enterprises. Such a change is unlikely to be compatible with a regime of taut production targets — if indeed it is compatible with any sort of mandatory targets for enterprises. In stressing the innovation issue and speaking of «fundamental restructuring» and «radical reform», Gorbachev has implied that something like this was part of his strategy for the long-term. In fact the package of organizational changes that is being introduced is not radical[5]. Nonetheless, it is meant to make Soviet enterprises capable of greater flexibility and initiative. This aim is incompatible with taut plans.

The 1986-90 plan embodies a strategy of pressure rather than reform. It sets generally high targets, including some that are downright extravagant. It treats the technology problem as amenable to closer central direction (the more centrally-controlled system of product-quality monitoring under the State Standards Committee, for example) and to shifts in centrally-decreed resource allocation. Current expenditure on science is to grow at 5.9 percent a year and capital investment in science at 11.2 percent a year (Ryzhkov's report to the Supreme Soviet, *Izvestiya* June 19, 1986). In general, inputs into the research, development and innovation process have been set to grow much faster than before.

The working assumption seems to be that, at any rate in the medium term, faster growth is to be obtained by pressure to reduce organizational slack and by policy changes (not reform) involving three main visible changes in priorities: a larger resource share for investment as against consumption, for investment in the engineering sector as against investment in agriculture, light industry, transport and social infrastructure, and for R and D and high-technology industries as against everything else. A resource shift which may be present but is hard to detect with any reliability is from investment in military hardware production plants to investment in civilian engineering. The rationale of this, if it is indeed being attempted, would be that a cluster of electronics-based technologies with both military and civilian applications needs to be given a stronger foundation now for the sake of both the civilian economy and military hardware capabilities in the future.

Tables 2-4 illustrate these points. Table 2 shows that the main aggregate targets have been set (in terms of the growth rates required) above the performance levels of 1981-85, and in most cases above the planned growth of the previous five-year plan period. Investment is supposed to grow much faster than was planned for 1981-85, and will probably be reported to have grown faster than planned. Reported investment growth usually exceeds planned; it contains an element of concealed inflation, which helps, and it is an input rather than an output measure, and the system is good at using lots of inputs. By contrast, the planned growth of per capita real income, an official number whose derivation is mysterious but whose purpose is clearly to flatter, is below what was planned for 1981-85. The figures in the table for 1991-2000 are inferred from the guideline targets for 1986-2000 and the guideline targets for 1986-90. Unlike the real per capita income figures, these perspective-plan numbers are mysterious in both derivation and purpose. It appears, for example, that the labour force in material production in the 1990s is planned to shrink (assuming that national income produced grows at not more than 0.5 percent per annum faster than national income utilised — though why it should be in the habit of doing that in the first place is yet another mystery). I assume that the targets in the long-term plan are derived by what Soviet managers call the 2P4S formula[6].

Table 3 contains a selection of major product targets in physical terms. The tendency has been to set relatively slack targets for those few items amongst the key materials which have had quite strong growth recently — natural gas and mineral fertilisers, for instance — but to set distinctly ambitious targets for the more numerous items whose recent growth has been slow or negative. One possible interpretation is that there has been some effort to avoid taut planning — but only in those relatively few cases where this was compatible with the aim of faster overall economic growth.

So far as output targets are concerned, the really exotic targets are mostly in electronics. The output of industrial robots is supposed to rise from 13,200 to 28,600, that of machining centres from 2,500 to 10,700, numerically controlled machine tools from 17,700 to 34,200 and process control devices containing microprocessors from 200 to 2,000 (the last of these probably excludes devices containing imported microprocessors)[7].

The expansion of engineering output is at the heart of Gorbachev's strategy. The emphasis is on a linked set of priorities: investment to expand and modernise the engineering sector itself (probably mostly in capacity to produce civilian and dual-purpose items rather than items that are exclusively military, like ships, tanks and guns — see below); a rapid increase in engineering output and the supply of domestic machinery for domestic investment; a rapid growth in equipment investment, with the share of equipment in total investment spending set to rise; a rapid growth in the volume of research and development (R and D) activity and testing and pilot-plant facilities. The direction of these priority changes is surely sensible; technological change affects all sectors of a modern economy, but R and D and engineering are the sectors which generate most of it. The problem discussed in the next section is whether the scale and speed of the planned shift, rather than its direction, are a source of risk.

Table 4, together with its footnotes, is from a forthcoming paper by Robert Leggett. It is doubtful if we can go much further at present in assembling a picture of the planned allocation of investment. The shifts in that allocation are marked. As has already been observed, the engineering sector is assigned a substantially increased share of investment. So are communications, the chemical sector and (continuing a past trend) the fuel and energy sector. Apparently the total share of light industry, timber and woodworking, building materials, construction and the service sector is being cut back. Indications that the share of military industry in investment is also being cut back are given in footnote 3 of the table; Campbell, in a recent paper, reaches the same general conclusion[8].

The consumer's share of output, and the consumer sector's share of investment are both, apparently, being squeezed. It is not simply that gross investment is set to grow faster than national income utilised (a somewhat inconclusive comparison, since the latter is net of depreciation); the «accumulation» share of national income utilised is set to increase[9]. It is true that in a generally ambitious plan this still leaves room — on paper — for useful growth in per capita consumption, but the informal priorities of the established planning tradition tend to work against consumption when the plan is being implemented. The shift from Brezhnevian priorities is clear. The only proviso to be attached to that conclusion is that the planners probably envisage some efficiency gains in the consumer sector from an enlargement of the legal private sector and the small-cooperative sector. What gains can really be expected from the very limited liberalization of ownership arrangements, however, is not clear.

Consistency and Feasibility

The plan is obviously ambitious. This is true both of the aggregates of output relative to inputs and in several important sectors and product-groups. The slowdown in the growth of capital and labour inputs, evident in the past decade (Table 1), is expected to continue in 1986-90. Ryzhkov at the XXVII Party Congress said that «basic production funds» (fixed capital in material production) were expected to increase by only 30 percent (5.4 percent a year) and the labour force in material production by only 0.5 percent (0.1 percent a year)[10]. So output per unit of inputs, in a highly aggregated and abstract sense, is expected to grow faster than in the past. How far so-called «total factor productivity» growth has slowed (or even gone negative) in recent years, compounding the effects of slower input growth, is a controversial question. If it has, there is an even more controversial question: why? Worsening innovation performance? Deteriorating morale and effort, affecting activities other than innovation? Deteriorating average weather or deteriorating natural-resource conditions, not captured in the input measures?[11] What is clear is that an enormous improvement is required in productivity on almost any measure: apparent total factor productivity, labour productivity and capital productivity.

Soviet economists share this assessment. Academician Abel Aganbegyan has a rather idiosyncratic (and mysteriously derived) measure of total factor productivity growth, which is a stable 1.4 percent a year in 1976-85 and has to accelerate to 2.1-2.7 percent a year if the five-year plan targets are to be met[12]. Shatalin has what looks like a CIA-type measure of total factor productivity growth, according to which it has been declining over time to only 0.6 percent a year in 1981-85; he estimates that it has to accelerate to about 2 percent a year for the 1990 plan targets to be met[13].

Several Western specialists have looked at the international consistency of the plan and the feasibility of particular elements in it. Only a very broad summary of the conclusions will be given here[14]. So far as the key area of industrial strategy is concerned, Noren concludes that the planned growth of machinery output and steel output are not obviously out of line with one another, and that machinery output growth is not obviously out of line with equipment investment growth. In these respects Noren agrees with Levine and Roberts, and they also agree that supplies of non-energy raw materials may be a bottleneck. Levine and Roberts, however, are doubtful about the feasibility of planned equipment investment growth, given the planned growth of machinery output. Leggett tends to agree with them on this point, rather than with Noren. The crucial matter on which all three analyses are agreed is that achievement of the overall output target depends on an implausibly large improvement in productivity growth[15].

All these assessments, whether the method is simple or sophisticated, rest on the extrapolation of past input-output relationships. One problem is the influences on input productivity which are particularly hard to gauge, such as changes in morale and effort, changes in average weather and changes in inter-branch supply imbalances, or bottlenecks. It is possible that there is considerable scope for luck with the weather, the correction of past imbalances and the new-broom effect of the new leader to improve factor productivity growth more than is generally thought plausible. On the whole, though, the likelihood is that the targets for industrial and for total material output are simply too high to

15

be reached.

Shortfalls in agriculture have played a large part in recent Soviet economic difficulties. The farm sector contributes about a fifth of national income (the share happens at present to be about 19 percent both in the CIA calculations of Soviet GNP and in Soviet official measures of NMP produced). In addition to the direct effect of fluctuations in agricultural output on total output, the indirect effects through supplies to the food processing and textile industries are considerable. The effects of food shortages on workers' incentives and political stability are unknowable, but Soviet policymakers in the post-Stalin era have generally acted as though they feared the worst, and have committed large resources to agricultural investment and food imports. The present plan is not so investment-oriented as to downgrade the farm sector in any marked way. The investment share of the agro-industrial complex as a whole seems to be at least maintained (Table 4). Within the « complex » there has been a reduction in investment priority for agriculture proper and an increase for the storage, transportation and processing of food[16]. Soon after he took office, Gorbachev had seemed to threaten some drastic changes in the priority for agriculture. In June 1985 he said about agriculture : « We have reached here the rational limits of building up investment. » In September 1985 he hinted that food price subsidies might be cut[17]. In the event his revisionism over farm and food policy has not so far been as striking as these early speeches suggested. He has moderated the growth of the enormous farm investment programme (inter alia by halting the grandiose scheme for diverting Siberian rivers), but that is all.

The targets for farm production are ambitious, but not uniformly so. As with basic industrial materials and intermediates, a sharp and implausible growth acceleration is sought in the output of those products whose output has been lagging badly, while the growth targeted for more successful branches is modest. The livestock sector (particularly poultry) has been growing tolerably well since 1982, but the original Brezhnev Food Programme targets for meat and eggs in 1990 have been revised slightly downwards in the plan; the target for meat remains high by the standards of the recent past, but it is much less demanding than what is expected for grain (Table 3), and the growth targeted for milk and eggs is actually below what was achieved in 1981-85.

There is a fair chance of better average weather in 1986-90 than in 1981-85. The contribution that can make to grain output has already been illustrated by the 1986 harvest. In addition, the area sown to grain will probably be stabilised after its recent reduction, and an extension of the planting of high-yield varieties and of the use of agrochemicals could generate at least some significant increase in grain production, even if

16

the outcome remained well short of the target. That in turn is compatible with a substantial growth of output from the livestock sector. An assessment by Barbara Severin of the livestock feed requirements in the plan suggests that continued improvements in the balance of concentrates and roughages in the feed supply, on top of the simple quantitative improvement in feed supply could bring livestock herds and output closer to planned levels than the likely shortfall from feed unit targets might suggest. Severin concludes that a substantial improvement in food supplies to the population is by no means impossible. Per capita supplies of meat grew at only 0.6 percent a year on average between 1975 and 1985 (and actually fell for a time in the early 1980s); if meat imports are not cut, per capita meat supplies could rise by 3 percent a year, Severin concludes, between 1985 and 1990; if meat imports were ended the increase could be about 2 percent a year[18].

The tensions in the plan, therefore, are to be found in the industrial sector above all. From the relationships in the past between large aggregates like « machinery output » and « equipment investment », it seems likely that they will arise mainly in bottlenecks between total industrial capacity and total industrial output (reflected in both labour and capital productivity improving less than planned); between capacity and output in the engineering sector in particular, and perhaps also between non-fuel material supplies and total industrial output[19]. The output of the machine-building and metalworking (MBMW) sector is supposed to grow at 7.4 percent a year and investment in that sector (with particular emphasis on machinery investment) at no less than 12.5 percent a year.

This problem is not, in my view, one that will necessarily show up in official Soviet data for large aggregates like MBMW output. There is an element of concealed inflation in that output series already. If the central authorities exert pressure for higher growth rates, the engineering enterprises and branch ministries can cope in part by obtaining more covert price rises — mainly on phoney « new » products — than before. The increased emphasis on technological change will make this easier. It is true that the new quality control arrangements are designed to restrict this kind of fudging, but nothing has been done so far to reduce the *de facto* supremacy of output targets, and the reckoning at present must be that the old-style priorities will prevail. In the civilian engineering sector those priorities can be met by appearances rather than reality. To some extent (the precise extent is a matter of controversy[20]), the concealed inflation in machinery output carries over into the machinery investment figures; to that extent the apparent outcome there is also likely to be better than the real outcome. In this sense, Gorbachev's priorities happen to be those which the Soviet system is good at pretending to meet.

What this means in practice is that the problems are likely to show up in only limited gains in the output of consumer goods, basic materials and intermediates despite apparently large gains in the size and modernity of the capital stock; export performance in manufactures will probably also improve less than it should do, given the accelerated growth of R and D and production of new types of machinery.

This is not to say that there will be no improvements in these areas. The prospects can be illustrated by the case of computers. Total output of computers and related equipment is supposed to rise by 18 percent a year. It would be odd if that did not include some improvement in the USSR's annual increments of computer capacity. But a real, 18 percent per annum improvement? Where exactly will all the additional good-quality microprocessors come from, and the sophisticated design and manufacturing equipment to support this rate of increase? Two answers which suggest themselves — the military and the West — are considered below. On the whole, however, the odds are that the main shortfalls will be in quality, technical level and real output, but that such shortfalls will be only poorly reflected in offical Soviet statistics.

Foreign Trade

The likely role of foreign trade in the 1986-90 plan is discussed by other contributors to this Colloquium. It cannot, however, be left entirely out of a general overview of the plan. My guess is that the Soviet planners are not counting on any very substantial contributions from trade with the West. They may end up obtaining them but they would not be wise to count on them at present, and they show no signs of doing so. Both Gorbachev and Ryzhkov have spoken of the political need to avoid dependence on the West, while at the same time stressing their readiness to engage in some « equitable and mutually beneficial trade with industrially developed capitalist countries » — an assurance that has been programmed into all plan guideline statements for years and reveals nothing about the balance of policymakers' intentions at the time the assurance is uttered. Political considerations are hardly favourable at present (though they might become favourable if there was a breakthrough in superpower arms control negotiations). Moreover, Soviet hard-currency purchasing power prospects have been severely damaged by the fall in world energy prices (despite the recent partial recovery engineered by OPEC).

In these circumstances, the Soviet policymakers and planners must be reckoning to continue the policy of the early 1980s in which machinery and equipment imports from the West grew relatively slowly, amounting to about 8.5 percent of Soviet equipment investment in 1985, against an apparent share of about 30 percent for imports from socialist countries (mainly in Eastern Europe). Moreover, the balance of machinery production and supply, considered merely in terms of aggregate quantities as officially measured, is probably reckoned to require only a modest increase in total imports (see Table 5).

There are, however, some considerations that point to rather more demand for Western machinery. The domestically-produced equipment will often not do, or will perform only poorly, the tasks assigned for it. Pressure from enterprises and ministries for more imported Western machinery will be generated to a greater extent than usual by the high output and investment targets that have been imposed. Neither East European capacity nor Soviet purchasing power within Comecon seems likely to support a further rapid real growth (concealed inflation apart) of equipment imports from Eastern Europe. Soviet capacity to purchase more Western machinery without departing from the low-debt tradition will be enhanced by the probable fall in the volume of food import requirements. Moreover, the Euopean Community's taxpayers seem likely to go on investing enthusiastically in low food prices for the rest of the world, and that helps. (Even when oil is trading at around $15 a barrel the Soviets can obtain grain on world markets via oil (or gas) a great deal more cheaply (in domestic resource costs) than they can produce it at home, and with grain prices currently around $85 a ton, the Soviet gains from trade in grain for oil seem to be not much less than they were three years ago[21].)

Just how these problematic and variable influences on Soviet-Western trade during the plan period are likely to work out, is impossible to say. The best guess seems to be a somewhat lower average volume of food imports from the West and a modest increase in machinery and equipment imports — the latter probably contrary to the central planners' present intentions.

Gainers and Losers

The present five-year plan has been politically contentious. From an early stage in its preparation, Gorbachev seems to have been at loggerheads with the State Planning Committee. The bone of contention was the growth rates to be incorporated in the plan[22]. Eventually higher targets were included in the final version of the plan than had been envisaged in the guidelines. I for one thought that this had something to do with the replacement of Baibakov by Talyzin as the chairman of Gosplan in late 1985. Whether or not Talyzin is in some sense Gorbachev's man, however, the change of chairman has not in fact disposed altogether of the problem — at any rate if the samizdat transcript of Gorbachev's officially unpublished remarks to members of the Union of Writers in June 1986 is reliable. In a remarkable tirade about the resistance being put up against all his reforms, Gorbachev said, «Take Gosplan. For Gosplan we have no central authorities, no General Secretaries, no Central Committee. What they want, they do.» It is true that he went on to assert that he was gradually getting the upper hand over Gosplan. Still, these remarks suggest that the plan itself (not to mention its implementation) should be seen as the outcome of a difficult political struggle. As a result, it may well contain more compromise solutions and unresolved inconsistencies than most recent five-year plans.

What are the conflicts about? No doubt Gosplan is embroiled in disputes about organizational change in the economy, which need not directly concern the choice of national plan targets. It may be, however, that many of the planning officials hold a Brezhnevian set of views about priorities and about the dangers of imposing too much pressure on the system as a whole. That is suggested by some of the discussion in the Gosplan house journal, *Planovoe khozyaistvo*[23]. It is possible that there is a brand of cautious conservatism in the Soviet planning apparatus which is unhappy both about reforms and about the renewed emphasis on investment at the expense of consumption.

Important conflicts in Soviet politics are generally kept away from public view. The most significant conflict that might be going on around the priorities embodied in the plan, would be a conflict between defence and investment demands, rather than between investment and consumption. Several Western analysts have reached the view — already referred to — that part of Gorbachev's strategy is a diversion of investment from the strictly and directly military segment of the engineering (MBMW) sector to the civilian sector. Statements by Gorbachev and Ryzhkov about the allocation of investment within MBMW seem to imply that in 1981-85 the 11 civilian MBMW ministries received about 42 percent of the total, against the nine Military-Industrial Commission (VPK) ministries' 58 percent, whereas in the present plan both groups will get more investment but the proportions may shift to about 56:44 (civilian: military)[24].

What is not known is whether this shift has been upsetting to the military. A plausible interpretation is that the purpose is above all to modernise a cluster of electronics-based industries whose output is not final-stage military production, but whose long-run contribution to the technical level of Soviet military hardware, say in the mid-1990s, could be very large. If the military leadership is satisfied with the present capacity and technology levels of military industry for the needs of military programmes in the meanwhile, this may not be a politically contentious strategy.

There have been signs of friction, nonetheless, between Gorbachev and the military hardware producers, as well as some reduction of the symbolic military presence on big ceremonial occasions. In a speech in Krasnodar in September 1986 (though not in the text as published in the Soviet press), Gorbachev complained of the defence industries' reluctance to help solve problems in civilian equipment. Asked to come up with improvements in farm machinery, he said, they claimed that this was very difficult, apparently contending (Gorbachev asserted) that they found it easier to stick to rockets and the like[25]. Pressure on miliary producers to contribute more to the civilian economy, however, and their resistance to it, both pre-date Gorbachev. In short, there is some evidence of stress between the military sector and Gorbachev, but it is not clear whether it is acute or merely chronic.

Conclusions

Like more newsworthy goings-on at present in the Soviet Union, the five-year plan is hard to assess. It is over-ambitious, but then Soviet five-year plans always are. It incorporates some radical changes in priority from recent Brezhnevian practice. There is an old-fashioned, Stalinist element in it: machinery rules, and exotically high targets are set for it. On the other hand, the farm and energy sectors, which have absorbed such large shares of investment in the recent past, continue to do so, with the latter yet again increasing its share. The productivity gains and technological improvements that are sought are unlikely to be obtained in reality. On the other hand, the shortfalls are likely to be better masked than usual because the new priorities lend themselves so well to the concealed inflation treatment.

In addition, the new-broom effect of the new leadership, together with reasonable luck with the weather, is likely to yield some improvement in growth in the medium term, regardless of the plan. That seems already to have happened in 1986 (see Table 6), and there is no reason to envisage such effects as necessarily very short-lived.

There is a temptation for Western specialists to take Soviet five-year plans too seriously. I have succumbed to it in this paper — which ought to be shorter than it is. The sum of the annual plans frequently turns out to be very different from the five-year plan of which they are supposed to be part, and there is no reason to suppose that the practical importance of the annual plan has been reduced under Gorbachev. Presenting the 1987 annual plan, Talyzin claimed that there had been a change in this respect: instead of planning each year from the achieved level (the expected actual outcome of the current year), he claimed, the 1987 targets were based on the five-year plan — i.e., did not deviate from what was laid down for 1987 in that plan — and on the 1986 annual plan rather than the 1986 expected outcome.

Table 6 is an assembly of some evidence on the nature of the annual/ five-year plan connexion. There is some evidence that for activities where the 1986 target was overfulfilled the 1987 annual plan target has remained at its five-year-plan level instead of being cranked up (the ratchet effect), and is therefore relatively modest. It is unlikely, however, that this treatment has been extended to activities which were below-plan in 1986. Nor is it likely that ad hoc increases above five-year-plan targets for 1987 have been scrupulously avoided; indeed Talyzin several times in his speech remarked that a target was above its originally-planned level. There may have been some move towards a practice of stable five-year plans, but it is unlikely to have gone far. It would be very difficult indeed to make such a practice stick unless the original five-year-plan targets were uniformly slack, so that downward adjustments were seldom forced on the central planners during the five years. The most striking conclusion from Table 6, however, is that it is still virtually impossible to relate published annual to published five-year plan targets. The final version of the five-year plan, as published, contains annual targets for very few items, and in several cases (e.g., investment) different definitions are employed in the annual series in the five-year plan and in the annual plans. I suspect that the five-year plan should still be studied more for the general policy directions and priority changes that it contains than for the particular numbers in it.

The present plan is unlikely to achieve the ambitious technological and industrial goals which the Soviet leadership wants to achieve. On the other hand, the numbers that eventually appear in *Pravda* in January 1991 may play quite well in the Kremlin.

Notes

1. The Soviet measure shows Soviet net material product (NMP) at about two-thirds of US since 1974. The CIA assesses Soviet GNP at about half of US in 1985 (geometric mean of ruble and dollar comparisons) and tending to decline relative to US since 1975 (CIA, *Handbook of Economic Statistics 1986* pp. 38, 39).
2. Speech in Leningrad in May, 1985, published as M.S. Gorbachev, *Nastoichivo dvigat'sya vpered*, Moscow: Politicheskaya literatura, 1985, at. p. 11.
3. Retail sales of «other food goods» (probably mainly alcoholic) were 57.3 bn rubles in 1984, equivalent to 10.3 percent of national income utilised in current prices (derived from *Narkhoz 85* pp. 469 and 409). Something of the order of a 15 percent cut in the volume of alcohol sales between 1984 and 1985 can be inferred from the same source, equivalent to 1.5 percent of national income utilised in 1984. The official national income growth figures given in Table 1, unlike other Soviet official figures which are more obscurely presented in the annual handbook, seem to have been manipulated to conceal this effect — which appears not to have been offset by any significant enhancement of supplies of other consumer goods and services.
4. See R.W. Campbell, «Resource Stringency and the Civilian-Military Resource Allocation,» mimeo, October 1986; Robert E. Leggett, «Soviet Investment Policy: the Key to Gorbachev's Program for Revitalising the Soviet Economy,» forthcoming in US Congress Joint Economic Committee 1987 compendium on the Soviet economy; James Noren, «Soviet Investment Strategy Under Gorbachev,» paper presented at the AAASS meeting in New Orleans, November 1986.
5. See Hanson, «The Shape of Gorbachev's Economic Reform,» forthcoming in *Soviet Economy*, 1987.
6. The 2P4S formula enables one to derive plan target numbers from the *pol. potolok i chetyre steny* — the floor, ceiling and four walls.

7. *Izvestiya*, June 19, 1986.
8. Campbell, op. cit.
9. Derived from Ryzhkov's speech at the Party Congress, *Izvestiya*, March 4, 1986.
10. Ibid.
11. For an analysis of several of these issues see V. Kontorovich, «Soviet Economic Growth Slowdown: Econometric vs. Direct Evidence,» *American Economic Review*, vol. 76 no. 2 (May 1986) and idem, «Utilization of Fixed Capital and Soviet Industrial Growth,» paper presented at the AAASS meeting in New Orleans, November 1986.
12. A.G. Aganbegyan, «Perelom i uskorenie,» *EKO*, 1986 no. 6, pp. 3-25.
13. S. Shatalin, «Sotsial'noe razvitie i ekonomicheskii rost,» *Kommunist*, 1986 no. 14, pp. 59-71.
14. I discuss some of these assessments in more detail in a «Commentary» in the forthcoming US Congress JEC compendium cited in note 4.
15. Noren and Leggett, works cited in note 4; H.S. Levine and B. Roberts, «Soviet Economic Prospects and their National Security Implications,» paper presented at the NATO Workshop on National Security Issues after the 27th Party Congress of the USSR, Brussels, November 1986.
16. Karl-Eugen Waedekin, «Agriculture», in M. McCauley (ed.), *The Soviet Union under Gorbachev*, forthcoming in 1987.
17. A full text of the June speech is in BBC *Summary of World Broadcasts* SU/7976/C/7-19 of June 1985; the Tselinograd speech was broadcast on Soviet TV on September 10, 1985.
18. Barbara Severin, «Solving the Livestock Feed Dilemma: Key to Meeting Food Program Targets,» forthcoming in the US Congress JEC 1987 compendium.
19. Noren, op. cit., Leggett, op. cit., Levine and Roberts, op. cit.
20. See the exchange of views forthcoming in *Soviet Studies* in 1987 between Abram Bergson, Alec Nove and the present author.
21. Author's calculations, updating calculations by Jan Vanous for 1981. A 25 percent increase in the average cost of production of Soviet grain in 1981-85 is assumed, along with the rise in domestic oil production costs projected by Vanous. I have assessed Soviet foreign trade prospects for the late 1980s in more detail in «Soviet Foreign Trade Policies in the 1980s», Berichte des Bundesinstituts fuer ostwissenschaftliche und internationale Studien, 41-1986.
22. See Ed. Hewett, «Gorbachev's Economic Strategy: A Preliminary Assessment,» *Soviet Economy*, Spring 1986.
23. See for example the round-table discussion of the Twelfth Five-Year Plan in *Planovoe khozyaistvo* 1986 no. 1, pp. 9-45.
24. Campbell, op. cit.; Leggett, op. cit., and see footnote 3, Table 4 (which is from Leggett's paper).
25. Soviet TV, September 19; BBC *Summary of World Broadcasts*, September 23, 1985.

Table 1

Soviet medium and long-term plans, 1981-2000

(Soviet official series; average percent per annum growth rates)

A. Soviet official measures

	1966-70	1971-75	1976-80	1981-85	1984	1985	1986
NMP produced	7.7	5.7	4.2	3.5	3.2	3.5[a]	4.1[a]
NMP utilised	7.1	5.1	3.9	3.2	2.6	3.1[a]	3.6[a]
Gross industrial output	8.5	7.4	4.4	3.6	4.2	3.9	4.9
Gross agricultural output[b]	3.9	2.4	1.7	1.1	0.0	0.0	5.1
Investment[b]	7.4	7.2	5.2	3.2	2.0	3.0	8.0
Capital stock	7.5	7.9	6.8	6.0	5.8	5.5	
Electric power	7.9	7.0	4.5	3.6	5.3	3.5	3.6
Three main fuels[c]	5.2	5.4	4.2	2.5	2.7	2.4	4.6

B. CIA estimates[d]

	1966-70	1971-75	1976-80	1981-85	1984	1985	1986
GNP	4.9	3.1	2.3	2.2	1.5	1.6	4.2
Industrial output	6.2	5.4	2.6	2.0	2.5	2.8	3.6
Agricultural output	3.9	−0.4	1.0	2.0	−0.5	−1.7	7.3
Investment	5.3	5.4	4.0	3.2	1.1	2.1	7.5
Capital stock	7.4	8.0	6.9	6.3	6.2	6.1	5.5
Labour (man-hour)	2.0	1.7	1.2	0.7	0.7	0.4	0.6

Notes: General: All output series and the investment and capital-stock series are, in principle, in constant prices, i.e., denote "real" changes. The Soviet official series, however, are known to contain an element of hidden inflation and therefore to be upward-biassed. See also note a.

a : Soviet reported growth rates for 1985 and 1986 are more than usually upward-biassed. See Philip Hanson, "Plan Fulfilment in 1986. A Sideways Look at the Statistics", Radio Liberty Research Bulletin RL 76/87 (February 26, 1987); Jan Vanous in PlanEcon Report, February 11, 1987; *Christian Science Monitor* February 26, 1987, p. 1.

b : For five-year periods, the growth rates shown are those between the total for the period and the total for the preceding five-year period.

c : Oil + gas + coal; author's estimates in terms of standard coal fuel units.

d : At 1982 ruble factor cost. 1986 figures are preliminary.

Sources: Narodnoe khozyaystvo SSSR (various years); *Pravda* January 18, 1987; CIA, *Handbook of Economic Statistics 1986;* CIA and DIA, "Gorbachev's Modernization Program: A Status report", paper prepared for the Subcommittee on Security Economics of the US Congress Joint Economic Committee, March 19, 1987.

Table 2

Soviet medium and long-term plans, 1981-2000

(Soviet official series; average percent per annum growth rates)

	1981-85 plan	1981-85 actual	1986-90 plan	1991-2000 implied plan (¹)
National income ut.	3.4	3.2	4.1	5.1-5.3
Labour productivity (²)		3.1	3.7-4.2	6.5-7.6
Industrial output	4.7	3.7	4.6	4.9-5.2
Ind. lab. productivity	3.6	3.2	4.6	
Agricultural output (³)	2.5	1.1	2.7-3.0	
Investment (³)	2.0	3.4	4.3 (?)	
Per capita real income	3.1	2.3	2.7	3.4-4.6
State & coop. ret. sales	4.2	3.0	5.9 (⁴)	4.1-4.3

Sources : Derived from the annual statistical handbook plus *Pravda* March 5, November 18 and 20, 1981; November 9, 1985; March 4 and June 19 and 20, 1986.

Notes:

(¹) Implied by the original plan guidelines, which gave only ranges for 1986-90 targets. The adoption of single, top-of-the-range figures for most of the 1990 targets implies that the output growth required in 1991-2000 to meet the year 2000 targets will generally be at the bottom of the range of growth rates given in this column.

(²) Labour productivity in net material product produced.

(³) Rates of increase between five-year periods.

(⁴) Non-alcoholic retail sales only. In 1985 "other food goods" (which are probably mostly alcolholic beverages) made up 16.4 % of retail sales.

Table 3

The Soviet Twelfth Five-Year Plan: Selected product-group targets

(Annual output in millions of tons except where specified, with average annual rates of change over the previous five years in parentheses)

	1985 actual	1990 plan
Electricity (bn kwh)	1,545 (3.6)	1,860 (3.8)
Oil	595 (–0,3)	635 (1.3)
Gas (bn cubic meters)	643 (8.1)	850 (5.7)
Coal	726 (0.3)	795 (1.8)
Total, three main fuels	2,096 (2.5)	2,448 (3.2)
Total, all primary energy	2,213	2,644 (3.6)
Rolled steel	108 (1.0)	116-119 (1.4-2.0)
Mineral fertilisers	33 (6.0)	41- 43 (4.3-5.3)
Grain	192 (0.3)	250-255 (5.6-6.1)
Meat (deadweight)	17 (2.5)	21 (4.2)
Milk	98 (1.6)	106-110 (1.5-2.3)
Eggs (bn)	77 (2.5)	80- 82 (0.8-1.3)

Sources : Annual statistical handbook; *Pravda* November 9, 1985 and March 4, June 19 and 20, 1986

25

Philip Hanson

Table 4

USSR: Distribution of investment in the 12th Five-Year Plan ([1])

Sector	Billion Rubles - 1984 Prices		Percentage Increase Plan 1986-90 over 1981-85
	1981-85 (Actual)	1986-90 (Plan)	
Total	843.2	1042	23.6
Productive	614.8	769	25
Industry	300.7	NA	NA
Fuels and power	108.4	147 ([2])	35
Chemicals	22.6	34	50
MBMW	73	100 ([3])	37
Agro-industrial complex	269	343 ([4])	28
Transportation	64.5 ([5])	67 ([5])	4.3 ([5])
Railroads	24.1	25 ([6])	4 ([6])
Communications	5 ([5])	7 ([5])	40[5]
Nonproductive	228.4	273	20

Notes:

([1]) Data for 1981-85 are from *Narodnoye khozyaystov SSSR v 1985.* Plans for 1986-1990 were culled from leadership speeches published in the open literature.

([2]) The Soviets have stated that 180 billion rubles will be spent on the development of the fuel and energy complex in the 12th FYP - a 35 percent increase over 1981-85. Netting out expenditures on pipelines - estimated at 31 billion rubles - yields an estimate for 1986-90 of about 147 billion rubles.

([3]) Estimated. Gorbachev, in a June 1986 speech, stated that the civilian sector of MBMW consumed 5 percent of the total volume of productive investment during 1981-85. This implies about 31 billion rubles was allocated to civilian machinebuilding and about 41 billion rubles for military machinebuilding. The value of total investment for 1986-90 was estimated by assuming an 80 percent growth in the civilian sector and an arbitrary 10 percent growth in the civilian sector and an arbitrary 10 percent growth on the military side.

([4]) Estimated as ⅓ share of total investment.

([5]) Estimated and rounded from data appearing in V. Biryukov, "Transportation and Communications in the New Five-Year Plan", *Planovoye Khozyaystvo,* no. 6, June 1986, pp. 17-26.

([6]) Estimated and rounded.

Source: Robert E. Leggett, "Soviet Investment Policy: the Key to Gorbatchev's Program For Revitalising the Soviet Economy". Forthcoming in US Congress Joint Economic Comittee 1987 compendium on the Soviet economy.

Table 5
Machinery supplies for Soviet equipment investment (bn 1984 rubles)

	1985			1990
	Levine-Roberts	Leggett	Hanson	
Eqpt. investment	66.4	66.4	66.4	91.6([1])
Of which:				
socialist imports	11.2	19.9([2])	20.0([3])	}
non-socialist imp.	7.1	6.6([4])	5.6([3])	33.3([5])
domestic prodn.	48.1	39.9	40.8	58.3([6])

Sources: Levine and Roberts 1986; Leggett 1987; *Vneshnyaya Torgovlya SSSR v 1985.*

Notes:

([1]) Total planned investment assumed to increase between 1985 and 1990 at the same rate as between 1981-85 and 1986-90, so plan 1990 = 1985 actual × 1.236. Planned rise in re-equipment share assumed, following Campbell 1986 and Leggett 1987, to lead to a rise in the equipment share from 37.0 to 41.3 percent. The planned equipment investment in 1990 therefore = 179.5 × 1.236 × 0.413 = 91.6 bn r.

([2]) Implied: "about 30 percent".

([3]) The reported foreign trade ruble values (ETN 1) treated as domestic ruble values. P. Bunich, "Samofinasirovanie osnovnogo zvena", *Voprosy ekonomiki* 1986 no. 10, pp. 14-24, says that machinery imports from the West are paid for domestically at "not less than their import value" and imports from other socialist countries at constant 1982 prices. The former, at least, appears to mean that the Deutschemark, etc. invoice values are simply converted into domestic rubles at the official exchange rates.

([4]) Implied: "about 10 percent".

([5]) Residual: 91.5-58.3.

([6]) Assumed to increase at same rate as total MBMW output between 1985 and 1990 plan (an overall increase of 43 percent).

Table 6
The relationship between the five-year and annual plans,
and why we know so little about it (1985 actual = 100)

	1986 FYP	1986 AP	1986 A	1987 FYP	1987 AP (¹)
National income ut	103.8	103.8	NA	108	NA
National income pr	NA	103.9(²)	104	NA	1.041y
Industrial output	104.3	104.3	104.9	108.9	1.044z, = 1987 FYP
Agricultural output	NA	105.8(³)	NA	NA	107.6
Total investment	NA	103.9(⁴)	NA	NA	1.046y
State centralised inv.	109.9	NA	NA	108.9	NA
Retail sales (⁵)	105.9	103.5/105.6	106	112.2	1.059y
Electricity	NA	103.9	104	"=1987 AP"(⁶)	y+60 bn kwh
Oil	NA	103.6	103	NA	103.7
Gas	NA	104.5	107	NA	"=y+40 bcm =712 bcm" so y=1986 AP
Coal	NA	101.0	103	NA	"=y+10 mn t" "=733.6 mn t" so y=1986 AP

Source (except as specified in footnotes) and definitions: 1986 and 1987 FYP are annual targets specified in the final version of the five-year plan, *Izvestiya* June 20, 1986. 1986 AP and 1987 AP are the annual plan targets given in *Pravda* November 27, 1985 and *Pravda* November 18 and 20, 1986. 1986 A is approximate, expected 1986 actual, derived from the Jan.-Sept. and Jan.-Nov. 1986 results in *Ekon. Gazeta* 1986 nos. 44 and 51. na means not known at the time of writing.

Notes:
(¹) Talyzin gave % planned increases or absolute increments without specifying whether the base from which the increase was measured was 1986 FYP, 1986 AP or 1986 A (expected). In this column y denotes the undentified base, and where available data make it possible to solve for y, the apparent identity is noted in the column. z denotes a base that must be either 1986 FYP or 1986 AP and cannot be 1986 A.
(²) Not announced at the time, but alleged retrospectively by Talyzin in introducing the 1987 annual plan.
(³) Inferred from a target of 220 bn r., assumed to be in 1983 prices.
(⁴) Originally described by Talyzin as a 7.6% increase – presumably over expected actual 1985. The ruble total amounts, however, to only a 3.9% increase over eventually reported 1985 actual in 1984 prices.
(⁵) It appears that some of the growth targets have been calculated for retail sales excluding alcoholic beverages and some including them. That is probably why it is possible to derive two different figures for 1986 AP.
(⁶) Asserted by Talyzin in introducing the 1987 plan.

Gorbachev's Approach to Economic Reforms

Hans-Hermann Höhmann

1. *Interdependence between Economic and Political Restructuring*

Since Gorbachev's coming to power as General Secretary of the CPSU in March 1985, the «acceleration of socio-economic development» (uskorenie) has been a central objective of Soviet politics, if not the prime concern of the present leadership. The reasons for this are obvious. The economic potential of the USSR is under strong pressure from all sides of the polygon of economic policy goals — the assurance of adequate capital formation, the stabilization of progress in the standard of living, the guaranteed ability to maintain the aspired military capacities, the provision of an economic basis for Soviet hegemony policy, the restoration of legitimacy to the Soviet system. The crisis-scale slowdown in economic growth towards the end of the seventies was threatening to turn into a long-term constraint on the USSR's freedom of domestic and foreign policy action. With the same urgency as «uskorenie» itself, the establishment of the conditions required for more rapid economic growth was and still is advocated. At first, it was the call for a thorough «intensification» of the economic processes, i.e. for a profound transformation of the conditions for growth in the form of a switch from a primarily *resources-based (extensive)* to a predominantly *productivity-based (intensive)* course of economic development, that was in the foreground of these efforts. Even before coming to office as General Secretary, Gorbachev had already urged that the same resonance must now be afforded to these intensification efforts as had been given to industrialization in the early phases of Soviet history [1]. Later, and in particular after the 27th Party Congress of the CPSU held in February/March 1986, other guiding formulae came to the fore. The concept of «reform», which the General Secretary stressed even further by adding the amplifier «radical» to lend decisiveness to the term, returned to political programme work and learned discussion, from which it had been banned since the early seventies. But even more it was the term «restructuring» (perestroika) that became the trademark of Gorbachev's policy of renewal [2]. Without restructuring of the workstyle, economic structure and management system, the goal of accelerated economic growth could never be achieved; this became the General Secretary's constantly repeated message. Such restructuring in turn presupposes «democratization» as a further consequence; it has been coming more and more to the fore since the January 1987 Plenary Session of the Central Committee of the CPSU [3].

Gorbachev's concept of « restructuring » is not limited only to the economy. In other fields of politics, society and culture in the USSR it has advanced even further. Especially in the media and in the cultural field, remarkable changes have come about under the slogan of « glasnost » (openness). Thus it can be assumed that « restructuring » is, above and beyond its economic functions, part of an overall political plan geared towards a comprehensive revitalization of socialism in the USSR on the basis of its Leninist foundations. Of course, changes in the media and cultural scene in turn have an economic function. It is hardly a coincidence that, when his initial hopes of a rapid « redynamization » of the Soviet economy failed to be fulfilled and resistance was making itself felt at all levels of economic decision-making and action, Gorbachev called to the cultural and academic intelligentsia for aid. His major objectives in this course of action are apparently twofold. Firstly, his intention is to create a more profound awareness of the fact that, despite some improvements since 1985, the difficulties experienced by the Soviet economy in the late seventies and early eighties, and which he himself rates as critical, have not been overcome and thus make more sweeping countermeasures necessary. And secondly, by elimination of antiquated ideological and theoretical positions and by intensified specialist discussion and communication between economic research and practice, the conditions essential to the elaboration of an operational strategy for more drastic changes of planning, management and the economic mechanism are to be established. So, under pressure from actual conditions, some « restructuring » took place even within the General Secretary's own concept of reform, too : his modernization programme, originally predominantly technocratic/conservative in character, gradually took on more and more elements of openness for more extensive reforms.

The following discussion is based on the hypothesis that Gorbachev has recognized the need to take urgent action towards the modernization of the USSR and that in his own perception of socialism it is not enough merely to stabilize State power but that instead the aim must be to restore the capability to engage in successful politics both internally and with the outside world, even if this involves giving up some traditional positions on Party and State rule and some paradigms of ideological legitimation. At the same time, there is much to indicate that the restructuring to which he aspires is coming up against barriers of the most varied nature : Gorbachev's own as yet unclear conceptions of the concrete configuration to be given to economic and political restructuring, the too hesitant support given to him at the top levels, resistance from all social groups affected, tight constraints on economic manoeuvrability, ingrained perception and behaviour patterns, inadequate resonance in the foreign-policy field. Thus, what is under way is the toilsome process, of as yet highly dubious outcome, of a modernization from above which has to be imposed and pushed through under onerous economic restrictions and against pockets of serious social resistance.

2. *The Gorbachev Approach*
a) *Economic Policy as a « Policy Mix »*

As has already been pointed out, Gorbachev from the very start placed the main emphasis of his policies on the revitalization of the still crisis-ridden economy. Even as early as in his « government policy statement », his speech to the April 1985 CC Plenum, he recited numerous variations on the central theme of his programme: « The most important question at this time is as follows: how and by what means can the country achieve an acceleration of its economic development? ... The historic fortune of the country and the position of socialism in the modern world depend in many ways on how we carry on this matter » [4]. At the same time it became apparent that the Soviet perception of the problems to be dealt with suggested a number of different courses of action but that, especially as regards reform policy, there were only general principles but no operational strategy to offer.

The reasons for the difficulties facing the Soviet economy at the turn of the eighties, and which Gorbachev himself eventually described as crisis-ridden [5], are generally attributed to three groups of maldevelopments: the progressive degeneration of the « subjective factor » (i.e. the drop in human performance at all levels of decision-making and action), inappropriate structure and investment policy (i.e. reduced capital formation, neglected re-investment, inadequate promotion of sophisticated technologies in the branches of industry that could profit from them) and unsatisfactory performance by the economic management system, generally expressed in politico-economic/ideology language as growing contradictions between the productive forces and the conditions of production. Thus, the causes of the difficulties are not seen in any failure of the system as such but rather in the failure of the leadership team around and under Brezhnev, which had lost the ability to develop the systemic qualities of socialism, above all its « planomernost ».

This perception of the difficulties to be handled, accordingly, determines the conception of the economic policy reorientation required to combat them. More than with any specification of material substance, Gorbachev and his followers are concerned first and foremost with how to strengthen central economic authority and bring about a significant improvement in economic-policy style. For the imageless « muddling through » of the latter Brezhnev years had its roots precisely in persistent deficits in this field. The aims for the future are more freedom from contradiction, more stringency, and better labour discipline; in short, better central economic management as a whole. As expedient and promising as these intentions may be, their implementation is for the time being hampered by the fact that the role of the central organs of economic policy, for instance the State Planning Committee (Gosplan), first has to be redefined.

In terms of substance, Gorbachev's economic policy is best conceived of as a «policy mix», combining elements of labour policy, structure and process policy, and system policy. As such it in principle continues the line followed in the past, while now stressing that the elements from the various fields must be packaged into a «total system» of measures that are to be better tailored to each other than in the past. This is to apply first of all to the «timewise division of labour» between the above fields of policy. Some of the envisaged measures — above all those in the field of labour policy and the intended improvement of organization — are to serve the short-term mobilization of available reserves. Others, in particular in investment and system policy, are geared towards long-term improvements in performance. These hopes are certainly realistic. Since the Soviet economy has in the more recent past fallen significantly short of its achievable performance limits, it is quite right to give priority to the mobilization of reserves. Thereafter, the changes in investment policy are likely to be the next to take effect. The system policy reforms, on the other hand, are unlikely to make themselves felt much before the beginning of the nineties. But the reforms in the various policy fields are intended not only to produce their results on a staggered time-scale; it is hoped that in the long term they will back each other up better than in the past. For past changes to the system were impeded not only by a limited-scope, inconsistent, and unstable reform policy but also by the fact that they were not accompanied by an adequate labour, structure and process policy. «Re-conception» of economic policy, of course, is not in itself enough to ensure that a really new quality of economic policy can actually be achieved; whether the envisaged measures are consistent in and among themselves and what effects they promise in terms of the aspired goal of accelerated growth will be reviewed later. But first a summary outline of the essential elements of the «policy mix» as it appears at this time.

In the field of *labour policy,* a number of measures have been introduced (under the slogan of the «activation of the human factor») with the aim of improving work effort and labour discipline, reducing worker delinquency of all kinds, and improving motivation through the by no means new approach of a mixture of pressure and incentive. These measures include wide-scale «cadre replacement», anti-alcohol campaigns, tightening up of legislation on economic and labour crime, stricter application of existing labour law provisions, measures to counteract what is referred to as «non-earned income» of all kinds [6], and on the incentives side wage reforms and measures towards controlling and extending the scope for legal private work activities by the individual.

Structure policy consists above all in the contents of the 12th Five-Year Plan and comprises changing the structure of the goals of economic development with a view to modernizing production, promoting scientific-technological progress, and renewing the capital stock. The latter includes, in just a few keywords, raising the growth of capital formation, reducing the share of machine-building in investment (while at the same time promoting its «most progressive» sectors), raising the proportion of re-investment, and promoting the development of resources-saving technologies of all kinds. The *foreign trade and payments economy,* too, is to be integrated as far as possible into the strategy for the modernization of the structure of the economy. And in *process policy,* noteworthy efforts are those being made to improve the constancy of planning, to bring more equilibrium into the production processes, to reduce deficits, to relax bottlenecks, and to open up new reserves for acceleration by better «bottleneck management». *System policy,* finally, encompasses the whole reform approach of Gorbachev.

b) *Gorbachev's Reform Approach*

Since his coming to power, Gorbachev's statements on economic policy have documented his view that economic upswing and the intensification of the economic processes cannot be achieved without profound «perfecting», «improvement» or «restructuring» of planning, management and the economic mechanism. As early as at the April Plenum of the CC (1985), the General Secretary had declared: «Whatever question we discuss, from whichever side we tackle the economy — it all eventually boils down to the need to seriously improve management and the economic mechanism as a whole» [7]. At the 27th Party Congress, Gorbachev established further points of emphasis. As already mentioned, the concept of reform returned to Soviet economic language, and the use of the epithet «radical» gave an indication of the resoluteness with which it was meant. The reform discussion within the USSR — which had already picked up noticeably under Andropov — took on new intensity. Considering the pressure for reform and the course of the discussion on economic policy, the revised Party Programme laid comparatively little emphasis on system-policy changes, a reflection of its origins in the pre-Gorbachev era which have, in the meantime, made the entire document obsolete.

Gorbachev's concept of reform was most clearly expressed in his «Political Report» to the 27th Party Congress [8]. It links up on the one hand with the reform policies pursued since the mid-sixties, but also reveals new, more far-reaching features that bear the marks of such reform-oriented economists as Aganbegyan and Fedorenko. It is not (yet?) the concept of a «socialist market economy», but it is the concept of a relaxed and rationalized planned economy which attempts to make more use of market mechanisms especially in the areas of lower political priority closely related to the private consumption sector. This includes limited corrections to the conditions of ownership (somewhat more private enterprise), which, at the same time, bears stronger participatory features. Gorbachev outlined this concept in his «Political Report» with the following elements:

— concentration of the central economic authorities on the solution of major structure and process policy tasks and on the implementation of the principal economic targets;
— streamlining and reduction of the economic administration apparat, re-organization of planning and economic management in accordance with more complex branch-related and regional aspects, diversification of the structures of the production units;
— extension of the leeway for decision-making by the production units themselves, reduction of planning indicators, more widespread application of the principle of economic accountability by the production units, and more indirect ways of bringing influence to bear on the production units' decisions by economic parameters (normatives, economically better substantiated prices, etc.);
— more worker participation in the production units («democratization») with a view to improving worker motivation and enhancing the system's legitimation.

The generalized nature of this conceptual approach, probably more appropriately characterized as a bundle of principles, made it necessary from the very beginning to find concrete operational programmes for its implementation. This programme definition process has by no means been concluded yet. It is suffering from the traditional deficit of empirically substantiated theory of economic policy. However, an expanded discussion among economists is by now under way. We will return to this and to potential further conceptual development on the part of Gorbachev himself following a look at the reform measures which have been introduced to date.

But first a word on the support given to Gorbachev by the other members of the Politburo. Because of the division of labour within this body and the resultant concentration on other than economic topics in the speeches made during public appearances by the Politburo members, it is not possible to give a conclusive documentation of the attitude to economic reforms prevailing within this top-level political body of the

USSR. Perhaps there are three things that can be said with reasonable certainty: the strongest impetus for reforms in politics and the economy is that exerted by Gorbachev himself; loyal support is displayed above all by Prime Minister Ryzhkov (most recently in a speech made in Sverdlovsk); on the other hand there are certainly those who prefer to exercise reserve and even latent opposition, but the weak point of this attitude is the lack of any convincing alternative.

3. *Soviet Reform Policy in Practice*

The reform measures implemented, introduced, decided upon or planned to date are diverse and can thus be discussed only by way of outline and a few examples in the present context. For this purpose we shall distinguish *four fields of reform*:
— the organizational structure of the administration of the economy, planning and production units;
— the principles, methods and reach of *central planning;*
— the «economic mechanism», i.e. the *instruments connecting central planning and the economic processes in the production units;* and
— the *system of ownership* and the *control of the individual's private economic activity.*

In the first three of these fields, numerous changes had already been made in the past, even if overall they had met with little success [9]. The system of ownership and private economic activity have been made the subject of reform — albeit within narrow bounds as yet — only under Gorbachev.

In the *field of organization,* the first reform worthy of mention is the attempt to streamline the decision-making processes by the introduction of new, centralizing management authorities («Superministries»). These arose in various types. In the case of the agro-industrial complex, a new supreme authority (Gosagroprom) was formed from the dissolution of existing ministries. In other cases, the newly created bodies were superimposed upon the old ministries, which remained in existence (Bureaux of Machine-Building and of the Fuel and Energy Complex). In the case of the construction industry, an existing authority (Gosstroi) had its functions changed and was given supervision over newly formed ministries. And finally, the «State Foreign Economy Commission» was founded as the co-ordinating supreme authority on international economic affairs.

The industry associations, formed in 1973 as intermediate-level economic administration organs by commutation from Main Sections of the ministries, were disbanded again, but there had not been many of them anyway. At the lower level, by contrast, the concentration of production in production associations and scientific production associations has

35

been continued and even intensified.

In the *field of central planning,* i.e. above the production unit level, the 12th Five-Year Plan brought a new attempt at continuous, consistent and at the same time better-balanced planning. The major problem to be resolved in this field of reform, the re-definition of the functions of the central economic organs (principally Gosplan, Gossnab and Gosbank but also the Union Ministries) and the introduction of institutional and legal provisions to this effect, is still awaiting decision. Gorbachev has repeatedly made reference to the forthcoming approval of such statutes. However, this area of problems is particularly sensitive, because it touches upon the very nature of the Soviet economic system and also upon the vested interests of the higher and intermediate-level economic bureaucracy.

The main theatre of the restructuring efforts at present under way in the economic system is the *interplay between central planning and the economic processes in the production units,* often referred to as the « economic mechanism » in the narrower meaning of the term. Of particular significance in this context are the new provisions governing industry, light industry, agriculture and foreign trade and payments. As of 1987, « new economic methods » derived from the « large-scale economic experiment »[10] launched in 1984 apply to industry, but also to the construction sector, transportation and communications, and to service enterprises. The four principal elements of the « new economic methods » are :

— re-organization of the time-frame for planning by drawing up plans in good time and ensuring the medium-term stability of the plans for the duration of the five-year planning period;

— extension of the production units' leeway for decision-making by involving the production associations (enterprises) in the drawing up of the plans, by reducing the numbers of obligatory planning indicators, and by emphasizing the importance of contracts between production units;

— extension of the production « units » financial leeway by giving them access to various « funds », depreciation facilities and credits, and by changing over from the practice of requiring the production units to surrender their profits to one of profit-related taxation (application of normative contributions to the state budget);

— re-organization of the incentives system in the production units by linking bonuses to indicators that are intended to reflect improved co-ordination (fulfilment of delivery plans on the basis of contracts concluded) and enhanced efficiency (increased productivity, quality improvements, innovation), for which reason the development of the

36

wages fund is coupled via normatives with the growth of net production.

Of importance in the context of the re-organization of the incentives system in the production units is the *reform of the wage and salary system* which comes into effect for about 75 million employees in the State sector as of 1st June 1987 and is intended to re-vitalize the current strongly egalitarian structure of labour-related incomes by introducing wage differentials dependent upon function and qualification [11].

Comments and criticism from within the USSR and which have lined the path from the experiment to the « new economic methods » make it plain why, in addition to the extension of the experiment, a new wave of further restructuring is already under way, this time under the motto of the « transition to full economic accountability ». For apart from the encouraging aspects in terms of increased efficiency and improved co-ordination, some adverse developments were also observed which give rise to doubts as to whether the new methods will have a sufficiently positive net effect. For one thing, pressure towards increasing efficiency is still considered too weak. Particular targets of criticism are the links between wages funds and the growth of production and other « soft budget constraints » on the production units. But there are also frequent complaints about the ineffectiveness of both horizontal and vertical relationships: the former about the lack of sales opportunities on the one hand and irregular deliveries of the means of production on the other, both the result of the deficient distribution system, and the latter over persistent intervention by the ministries. The changeover to « full economic accountability » — first in a few large production units, then as of January 1987 in the production units of seven ministries and in 36 further enterprises — is intended to promote both pressure towards economization and also the willingness to undertake entrepreneurial risks and the production units' disposition to innovate [12]. The principle of this « second stage » of new economic methods (A. Aganbegyan) is generally summed up by the slogans of « self-sufficiency », « self-financing », « self-funding » and « self-administration », and is intended to bring about a change in the function of the production unit from being the lowest rung in the ladder of economic management to being an autonomous economic entity. This is reflected, for instance, in the fact that profit is made the decisive factor in the assessment of the success of the production unit, from which running costs, wages and salaries and also contributions to the State budget (as taxes) have to be financed. The *new Soviet Enterprises Act,* the draft of which was published in early February 1987 for the purpose of public discussion [13], can be seen as the legislative counterpart to the extension of « full economic accountability ». The Act is intended to supersede an Ordinance dating

37

from 1965 and may be of twofold significance for the further process of reform. Firstly, it is intended to consolidate the institutional demarcation of the production units from the economic administration. Secondly, it establishes in formal legal and legislative terms a number of further reform steps which up to now have found their way only rudimentarily and informally into economic-policy practice. These include, for instance, more wholesale trade in means of production, freer competition between the production units (as opposed to the traditional «Socialist competition»), flexible pricing, and more democracy within the production unit.

At the same time, no doubt, it is apparent that the reform steps undertaken to date are inadequate and make *further reforms indispensable*. This situation provokes some quite contradictory developments. The call by A. Aganbegyan and others for a «third stage» of restructuring to make «full economic accountability» functional as a new economic category and to concentrate above all on thorough reforms in pricing and in credits for material/technology supplies [14], as well as the announcement of a forthcoming legislative redefinition of the functions of some central economic organs, indicate a trend towards a further extension of reform efforts. But the introduction of an independent *« State Quality Control »* organization (gospriemka) in 1,500 large production units, which is to have the right to reject sub-quality products and thus to disqualify them from consideration as a contribution towards planning target fulfilment, is an element of traditional state intervention from «outside the economic mechanism» and one which, according to reports in the press, has caused some considerable concern in the production units affected [15].

Reforms to the economic mechanism go further (at least in the wording of the new legislation) in light industry and agriculture than in industry as a whole. Planning and evaluation of production in *light industry*[16] (textiles and clothing, furs, the leather and shoe industry) are to be geared towards satisfying the «real demands of the populace», as expressed in orders from the retail trade. Accordingly, planning from above is intended essentially to re-affirm market processes, with «wholesale markets» serving as interface between production and retail trade. In *agriculture*[17], decision-making by the kolkhozi and sovkhozi is to be extended on the basis of stable medium-term planning targets, of a cutback in planned State purchasing of agricultural produce coupled with the producer's right of free disposition over any surpluses produced, of higher prices for grain deliveries above plan targets, of expanded financial leeway under the terms of reference of «full economic accountability», of the use of normatives to control relations between the planning and State budget authorities on the one hand and the production units on the other (Gorbachev made much-heeded reference to Lenin's « taxes in kind »), and of extended application of the work contract system at the brigade, work group, and family levels within the agricultural production units.

However, the new ordinance governing the economic mechanism in the agro-industrial complex — like comparable developments in industry — leaves open some cardinal questions, in particular how can relations between the agricultural production units and their suppliers be shaped and how can the tendency of the administrative and political authorities to intervene in production unit decision-making be curbed?

And finally, the *foreign trade and payments* mechanism[18] is to be made the subject of a reform for the first time ever. As at the beginning of 1987, 21 ministries and over 70 large-scale production units have been given the right to engage in independent, even if still administratively controlled, foreign trade activities, with the right of disposition over the accumulated « foreign currency funds » being intended as an incentive to improve export efficiency.

Turning now to the *fourth field of reform,* that of the system of ownership and the control of private economic activities by the individual, there are two indicators, albeit as yet of minor significance, that are worthy of mention. The first is the passing of an Act re-defining the legal basis for the *exercise of private gainful activity,* especially in the services sector, by restricted categories of persons. This means first and foremost persons not otherwise in gainful employment — such as pensioners, housewives and students — and employed persons in their spare time [19]. Such activities require official approval and earnings from them are subject to tax. In the light of the widespread « grey labour » already going on in the USSR, this Act serves not so much to promote private work as rather to bring it to the surface and to place it on a legal basis. This limits the Act's economic efficacy, especially since another act passed at almost the same time with the aim of combatting illegal incomes has caused some considerable confusion amongst the populace. This all means that a new, stable balance of conduct is yet to be found in this field. The prospects of the second new development in the private activity sector would appear to be more promising: the opening up of new opportunities for the founding of « co-operatives » and associations for the production of consumer goods and in the services sector [20]. Gorbachev, too, has placed a lot of emphasis on this development. Nevertheless, the freedom of action of the new co-operatives remains limited at present, mainly by their being restricted to the same categories of person as for private activity by individuals, i.e. to persons not otherwise in gainful employment and to employed persons in their spare time. Thus, recourse to elements of private initiative in complement to

State planning is, despite a number of new steps, very hesitant. This is probably due less to ideological reservations than to the conviction that the success of attempts to improve the economy depends more on progress made in the State sector, that more private economic activity may give rise to new problems, and that the experience of other Socialist countries in this respect has not been totally positive.

4. *Evaluation and Outlook*

A review of the changes to the planning and economic management system of the USSR since Gorbachev took office reveals that the measures introduced to date take their orientation from traditional reform policy. There are, however, some new accentuations discernible, in particular endeavours to pursue a sectorally more differentiating reform policy. Some other approaches, familiar from the past but never put into practice, are now re-appearing with new emphasis in the economic-policy programme. But for the current reform policy to be able to manage the transition from the traditional modifications «within the system» to real «radical reform», i.e. to a new systemic equilibrium, that it has not brought about to date, there is still a need for further conceptual clarification and for numerous further measures towards practical implementation in concrete economic policy. This applies especially to the provisions in connection with the transition to «full economic accountability». In this context, in turn, particular importance attaches to future pricing policy, to the modalities of ensuring an adequate supply of means of production to the production units, and to the legal and institutional demarcation of responsibilities between planning and administrative authorities on the one hand, and the production units on the other. Attempts to bridge the gaps identified are hampered on the one hand by the lack of experience with more strongly decentralized forms of planning and management and on the other by the state of the art in economic theory, which for numerous reasons is too underdeveloped to be of satisfactory use for the purposes of practical economic policy. Thus, as Aganbegyan in his capacity as acting Secretary of the Economics Section of the Academy of Sciences pointed out in the spring of 1986, there was still no operational strategy for a new economic mechanism available [21]. By November he was voicing more optimism [22], but it is safe to assume that even today the conceptual basis for the transformation of Soviet system policy from the traditional approach of «improving» and «perfecting» to one of really «radical reform» is still inadequate.

The course of events to date has shown not only Gorbachev's continued interest in reform but also that his policy of «restructuring» is meeting with resistance from many sides. This is not surprising and only confirms the opinions of many Western analysts who have long been calling attention to the existence of broad-scale opposition and to the lack of any effective lobby for reform within Soviet society. However, it is likely that this opposition is directed not solely or even primarily against the system reform measures introduced to date but rather against Gorbachev's policy as a whole, which in effect amounts to the elimination of ingrained patterns of working and behaviour, to the unilateral termination of the « contrat social » of the Brezhnev era, which consisted of allowing Soviet society personal « restructuring » to the benefit of the individual in return for the individual's recognition of nomenklatura rule. Gorbachev is at pains to break this « exploitative mentality » and to replace it by a « productive mentality ». The « activation of the human factor » has turned into a handy formula for this endeavour. However, this policy demands that the Soviet populace works harder, accepts a re-distribution of incomes within the social groups, and renounces consumer spending now in favour of (perhaps) better satisfaction of consumer demand in the future, without having proved to the population any well-substantiated hope of real improvements to come.

The realisation that it is not going to be possible to revitalize society or to achieve an economic upswing without political mobilization of the masses has, in the course of time, shifted the emphasis in Gorbachev's policies. On the one hand, political and ideological accentuations have come to the fore to replace the original technocratic weighting. More « openness » and « democratization » are now intended, in conjunction with an improvement in economic performance, to assure the irreversibility of « restructuring », to restore Soviet socialism to its model status and, at the same time, to act as an instrument of economic restructuring and acceleration [23]. Since the economic policy reform measures introduced to date have as yet failed to bring any real improvement and the reforms to the economic mechanism have not yet brought about the desired « productive orientation » in administration and in the production units, political mobilization within and outside the production sites indeed remains the only option open for imparting new dynamism to economy and society. Political activation at the same time is intended to widen the latitude for reform, thus linking up with the other aspect of the shift in emphasis in Gorbachev's policies : the enrichment of modernization policy by elements of more far-reaching reform. This assessment can be derived, at least indirectly, from the General Secretary's more recent speeches and statements. His more far-sighted perception of the problems involved, his repeated emphasis on the need for radical, indeed revolutionary restructuring, his frequent references to Lenin's « New Economic Policy » (NEP), etc. make it apparent that — given

41

continuity in the leadership — drastic changes to the system can be considered not quite so unreasonable as they still were even in the first half of the eighties.

A further indication of the possibility of a really radical reform is the progress of the specialist discussion and its increasing interaction with conceptual debates in this context is a conference which was held in Moscow in November 1986 on the topic of « Problems of the Scientific Organization of Economic Management » in co-operation with the Reform Commision of Gosplan. It involved well over 1,000 scholars in its preparation and implementation, and was described by Aganbegyan in an interview with « Ekonomicheskaya gazeta » as an important step on the path to a scientifically based operational strategy of reform [24]. Highly indicative are, above all, Aganbegyan's references to a « third stage » of reform (to follow on from the extension of the « large-scale economic experiment » as the first stage and the transition to « full economic accountability » as the second), which would in actual fact be tantamount to radical changes along market-socialism lines, as became apparent from his use of catchwords such as the « cutback of imperative planning », « abolition of the traditional material-technical supply (system) », « transition to horizontal co-ordination between the production units » and « termination of the dictatorship of the producer ». The actual term « market socialism » is not used, however. At the same time, the discussion shows that there are numerous economists who would rather conclude the reform process at the second stage and who still adhere to a rationalized planned economy as their terms of reference.

Even if the determination to proceed with further reforms has grown on the whole, there are still serious obstacles to be overcome. Reference has already been made to the still inadequate conceptual foundation of the reforms and to opposition from those social groups whose « vested interests » would be affected by the reform. A further complication is the need to push the reform through coherently and briskly as a complete package while the pressure is still on to stabilize the performance of the economy by more traditional means, because quick success yields an indispensable legitimation basis for further steps. Here there is a by no means vanquished contradiction potential, both on matters of principle and as regards the co-ordinated implementation of the « policy mix » in Soviet economic policy as outlined in the above. For instance, there is the contradiction between quantitative acceleration of economic growth and qualitative improvement, which is reflected in friction between labour policy (more discipline) and structure policy measures (extremely taut plans in some sectors) on the one hand and system policy measures intended to boost efficiency, accelerate innovation and improve co-ordination on the other — even if stricter discipline does not necessarily have to be detrimental to quality in all cases. A second contradiction lies in the fact that it is left to administrative efforts and political mobilization to bring about a «radical reform» which by its very nature is expected to replace the traditional forms of political and administrative mobilization by a form of economic activation that is to emerge from within the production units themselves.

Finally, it must be remembered that any thoroughgoing reform is also bound to come up against certain limitations which are inevitable in the light of the socio-economic and political structure of the USSR and which would influence scope and pace of a reform no matter how resolute the determination to carry it through. The essential elements of this structural configuration are as follows:

— the size of the country and its unbalanced economic structure, which adds its own specific risks to those of any extensive reform;
— the Soviet national minorities problem, which harbours the danger of centrifugal tendencies to the detriment of the central State in the event of far-reaching reforms;
— the traditional lack of market economy thinking and entrepreneurial potential in Russia and the USSR, coupled with the likewise traditionally strong tendency towards intervention on the part of the State authorities;
— the USSR's role as a world power, with the tendency to keep the economic forces under permanent tension and thus to preserve the traditional rationale for central planning;
— the special weight of the military industrial complex, but also of other State tasks and expenditures (for instance in connection with regional policy);
and last but not least:
— the by now long time spent under the centralized administrative planned economy system, with all its behaviour-forming and structure-shaping effects.

Neither would the NEP have any chance of being accepted in its entirety as a model for the USSR. For one thing, the present agricultural structure of the USSR would not allow a pure NEP solution. For instance, the individualization of the agricultural production units would be impracticable. At most a relaxation and complementation of the present-day socialist structure of the agricultural production units — i.e. the kolkhozi and the sovkhozi — perhaps along the lines of the Hungarian model, might be possible. And for the other, Lenin's «commanding heights», those sectors of big business that were intended to remain under direct State influence even in the twenties, have by now multiplied into whole «commanding mountain ranges» comprising, for instance, the military industrial complex but also many sectors of the basic materials economy. This puts tight constraints on the leeway available for market-economy co-ordination and relegates the latter to a more restricted role even in the long-term perspective.

To recapitulate by way of conclusion: in terms of changes already achieved, the present-day system-policy situation in the USSR differs hardly at all from developments under Gorbachev's predecessors. Instead, its prominent feature is that, for the first time since Khrushchev's days, the status quo has been plainly censured, new objectives have been formulated, and processes of change have been initiated in the economy, politics, and society of the Soviet Union.

Where these processes may lead is at present an open question. But even an open question would have been non-typical of the Brezhnev era and its characteristic ossification and stagnation. The future of the «radical reform» depends on many preconditions that have been referred to either directly or implicitly: on the extent to which Gorbachev is able to consolidate his authority and gain further support at the top political echelons; on growing appreciation for the necessity and irreversibility of change; on adequate support from society; on the detailed elaboration of an operational strategy for the implementation of a specifically Soviet «mixed economy», and last but not least on a benign foreign-policy milieu — and on luck. These conditions do not all apply as yet, but appear all in all to be improving at present. Failure in system policy would hardly mean a return to the «contrat social» of the Brezhnev era. Stronger administrative pressure in the economy, a harder line in domestic policy, and an intensification of tensions with the outside world would be the more likely alternative.

NOTES

1. Pravda, 10.12.1984.
2. Cf. Gorbachev's speeches in Khabarovsk and at the January Plenum of the Central Committee (Pravda, 31.8.1986 and 28.1.1987).
3. Pravda, 28.1.1987.
4. Pravda, 24.4.1985.
5. Pravda, 28.1.1987.
6. Cf. for a law to this effect, Ekonomicheskaya Gazeta, 23/1986.
7. Pravda, 24.4.1985.
8. Pravda, 26.2.1986.
9. Cf. H.-H. Höhmann, Sowjetische Wirtschaftsreformen, in: Sowjetunion 1984/85, Munich 1985, pp. 201 et seq.
10. Cf. G. Seidenstecher, The «Large-Scale Economic Experiment in the Soviet Economy», Reports Nos. 36, 37/1986 of the Federal Institute for East European and International Studies (BIOst).

11. Izvestia, 26.9.1986, Ekonomicheskaya Gazeta, 43/1986.
12. Ekonomicheskaya Gazeta, 1/1987.
13. Text in Pravda, 8.2.1987, Cf. also R. Götz-Coenenberg, Aktuelle Analyse des BIOST, No. 5/1987.
14. Ekonomicheskaya Gazeta, 48/1986.
15. Cf. Ekonomicheskaya Gazeta, 50/1986.
16. Ekonomicheskaya Gazeta, 20/1986.
17. Ekonomicheskaya Gazeta, 17/1986.
18. Cf. C. Meier, BIOST Report, No. 51/1986.
19. Pravda, 21.11.1986.
20. Cf. Pravda, 6.2 and 12.2.1987.
21. Voprosy Ekonomiki, 6/1986, p. 111.
22. Ekonomicheskaya Gazeta, 48/1986.
23. Cf. especially Gorbachev's speech at the January Plenum (1987), Pravda, 28.1.1987.
24. Ekonomicheskaya Gazeta, 48/1986, cf. also P. Hanson, The Reform Economists make their Pitch, in: Radio Liberty, RL 459/86.

Consumption, Income Distribution and Incentives

Hans Aage

1. Achieved Levels of Consumption

The impressive achievements in Soviet consumer goods production during the last four decades have not only partly satisfied existing needs, but have also contributed to the creation of new ones and also to the formation of great expectations for their fulfilment — as correctly anticipated in Marx's statements

«... dass das befriedigte erste Bedürfnis selbst, die Aktion der Befriedigung und das schon erworbene Instrument der Befriedigung zu neuen Bedürfnissen führt — und diese Erzeugung neuer Bedürfnisse ist die erste geschichtliche Tat.»[1]

«Mit seiner Entwicklung erweitert sich dies Reich der Naturnotwendigkeit, weil die Bedürfnisse...»[2]

As expectations have their own inertia they may continue to grow irrespective of the slowdown of the Soviet consumption growth rate after 1975, and they were not damped by Gorbachev, when he recently remarked that

«Over the eight years before the Plenum (in May 1982), however, both the population and effective consumer demand grew. The people want to spend the extra money that they have enjoyed through pay rises. This is an issue that brooks no delay whatsoever. It is inadmissible to let this problem take further years upon years to solve.»[3]

This major challenge for the Soviet leadership is part of the reason why Gorbachev explained acceleration (uskorenie) of social and economic development in this way:

«Above all, it means increasing the rates of economic growth.»[4]

According to a 1982 study of the U.S. Congress, Soviet consumption per capita increased at an average rate of 3.0 % per year during 1951-1979 compared to 2.2 % in the USA, 6.6 % in Japan and 2.2 % in the U.K. Growth rates for GNP were 4.8 % in the USSR, 3.4 % in the USA, 8.3 % in Japan and 2.7 % in the UK.[5] In 1976 Soviet per capita consumption was about one third of that in the USA.[6]

The structure of Soviet production by origin and end use has changed markedly:[7] during the years 1951-80 industrial production grew at an average rate of 6.8 % a year (according to the CIA SPIOER index, 8.7 % according to official data). For agricultural production the growth rate was 2.8 % (3.1 % according to offical data). These differences are reflected in the changing structure of production. Industry and construction increased its share from 24.7% to 44.7%, and the share of agriculture decreased from 30.6% to 13.9%. But most remarkable is the decline in the share of services from 29.5% in 1950 to 20.3% in 1980, contrary to the experience of most countries with increasing income levels, which normally entail increasing shares of services. During the same period investment has increased its share of GNP by end use from 14.2% in 1950 to 33% in 1980, consumption dropping from 59.9% in 1950 to 53.6% in 1980, and an increasing share of investment has been allocated to agriculture and energy extraction. The remaining 13% in 1980 were supposed to be allocated to military spending.

The trend in growth rates has been strongly downward, and this also applies to consumption, cf. the estimates by Schroeder[7] in Table 1:

Table 1

Average annual rates of growth of per capita consumption by major category, 1950-1979. Structure of consumption

	1951 −60	1961 −70	1971 −79	Structure of consumption		
				1960	1970	1979
Food	3.4	3.0	1.4	55	51	46
Soft goods	6.9	4.4	2.9	20	21	22
Durables	14.2	6.8	7.6	5	7	11
Household services	3.9	5.0	3.8	20	21	22
Education	1.5	4.1	1.5	—	—	—
Health	3.9	2.6	1.5	—	—	—
Total consumption	4.3	3.8	2.5	100	100	100

Source: Schroeder, 1983: 312, 320.

Note: The structure of consumption is computed for private consumption only. The corresponding numbers for education are 7, 7 and 6 for the three years considered, and for health 5, 4 and 4 respectively.

Table 2

Annual average rates of growth of per capita retail trade turnover 1976-1990

	1976 −80	1981 −85	1986	1986 −90
Food	2.6	1.5	—	—
Non-Food	4.5	3.0	—	—
Services	6.6	4.8	—	—
Total retail plan	4.3	3.3	4.5	5.9
Trade turnover actual	3.6	2.2	5.6	—

Note: Population annual rates of growth assumed are 0.9% 1976-80, 0.9% 1981-85, and 0.8% 1986-90 (Baldwin, 1979:8). Data for the three subgroups 1981-85 are based on the assumption that 1984 data are identical to 1985 data which are not available.

The 1986-plan for total retail turnover (not per capita) increase was 3.6% in November 1985 (6% exclusive of alcoholic beverages). However in the report in February 1987 the plan was stated at 5.3% and 6% respectively, apparently due to changes of method.

Sources: U.N.ECE, 1986:189; Ekonomičeskaja Gazeta (November 1985, no. 48): 11-16, (February 1986, no. 6): 11-14, (June 1986, no. 26): 14, (January 1987, no. 5): 10.

The downward trend in consumption growth, especially for food consumption, is apparent in Tables 1 and 2. The data in Table 2 may be subject to changes in statistical methods, especially the data for 1986, and also the price index. Retail trade prices increased 1.0% in 1981, 3.8% in 1982, 0% in 1983, −1.0% in 1984 and 1.0% in 1985.[8]

The growth of total consumption has been accompanied by changes in its composition. Although the share of food has dropped from 55% in 1960 to 46% in 1979 it is still well above the shares in countries like the USA (17%), Japan (29%) and the UK (32%).[9] The growth rate has differed for various components of consumption as documented by selected physical indicators.

Food. The main conclusion from Table 3 is the impressive growth in Soviet per capita food consumption since 1960.

Table 3
Food consumption 1960-1985 (kilograms per capita per year)

	1960	1975	1980	1985	Plan 1990	Rational norm
Meat and meat products	39.5	56.7	57.6	61.4	70.0	82.0
Milk and dairy products	240	316	314	323	330-340	405
Eggs (number)	118	216	239	260	260-266	292
Fish and fish products	9.9	16.8	17.6	17.7	19.0	18.2
Sugar	28.0	40.9	44.4	42.0	45.5	40
Vegetable oil	5.3	7.6	8.8	9.7	13.2	9.1
Potatoes	143	120	109	104	110	110
Vegetables and melons	70	89	97	102	126-135	130
Fruit and berries	22	39	38	46	66-70	91
Bread and cereals	164	141	138	133	135	115

Sources: Nar. Khoz. 1985: 445; Možin & Krylatykh, 1982; Trehub, 1986: 21; Sarkasjan, 1983: 165; Pravda, 25 May 1982, pp. 1-2.

Table 4
Consumption of calories, protein and fat in various countries 1983-1984

	GNP per capita 1980, US $ World Bank Estimates	Total: animal and vegetable products	Animal products	Total: animal and vegetable products	Animal products	Total: animal and vegetable products	Animal products
		Calories, number		Protein, grams		Fat, grams	
		Per capita, per day 1983-1984					
Sweden	13520	3186	1357	94.7	64.9	148.2	107.0
Denmark	12950	3564	1582	100.0	67.5	174.4	136.8
USA	11360	3644	1280	105.8	70.9	167.3	98.8
Japan	9890	2858	604	92.3	50.6	83.3	38.7
UK	7920	3162	1160	86.8	52.1	142.6	95.8
Italy	6480	3542	923	105.6	54.5	139.3	70.1
Spain	5400	3335	935	96.8	53.3	136.7	70.6
USSR	4550	3426	883	100.9	51.8	98.1	65.3
Poland	3900	3301	1030	103.4	54.5	105.5	81.1
Yugoslavia	2620	3621	821	102.5	38.9	107.8	67.5
Brazil	2050	2564	389	60.6	22.4	51.1	28.0
India	240	2088	113	50.8	5.8	33.8	7.8

Sources: FAO Production Yearbook, 1985: 271-276; World Bank: World Development Report 1982: 110.

Note: Official East European and Soviet data include some animal products, not included in Western statistics, possibly 5-20%, cf. Gray (1981: 38,41).

Although growth rates have stagnated since 1975, especially for meat consumption which is still below the OECD average of about 83 kilograms per capita in 1983, it is apparent that the Soviet food problem is not a matter of insufficient amounts of calories, but rather a matter of the composition of the diet and of demand being in excess of supply at prevailing prices. The share of animal components is below that of the USA, but it is comparable to that of Italy and Spain, cf. Table 4. The consumption of dairy products, fresh vegetables and fruit is also comparatively low, to a large extent due to lack of storage and transport facilities for agricultural produce, of which approximately 20 % is lost in transit from the country-side to consumers according to some estimates.[10]

The consumption of meat, dairy products, fresh vegetables and fruit is also below the «rational norms of consumption» computed by Soviet scientists, and these norms are not fulfilled by the plans for 1990 either, cf. table 3.[11] However, rational norms according to consumers' preferences and to physiological needs are different things. It is ironical that recent tendencies among Western nutrition experts are in the direction of urging us to eat less animal food and more bread, potatoes and coarse vegetables, like cabbage, in which the Soviet diet is rich.

The problem of Soviet food consumption is not only a problem of composition but also of distribution:

« The overall gap between actual per capita consumption and recommended levels is one aspect of the problem. Another is the irregularity of the supply of meat, dairy products, fruits and vegetables in many regions of the country, and seasonal fluctuations in the availability of various foods in the stores. »[12]

The plans for 1990 may be modest compared to the rational norms of consumption, but it presupposes considerable increases in Soviet grain production and/or grain imports, which are at best very uncertain.

Industrial consumption goods. The supply of goods, particularly durables, has increased even faster than the supply of food. For goods like clothes and shoes the problem has often been a lack of demand due to insufficient quality and fashion. There are even unused services like dry cleaners and shoe repair stores.[13] In light industry, almost 10 % of output is considered « not demanded ».[14] Clearance sales as well as more flexible prices have been introduced as a way of cutting down the stocks of unsold goods.[15]

Table 5 shows the increase in household stocks of selected durables, which are however still below « recommended, optimal » levels.[16]

Table 5

Household stock of durables. Number per 100 families

	1965	1975	1985
Radio sets	59	79	96
Television sets	24	74	97
Refrigerators	11	61	91
Washing-machines	21	65	70
Vacuum cleaners	7	18	39
Motor cars	—	5	15

Sources: Nar. Khoz. 1979: 433; Nar. Khoz. 1985: 446.

The family car is high on the want list of consumers in the Soviet Union as everywhere. Production in 1986 was 1.3 million, slightly above plans, which were reduced a little compared to 1985[17], and waiting lists

51

are long, about 8 years.[18] This also applies to telephones. In 1985, 23 % of urban families and 7 % of rural families had telephones.[19]

Housing. The housing shortage is the most serious problem for the Soviet consumer. Being constant since 1928, rents in state housing are nominal, and waiting lists are long and unpredictable. Private and co-operative housing (20-30 % of the total) is expensive, 10,000-15,000 rubles for a two- or three-room cooperative apartment with a 30 % downpayment, and 25,000-30,000 rubles for a private house.[20] After a period of shrinking, cooperative and private housing is now encour-aged[21], but it still competes with state housing for scarce materials and capacity, and housing is not top priority for investment allocations.

Despite substantial improvements, average per capita living space for city dwellers having increased from 8.9 square meters in 1960 to 14.1 in 1985[22], the lack of housing is not only a shortage, but a genuine scarcity, as repeatedly stated during the 27th Party Congress:
«More than 80 % of all urban families now live in separate apart-ments».[23]
«To provide every family with a separate apartment or house by the year 2000 is in itself an enormous task, but a feasible one».[24]

This promise has wide social significance, for family problems and for labour allocation as well. Complaints about poor housing are numerous in the press, particularly in the cities in the far North and East and,
«It's hard to find a worker who would change jobs just to get an extra 20 rubles a month. But if he's promised an apartment, sometimes even a longtime employee can't be retained».[25]

Services. Household services showed very high rates of growth, es-pecially public transport and communications, cf. tables 1 and 2.[26]
«But, as the saying goes, man does not live by bread alone».[27]

And in the field of education, the Soviet Union has achieved a level on a par with the highest in the world. Average educational attainment for Soviet citizens aged 16 and above has increased from 5 years in 1950 to 9.1 years in 1980 according to Western estimates.[28] Large groups of the population have benefited from educational progress. This also applies to health care, which is universally available without direct charge, although not in quantities and qualities comparable to the most advanced countries in the world. There are shortages of medicines, side-payments to doctors and nurses are widespread, and the best service is reserved for the elite. The health system has not prevented general problems of health in the population as expressed by the stagnating average life expectancy.[29]

The military sector also increased its output of services to the population. National security and the proud feeling of being a super-power are significant from a consumer point of view.

Consumption in 1986. The reported 6.4 % increase in real trade turnover seems to overrate the real improvement for the Soviet consumer. Real per capita incomes were reported to increase 2.3 %[30]. Retail trade turnover exclusive of alcoholic beverages increased 7.1 %. The difference in the growth rate of 0.7 % due to lower alcohol sales seems to be small, as alcohol sales were about 15 % of total retail sales in 1985 (in 1985 it dropped about 15 %, and prices increased on average 8 %). The reported drop in alcohol production was 35 % in 1986 and in sales 37 %.[31] This should produce an effect of approximately −5.5 %. Maybe the price weights have been changed. Retail prices for alcoholic beverages were increased 20-25 % in August.[32] Plans for retail trade were changed during 1986, cf. the notes to table 2. One may wonder whether there is sufficient substitution in the production of soft drinks, or in consumption, to make up for this loss.

For the majority of consumption goods, plans were fulfilled, but the report plainly stated that

« The quality of consumer goods, especially of TV sets and refrigerators remains poor ».[33]

For broad categories of goods like meat, milk and vegetables, the gap between supply and demand has increased during 1987. This is also the case for coffee (a 70 % drop in processing) and tea. This was reported in Izvestia in January[34] in a new column appearing every Saturday entitled « Kommerčeskoe obozrenie » (Commercial review). Despite frequent complaints in the press about local and specific shortages of a variety of goods, like toasters[35], eyeglasses[36], yeast[37] and sewing machines[38], it seems to be due to the glasnost' campaign that these matters are treated in more general terms. The newspaper also warned about impending shortages of shoes and woollen and cotton clothes, and estimated total unsatisfied demand in 1986 at 21-25 milliard rubles, i.e. 6.3 %-7.5 % of total retail trade.

2. *Other Aspects of the Standard of Living*

Imbalances caused by prices being below market clearing levels are often considered evidence of consumer deprivation, as « there are no goods on the shelves » (by Western observers), or of consumer prosperity, as « prices are low, so that everybody can afford to buy the goods» (by Soviet consumers).[39] Of course both are wrong, if consumer prosperity is defined by the amount and quality of goods and services available for consumption. A distinction should be made between shortages due to excess demand at low prices, and scarcity, i.e. shortfalls from some absolute standard of need.[40] However, the former entail nuisances of their own, which together with other peculiar features of Soviet consumption and distribution influence the standard of living.

Queuing and shopping take up huge resources of time, partly during working hours. The total amount has been estimated at 37 milliard hours a year in 1981[41] or roughly 190 hours per adult person, which is close to the amount of working time lost per year per capita in a country like Denmark due to unemployment.

Irrational use of goods appears everywhere, when prices are subsidized, and the Soviet Union is no exception. Cheap bread is widely used for feed, in 1975 as much as 4% of bread and grain products sold, corresponding to 5-6 kilograms per capita.[42] Meat is used profitably to raise fur animals, and in 1982 a ban on private keeping of carnivorous fur-bearing animals was necessary.[43] A resolution was adopted by the Central Committee in May 1985 calling for

«greater strictness in adhering to established procedures for the use of bread and other food products».[44]

In 1984 agricultural subsidies amounted to 54.7 milliard rubles, including 21.0 milliard for meat. The cost of producing one kilogram of beef in 1983 came to 4.75 rubles, while the average retail price was 1.77 rubles.[45]

Savings deposits of the population have increased from a total of 10.9 milliard rubles in 1960 to 220.8 milliard rubles in 1985[46], or about 1,100 rubles per adult member of the population. They are unequally distributed, 3% of the accounts amounting to 50% of total deposits.[47] Whether this increase is a sign of shortages of consumer goods has been debated among Soviet as well as Western observers. However, the role of shortages should not be overrated. Annual net savings have not increased as fast as total savings deposits, and these have not grown much faster than expenditures for which people save.[48] Compared to prices of e.g. cooperative housing (cf. above) and motor cars (7,500-15,000 rubles), deposit increases may not be excessive.

Retail trade is endowed with much less resources in the Soviet Union than in other industrialized countries. Besides the shortage of goods there is also a shortage of shops, of which the number is about one fourth of that in the USA.[49] In 1979, 8.2% of the labour force was employed in trade compared to 28.6% in the USA and 20.4% in

Denmark.[50] Official wages are low, but they are supplemented by significant side-payments.[51] Corruption would be less if market clearing prices prevailed. It is possible that the newly adopted more flexible price system for theatre tickets, allowing price increases as well as discounts of 50 %[52], may reduce the number of

«tie-in deals, which everybody is sick and tired of. ... All cashiers know that this form of selling tickets is illegal. Nevertheless it is alive and well».[53]

The market for consumer goods is not very transparent as a significant share, probably about one third, is sold in special shops in enterprises, where producers often sell their produce from an «avtolavka», and in closed shops for the elite.

3. *Future Trends in Consumer Goods Production*

The element of sobriety in the draft guidelines for the 1986-1990 plan was considerably reduced in the final law, cf. Table 6. Most targets were slightly increased, but the target growth rate for retail trade turnover (excluding sales of alcoholic beverages) jumped from 3.4-4.1 to an ambitious 5.9 % (unless covert inflation is supposed to contribute a significant share). Consumer services are planned to grow even faster at 8.4 % per year, and the whole of the modest net addition to the labour force is expected to find employment in services.[54] Per capita real incomes will grow 2.7 %, which means that growth in education, health and other types of public consumption must be small.

For food consumption, the goals of the food program from 1982 have been restated by Gorbachev[55], cf. table 3, and the projected increase in agricultural production is based on an expected growth in the grain harvest to 250-255 million tons[56], i.e. an annual growth rate of 6.8 %-7.2 % compared to the official 1981-1985 average of 180.3 million tons, and 3.5 %-4.0 % compared to the 1986 harvest of 210 million tons. The agro-industrial complex almost retains its 33 % share of total investments.

The share of total investment in national income will increase from 25.9 % in 1985 to 27.6 % in 1990. This is itself a drag on other uses, including consumption. The increase will be channelled exclusively into the productive sphere, and top priority is given to the machine building industry with an 80 % increase, and the fuel and power complex (35 %, reduced from 47 % according to the draft guidelines). This leaves relatively smaller increases for light industry, and the pay-off in terms of increased consumer goods production will therefore show up relatively slowly.[57]

Table 6
The Eleventh and Twelfth Five-Year Plans.
Average percentage growth rates per year.

	Plan 1981-1985	Actual 1981-1985	Draft guidelines 1986-1990	Approved plan 1986-1990
National income utilized	3.4	3.1	3.5-4.1	4.1
Gross industrial output	4.7	3.7	3.9-4.4	4.6
Group A: means of production	4.6	3.6	3.7-4.2	4.4
Group B: consumer goods	4.8	3.9	4.1-4.6	4.9
Gross agricultural output	2.5	1.1	2.7-3.0	2.7
Gross investment	2.0	2.9	3.4-4.1	4.3
Per capita real incomes	3.1	2.1	2.5-2.8	2.7
Retail trade turnover	4.2	3.1	3.4-4.1	5.9
Consumer services	7.6	5.8	5.4-7.0	8.4
Average earnings	2.7	2.5	2.5-2.8	2.8

Note: For agricultural output and investment: rate of increase between five-year periods.

Sources: Ekonomičeskaja Gazeta (November 1985, no. 46): 3-15, (February 1986, no. 6): 11-14, (June 1986, no. 26): 14. K. Bush in Radio Liberty Research, RL 250/86.

However, a significant share of consumer goods is produced by heavy industry, and

« all branches without exception have been oriented, to a greater degree than before, to the output of consumer goods and the development of the service sphere».[58]

In 1983 the production of consumer goods per ruble of wages fund was introduced as a bonus indicator, but only with partial success because it threatens productivity, and bonuses are encumbered by restrictions.[59]

The expansion of paid services will also to a large extent be provided by industrial enterprises. It is possible that the very high increase (50 % over the five years) means that some free services will be charged a price, maybe even in education and in health care where « improvements in the organization» have been announced.[60]

In housing much emphasis is put on cooperative and individual construction and do-it-yourself methods of construction, which are also encouraged for industrial reconstruction.

Even if these plans are consistent it is nevertheless relevant to ask which consequences are most likely, if the growth targets are not met. There have been many declarations about the importance of improved consumption and housing for the Soviet population with reference to the need of fulfilling growing aspirations[61], to better family life[62], to curbing speculation and unearned income[63], and, most important, to the incentive problem, which demands that

«... needs and requirements should be satisfied more fully. This is advantageous to the state as well».[64]

«Its solution is directly linked to the strengthening of material incentives to labour, the rational use of non-working time, the mood of the Soviet people, and the overcoming of the negative phenomena engendered by shortages».[65]

But the commitment to increasing investment appears to be even stronger, and furthermore, there are powerful systemic forces promoting expenditures in this area, where the problem is not so much to obtain plan fulfilment, but rather to prevent overfulfilment (cf. Table 6). Also, the military complex has strong arguments in favour of its claims. It is also repeatedly stated that a condition for obtaining pay increases is that

«the needed money is to be earned by labour collectives on the basis of improvements in the organization of production and the performance of a growing volume of work by a smaller number of people».[66]

Table 7

Numerical examples showing possible outcomes of the Twelfth Five-Year Plan
(shares of total output 1990, and average percentage growth per year)

	Assumed output shares 1986 (1)	Plan (2)		As (2) with 0% agricultural growth (3)		3% industry 1% agriculture 2% total (4)		As (4) with 4.5% military spending (5)	
Origin:									
Industry, construction	45	46	4.6	47	4.6	47	3.0	47	3.0
Agriculture	14	13	2.7	12	0.0	13	1.0	13	1.0
Services, trade etc.	41	41	4.0	41	4.0	40	1.2	40	1.2
Total	100	100	4.1	100	3.8	100	2.0	100	2.0
End use:									
Consumption	46	46	4.0	45	3.3	44	1.1	43	0.5
Food	21	20	2.7	17	0.0	20	1.0	20	1.0
Goods	15	16	5.7	18	6.6	14	1.0	13	-0.7
Services	10	10	4.0	10	4.0	10	1.2	10	1.2
Public consumption	7	7	4.0	7	4.0	7	1.2	7	1.2
Investment	32	32	4.3	33	4.3	34	3.0	34	3.0
Military spending	15	15	4.1	15	4.1	16	3.0	17	4.5
Total	100	100	4.1	100	3.8	101	2.0	101	2.0
Consumption per capita	—	—	3.2	—	2.5	—	0.3	—	-0.3

Note: Each numerical example shows output shares 1990 and average percentage growth per year.
Output of services, etc. is computed as residual.
Food consumption: same growth rate as agricultural production.
Goods consumption: computed as a residual.
Services consumption and public consumption: growth rate as service production.
Investment: as plan in (²) and (³), as industrial growth in (⁴) and (⁵).
Military spending: as total output in (²), same absolute growth in (³) as in (²), as industry in (⁴), 4.5% in (⁵).
Population annual percentage rate of increase: 0.8% (Baldwin, 1979:8).

Therefore, the most likely claimant to suffer in case of shortfalls in growth performance is consumption, as has been the case in the past. In his recent speech in Riga Gorbachev warned that

«... perestrojka cannot be regarded from a pure consumer position ... Its significance cannot be evaluated from immediate results ... This will not be manna from heaven but fruits of our work for fulfilling the 12th Five-Year Plan».[67]

To illustrate the room for manoeuvre it is tempting to combine planned growth rates with Western estimates of aggregate shares of production by origin and by end use. This is how the numerical examples in Table 7 are computed. The input-output assumptions are very crude, and implied input proportions are not the same in the four examples. A high degree of flexibility in production is assumed. Therefore the computations are easy to criticize, but also easy to use, and they may illustrate a few points.

First, given the planned growth rates there is room for a considerable increase in consumption of goods and services per capita. Consumption of goods is in every case computed as a residual — despite Ryzkov's express denunciation of the «residual (ostatočnyj) approach to the planning of the social sphere».[68] The share of non-food items in household consumption increases 2 percentage points, not 9 points as stated in the plans.[69] But retail trade turnover of goods increases at a rate comparable to the high planned rate, cf. Table 6. The planned 8.4% increase in consumer services is not reflected in the example because service production growth is computed as a residual. Part of the increase may be expressed in the output of industrial enterprises, which are supposed to provide half of the increased output of services.

Second, if there is no agricultural growth total consumption declines, but goods consumption increases because industrial capacity needed to process agricultural output is released for goods production.

Third, if growth rates are smaller with a probably more realistic total of 2%, per capita consumption growth almost vanishes, and finally if this is combined with an increased military burden, it becomes negative.

Thus, although the new party program is careful to define full communism in terms of «full satisfaction of reasonable (razumnyj) needs»[70], the 12th Five-Year Plan nevertheless seems to be very ambitious with respect to consumer promises.

4. *Recent Measures Affecting Consumption*

The main determinant for consumption growth is total production, and all measures of economic policy are relevant for future consumption. Some measures specifically directed towards consumption are listed below.

Complex programmes. Two major «complex programmes», the Food Programme from 1982[71] and the Comprehensive Programme for the Development of Consumer Goods Production and the Service Sphere from 1985[72] specify goals for consumption growth which are incorporated in the 12th Five-Year Plan. Output of consumer goods in light industry is supposed to increase 3.5 % annually during 1986-1990, and selling floor space should be increased to 200 square meters per 1,000 inhabitants in the cities. In England the corresponding area was about 600 square meters in 1972.[73]

Other resolutions have called for increased production of consumer goods[74], particularly in light industry[75], a network of manufacturers' outlets for consumer goods[76], and better organization of retail trade, including more flexible opening hours.[77]

Consumer prices. At the 27th Party Congress Gorbachev declared that «Prices must be given greater flexibility, and their level must be linked not only to outlays but also to the consumer properties of goods, the effectiveness of manufactured articles, and the degree to which the product in question meets the requirements of society and public demand. It is planned to make wider use of ceiling (limitnye) and contract prices».[78]

There have been some discussions in the press[79], and a few further measures include the experiments with theatre tickets, the introduction in January 1987 of new kinds of high quality bread and pastry sold at higher prices than the normal types[80], and cooperative production and sales. Vegetables are sold directly by producers to consumers, and cooperatively produced sausages are sold through state shops. Prices are higher than state prices, but lower than kolkhoz-market prices, for sausages often about 7 rubles per kilogram, compared to the 4-5 rubles state price and maybe 10 rubles kolkhoz-market price. Quality is also said to be higher than for state produce. A newly opened cooperative «kafé» in Moscow charges prices that seem to be 50-100 % higher than in other restaurants. One possible purpose of encouraging the cooperative sector — maybe even the main one — might be to introduce very unpopular price increases through the back door.

Changes in agriculture may directly influence the food supply. A resolution in March 1986[81] allowed for a 50 % bonus on production above the 1981-1985 average, gave kolkhozes and sovkhozes the right to sell 30 % of planned production of fruit and vegetables as well as above plan output directly to local shops, and allowed for local variation in prices. Family teams and private plot production is further encouraged, also outside agricultural enterprises.

«... in most industrial ministries the production of livestock and poultry (live weight) will reach 15 to 20 kg. per year per worker by the end of the Five-Year Plan».[82]

The quality campaign also refers to consumer goods, and
« Quality, and once again quality — that is our slogan today ».[83]

A new system of «state acceptance» (gosudarstvennaja priemka) is gradually being introduced in Soviet industry. Quality control is performed by a network of state control bodies, not by enterprises themselves as before, but apparently not without difficulties.[84]

Individual enterprise. By a law from November 1986[85] the scope for individual enterprise was broadened and some existing forms were legalized. The law specifies a list of permitted activities including taxi-service using private cars, tutoring, guesthouse services, handicrafts, and repair services. In 1985 it was reported that about half of consumer services were produced outside the social sector engaging 17-20 million people, including 45 % of apartment repairs and 40 % of automotive repairs, in rural areas as much as 80 %.[86] However, the purposes of the law also is to enforce stricter controls, and in most cases certificates of registration are needed.

Even more important for consumer welfare is, maybe, the developing cooperative sector, which is not restricted to employing only family members. It was actively encouraged by Gorbachev at the 27th Party Congress :

« We also favour total clarity in the question of cooperative ownership. It has by no means exhausted its possibilities in socialist production and in the better satisfaction of peoples requirements. ... They should become widespread in the production and processing of output, in housing and orchard-and-garden construction, and in the sphere of consumer services and trade. It is also time to overcome prejudice concerning commodity-money relations and their underestimation in the practice of planned economic management ».[87]

In February 1987 a model statute for public catering was published.[88] The crucial test for the success of individual and cooperative enterprise will be, whether the necessary materials and tools will become available, not only for a few experimental enterprises, but on a broad scale.

The anti-alcohol drive. Finally, it could be mentioned that the decrease in alcohol consumption (35 % in 1986), besides its immediate effects upon consumption, health, labour, consumer satisfaction etc., also exerts a pressure on total demand, because of the significant amounts of purchasing power (maybe 5 % of total consumption) seeking other outlets.

The production of moonshine (samogon) has increased, also in the towns, «even in Moscow».[89] In one rajon sugar consumption increased 70 % last year, in others it has disappeared from the shelves, and yeast has become more deficit than it used to be.

These institutional changes, even «radical reforms», may have a certain impact on consumer welfare, but the main determinant is total production. Not even the best economic reforms can escape material restrictions, economic priorities and economic policy.

5. The Distribution of Income and Consumption

However, changes in the general mood of the workforce, the «čelove-českij faktor», is ascribed decisive importance for the restructuring (perestrojka) of the economy, and it is influenced not only by institutional changes, but also by consumption itself, its total amount as well as its distribution.

Table 8

Wage inequality in various countries during the latest decades as measured by the decile ratio (P90/P10)

	1947	1950	1952	1955	1960	1962	1965	1967	1970	1975	1981
Bulgaria				2.3		2.5		2.5	2.5		
Czechoslovakia	5.6	3.6			2.9	2.7	2.7	2.7	2.8		
Hungary			2.9	2.8	2.6		2.5	2.6	3.0	2.7	
Poland				3.4	3.2		3.5		3.1	3.4	
Romania									2.3		
USSR	7.2			4.4	4.0		3.2	2.8	3.2	3.3	3.0
Yugoslavia						3.2	3.8	2.9	3.0		
USA		7.1								6.3	
U.K.			3.7						3.9		
Sweden								3.7	3.6		

Note: The decile ratio is the proportion between the 90th percentile (P90) and the 10th (P10). The percentiles are amounts of income, and the size of P10 is determined so that 10% of the population earns less than P10 and 90% earns more. Likewise for P90: 90% earns less and 10% more.

Comparability is a very difficult question due to differences in taxes, price systems, fringe benefits and the structure of outlays, e.g. the weights of housing rent. One investigation shows that correcting for taxes and privileges eliminates differences in inequality between East and West (Morisson, 1984).

Western data are exclusive of taxes. The income year may deviate one year from that stated in the table. For Denmark, P90/P10 is 5.75 for the total workforce, but merely 2.33 if part-time workers are excluded.

Sources: Bulgaria: Levcik in Fallenbuchl, 1975, vol. 1: 337; Kiuranov, 1975.
Czechoslovakia, Hungary and Yugoslavia: Michal, 1973: 410; Michal, 1975: 264; Asselain, 1984: 50.
USSR: Bergson, 1984: 1077; McAuley, 1979: 220-222; Aleksandrova & Federovskaja, 1984; computations using data from Rabkina & Rimaševskaja, pp. 175-192 in Fedorenko & Rimaševskaja, 1979.
Poland: Vielrose, 1978: 231; Asselain, 1984: 50.
Romania: Connor, 1979: 218.
U.K., Sweden, U.S.A.: Wiles in Krelle & Shorrocks, 1978: 191.

The general trend since the war has been towards relatively narrow income differences. Skill differentials have contracted as a consequence of successive increases in the minimum wage, reductions of top salaries and two general wage reforms. Production workers have improved their position at the expense of technical and administrative staff. Differences between sectors have also narrowed, and peasants are approaching the national average (peasants now earn about 90 % of the average, compared to 70 % in 1960). Women's incomes are about two thirds of men's on average, not far from the proportion found in many other countries. Regional differences still exist, although smaller than in other parts of the world. Higher wages in the far North and East are almost neutralized by higher prices and by non-availability of goods, particularly in the newly created cities.

With many reservations, table 8 shows that income differences are relatively narrow in the Soviet Union. The trend towards decreased differences, deplored by many economists in the seventies, was reverted after a low in 1968, but this proved to be temporary, as previewed by the economists.[90]

The mechanisms of income inequality in the Soviet Union differs in two important aspects from that in the West. First, unemployment does not create inequality — so far. There is a job for everybody, due to the labour shortage. But,

« If you look into the matter more deeply, you may find that there is no manpower shortage »[91]

as Gorbachev said, referring to overmanning and unproductive employment. There have been some debates about the consequences of reducing overmanning[92], and also proposals for a system of unemployment relief with an obligation to take up unskilled work.[93]

Second, much inequality is created not by the distribution of jobs, but by the distribution of goods. Erratic availability of goods, special shops and privileges reduce the correlation between income and consumption, and have to a large extent replaced the use of the denounced, but in a certain sense rather democratic, money. For many years the consumer goods market and the public's understanding of the allocative functions of prices have been systematically destroyed by preventing price in-

creases necessary for equilibrium. But the total impact of privileges should not be overrated.[94] In most cases the living standards of the elite does not exceed a Western middle class level, as witnessed by these excerpts from a young girl's letter:
« My parents also earn a lot. We have a Volga, a three-room cooperative apartment, a garden and a dača ».[95]

6. Recent Measures Affecting Distribution
The wage reform. The overall purpose of the wage reform, which has been announced and discussed[96], but still not published in full detail, are incorporated in the law on the 12th Five-Year Plan and they are
« To enhance the effectiveness of the pay system, more closely link the remuneration of personnel with their labour contribution, resolutely eliminate elements of wage-levelling (uravnilovka), and increase material and moral responsibility for shortcomings and deficiencies in work ».[97]

It is implicit that the incentive effect is the stronger the more closely the first principle of socialist justice — payment according to work — is adhered to. The second principle, i.e. equalization between groups, is applied to differentials between branches in the economy. Inequality due to different labour efficiency is accepted to a certain degree, but excessive differences, e.g. between production brigades, has evoked complaints from the public.[98]
Wages should be more decisive for consumption possibilities.[99] Hence the sharp increase in paid services, and the intentions to reduce shortages. Wage increases should be contingent upon productivity increases, contrary to past experience[100], and this should even apply inside each enterprise. Wage increases should be provided by the money of the enterprises themselves. The model should be like the experiment in the Belorussian railways.

The bonus fund should be determined mainly by cost reductions for enterprises in group A and profits — nothing less — for enterprises in group B according to the 1986 regulations.[101] If output has been decided these two criteria amount to the same thing, but using profits in group A probably means that greater freedom concerning output mix will be allowed for consumer goods enterprises.

Occupational groups. The position of engineers, including their « prestige », and for teachers, doctors and other « non-productive » groups will be improved, and the advantage of production workers consequently reduced.[102] Teachers have already received 30 % wage increases according to the 1985-plan fulfilment report.[103]

Unearned incomes (netrudovye dokhody), as they show up in the very unequal distribution of savings deposits[104], are the targets of two resolutions and one decree of May 1985.[105] The purpose is to combat corruption, speculation, use of state owned motor cars for private purposes, excessive rents for private hiring out, etc. The means are reduction of shortages in a variety of fields, fines of 50-100 rubles in cases of violation, declaration of money sources when concluding deals totalling more than 10,000 rubles or when building a house (dača) valued at over 20,000 rubles. The internal passport system will be reinforced, and stricter control with kolkhoz market sellers enacted.[106]

Social policy. A new pension system is being prepared in order to improve the position of various groups, but also with a view to incentive effects, particularly concerning pensioners' propensity to continue working.[107] It has also been pointed out that higher pensions will increase the incentive effect of wages by reducing the burden of dependent members of the family.[108]

7. *Consumption, Equity and Incentives*

The conclusion can be phrased in Marxian terms, i.e. in terms of several contradictions facing Soviet policy on consumption, equity and incentives.

Legitimacy versus consumerism. Apart from military strength superpower status, the main legitimation of the CPSU's monopoly of political power is the ever increasing welfare of the Soviet consumer and the future abundance in full communism. At the same time excessive «consumerism» (potrebitel'stvo) is criticised.[109]

Equality versus equity. It is generally accepted that equity or social justice (social'naja spravedlivost') does not mean equality, but rather remuneration according to work and equal opportunities. Nevertheless equalitarian attitudes are widespread among the population.[110]

Equity versus motivations. It is generally agreed that wage differentials should be based on 1) productivity (quantity and quality of work), 2) incentive effects, 3) compensation (for adverse working conditions), and that 4) social considerations are alien to wage fixing. But it is seldom acknowledged that the two first criteria may often contradict each other. Very big incomes are not accepted. Rogovin simply proposes a maximum acceptable per capita income[111], but ignores that the possibility of the big jackpot, however tiny, whether earned, unearned or due to sheer luck, is an immense motivating force.[112] Gorbachev retains a clear distinction:

« But, in curbing unearned income, we must not allow a shadow to fall on those who receive additional earnings through honest labour ».[113]

Individual private enterprise versus control. The types of « honest labour » allowed are narrowly defined, and strict controls are to be enacted.

Motivation versus macro-economic balance. The total amount of consumption goods available severely restricts the expansion of wage incentives.

The ultimate contradiction is the one between:
Consumption targets versus production possibilities.

Is there a synthesis of all these theses and antitheses? Perhaps one could say about glasnost' and demokratizacija, what Marilyn Monroe once said about money: maybe it does not solve all your problems, but it helps.

Notes

1. K. Marx & F. Engels: Die Deutsche Ideologie (1845-46). MEW 3 p. 28.
2. K. Marx: Das Kapital III, Chap. 48 (1894). MEW 25 p. 828. However, Marx seems to miss the point when stressing that « In den meisten Fällen entspringen die Bedürfnisse aus der Produktion...» (Das Elend der Philosophie (1846-47). MEW 4 p. 76). And A. Marshall made the same mistake in his comments on topical problems of economic policy in the Soviet Union and elsewhere: «... each new step upwards is to be regarded as the development of new activities giving rise to new wants, rather than new wants giving rise to new activities». (Principles of Economics (1890), Book III, Chap. II). But it is not at all impossible that « In einer höheren Phase der kommunistischen Gesellschaft, nachdem ... die Arbeit ... selbst das erste Lebensbedürfnis geworden ... - erst dann kann ... die Gesellschaft auf ihre Fahne schreiben: Jeder nach seinen Fähigkeiten, jedem nach seinen Bedürfnissen». (K. Marx: Kritik des Gothaer Programms (1875). MEW 19, p. 21).
3. Speech at CPSU Central Committee conference on labour productivity in agriculture, January 23, 1987 (Pravda, January 25, 1987, p. 1).
4. Gorbachev, 1986, p. 6.
5. U.S. Congress, 1982, pp. 20-22. These estimates have been questioned, e.g. by Ellman (1986) especially for overrating growth in recent years due to neglect of increased inflation.
6. Schroeder, 1983, p. 318; Schroeder & Edwards, 1981. Soviet consumption is 42.8 % of USA consumption according to the dollar comparison, 27.6 % according to the ruble comparison, and the geometric mean is 34.4 %.
7. U.S. Congress, 1982. pp. VIII, 18, 59-61, 76-78. Growth is higher if weights in established (prevailing) prices are used (3.5 % per capita consumption growth 1950-79), rather than factor cost weights (3.0 % per capita consumption growth 1950-79), cf. Schroeder, 1983 pp. 312-313 and table 1.
8. Nar. Khoz. 1985, p. 478: U.N. E.C.E. 1986, p. 188.
9. Schroeder, 1983, p. 323: cf. Kunel'skij, 1981, p. 22.
10. Trehub, 1986, p. 21; Kommunist (September 1986, No. 14), p. 60; Herlemann, 1987.
11. Sarkisjan, 1983, p. 116; Fedorenko & Rimaševskaja, 1979, p. 34.
12. Možin & Krylatykh, 1982. Translation from The Current Digest of the Soviet Press 34 (September 1, 1982, No. 31), p. 4.
13. Herlemann et al., 1987.
14. Levikov in Literaturnaja Gazeta, March 20, 1985; Karup Pedersen, 1986, p. 291.
15. Izvestija, June 30, 1984, Ruban, 1986, p. 670; Petrov, 1986, p. 26; Schroeder, 1983, p. 325.
16. Ruban, 1986, pp. 666, 670; Orlov & Saenko, 1982, p. 100.

17. Ekonomičeskaja Gazeta (January 1987, n° 5), p. 12.
18. Ruban, 1986, p. 667; Andrienko, 1985, p. 106.
19. Pravda, September 26, 1985, p. 1.
20. Trehub, 1986, pp. 32-33.
21. Gorbachev, 1986.
22. Nar. Khoz, 1985, p. 426; Trehub, 1986, p. 31; Karapetjan & Rimaševskaja, 1977, pp. 117-119.
23. Ryžkov's report, Pravda, March 4, 1986, p. 4.
24. Gorbachev, 1986.
25. Pravda, January 11, 1983, p. 2. Translation from The Current Digest of the Soviet Press 35 (February 9, 1983, n° 2), p. 20.
26. Schroeder, 1983, p. 313.
27. Gorbachev, 1986, p. 11; cf. The Mosaic Law, Book 5, Chap. 8.3.
28. Schroeder, 1983, p. 314; cf. Connor, 1986, pp. 36-39.
29. Trehub, 1986, pp. 13-24.
30. Ekonomičeskaja Gazeta (January 1987, n° 5), p. 10.
31. Ekonomičeskaja Gazeta (January 1987, n° 5), pp. 13-14; P. Hanson in Radio Liberty Research 439/86, p. 3; cf. Schroeder, 1983, p. 322; Ekonomičeskaja Gazeta (December 1986, n° 51), p. 23.
32. Pravda, August 1, 1986, p. 2.
33. Ekonomičeskaja Gazeta (January 1987, n° 5), p. 12.
34. Izvestija, January 3, 1987, p. 2.
35. Nedelja, 1982, n° 8, p. 8.
36. Izvestija, September 8, 1983, p. 2.
37. Nedelja, 1983, n° 47, pp. 6-7.
38. Pravda, April 16, 1984, p. 7.
39. Cf. the results from the Soviet Interview Project, Millar & Clayton, 1986, p. 10; cf. also Connor, 1986, p. 44.
40. Cf. Gray, 1981, p. 45.
41. Rutgajzer, 1981. In 1974 the amount was lower, 30 milliard hours (Pravda, June 9, 1984, p. 3). Cf. also EKO (March 1978, n° 3) p. 91 and Schroeder, 1983, p. 326. For literary treatment, see J. Wishnevsky in Radio Liberty Research RL 397/85. Cf. Wiles in Gumpel, 1985, p. 55; Wiles, 1982, p. 131.
42. Lane, 1982, p. 28; Lokšin, 1975, p. 91. The problem has been widely debated in the press, cf. e.g. Pravda, December 7, 1982, p. 3.
43. Vedomosti Verkhovnogo Soveta RSFSR, n° 47 (1257), November 25, 1982, Items 1726, p. 1042. Translated in The Current Digest of the Soviet Press 35 (March 2, 1983, n° 5), p. 21. Cf. also the debate in Pravda, March 15, 1981, p. 3.
44. Pravda, May 7, 1985, p. 1. Fines of 50-100 rubles were specified in a decree in May 1986, Ekonomičeskaja Gazeta (June 1986, n° 25), p. 5.
45. Ekonomika sel'skogo khozjajstva (March 1986, n° 3), pp. 59-64. Radio Liberty Research RL 295/86; Pravda, September 11, 1985, p. 1.
46. Nar. Khoz. 1985, p. 448.
47. Sverdlik, 1982.
48. Cf. D. Sedik in Radio Liberty Research, RL 321/85.
49. Schroeder, 1983, p. 326; EKO (March 1978, n° 3), p. 91.
50. Statistik tiarsoversigt 1982; Labour Force Statistics, OECD; Yearbook of Labour Statistics ILO, cf. Aage, 1986.
51. Cf. Izvestija, May 30, 1986, p. 3.
52. Izvestija, June 11, 1986, p. 6.
53. Izvestija, January 15, 1983, p. 3. Translation from The Current Digest of the Soviet Press 35 (February 9, 1983, n° 2), p. 23.
54. Ryžkov at the 27th Party Congress, Ekonomičeskaja Gazeta (March 1986, n° 11), pp. 23-30.
55. Pravda, May 25, 1982, pp. 1-2; Pravda, September 7, 1985, pp. 1-2; Pravda, June 19, 1986, pp. 1-5.
56. Ekonomičeskaja Gazeta (March 1986, n° 11), pp. 23-30.
57. Ryžkov in Pravda, June 19, 1986, pp. 1-5. The growth rate of light industry was 3.9 % annually 1986-1990 according to the Consumer Goods Programme, Pravda, October 9, 1985, pp. 1-3.
58. Ryžkov, Ekonomičeskaja Gazeta (March 1986, n° 11), p. 27.
59. Izvestija, May 19, 1983, p. 2, December 18, 1985, p. 2, December 19, 1985, p. 2.
60. Ryžkov, Pravda, June 19, 1986, cf. the Consumer Goods Programme, Pravda, October 9, 1985, pp. 1-3.
61. Cf. note 3.
62. Gorbachev, 1986, p. 6.
63. Ekonomičeskaja Gazeta (June 1986, n° 23), p. 5.
64. Gorbachev, Pravda, April 24, 1985, pp. 1-2.
65. Ryžkov, Pravda, March 4, 1986, p. 5.
66. Ryžkov, Pravda, June 19, 1986, p. 3.
67. Pravda, February 20, 1987, p. 2; cf. The Mosaic Law, Book 2, Chap. 16. 13-31. Cf. K. Bush in Radio Liberty Research, RL 250/86, pp. 7-9.
68. Quoted from K. Bush, Radio Liberty Research, RL 250/86, p. 8.
69. Pravda, June 19, 1986, p. 3.

Hans Aage

70. Quoted from D. Dyker in Radio Liberty Research, RL 363/85, p. 1.
71. Pravda, May 27, 1982, pp. 1-4.
72. Pravda, October 9, 1985, pp. 1-3.
73. Skurski, 1983, p. 149. D. Dyker in Radio Liberty Research, RL 351/85, p. 2.
74. Pravda, May 7, 1983, p. 1.
75. Ekonomičeskaja Gazeta (May 1986, n° 20), p. 2.
76. Izvestija, June 7, 1986, p. 2.
77. Pravda, August 5, 1986, p. 1.
78. Gorbachev, 1986, p. 8.
79. Petrov, 1986; Khasbulatov in Pravda, June 15, 1986; Kazakevič, 1986: 38-39.
80. Pravda, November 13, 1986.
81. Pravda, March 29, 1986, pp. 1-2.
82. Ryžkov, Pravda, June 19, 1986, p. 3.
83. Gorbachev, Pravda, April 24, 1985, p. 1.
84. As reported by Gorbachev, Pravda, November 16, 1986, pp. 1-2; cf. the resolution in Ekonomičes-kaja Gazeta (July 1986, n° 28), p. 4.
85. Pravda, November 21, 1986, pp. 1,3. The term «individual enterprise» (individual'naja trudovaja dejatel'nost') is used, and the term «private» (častnaja) is avoided.
86. Izvestia, August 19, 1985, p. 3; cf. Sovetskaja Rossia, August 11, 1983, p. 3.
87. Gorbachev, 1986, p. 9.
88. Ekonomičeskaja Gazeta (February 1987, no 9), pp. 11-14; cf. E. Teague in Radio Liberty Re-search, RL 319/86. A cooperative «Kafé» was opened in Moscow in March 1987; cf. Moskovskie Novosti, March 29, 1987, p. 14.
89. Sovetskaja Rossia, March 17, 1987, p. 4.
90. Rabkina & Rimaševskaja, 1978.
91. Gorbachev, 1986, p. 10.
92. V. Kostakov in Sovetskaja kultura, January 4, 1986, p. 3 and February 1, 1986, p. 3.
93. G. Popov in Pravda, December 27, 1980, p. 3.
94. Cf. the letters in Pravda, February 13, 1986, p. 3; February 15, 1986, pp. 1-2.
95. Komsomol'skaja pravda, November 13, 1983, p. 2. The Current Digest of the Soviet Press 36 (May 9, 1984, n° 15), p. 9.
96. Ekonomičeskaja Gazeta (October 1986, n° 43), pp. 6-7; Kunel'skij, 1987.
97. Ekonomičeskaja Gazeta (June 1986, n° 26), pp. 14-15.
98. Maksimova, 1985.
99. Cf. Connor, 1986, pp. 32, 42.
100. D. Sedik in Radio Liberty Research, RL 321/85, p. 7.
101. Ekonomičeskaja Gazeta (February 1986, n° 8), pp. 11-14, (July 1986, n° 28), p. 6.
102. Ekonomičeskaja Gazeta (June 1986, n° 26), Gorbachev, 1986, Loznevaja & Khejfec, 1986.
103. Ekonomičeskaja Gazeta (January 1987, n° 5), pp. 10-14.
104. Cf. note 45.
105. Ekonomičeskaja Gazeta (June 1986, n° 23), pp. 4-5, cf. (September 1986, n° 39), pp. 6-7.
106. Cf. Giroux, 1986.
107. S. Voronitsyn in Radio Liberty Research, RL 387/86.
108. Rabkina & Rimaševskaja, 1978, p. 29.
109. E.g. V. Rogovin in Komsomol'skaja Pravda, June 7, 1985.
110. Cf. A. Trehub's analysis of the articles by Rogovin (1986) and Zaslavskaja (1986) in Radio Liberty Research, RL 382/86.
111. V. Rogovin in Komsomol'skaja Pravda, June 28, 1985.
112. G. Lisičkin ridicules Rogovin in Literaturnaja Gazeta, February 19, 1986, n° 8.
113. Gorbachev, 1986.

References

Aage, H.: «Unemployment: Lessons from the Socialist Countries». Nordic Journal of Soviet and East European Studies 1986 (forthcoming).

Aleksandrova, E. & E. Fedorovskaja: «Mekhanizm formirovanija i vozvyšenija potrebnostej». Voprosy ekonomiki (January 1984, n° 1), pp. 15-25.

Asselain, J.-C.: «La répartition des revenus dans les pays du Centre-Est Européen». Chap. 1, pp. 33-85 in Kende & Strmiska, 1984.

Baldwin, G.: Population Projections by Age and Sex for the Republics and Major Economic Regions of the USSR: 1970-2000. International Population Reports, Series P-91, n° 26, Washington, D.C.: Bureau of the Census 1979.

Bergson, A.: «Income Inequality Under Soviet Socialism». Journal of Economic Literature 22 (September 1984, n° 3), pp. 1052-1099.

Bergson, A. & H.S. Levine (eds.): The Soviet Economy: Toward the Year 2000. London: Allen & Unwin 1983.

68

Connor, W.D.: Socialism, Politics and Equality: Hierarchy and Change in Eastern Europe and the USSR. New York: Columbia University Press, 1979.

Connor, W.D.: «Social Policy under Gorbachev». Problems of Communism 35 (July-August 1986, n° 4), pp. 31-46.

Ellman, M.: «The Macro-Economic Situation in the USSR-Retrospect and Prospect». Soviet Studies 39 (October 1986, n° 4), pp. 530-542.

Fallenbuchl, Z. (ed.): Economic Development in the Soviet Union and Eastern Europe. Vols. 1-2. New-York: Praeger 1975.

Fedorenko, N.P. & N.M. Rimaševskaja (eds.): Potrebnosti, dokhody, Potreblenie: Metodologija analisa i prognosirovanija narodnogo blagosostojanija. Moskva: Nauka 1979.

Giroux, A.: «Les marchés kolkhoziens sous surveillance». Le Courrier des Pays de l'Est (Novembre 1986, n° 312), pp. 57-61.

Gorbachev, M.S.: «The Political Report of the CPSU Central Committee to the 27th Congress of the Communist Party of the Soviet Union». Ekonomičeskaja Gazeta (March 1986, n° 10), pp. 3-18.

Gray, K.R.: «Soviet Consumption of Food: Is the Bottle «Half-Full», «Half-Empty», «Half-Water» or «Too Expensive»?» The ACES Bulletin 23 (Summer 1981, n° 2), pp. 31-50.

Gumpel, W. (ed.): Das Leben in den Kommunistischen Staaten. München: Hans-Martin Schleyer Stiftung 1985.

Hanson, P.: «Economic Constraints on Soviet Policies in the 1980s». International Affairs (Winter 1980/81), pp. 21-42.

Hanson, P.: «Brezhnev's Economic Legacy», pp. 41-54 in P. Joseph (ed.): The Soviet Economy after Brezhnev. Bruxelles: NATO, Economics Directorate 1984.

Herlemann, H.G. (ed.): The Quality of Life in the Soviet Union. Godstone: Westview Press 1987. (forthcoming)

Karapetjan, A.Kh. & N.M. Rimaševskaja (eds.): Differencirovannyj balans dokhodov i potreblenija naselenija. Moskva: Nauka 1977.

Karpukhin, D.: «O Sootnoženii rosta proizvoditel'nosti truda i zarabotnoj platy». Planovoe Khozjajstvo (October 1983, n° 10), pp. 87-92.

Karup-Pedersen, J.: «USSR midt i et sporskifte». Okonomi og Politik 59 (1986, nr. 4), pp. 287-298.

Kazakevič, D.M.: «K soveršenstvovaniju potrebitel'skikh cen». EKO (January 1986, n° 1), pp. 33-43.

Kende, P. & Z., Strmiska: Égalité et inégalités en Europe de l'Est. Paris: Presses de la Fondation nationale des sciences politiques 1984.

Kiuranov, C.: «Aspects of the Distribution of Personal Earnings and Earnings Stratification in Bulgaria». Chap. 10, pp. 276-286 in Fallenbuchl, 1975.

Krelle, W. & A.F. Shorrocks (eds.): Personal Income Distribution. Amsterdam: North-Holland 1978.

Kunel'skij, L.: «Novoe v systeme organizacii zarabotnoj platy». Kommunist (January 1987, n° 2), pp. 30-40.

Kunel'skij, L. E.: Zarabotnaja plata i stimulirovanie truda. Social'no-ekonomičeskij aspekt. Moskva: Ekonomika 1981.

Lane, A.: «USSR: Private Agriculture on Center Stage». Part 2, pp. 23-40 in U.S. Congress, Joint Economic Committee (ed.): Soviet Economy in the 1980's: Problems and Prospects. Washington, D.C.: U. S. Government Printing Office, 1982.

Lokšin, P.A.: Spros, proizvodstvo, torgovlja. Moskva: Ekonomika 1975.

Loznevaja, M. & L. Khejfec: «Oplata inženernogo truda». Voprosy ekonomiki (June 1986, n° 6), pp. 33-42.

Maksimova, N.: «Brigady na perepute». EKO (August 1985, n° 8), pp. 152-199.

McAuley, A.: Economic Welfare in the Soviet Union: London. Allen & Unwin 1979.

Michael, J.: «An Alternative Approach to Measuring Income Inequality in Eastern Europe». Chap. 9, pp. 256-275 in Fallenbuchl, 1975.

Michal, J.M.: «Size-Distribution of Earnings and Household Incomes in Small Socialist Countries». Review of Income and Wealth (December 1973, n° 4), pp. 407-427.

Millar, J.R. & E. Clayton: «Quality of Life: Subjective Measures of Relative Satisfaction». Soviet Interview Project (SIP) Working Paper n° 9, Urbana-Champaign, IL., February 1986.

Morisson, C.: «Income Distribution in East European and Western Countries». Journal of Comparative Economics (June 1984, n° 2), pp. 121-138.

Možin, V.P. & E.N. Krylatykh: «On Drawing up the Food Programme». EKO (June 1982, n° 6), pp. 5-18.

Narodnoe khozjajstvo SSSR v 1985 g. Moskva: Finansy i statistika 1986.

Orlov, A. & D. Rubval'ter: «Perestrojka proizvodstva tovarov narodnogo potreblenija». Voprosy ekonomiki (October 1982, n° 10), pp. 97-107.

69

Peebles, G. : «Aggregate Retail Price Changes in Socialist Economies: Identification, Theory and Evidence for China and the Soviet Union». Soviet Studies 39 (October 1986, n° 4), pp. 477-507.

Petrov, A.M. : «Kak osušit'potok nekhodovykh tovarov». EKO (January 1986, n° 1), pp. 18-33.

Rabkina, N.E. & N.M. Rimaševskja: «Raspredelitel'nye otnošenija i social'noe razvitie». EKO (May 1978, n° 5), pp. 17-32.

Rimaševskaja, N.M. : «Strukturnye izmenenija v tendencijakh rosta blagosostojanija». Sociologičeskie issledovanija (April 1985, n° 4), pp. 22-33.

Rogovin, V.Z. : «Social'naja spravedlivost' i socialističeskoe raspredelenie žiznennykh blag». Voprosy filosofii (September 1986, n° 9), pp. 3-20.

Ruban, M.E. : «Lebensstandard - Rückkehr zu Nüchternheit und Realismus?» Osteuropa 36 (August-September 1986, n° 8-9) pp. 663-671.

Rutgajzer, V.M. : «Čelovek truda v sfere raspredelenija i potreblenija». EKO (September 1981, n° 9), pp. 46-62.

Sarkasjan, G.S : Narodnoe blagosostojanie v SSSR. Moskva 1983.

Schroeder, G.E. : «Consumption», Chap. 10, pp. 311-349 in Bergson & Levine (1983).

Schroeder, G.E. & I. Edwards: Consumption in the USSR : An International Comparison. Washington: Joint Economic Committee, U.S. Government Printing Office 1981.

Seljunin, V. & G. Khanin : «Lukavaja cifra». Novyj Mir (February 1987, n° 2), pp. 181-201.

Skurski, R. : Soviet Marketing and Economic Development. New York : St. Martin's Press 1983.

Sverdlik, Š.B. : «Rost sbereženij naselenija: pričiny i sledstvija»; EKO (June 1982, n° 6), pp. 115-130.

Trehub, A. : «Social and Economic Rights in the Soviet Union : Work, Health Care, Social Security and Housing». RL Supplement 3/86 (December 29, 1986).

U.N. ECE : Economic Survey of Europe in 1985-1985. Geneve: U.N. Economic Commission for Europe, 1986.

U.S. Congress, Joint Economic Committee (ed.) : USSR : Measures of Economic Growth and Development, 1950-1980. Washington, D.C. : U.S. Government Printing Office 1982.

Vielrose, E. : «Patterns of the Distribution of Earnings in Poland». Chap. 9, pp. 229-240 in Krelle & Shorrocks, 1978.

Wiles, P.J.D. : «What We Still Don't Know About the Soviet Economy» pp. 117-138 in NATO (ed.) : The CMEA Five-Year Plans (1981-1985) in a New Perspective. Bruxelles : NATO, Economics Directorate 1982.

Zaslavskaja, T. : «Čelovečeskij faktor razvitija ekonomiki i social'naja spravedlivost'». Kommunist (September 1986, n° 13), pp. 61-73.

Zaslavskaja, T.I. : «Tvorčeskaja aktivnost' mass: social'nye rezervy rosta». EKO (March 1986, n° 3), pp. 3-25.

Soviet Labour-Saving Policy in the Eighties

Silvana Malle

Introduction

Labour-saving has been a primary concern to Soviet planners since the bleak perspective of stagnation emerged as a consequence of failing rates of growth of productivity and of the able-bodied population in industrialized areas. In the seventies labour shortage and productivity growth were discussed primarily from the demographic point of view, that is from the labour supply side. Finding unused labour reserves, tightening up labour discipline and curbing the rate of unplanned turn-over were policies of control of labour. In the eighties the focus has moved to the demand side, that is to the causes of overemployment mainly in the secondary sector of the economy, which for decades had benefited from comparatively higher rates of investments and capacity growth. After two years of bad economic performance, economic experiments were started in 1984 with the purpose of improving managerial discipline and the utilization of material and labour resources, reshaping branch capital-labour balances and channelling efforts towards technological change.

The main target of the 12th Five-Year Plan is the implementation of the ambitious programme of industrial modernization with no additional workforce. M. Gorbachev's assertion that there is no labour shortage[1] is a provocative message to planning authorities and managers that the present leadership does not intend to accept demographic constraints to economic growth and to bend labour and wage policies to managerial interests. Gorbachev's approach is not original, because the main lines of the present labour-saving policy had been worked out, planned, and in part implemented before he was appointed Party General Secretary. However, his emphasis on correct managerial policies and acceleration of technical progress is a sign that an effective labour-saving policy is needed to avoid stagnation and that planning will have to adapt to this priority.

The paper discusses the nature, aims and limits of the Soviet labour-saving policy in the eighties as compared with the approach of the seventies, focusing on those measures which are likely to survive the economic re-modelling which is gaining impetus under Gorbachev's leadership. Capacity-labour balances, technically substantiated production norms and limits to employment, labour-saving indicators and in-

71

centives are examined as interrelated policies. Separate attention is devoted to the recently approved wage reform which hints at an increasing concern for financial balances.

The Labour Demand versus the Labour Supply Approach to Output and Employment Planning. The Priority of Output versus Employment Planning

The Soviet model of industrialization has long been based in theory and practice on the support of agriculture in terms of low state purchase prices, low peasant incomes and controlled labour outflows. Hidden unemployment mainly in rural areas served as the large reserve of industrial manpower as long as earnings and living standard differentials provided incentives to potential mobility. The estimated labour reserve was significant until the end of the fifties (see Table 1).

Table 1
Not employed in social economy and attending full time schooling.
Percentage of the total able-bodied population.

1926	1939	1959	1970	1979
80.8	37.7	18.9	9.6	6.0

Source: *Trudovye resursy. Ekonomiko-demograficheskie problemy zaniatosti. Sbornik nauchnikh trudov*, Moskow, 1984, p. 12

The source cited above may tend to overestimate employment in census years, because employment census data include also seasonal workers, see V.G. KOSTAKOV, *Prognoz zaniatosti naseleniia. Metodologicheskie osnovy*, Moscow 1979, p. 64. V. KOSTAKOV, ("Balans trudovykh resursov v sovremennykh usloviiakh", *Sotsialisticheskii trud*, 1980, no 6, p. 80) maintains that in 1980 about 10% of the able-bodied were not employed in social production and that this percentage had been stable for a long time, thus suggesting that it could not be considered a source of supplementary labour. However, State Control officials (*Trud*, 19.5.1983) maintain that the rate of "unused" labour is unknown.

Internal passports and residence permits worked as institutional, albeit imperfect, regulators of labour mobility. In this model, the planning of industrial output was by and large independent of labour supply and labour balances constraints. In other words, the increasing démand for labour was the result of taut production plans, based on physical indicators and on fixed capital-labour ratios, rather than the consequences of full employment targets[2]. Industrial planning was also quite independent of location of potential labour supply. Systematic efforts to collect data on manpower at the republican, *oblast, raion* and town level started only in the seventies, under the incipient labour shortage.

Lack of preparatory work and disregard for labour supply in traditional Soviet planning explains why long range and annual labour balances, much discussed in the seventies, have not yet been completed, nor are they so far a structural component of output planning[3]. The branch/ enterprise demand for labour is not modelled on available local resources, but on hierarchically determined indicators of output and productivity growth. These indicators are directly related to labour inputs via prices determined as a function of direct (material and labour) cost. Employment and labour policies, therefore, have been so far a subsidiary of the *output oriented approach* of Soviet planning.

Labour shortage has provided a strong incentive to discuss the premises and goals of Soviet planning and its performance in terms of productivity growth. With decreasing rates of increase of employment, productivity started falling (see Table 2).

Table 2
Employment* and productivity growth, 1961-1985. Percentage rates of growth of labour productivity and average annual increase of employment in millions.

	1961-1970	1971-1975	1976-1980	1981-1985
Labour productivity	6.4	4.5	3.3	3.1
Employment	2.3	2.1	1.7	0.9

* Total employment in the social economy including *kolkhozniki.*

Sources: For labour productivity, V. KOSTAKOV, "Zaniatost: defitsit' ili izbytok?", *Kommunist,* 1987, no 2, p. 79. For employment, *Narodnoe khoziaistvo SSSR v 1985,* Moskow 1986, p. 390.

The tensions that labour shortage provoked in intersectoral labour balances are revealed by the increasing number of workers temporarily transferred from other sectors to agriculture. In 1970 the estimated average annual number of workers transferred was 650,000, in 1984, 1.5 million. However, in terms of the actual number of *workers,* each working for an estimated 2-3 weeks, more than 30 million workers were involved[4].

Expected falling rates of growth of the able-bodied population up to 1995[5] have provided grounds for what can be defined as a *demographic approach* to planning and employment. This approach, which was developed in the seventies, contains both conservative and reformistic aspects, some of which have survived in the eighties. From the point of view of labour productivity, this approach appears to be a conservative one, since its arguments may be used to find transitory solutions to labour shortage. By focusing on demographic aspects, projected capacity-labour imbalances may be adjusted by drawing unused labour resources into production and increasing the effective working time. In the seventies this approach led to a better knowledge of available labour resources and prompted research into labour expectations, motivations and mobility. Potential resources were identified in the field of domestic labour, pensioners, invalids, part-time students, and, in general, in a

73

better utilization of the so-called time budget. Efforts to improve the information on available manpower produced an impressive number of labour balances. Job Placement Bureaus were supposed to provide correct information on vacancies and shorten the time lag between jobs. With the aim of encouraging a greater degree of planned labour mobility, the State Committee for Labour and Wages was reorganized into a State Committee for Labour and Social Questions (Goskomtrud) and charged with functions of coordination and control over the utilization and territorial redistribution of labour[6]. The reformistic aspect of the *demographic approach* may be found in arguments against the traditional organization and goals of Soviet planning. Some forms of territorial planning were advocated to overcome the negative effects of branch planning in regions badly equipped to sustain industrial growth[7]. Criticism of production planning versus employment planning emerged among sociologists and labour economists who claimed that output plans should adapt to labour needs and aspirations, rather than the latter to production goals[8]. By and large, however, the reformistic aspects of this approach have not been developed into a comprehensive and consistent alternative to traditional Soviet planning.

The 11th Five-Year Plan (1981-85) reflected the conflicting impulses generated in part by the demographic approach and in part also by the need to adapt rapidly the branch-output oriented approach to labour constraints. The principle of territorial labour balances was used to introduce into the set of existing planning indicators limits on maximum branch employment to be agreed with territorial organs. But labour balances were ill-suited to this purpose. Being territorial averages, the labour balances do not provide useful information for labour redistribution from excess labour to deficit labour areas. The larger the territory covered, the worse the « averaging » effect of the balances. If circumscribed to smaller areas the analysis of labour demand and supply is complicated by commuter flows[9]. The principle of territorial labour balances, which should have brought about a new investment policy adapted to local labour resources, was sacrificed to the imperative of higher rates of growth from existing capacity. Valuable data on the causes of labour turnover were used to enforce stricter disciplinary rules aimed at stabilizing the workforce, rather than removing the causes of unplanned turnover[10].

Capacity-Labour Balances and Certification of Capacity

The cornerstone of the Soviet approach to labour saving, worked out during the 11th Five-Year Plan and embodied in the 12th FYP, is that excess-demand for labour is sustained by excess-production capacity. That is, new capacity is demanded and added even if the existing capacity is not fully utilized. The main indicator of capacity utilization is identified with the shift coefficient. The difference between the normative branch shift coefficient, decided by planners, and the actual factory coefficient is used to estimate unused capacity. Since in most industry, and particularly in engineering, the shift coefficient is measured as the ratio between the total number of blue collar workers on the payroll and the number of blue collar workers employed in the first (most numerous) shift, that is, in relation to machine operators rather than to equipment as such, the discrepancy between normative and actual shift coefficient portrays unused capacity in terms of vacancies. In other words, from the point of view of normative planning, labour shortage is estimated in relation to the full loading of capacity, according to the shift regime which applies to each branch. In order to increase capacity utilization, vacant and not fully loaded workplaces should be written off and the «released» workforce should be used to fill other shifts, e.g. to sustain the higher utilization of approved workplaces[11].

This approach is but a *refined version of the traditional output approach to planning,* in so far as output growth remains the primary target of planning, capacity-labour balances are sought within the branch/enterprise, and labour mobility (or stabilization) is supposed to adapt to industrial planning, rather than having an impact on the quality and distribution of economic growth. The tensions in the industrial labour market provoked by negative growth rate of the able-bodied population in industrialized areas do not have the effect of improving work conditions for the workforce, but on the contrary call for a worse shift regime. At the same time excess labour resources in Central Asia are not matched with adequate investments and offered broader employment opportunities.

This new version of the output approach to planning was used in 1984 to plan capacity-labour balances in the engineering industry and to promote a nation-wide industrial certification of capacity (*attestatsiia*), to single out unused (and unusable) capacity to be scrapped and to stimulate the rationalization of outdated and inefficient workplaces. The capacity-labour balances model discussed in this section has been inherited by the 12th Five-Year Plan. There is no sign that under the present leadership alternative solutions have been worked out.

The link between the working out of branch capacity-labour balances and a cumbersome procedure of certification of capacity expressed by number of workplaces can be explained by the poor quality of current information on existing and usable capacity conveyed to planners. It is known that ministries/enterprises tend to overestimate capacity utilization, whilst the census, carried out each two-three years by the USSR Central Statistical Administration, tends to underestimate it. The estimates of capacity utilization, moreover, are complicated by the fact that enterprises producing homogeneous commodities, but belonging to different ministries, have their capacity utilization rated on different branch shift regimes[12]. Rules and indicators of assessment of capacity applied, firstly, to the machine-building branches and extended to all industry in 1986[13], therefore, are meant to (a) reveal excess capacity, (b) detect the reasons for idle capacity, (c) oblige managers to update the technology and dispose at once of totally inadequate equipment, and (d) bring output norms to what is considered a technically substantiated level.

The definition of workplace adopted for the assessment of capacity and the drawing up of capacity-labour balances in the engineering industry suggests that labour-saving is sought primarily in this branch. Innovating with respect to the former assessment used by Ministries[14], the 1984 Gosplan instructions for the engineering industry define the workplace as a zone of application of labour, determined on the basis of labour and other normatives, and endowed with the necessary means for the working activity of *one worker,* regardless of the number of shifts[15]. The new indicator is supposed to have three advantages. First, by relating the workplace (as a unit of capacity) to only one worker, a rigid link between capacity replacement and instalment on the one hand and labour demand on the other is introduced[16]. Second, being workplaces unrelated to the shift regime, their number is lower than the number of workers employed, at least by the shift coefficient factor. The writing off of a certain number of workplaces should be matched at least by an equal number of released workers, giving the volume of the minimum labour-saving. Third, the assessment of the cost of additional capacity is improved.

Ministries used to plan new capacity on the basis of the average capital-labour ratio[17]. Thus, enterprises and branches underutilizing capacity, e.g. having a comparatively lower shift coefficient, thus a higher capital-labour ratio, were assigned a relatively higher volume of investment for each additional workplace as compared with enterprises and branches making better use of their capacity, e.g. with a higher shift regime. In other words, other things being equal, labour intensive production working at full capacity obtained a relatively lower volume in investment than capital intensive production because of the planning indicator used for this purpose. The gap between well-equipped and badly-equipped enterprises was made worse. Now, new capacity is to be planned on the basis of a capital-workplace indicator, which — given the definition of workplace adopted in engineering — is the ratio between capital and labour employed in the first shift, that is a much higher cost-value indicator. The normative (admissible) number of workplaces in the engineering industry (rated in a two shift-regime) is equal to half the number of workers. The actual number of workplaces is equal to the number of workers divided by the actual shift coefficient[18]. Since the latter is lower than two, the actual number of workplaces is higher than the norm. The difference between the two estimates gives the volume of idle (partially unloaded) capacity. The capacity-labour balance is to be restored by getting rid of superfluous capacity and by a more intensive utilization of the approved workplaces.

This model assumes that higher rates of growth of capacity as compared to manpower rates of increase are the primary cause of idle capacity. Thus, the focus falls on a higher shift coefficient as an intensification factor, rather than on a better utilization of existing working time, although intra-shift break-downs due to irregular supplies, repair and other technical and organizational failures are recurrent[19]. The implicit assumption is that a higher shift coefficient does not need additional manpower because excess factory labour reserves may be used for this purpose and because technical-managerial staff will not need to increase.

However, results may be perverse for capacity as well as labour utilization. By employing half of their workforce in the first shift and the other half in the second shift, managers may give the appearance of conforming to the targets of capacity utilization, although 50 % of capacity is not used in either shift[20]. On the other hand, with no appropriate infrastructure either within or outside the factory[21], the productivity of labour redeployed in the second shift may even decrease.

From the point of view of labour-saving, the limit of the new capacity-labour balance model is that it is not innovating with respect to the principle of fixed capital-labour proportions (or zero elasticity of substitution) on which Soviet planning is based. The upward adjustment of the capital-labour indicator means that additional capital investment will command a proportionate (although lower than before) increase in the demand for labour.

Labour-saving based on the release (*vysvobozhdenie*) of workers is not matched by a corresponding inter-factory labour mobility, because workers are supposed to be redeployed, in the first place, within the factory in other shifts. What seems peculiar in the selection of labour-saving indicators is that mechanization plays a more important role than automation. The indicator of percentage mechanization of manual labour was introduced in planning from 1982 [22]. It is still considered an important labour-saving indicator, although the information it conveys to planners is not unequivocal. The blue collar workforce is divided into five groups, according to the degree of automation and mechanization of labour operations. The programme of mechanization concerns only the last two groups of workers: manual labour working at (*pri*) machines and motors and manual labour not working at (*pri*) machines and motors. The great bulk of repair workers is excluded from this programme. It is widely held that mechanized work increases slowly. A compilation of scattered and incomplete figures on the rate of labour mechanization is presented in Table 3.

Silvana Malle

Table 3
Industrial manual labour in the USSR, 1959-1985, thousands.

	Total blue collar workers	1	%	2	%	3	%	3a	3b	%
1959	18,888	6,819	36.1	1,794	9.5	10,275	54.4	1,828	9,121	40.4
1965	22,576	9,099	40.3	2,528	11.2	10,949	48.5			
1969	25,135	10,656	42.4	3,041	12.1	11,435	45.5			
1970	25,631									
1972	26,418	11,703	44.3	3,329	12.6	11,386	43.1	2.034	9,352	35.4
1975	27,507					11,525	41.9			
1979	29,228	13,649	46.7	3,858	13.2	11,720	40.1	2,133	9,587	32.8
1980	29,497									
1981	29,713	14,301	48.1	3,900	13.1	11,513	38.7			
1982	29,981					11,213	37.4	1,670	9,543	30.2
1983	30,154									
1984	30,253					10,887	36.0	1,387	9,500	31.4
1985	30,381					10,390	34.2			

Note: column 1 lists manual labour working with motors and automated equipment;
column 2 lists manual labour in repair work;
column 3 lists together manual workers working at machines and motors (3a) and not working at machine and motors (3b).
Data on blue collar employment are found in the corresponding years of *Narodnoe khoziaistvo SSSR v 1959...1984g.*
Column figures 3a are derived from the difference between colums 3 and 3b figures.

Sources: For percentage data listed under columns 1-3 from 1959 to 1979, see G. Ia. Rakitskaia and A.N. Shokin, "Preobrazovaniia v sfere truda v 80e gody", *Znanie: Ekonomika*, 1984, no. 2, p. 14. The absolute figures under columns 1-3a, if other sources are not specifically mentioned below, are my estimates from percentage data published in several sources (see below) and data on total blue collar employment. The figure under column 3 for 1975 is in D. Karpukhin and I. Oblomskaia, "Sotsial' no-ekonomicheskie problemy truda na etape razvitogo sotsializma", *Planovoe khoziaistvo*, 1980, no. 2, p. 95. A. Bachurin, "Problemy uluchsheniia ispol' zovaniia trudovykh resursov", *Planovoe khoziaistvo*, 1982, no. 1, p. 35, however, mentions a slightly lower percentage (41.4) of manual labour in the same year. The absolute figure under column 3b for 1984 is in M.A. Vilenskii, "Nauchno-tekhnicheskii progress: sotsial'no-ekonomicheskie aspekty", *Znanie: Ekonomika i Organizatsiia Proizvodstva*, 1985, no. 4, p. 33 under my assumption that this source refers only to manual labour not working at machines, since another authoritative source (*Ekonomicheskaia Gazeta*, 1984, no. 10, p. 5) indicates 36% workers under the group 3, which is a more likely percentage (than 31% which would result if Vilenskii's data were to be referred to the aggregate under column 3). Figures for 1979 are found in Iu. Baryshnikov, "Khoziaistvennyi mekhanizm i upravlenie trudom", *Ekonomicheskie Nauki*, 1981, no. 6, p. 87. L.A. Kostin (*Trudovye resursy v odinnatsatoi piatiletke*, Moscow: Ekonomika, 1981, p. 32) reports 32.8% (8.1 million industrial workers) not working at machines on August 1st, 1979. The 1979 absolute figure for workers under column 3b is estimated on the assumption that this percentage remains valid for the end of the year, when total blue collar employment tends to increase. The 1982 absolute figure for column 3 is estimated from percentage data in V. Mart'anov and V. Tambovtsev, "Razrabotka tselevoi kompleksnoi programmy po sokrashcheniu primenenii ruchnogo truda", *Planovoe khoziaistvo*, 1985, no. 3, p. 93 and for column 3b from L. Kostin, *"Rezervy ispol'zo vaniia trudovykh resursov" EKO*, 1984, no. 1, p. 24. The 1985 percentage is estimated from indirect data provided in R. Grigor'iants, "Ispol'zovanie rabochei sily v otraslei", *Sotsialisticheskii trud*, 1985, no. 11, p. 100. The absolute figure under column 3 for 1981 is estimated from data for 1981 and B. Gavrilov's assertion in *Sotsialisticheskii trud*, 1983, no. 11, pp. 32-33 that manual labour decreased by 300,000 units in 1982.

Until 1979 the absolute number of industrial manual workers was increasing. After that date it started to decrease. It is not evident that this is the consequence of technological change, rather than the effect of labour shortage and/or biased information. The fact that most vacancies are concentrated in manual jobs[23] suggests that labour shortage could be an important cause of the relative decrease in the number of manual workers. Moreover, the classification of workers into manual and mechanized labour is conventional and ambiguous. It depends on whether more or less than 50 % of working time is spent in manual or mechanized work[24]. On the border between alternative classifications, an insignificant amount of mechanization could have an impact on the size of the mechanized workforce with no significant effect on labour productivity. On the other hand mechanized plants with a relatively lower number of manual workers may appear to be lagging behind the process of technological change. Furthermore, the fact that some skills classified under heavy[25] and dangerous manual jobs are granted some monetary and material benefits may cause a statistical overestimation of the number of workers engaged in such jobs.[26]

Physical labour-saving indicators have not yet been applied to adjusters and repair workers (classified as a rule under the category of auxiliary workers), although it is known that most of the latter operations are performed manually. Available statistics aggregate automated labour with mechanized labour, thus blurring the distinction both between direct and indirect labour and between traditional and technically advanced skills. In 1985, six million workers were employed in capital repair[27]. Gosplan officials maintain that the work of half a million adjusters and repair workers could be saved if superfluous obsolete equipment was scrapped[28]. However, it is not clear, as it does not emerge statistically, what the actual work performed by auxiliary workers is. Workers of auxiliary workshops are considered basic production workers if their output is delivered outside the enterprise, and auxiliary workers if it is used by the enterprise itself. Thus, the mere regrouping of enterprises into production associations or other conglomerates could produce a statistical increase of auxiliary workers in total employment. It is likely that an indicator of auxiliary labour-saving has not been introduced so far, because planners do not know the actual need for auxiliary labour.

Constrained by the equivocal information conveyed by physical labour-saving indicators, Soviet planners are deprived of a correct picture of the technological capacity of industry. If, as an alternative, labour-saving instructions were to be based on international parameters, they would be likely to clash with the balance of skills and functions which single production units have adapted to the needs of their installed technology, maintenance requirements, formal and informal contacts with other organizations, i.e. to the needs of an economic system which remains by and large unchanged.

Labour-Saving: Programmes and Facts

Total labour resources are expected to increase from 1986 to 1990 by 3.2 million people[29] mainly located in non-industrialized areas. During the 12th Five-Year Plan 2% of the total number of workplaces should be scrapped each year[30]. Manual labour in the economy as a whole, should decrease by 5-6 million people[31]. Engineering branches should work on an effective 2-shift regime, following the example of Leningrad industry[32].

However, the outcome of the 11th Five-Year Plan from the point of view of methods and results in labour-saving was not promising. Among the branches which carried out the process of certification of capacity, the building materials, and meat and dairy industries did not write off any workplaces, nor did they release any workers. Animal husbandry, machine-building and power engineering scrapped respectively 0.9% and 0.8% of their workplaces. Better results were obtained in the agricultural machine-building and automobile industries, where 1.9% and 1.6% of respective workplaces were written off with an estimated respective labour release of 4% and 3.7%[33]. However, one must bear in mind that initial success in labour-saving often depends on the one-off scrapping of unusable capacity, which does not imply any significant technical or organizational improvement. The capacity-labour expansion drive emerges again thereafter, as is apparent from the experience of the K.S. Voroshilov combine building association, the first to implement a system of *attestatsiia* (see Table 4).

Table 4

Rate of increase of employment and capital-output ratio, 1981-1985 at the Dnepropetrovsk K.S. Voroshilov combine building association, (1980=100).

	1981	1982	1983	1984	1985
Employment	99.9	99.8	105.7	102.1	102.5
Capital-output	111.5	115.7	114.1	121.2	128.8

Source: My estimates from V. BOIKO, "Ekonomicheskii mekhanizm attestatsiia rabochikh mest", *Voprosy ekonomiki,* 1986, no. 9, p. 98.

In 1985 38 % of industrial enterprises carried out the certification of workplaces. Seven million workplaces were examined. A «conventional» release (e.g. labour-saving obtained by increasing labour productivity as compared with estimates based on the «achieved level» of productivity growth) of 600,000-650,000 workers was expected for 1986[34]. However, formalism in this process cannot be ruled out. At the ministerial level a success indicator called «workplace certification» has been adopted, which may stimulate biased information. According to the USSR Goskomtrud, data presented by enterprises on the conventional release of workers and on lower production costs after the introduction of robotized techniques, do not correspond to reality[35].

From 1980 to 1985, out of a projected increase of the total Soviet able-bodied population of 3,646,000[36] industry (whose share in total average annual national employment was 32.3 %) absorbed one third[37]. This indicates that there has not been inter-sectoral labour distribution and that the increase of industrial output still needs additional manpower. The implicit industrial employment growth estimated from the rate of output and productivity increase planned for 1986 was 0.19 %. The actual rate of growth has been 0.29 %, which amounts to about 110,500 additional workers, i.e. 55 % more than planned. A conventional release of 700,000 workers reported for 1986 (a figure higher than planned) has been due to technical change, even though it is admitted that *attestatsiia* is proceeding slowly and is not producing the expected results[38]. It is, perhaps, not a coincidence that the Communist Party Plenum of June 16, 1986, was informed that 700,000 industrial workplaces were unfilled, with industry working practically on a one shift regime[39]. The planned conventional labour release from industry seems to have been estimated on the basis of vacancies in the first shift, meaning that even in the 12th Five-Year Plan (best variant) industry will not release workers to other sectors. This may jeopardize any improvement in the service sector, unless agriculture, which however is not faring well, provides the necessary workforce.

The need for labour-saving depends to a great extent on how labour shortage is estimated, given the installed technology. Industrial labour shortage has been estimated at 1.6 million workers in 1970, when the rate of growth of the able-bodied population was still high, and was estimated at 2 million workers in 1980[40]. According to other estimates total labour shortage was 2.5 million workers during the 9th Five-Year Plan, 1.4 million workers during the 10th Five-Year Plan, and again 2.5 million from 1981 to 1984[41]. The most recent information is that 4 million workplaces are vacant[42]. In an industrial sample monitored by the CSA in 1983, 10 % of workplaces were vacant in the first shift. In another monitoring of the engineering industry carried out in 1984, 14 % of workplaces in the first shift were vacant[43].

But if estimated on the basis of the optimal loading of capacity, e.g. with the normative shift coefficient, labour shortage is even higher[44]. A. KOTLIAR estimates that if the shift coefficient had to be increased from 1.4 to 1.7 (the present plan target) the demand for industrial productive labour would increase by 7.9 million units[45]. As a matter of fact, the shift regime applies, as a rule, only to blue collar workers. Labour regulations by and large do not even provide for extra pay for evening and night shifts for technical-managerial and clerical staff. Part of the auxiliary blue collar workers are also excluded from other shifts. If the shift regime was to include only mechanized and automated industrial blue collar labour, it is likely that less than three million additional workers would be required. This figure, however, is still high if compared with the programme of increasing the rate of capital replacement[48] and with the location and skills of additional labour resources, and certainly inconsistent with the outdated programme of labour mechanization. The awareness that «machines and equipment capable of working in the second and third shift with no need for labour participation» are badly needed is emerging only now[47], while the process of implementation of the 12th Five-Year Plan still conforms to rules, indicators and parameters based on the principle of the zero substitutability between capital and labour.

Technically-Substantiated Output Norms and Limits on Branch Employment

Output norms, in principle, should provide the information needed to determine necessary labour for a given output volume. However, only in machine-building branches, are norms on technological labour intensity per unit of output used, given the approved wage rates, to determine the total wage fund of basic workers and part of the wage fund of auxiliary workers[48]. At the end of 1985 it was claimed that 80 % of all industrial labour, and 90 % of engineering workers, worked on the basis of technically substantiated norms. But in engineering norms were still overfulfilled by 29 %[49]. Twenty percent of time workers, technical-engineering and clerical staff remained outside «normed» work[50].

Given the labour constraint to new capacity-labour balances, the fixing of technically-substantiated norms, as distinguished from norms based on statistical experience, has acquired increasing importance. It is claimed that the labour intensity of new products is overestimated by as much as 3-5 times[51].

One needs to recall that labour intensity norms at the factory/branch level still refers only to basic production workers. Labour intensity norms are either derived from the rate of growth of a given output established by the annual or Five-Year Plan or from what is considered the branch average normative labour intensity. The assumption is that

83

once the «technical» output norm is established, the necessary number of direct workers is obtained and the complete staffing may be estimated on the basis of regulated direct proportions between basic production workers and other staff. This outdated staffing scheme has produced perverse consequences. On the one hand, the growing employment of blue collar workers has been associated with an increasing number of other staff. On the other hand, in particular cases of technological advancement, fixed proportions between different categories of workers have hindered the replacement of blue collar labour with technical-auxiliary staff.

In the late seventies, work started to uncover hidden labour reserves among technical, clerical and managerial staff. Efforts were made to work out technically substantiated norms for all factory production personnel. The purpose was to get reliable estimates of the *full* labour intensity of output. In 1977 new staffing norms on the basis of direct indicators were worked out for ferrous and non-ferrous metallurgy, the coal industry, electrotechnical, chemical and oil machine-building, and light industry. The managerial time budgets were examined and super-fluous operations removed in order to obtain the actual volume of true managerial operations and a less generous estimate of necessary managerial staff. In branches where the volume of staff was also a function of the value of production funds, correction coefficients were introduced to take into account the introduction of labour-saving technology[52].

This approach has been carried further in the eighties. In 1980 limits on branch employment were approved for all union ministries and for some republican ministries. However, this policy has not been substantiated in rigid norms. Limits are by and large branch indicators related to gross or net output volume, that is they are not absolute but relative to output growth. Up to 50 % of the managerial bonus can be lost if limits are exceeded, but this sanction only applies if the target increase of labour productivity is not met. In 1982 new instructions tried to enforce limits on additional branch employment, regardless of their departmental subordination on the basis of territorial labour balances. Under the new rules the enterprise wage fund was to be approved by financial institutions, such as the Investment Bank, only if backed by certification for the additional employment by territorial organs[53]. However, relations between ministries/enterprises and territorial organs, at any level, are either uncooperative or inconsequential. Ministries do not always inform the enterprises on employment ceilings. Labour-intensive enterprises are often unable to adapt to such constraints, whilst techno-logically-advanced factories are able to agree with local organs on limits well above available local labour resources[54].

The application of internal branch normatives referring separately to particular categories of workers appears to be more successful. Aggregate normatives for engineering-technical and clerical staff have been worked out for 80 branches, with the purpose of enforcing factory labour-saving primarily on these categories. Although the quality of such norms is debatable[55], limits on branch employment for those categories have been justified with the rationale of job evaluation. As a matter of fact, these normatives are more an attempt to check intra-factory upward mobility which could have resulted from the conjuncture of labour shortage and fixed wage differentials, than to realise an actual interbranch redistribution of labour. They have succeeded in curbing the relative growth in total employment of the engineering-technical staff and in bringing down over a period of ten years both the absolute (by 27,000 workers) and relative share of clerical staff[56].

The nature of this success is, however, questionable. The very working out and control of norms is labour-consuming[57]. Moreover, as in any rationing policy, limits are bad substitutes for correct scarcity ratios. Functions under control tend to re-emerge under other headings: accountants are concealed under economist positions, technicians under engineering positions, clerical workers under technicians or blue collar positions. Labour-saving is fictitious. Workers released from their positions are redeployed within the same production units to other jobs. The resulting labour redistribution conveys biased information on relative skill scarcities, may affect perversely educational planning and hinder future capacity labour balances.

Plan Indicators and Labour-Saving Incentives

Branch limits on employment which had been given much emphasis by the 1979 economic reform, were quietly disregarded in the economic experiment applied in 1984 to two unions and three republican ministries. The « experiment » which is supposed to encompass all industry in 1987 focuses on three main performance indicators: output volume (i.e. total sales), net productivity growth and fulfilment of delivery contracts. Enterprises are not set from above planned limits on employment, rates of decrease of manual labour and wage fund[58]. A labour-saving incentive is supposed to be built into the enterprise right to retain the annual wage costs saved and to use them for its own purposes.

The assigned annual wage fund may increase or remain stable depending on output targets. The basic wage fund is separated from the wage increase and is not subject to intra-branch adjustments. The unused part of the wage fund is transferred into the enterprise Material Incentive Fund[59]. The branch norm of average wage increase related to the rate of productivity growth replaces the 1979 norm of unit wage cost of output. The enterprise wage fund includes, besides production personnel wages, wages accruing to other workers (formerly excluded from this indicator), such as non-production personnel, workers not on the payroll (*nespisochnyi*)[60], and labour which will be needed to utilize new capacity. The new estimate of the wage fund is a step towards full labour cost estimates of output. The norm of average wage increase is supposed to compel management to either dismiss excess manpower or to diminish wages, if the rate of productivity growth is both below the planned target and below the average productivity of the preceding Five-Year Plan[61]. For industry as a whole, the norm of wage increase has been fixed 3-4 times below the initial proportion between the wage fund and net output. It is a taut norm, which according to some, could work as a disincentive to productivity growth[62]. However, in spite of initial commitments, it has been differentiated not only across branches, but also through industry[63]. From the economic point of view, positive effects were expected from the combination of a labour productivity indicator estimated on the basis of the Net Normative Output and the utilization by the enterprises of wage costs saved to increase wages[64]. From the financial point of view, it was expected that bank control of wage and bonus expenditure would improve. The bank may request the curtailment of the planned bonus if wage expenditure is higher than planned[65].

However, the volume of the Material Incentive Fund (MIF) and bonuses out of this fund are still by and large unrelated to productivity growth, since the main indicator remains output growth. Being also unrelated to the profit volume, the MIF may increase more than the latter. It occurred, indeed, that higher bonuses had to be financed by writing-off capital charges and reducing profit deductions into the State Budget[66]. It is unclear, however, whether the MIF has been used to increase managerial bonuses, or, a recurrent feature, to pay for unplanned overtime and work on rest days and holidays.

It is unlikely that the present financial constraints and incentives will have a positive effect on labour-saving *per se*. In 1985 out of nine civilian machine-building ministries, working under the new regulations, only the Ministry of Heavy Machine-Building and the Ministry of Instrument Making increased labour productivity more than output. The other seven attained the output target only by employing additional labour[67].

The would-be material incentive to labour-saving is restrained by detailed regulations issued by Gosplan, Goskomtrud and the Ministry of Finance, limiting the enterprise right to use the wage costs saved to the benefit of its personnel[68]. Extra-wage payments to multi-machine operators, for instance, may be assigned only when they are employed on higher than planned norms of machine servicing. Thus, they are implicitly ruled out in engineering jobs where norms are dictated by technological synchronization. Combining different functions, which in principle entitles the worker to extra-wage payments, is only allowed if the basic job is not fully loaded. Wage supplements for skill mastery may be awarded only to workers with above-average skill ranking[69].

One may estimate that the wage savings due to the conventional labour-saving (that is, to higher than planned productivity growth) is quite small[70]. The unused part of the wage fund, which by the new regulations is to be transferred to the MIF, is not significant, either. Moreover, although there is no need for the agreement of the Council of Ministers on top level salaries, there is still a centrally-fixed maximum to managerial bonuses.

The 1984 economic experiment (which now covers all industry) shows that labour-saving induced by financial norms is by and large illusory and that initial gains are rapidly exhausted. In 1984, 78 % of electrotechnical enterprises did not increase or even decrease employment while keeping a 5 % rate of productivity growth. In 1985, only 35 % of those enterprises were still able to increase productivity at higher rates than output. It is possible to estimate that light industry reduced employment by 1.4 % (while output increased only by 1.3 %) and the food industry, after a modest discharge of labour, increased employment again by 0.4 %. Heavy machine-building discharged labour, but had a negative wage fund saving and was exonerated from limits on capacity expansion[71].

Productivity gains may be unreal. The five ministries which started the 1984 experiment, did not fulfil their plan for capital re-equipment and capital investment out of their own funds[72]. These facts suggest that absolute labour-saving, when it occurs, is not the result of newly in-built incentives for technological change, that is, of a capital-labour substitution approach on the part of the enterprise, but of a short-lived feedback to central indicators, the drawbacks of which may appear, in the long run, in terms of improper maintenance and attendance of the equipment and/or of lower output quality[73].

Self-Financing Schemes and Labour-Saving. The Wage Reform

The 12th Five-Year Plan will be carried out by and large on the basis of the economic rules and indicators discussed in the former section. However, since 1986 the emphasis has progressively shifted to the new economic experiment based on the self-financing schemes tested at the Sumy Production Association « M. Frunze » and at the « Autovaz » car producing association. In 1987 this economic model will be applied to the industrial Ministries of Chemical and Machine-Building, Instrument Making, Petrol and Oil Refining Industry, the Automobile Industry and to 36 large-scale industrial enterprises[74]. Re-equipment, restructuring and enlargement of capacity must be financed in part or in whole by the enterprise itself.

In principle, this experiment should stimulate labour-saving indirectly, by incentives related to a higher degree of utilization of existing capacity. The MIF is a function of the profit volume, after predetermined deductions (at fixed or progressive rates) into the State Budget. The necessary condition for the assignment of the bonus is a 100 % percent plan fulfilment. The size of the bonus depends on the target of capacity utilization[75]. An implicit goal seems to be, therefore, the scrapping of unused capacity which sustains excess-demand for labour and, if necessary, the redeployment of manpower to other shifts.

So far the labour-saving effects of this experiment are debatable. Since the rate of productivity growth is still lower than the rate of output growth, one may estimate that there has been a 1.2 % increase in employment at the Sumy production association since the beginning of the experiment. It is also interesting to note that the rate of average wage/productivity increase has been lower (0.45 %) than planned (0.52 %), as a result of lower bonuses accruing to technical-managerial and clerical staff. This suggests that within the rationale of Soviet planning and price indicators, financial constraints are not sufficient to induce absolute labour-saving. Faced with the choice of either higher wages with lower employment or lower wages with more labour, the enterprises still seem to prefer the latter. (This behaviour may have contributed to the levelling of industrial wage differentials when productivity growth started falling.)

The wage reform approved on September 16, 1986 aims at reversing this trend[76]. Following the reform blue collar wages should increase on average by 20-25 % and white collar wages by 30-35 %. Blue collar skill wage differentials should increase. Wage supplements for heavy and dangerous work will have to be rated on the actual job conditions, rather than on skill lists. The number of functional rankings of technical staff will increase from the present two to four. Improvements and wider salary differentials accrue also to managers, whose salary grouping is reduced from 7-5 categories to 3-5 categories and is made independent of the enterprise employment scale. Separate wage funds for each category of workers (blue collar workers, technical-engineering staff, managerial staff) are established.

This reform has been heralded as a major step towards increasing enterprises autonomy in matters of wage policy. As a matter of fact, it represents a shrewd attempt to restore central control over wages. Since 1975 the importance of centrally fixed and stable wage rates in the total wage has gradually diminished, since the bonus share, sustained by outdated output norms, has been steadily increasing. By 1985 bonuses, representing from 25 to 45 % of total wage, had become the enterprise regulator of wage differentials. The peculiarity of the reform is the fact that wage improvements and appropriate rankings of the technical-managerial staff will have to be financed by the enterprise wage fund, with the State Budget making no contribution to higher wage expenditure. In order to pay the new wages, therefore, most enterprises will have either to release labour or to syphon money out of the Material Incentive Fund.

It is believed that labour-saving will be stimulated by the rights granted to the enterprise to use the savings obtained within the wage fund allocated for each category of production personnel to increase the wages of each category. Blue collar workers may be granted different wage supplements related to performance, but with the limit of a 50 % increase of their basic wage. But there is no limit to wage increases for specialists. The enterprise should be free to determine their number, functions and extra-wage payments. This suggests that labour-saving is sought primarily within the category of technical-engineering staff, which seems a conservative approach in a phase of adaptation of industry to automated and computerized technology.

Higher wage rates at the expenses of lower bonuses and centrally reshaped wage differentials, suggest that planners intend to pursue a rigid incomes policy at a time of acute labour shortage and that they are trying to re-establish their control over the labour market. New wages rates and salaries should have been approved by the beginning of the eighties, but they were rescheduled because of worsening economic performance, and probably because of resistence on the part of the Ministry of Finance[77].

To the extent that the average wage increase which has to be paid by the enterprise is lower than the average extra-wage formerly accruing to workers as bonus, that is, as long as the Material Incentive Fund may be used to this purpose, total labour cost should not increase. Thus, the industrial wage reform does not incorporate a general labour-saving incentive. However, since the Material Incentive Fund is used mainly to pay technical-managerial bonuses, it is this category which may suffer in the short term, either by loss of income, or loss of posts. An implicit goal of the wage reform seems to be the redeployment of redundant staff in blue collar jobs[78]. But branches/enterprises endowed with lower financial sources may have to dismiss workers of any category to afford higher wage rates. This labour should be available for redeployment in expanding branches. However, the branch/enterprises financial sources depend on the price structure. Labour redistribution patterns may not lead to higher rates of productivity growth either in branches releasing labour or in expanding branches, unless an overall consistent price adjustment is provided.

Concluding Remarks

Labour-saving policies, a new imperative confronting Soviet planners, have been delayed in the seventies and part of the eighties due to a demographic approach to labour shortage. This approach was conservative, in so far as solutions to capacity-labour imbalances were sought through increasing employment of still unused labour time and resources, and was reformistic, in so far as a better utilization of local labour resources, a geographical reallocation of investment and better working conditions emerged as arguments for a revision of the traditional planning system.

The rapid economic deterioration in the first years of the 1981-1985 Plan and, possibly, political changes, made labour-saving a priority target in the last two years of the 11th Plan. Methods and solutions proposed at that time have been incorporated in the 12th Five-Year Plan. They belong to what can be called a refined version of the traditional output-oriented approach of Soviet planning. Labour imbalances are seen to be dependent on rates of capacity expansion higher than those of labour resources, e.g. in excess production capacity. The solution is sought in new branch and enterprise capital-labour balances. The method employed is the certification of capacity monitored from above, on the basis of indicators of utilization and rationalization of capacity. The estimated cost-value of one workplace has been increased, in order to curb the demand for new capacity and to have a better comparative assessment of relative capacity utilization. The limit of this approach is that the new capital-labour value ratios, although higher, are still based on the achieved level and rule out capital-labour substitutability. There is no incentive from below to save labour.

The inflationary tensions of the labour market have been brought under control, first, by delaying central wage increases, and second, by the 1986 wage reform which shifts the burden of new wage rates on to the enterprises. Average blue collar wages have been increased by 20-25 % and average white collar wages by 30-35 %. Skill wage differentials have been widened within each labour category. However, wage improvements are neither immediate, nor tangible, since they must be financed by the achieved enterprise wage fund. It is unlikely that industry will be able to afford new wage rates in the short term without drawing resources from the material incentive fund. Since the latter is used mainly for bonuses to the technical-managerial staff, their salaries cannot be increased in the short term, unless productivity gains are considerable and/or a significant number of such workers are dismissed. Labour-saving indirect indicators, therefore, still point to the release of technical, clerical and managerial staff.

The labour-saving strategy, therefore, is based on two main elements. On the one hand the cost of additional labour, in terms of capital investment, is raised, on the other hand, higher wages do not accrue to labour, as a scarce production factor, but are made dependent on higher labour productivity. The missing link between the two elements is the adjustment of the price system to the re-allocation of capacity and labour resources, which this strategy is supposed to bring about.

Notes

1. See M. Gorbachev's speech to the 27th Communist Party Congress, *Ekonomicheskaia gazeta*, 1986, n° 10, p. 10.
2. It is still claimed that unemployment has been «completely eliminated» since 1930, see A.E. KOTLIAR», «Defitsit rabochei sily i rol' demograficheskogo faktora», vol. *in Trudovye resursy. Ekonomiko-demograficheskie problemy zaniatosti. Sbornik nauchnikh trudov*, Moscow, 1984, p. 12.
3. See L. KOSTIN, «Rezervy ispol'zovaniia trudovykh resursov», *EKO*, 1984, n° 1, p. 34, and D.V. ZEMBATOVA, «Problemy planirovaniia zaniatosti naseleniia i effektivnost' obshchestvennogo proizvodstva», in A.G. AGANBEGIAN and D.D. MOSKOVICH (eds), *Povyshenie effektivnosti narodnogo khoziaistva*, Moscow 1984, pp. 224-5.
4. See L. S. CHIZHOVA, «Resursy truda v usloviiakh intensifikatsii ekonomiki i usileniia roli chelovecheskogo faktora», *Izvestiia A.N. SSSR, Seriia ekonomicheskaia*, 1986, n° 3, p. 20.
5. For projections on Soviet population growth in the eighties and nineties, see M. FESHBACH, «Soviet Population, Labour Force and Health», in *The Political Economy of the Soviet Union*. US Congress, Joint Economic Committee, 98th Congress, 1st Session, Washington D.C., US Government Printing Office, 1984, pp. 104 and 125.
6. See L. A. KOSTIN (ed.), *Trudovye resursy SSSR*, Moscow, 1979, pp. 238-242.
7. *Ibidem*, p. 249. See also A. KOTLIAR, «Polnaia zaniatost' i sbalansirovannost' faktorov sotsialisticheskogo proizvodstva», *Voprosy ekonomiki*, 1983, n° 7, pp. 107-108.
8. Cf. V.G. KOSTAKOV, *Prognoz zaniatosti naseleniia. Metodologicheskie osnovy*. Moscow, 1979, p. 6. A lasting echo of this approach is to be found in T.I. ZASLAVSKAIA's latest contribution, see «Tvorcheskaia aktivnost' mass sotsial'nye rezervy rosta», *EKO*, 1986, n° 3, pp. 10-15, which, however, is somewhat watered down in «Chelovecheskii faktor razvitiia ekonomiki i sotsial'naia spravedlivost'», *Kommunist*, 1986, n° 13, pp. 61-73.
9. See V. KOSTAKOV, «Balans trudovykh resursov v sovremennykh usloviiakh», *Sotsialisticheskii trud*, 1980, n° 6, pp. 85-86.
10. On 1980-83 regulations on labour discipline and turnover and their effects, see S. MALLE, «Planned and Unplanned Labour Mobility in the Soviet Union, under the Threat of Labour Shortage», *Soviet Studies*, 1987, n° 3, pp. 378-380.
11. One of the main theoreticians of this approach is I. MALMYGIN. On its developments, see: *Problemy intensifikatsii proizvodstva*, Moscow: Sovetskaia Rossiia, 1975; «Sbalansirovannost' rabochikh mest i trudovykh resursov», *Planovoe khoziaistvo*, 1982, n° 8 and (same title) *Voprosy ekonomiki*, 1983, n° 11; «Moshchnost'predpriiatiia i rabochee mesto», *Planovoe khoziaistvo*, 1984, n° 3; «Struktura i ispol'zovanie rabochikh mest v mashinostroenii», *Planovoe khoziaistvo*, 1985, n° 12, p. 101.
12. These issues are dealt with in detail in S. MALLE, «Capacity Utilization and the Shift Coefficient in Soviet Planning», *Economics of Planning*, forthcoming 1987.
13. See the Standard Instructions on *attestatsiia* in *Biulleten' Goskomtruda*, 1986, n° 7, pp. 3-28.
14. According to which, the workplace is «a zone endowed of the necessary technical means, in which *one worker or a group of workers* together fulfilling one task or operation perform their working activity», see I. MALMYGIN, cit., *Planovoe khoziaisto*, 1982, n° 8, p. 57 (emphasis added).
15. Cf. I. MALMYGIN, «Sbalansirovannost' rabochikh mest i trudovykh resursov», *Voprosy ekonomiki*, 1983, n° 11, p. 27 and V. CHEREVAN', «Uchet planirovanie rabochikh mest v protsesse ikh vosproizvodstva», *Vestnik statistiki*, 1984, n° 7, p. 49.
16. See A. TIKIDZHIEV, «Voprosy sbalansirovannosti vosproizvodstva osnovnykh fondov i trudovykh resursov», *Planovoe khoziaistvo*, 1981, n° 12, p. 50.
17. That is, the average annual budget value of basic production funds divided by the average annual number of workers.
18. This is a simplified version of the work needed to assess the useful number of workplaces. In practice, one does reckon that the number of machine operators is higher than needed under the particular shift regime, since additional labour is hired to replace workers on authorized leave, if the production process is not to be interrupted.
19. For recent data see V. KRIUKOV, «Planirovanie intensifikatsii proizvodstva», *Planovoe khoziaistvo*, 1986, n° 9, p. 41.
20. See M.S. GORBACHEV'S speech to the 28th Congress of Trade Unions in *Ekonomicheskaia gazeta*, 1987, n° 10, p. 5.
21. The social infrastructure needed to redeploy workers in evening and night shifts is a major obstacle towards the implementation of a multi-shift regime. This issue raised by experts (see I.U. CHARUKHIN, «Problemy smennosti v mashinostroenii», *Sotsialisticheskii trud*, 1984, n° 9, pp. 13-21) is tackled by a recent resolution establishing that multi-shift regimes must be introduced on a territorial

(town) basis by adapting to labour needs the system of transport, trade, catering and education as well as factory facilities (see *Ekonomicheskaia Gazeta*, 1987, n° 10, p. 12). Thus a contradiction emerges between the 12th FYP targets of industrial capacity utilization and the scope of the required adjustments.

22. See A.G. AGANBEGIAN, «Problemy perevoda narodnogo khoziaistva SSSR na puti intensivnogo razvitiia», in A.G. AGANBEGIAN and D.D. MOSKOVICH, (eds), *Povyshenie effektivnosti narodnogo khoziaistva*, Moscow, 1984, p. 28.
23. See S. MALLE, «Planned and Unplanned Labour Mobility», *cit.*, p. 376.
24. See FEOKTISTOVA E.N. and KAREV V.M., «Kompleksnyi podkhod k resheniiu problemy sokrashcheniia primeneniia ruchnogo truda v narodnom khoziaistve SSSR», *Izvestiia Akademii Nauk SSSR, seriia ekonomicheskaia*, 1986, n° 6, p. 38.
25. The definition of *heavy labour* agreed in 1982 is «the physical, dynamic loading of a worker during an 8 hour shift when the horizontal weight per shift is over 104,000 Kg (i.e. 13,000 Kg/hour; 216,7 Kg/minute, 3.6 Kg/second), see *Sotsialisticheskii trud*, 1983, n° 11, p. 33.
26. *Ibidem*, p. 38. Sample research indicates that up to one third of manual workers transferred into mechanized jobs suffer some disadvantages.
27. Cf. I.V. LEVCHUK, «Gosbank v reshenii i zadachii uskoreniia nauchno-tekhnicheskogo progressa», *Den'gi i kredit*. 1985, n° 11, p. 6.
28. Cf. I. MALMYGIN, *op. cit.*, 1985, p. 104.
29. See N.I. RYZKHOV'S speech to the 27th Party Congress, *Ekonomicheskaia gazeta*, 1986, n° 11, p. 25.
30. *Ekonomicheskaia gazeta*, 1986, n° 17, p. 4.
31. See interview with N.I. Ryzkhov in *Ekonomicheskaia gazeta*, 1986, n° 7, p. 2.
32. Cf. N.I. Ryzkhov speech to the Supreme Soviet, *Sotsialisticheskaia industriia*, 19 June 1986. From October 1986 virtually all main production units in Leningrad city and oblast switched to double-shift working, see. SWB-SU/8406/B/11, 3 November 1986, p. 4.
33. See A. A. PRIGARIN, «General'naia uborka v masshtabakh otraslei: kak k nei gotovy?», *EKO*, 1986, n° 4, p. 111 and I. MALMYGIN, *cit.*, 1985, p. 104.
34. *Sotsialisticheskii trud*, 1986, n° 2, p. 6 and *Ekonomicheskaia gazeta*, 1986, n° 17, p. 4. The average annual labour release due to technical progress is estimated to be about half million workers. Ninety percent of those workers are displaced to other jobs within the same factory, see N. AITOV, «Sotsial'nye problemy NTP», *Sotsialisticheskii trud*, 1986, n° 11, p. 16.
35. See *Ekonomicheskaia gazeta*, 1986, n° 14, p. 17.
36. See M. FESHBACH, *cit.*, p. 124.
37. That is, 1,212,000, see *Narodnoe khoziaistvo SSSR v 1985*, Moscow 1986, p. 107 and 391.
38. *Ekonomicheskaia gazeta*, 1987, n° 5, pp. 10-11.
39. Cf. quote from A. KATAEV, «Puti povysheniiu effektivnosti ispol'zovaniia osnovnykh proizvodstvennykh fondov», *Ekonomicheskie nauki*, 1986, n° 9, p. 57.
40. See D. KARPUKHIN, «Khoziaistvennyi mekhanizm i trud», *Voprosy ekonomiki*, 1981, n° 3, p. 131; *Trudovye resursy*, Moscow, 1979, pp. 265-6. However, in 1982, the Central Statistical Administration of the USSR estimated a 2.3 % industrial excess labour, as the difference between the actual number of employed and the planned limits to employment, e.g. some 865,000 workers, if the percentage is relative to total industrial employment, see R.N. TIKIDZHEV, «Rabochie mesta, trudovye resursy i kapital'nye vlozheniia» *EKO*, 1986, n° 4, pp. 116-117.
41. A. TSYGICHKO, «Sbalansirovannost' dinamiki osnovnykh proizvodstvennykh fondov i rabochei sily», *Voprosy ekonomiki*, 1986, n° 11, p. 63.
42. This figure has been reported by A. GALKIN at the Seminar on «Market and Planned Economies», Università Cattolica, Milan, 16-17 March, 1987.
43. *Ekonomicheskaia gazeta*, 1984, n° 10, p. 5 and A.A. PRIGARIN, *cit.*, p. 101.
44. According to I. MALMYGIN, in 1984, 45 % of workplaces in eleven engineering ministries were understaffed, see I. MALMIGYN, *cit.*, 1985, p. 100-101.
45. Cf. A.E. KOTLIAR, in *Trudovye resursy, cit.*, p. 4.
46. A 5-6 % rate of capital annual replacement is supposed to be achieved in the course of the 12th Five Year Plan, see A. KATAEV, *cit.*, p. 58.
47. See *Ekonnomicheskaia Gazeta*, 1987, n° 15, p. 2.
48. See *Metodicheskie voprosy sozdaniia sistemy norm i normativov*, (V.V. SOKOLOV ed.), Moscow, 1983, p. 174.
49. V. SHCHERBAKOV, «Mera truda i ego oplata», *Sotsialisticheskii trud*, 1986, n° 4, p. 29.
50. *Sotsialisticheskii trud.*, 1986, n° 2, pp. 12-13.
51. Cf. L. POPOV, «Nuzhna progressivnaia sistema upravleniia trudoemkostiu», *Sotsialisticheskii trud*, 1986, n° 3, p. 27.
52. See V.M. VERNIGORA et al., «Voprosy normirovaniia upravlencheskogo truda», *Organizatsiia i planirovanie otraslei narodnogo khoziaistva*, 1984, n° 77, pp. 45-5 and A. POLIANSKI and V. IL'IN, «Normativnyi metod planirovaniia chislennosti ITR i sluzhaishchikh na predpriiatiiakh otraslei», *Sotsialisticheskii trud*, 1981, n° 1, pp. 87-89.
53. See IU.N. KRASNOV, «Povyshenie effektivnosti ispol'zovaniia resursov truda», *Organizatsiia i Planirovanie otraslei narodnogo khoziaistva*, 1984, n° 75, p. 34.
54. Cf. G. SMOLIN, «Sbalansirovannost' trudovykh resursov s nalichem rabochikh mest'», *Sotsialisti-*

cheskii trud, 1983, n° 8, pp. 76-77, and N. ZENCHENKO, « Aktual'nye zadachi mestnykh planovykh organov», *Planovoe khoziaistvo,* 1983, n° 6, pp. 25-26.
55. The time job evaluation applies only to 3.5 of white collars, cf. A. PAVLENKO, « Regulator chislennosti», *Sotsialisticheskii trud,* 1984, n° 11, p. 73.
56. From 1970 to 1975, the number of industrial ITR increased by 16.3 %, from 1975 to 1980 by 19.7 % and from 1980 to 1985 by 9.5 %. Their relative share in total industrial production employment, which increased by 0.9 percentage points from 1970 to 1975 (when the rate of growth of labour resources was still respectable), grew from 1975 to 1980 by 1.3 percentage points and from 1980 to 1985 by 0.7, see *Narodnoe khoziaistvo SSSR v 1985,* Moscow, 1986, p. 107.
57. At the central level alone, some 20,000 workers are employed in fixing norms, see V. MARKOV, « Raspredelenie po trudu i sbalansirovannosti dokhodov tovarnymi resursami», *Sotsialisticheskii trud,* 1985, n° 1, pp. 47-48.
58. However, limits on additional employment are supposed to be agreed with local territorial organs, see *Khoziaistvennyi mekhanizm v dvenatsatoi piatiletke* (R.A. BELOUSOV and D.N. BOBRYSHEV eds), Moscow, 1986, p. 32. Branch and enterprise limits remain for enterprises of the Republican Ministries of Local Industry.
59. *Ekonomicheskaia gazeta,* 1985, n° 49. p. 18.
60. Such as staff working for research and development, design bureaus, technical organizers and staff of experimental units.
61. Aims and rules of the new indicator are explained in V. RZHESHEVSKII, « Povyshenie zainteresovannost' trudovykh kollektivov v rabote s menshei chislennost'iu», *Sotsialisticheskii trud,* 1984, n° 5, pp. 63-67.
62. G. KIPERMAN, « Ekonomicheskie normativy v upravlenii promyshlennym proizvodstvom», *Planovoe khoziaistvo,* 1986, n° 7, p. 24.
63. Interbranch differences go from 0.2 to 0.9, the rate of productivity increase. See A. DERIPASOV, « Regulirovanie sootnosheniia mezhdu rostom zarabotnoi platy i proizvoditel'nost'iu truda v promyshlennosti», *Planovoe khoziaistvo,* 1986, n° 7, p. 104.
64. See for the discussion of the potential advantages of new regulations, J.S. BERLINER, « Economic Measures and Reforms under Andropov», in *The Soviet Economy After Brezhnev,* NATO Colloquium 11-13 1984, Brussels, 1984, p. 62.
65. Cf. O.P. ZAROVETSKII et al., « O normativnykh sootnosheniiakh mezhdu prirostom proizvoditel'nosti truda i srednei zarplaty», *Den'gi i kredit,* 1985, n° 5, pp. 17-18.
66. See T. BORISOVA, « O povyshenii roli FMP v ulushenii konechnykh rezultatov proizvodstva», *Sotsialisticheskii trud,* 1986, n° 2, p. 53 and E.G. IASIN, « O normativnykh metodakh planovogo formirovaniia fonda oplaty truda», *Sotsialisticheskii trud,* 1986, n° 3, p. 9.
67. Cf. V.IL'IN, « Ekonomicheskii eksperiment i razvitie proizvodstva», *Planovoe khoziaistvo,* 1986, n° 5, p. 49.
68. *Sotsialisticheskaia industriia,* 30 July 1985, p. 2.
69. Cf. E. K. GORBUNOV, « Intensivnost' truda i povyshenie ego proizvoditel'nosti», EKO, 1986, n° 4, pp. 145-147.
70. From one percent of the wage fund in the Electrotechnical Industry to a maximum of 2.4 % in the Bielorussian Light Industry, see *Den'gi i kredit,* 1985, n° 11, pp. 35-37, *Finansy SSSR,* 1986, n° 2, p. 29, *Sotsialisticheskii trud,* 1986, n° 5, p. 36.
71. Cf. E.G. IASIN, « Ekonomicheskie normativy», *cit.,* 1986, p. 593; *Finansy SSSR,* 1986, n° 5, p. 28, and *Ekonomicheskaia gazeta,* 1984, n° 7, p. 15.
72. *Ekonomicheskaia gazeta,* 1985, n° 3, p. 9.
73. On some negative consequences of this approach to labour-saving, see *Sotsialisticheskaia industriia,* 30 July 1985, and G.I. GROTSESKUL, « Shchekinskii metod okhvatyvaet territoriiu», *EKO,* 1985, n° 6, p. 147.
74. *Pravda,* 22 September 1986.
75. See P.G. BUNICH, « Problemy perestroiki mekhanizma upravleniia ekonomikoi», *Ekonomika i matematicheskie metody,* 1986, n° 4, pp. 582-585.
76. *Sotsialisticheskii trud,* 1987, n° 1 presents the details of the wage reform.
77. A. BIM and A. SHOKIN (« Sistema raspredeleniia: na putiakh perestroiki», *Kommunist,* 1986, n° 15, p. 64) ascribe the rescheduling to «unplanned measures requiring extraordinary funds». In 1986 saving deposits reached 200 milliard rubles, 33 % of which took the form of ready cash (see BC SWB-SU/8298/C/21, 30 June 1986). The shortage of consumer goods is estimated, probably optimistically, to be about 10 milliard rubles. Imbalances in the consumer goods market may explain in part why pensions are still regulated by and large by the 1956 provisions, although it is has been said that the absolute standard of living of pensioners has been badly hit by price increases (see S. SHATALIN, « Sotsial'nye razvitie i ekonomicheskii rost», *Kommunist,* 1986, n° 14, pp. 67-70). A significant rise in pensions, moreover, could result in less labour offered by people of retirement age.
78. As it occured, in an experiment carried out in some Leningrad enterprises, see *Pravda,* 24 December 1985, p. 1.

M. Gorbatchev et l'agriculture

Chantal Beaucourt

Interrogée, en avril 1985, sur le secteur de l'économie soviétique qui pourrait être pionnier dans la « réforme radicale » que venait d'annoncer le nouveau secrétaire général du Parti, l'académicienne Tatjana Zaslavskaja, dont l'avis passe pour être écouté en haut lieu, avait aussitôt répondu : « L'agriculture ».[1]

Et de fait l'agriculture a été l'un des premiers secteurs concernés par les mesures de réorganisation entreprises par M.S. Gorbatchev.

A cela, il y avait deux bonnes raisons au moins : les performances agricoles ont été particulièrement faibles au cours de la dernière décennie, et elles ont contribué à freiner la croissance économique de l'Union soviétique. M. Gorbatchev a été confronté aux problèmes agricoles pendant toute sa carrière et possède une compétence indiscutée dans ce domaine.

Tatjana Zaslavskaja expliquait son choix d'abord par référence à l'expérience des pays socialistes qui ont déjà procédé à des réformes économiques, mais aussi par le fait que le complexe agro-industriel (APK) est le secteur le plus « sensible » aux formes économiques de gestion, et aussi « le plus souple ». Ce dernier argument peut surprendre, alors que depuis des décennies l'inertie des masses paysannes est rendue principalement responsable des déficiences de l'agriculture. Pourtant, « c'est dans les campagnes, constate-t-elle, que se développent le plus d'expériences, indépendamment de toute directive et au-delà de tout contrôle ... de nouvelles formes de gestion naissent, qui ne sont pas traditionnelles, mais ça marche et se marie bien au collectif ».

Est-ce là la voie dans laquelle s'engage M.S. Gorbatchev et peut-elle être qualifiée de « novatrice » et sa démarche de « révolutionnaire », comme il l'a laissé entendre récemment encore ?[2] On relève certaines ambiguïtés dans la façon de traiter les problèmes et les décisions qui ont été prises, et on peut se demander si les décisions les plus novatrices constituent une étape vers une réforme profonde ou une concession nécessaire pour atteindre un but qui, lui, n'a pas changé : il faut faire de l'URSS « le pays modèle du socialisme ». Les textes d'application issus du 27ème congrès se succèdent à une cadence rapide mais ils laissent en suspens autant de questions qu'ils en résolvent. En janvier encore, des dispositions « importantes » et « à grande échelle » ont été à nouveau annoncées. La reconstitution en cours est une opération de longue haleine. On essaiera cependant d'en dégager les principales orientations.

I - L'agriculture — Tremplin de la réforme

L'idée d'une réforme a mûri dans l'agriculture, depuis longtemps. «Celle-ci n'est pas tombée des nues», dira V.S. Murakhosky, l'actuel président du Gosagroprom.[3] «Il y a longtemps qu'on en discutait entre experts» — dix ans — précise T. Zaslavskaja.

En fait, on peut dater de mars 1965, la nouvelle approche du problème agro-alimentaire par les responsables de l'économie soviétique. L'agriculture devient alors un secteur prioritaire de la politique gouvernementale et s'inscrit comme tel dans la stratégie globale d'une croissance «intensive» décidée à cette date par L. Brejnev.[4] Mais, dans un premier temps, on s'attache principalement à fournir à l'agriculture plus de moyens matériels et financiers. «L'industrialisation de l'agriculture» est le mot clé de cette politique et, «de vache à lait de l'industrie», le secteur devient un des plus gros bénéficiaires de l'investissement. Assez vite cependant, il apparaît qu'une mauvaise exploitation de ces ressources les rend inopérantes. La croissance des productivités et des rendements ralentit. Dans un deuxième temps, qui débute avec le 10ème plan quinquennal 1976-1980, l'amélioration des méthodes de gestion et d'exploitation doit permettre d'utiliser les ressources existantes avec plus d'efficacité.

Depuis lors, on observe une certaine continuité dans la démarche entreprise. Faut-il s'en étonner lorsque l'on sait que M.S. Gorbatchev est chargé de ce secteur depuis 1978, date à partir de laquelle il occupe le poste de secrétaire du Parti pour les questions agricoles.[5] Le programme alimentaire adopté en mai 1982 qui, en 1987 encore, sert de référence à M. Gorbatchev, a bien été présenté par L. Brejnev comme une nouvelle étape de la politique introduite en 1965, mais s'il porte sa signature, nul n'ignore que l'actuel secrétaire général du PC en a été le principal artisan. Le décret du 29 mars 1986[6] vise pour l'essentiel à perfectionner le mécanisme économique du «complexe agro-alimentaire» (APK) mis en place en 1982 et 1985 : nouveaux organes de gestion au niveau du district — les RAPO — et regroupement de certains ministères de la filière agro-alimentaire en un seul organisme d'état — le Gosagroprom.

Ainsi, encore, le décret de décembre 1986[7] donne un rôle central aux «brigades sous contrat», parmi les formes d'organisation du travail qui permettent d'accroître la productivité des ressources; or la campagne en faveur de ces brigades, commencée en 1979, s'est développée en 1982 : le programme alimentaire en fait état; et, en 1984, M. Gorbatchev rappelait qu'il ne s'agissait pas là d'une campagne à court terme, mais d'une restructuration fondamentale de l'organisation du travail et de sa rémunération.

De même, la loi sur l'activité individuelle récemment adoptée[8] confirme une attitude favorable envers le secteur privé que l'on pouvait déceler dès 1981 dans un décret qui relance l'activité des lopins individuels (les «exploitations auxiliaires privées») ainsi que dans ceux de 1982 et 1985 qui réglementent les exploitations agricoles auxiliaires des entreprises industrielles ainsi que les vergers et jardins collectifs.

Les uns et les autres portent la marque du même maître d'œuvre, même si on ne peut pour autant lui imputer la paternité de toutes les expériences tentées dans les années 1970, ni celle de toutes les décisions prises : en 1984, M. Gorbatchev s'irrite contre le ministre de la bonification et des eaux qui «s'intéresse beaucoup plus à de grands projets coûteux qu'à l'amélioration et à la modernisation des systèmes d'irrigation existants».[9] Il n'empêche pas l'adoption en octobre de la même année d'un programme à long terme de bonification des terres, incluant un projet grandiose de transfert des eaux. Cet épisode marque cependant les limites de son pouvoir d'alors; et la lenteur avec laquelle le décret retirant le projet a été adopté montre qu'en 1986 les oppositions étaient encore fortes. Depuis sa nomination, pourtant, le changement des responsables en poste dans l'agriculture s'est accéléré, l'équipe en place lui est acquise. C'est un atout considérable.

Certes la réforme soviétique est une entreprise de longue haleine et la *reconstruction de l'économie forme un tout*. La «réforme radicale» dont le secrétaire général a fait état en 1985 s'applique à l'ensemble de l'économie et on ne peut concevoir de réorganisation efficace d'un secteur indépendamment des autres. La création du Gosagroprom n'a pas résolu le problème des autres ministères de l'APK; et le système de planification, celui de la formation des prix, le contrôle du Parti interfèrent sur chaque secteur.[10]

C'est pourtant sur les résultats de l'agriculture qu'on jugera en priorité du succès de l'entreprise : pièce maîtresse d'une accélération de la croissance, elle pèse directement sur l'approvisionnement de la population et son niveau de vie; et pour M. Gorbatchev, l'agriculture a les potentialités de gains de productivité les plus élevés et les plus rapides. En même temps le but n'a pas changé dans sa formulation et, si élevé qu'en puisse être le coût, l'autosuffisance alimentaire demeure l'objectif permanent de la politique économique soviétique.[11]

II - L'ANALYSE DE M. GORBATCHEV

2-1 L'approche de M.S. Gorbatchev concernant le problème agro-alimentaire se déduit d'une première constatation : *l'incapacité croissante de l'URSS à couvrir les besoins alimentaires* de la population.

• Certes la *consommation* par habitant a augmenté quelque peu ces dernières années, en particulier celle de produits «sensibles» comme la viande (4 kg entre 1982 et 1986). Mais, reconnaît-on, l'écart entre l'offre et la demande s'est accru, la production alimentaire n'a pas progressé au rythme des revenus monétaires alors que les prix restaient stables; et «les gens ne veulent plus vivre comme avant, s'accommoder d'une stagnation».[12]

Par ailleurs, les consommations alimentaires sont couvertes toujours davantage par des achats extérieurs. Vladimir Treml estime qu'en 1981, 22 % des biens consommés ont été importés.[13] Il est un fait que les importations ont augmenté de 80 % entre les deux derniers quinquennats. En 1984 et 1985, elles étaient supérieures de 60 % à celles des années 1975-1978.[14]

● Force est de le reconnaître, les performances au niveau de la *production* agricole ont été médiocres, M.S. Gorbatchev le constate en termes sévères, dans son intervention devant le comité central, en janvier dernier[15] : «nous nous sommes littéralement embourbés dans ces affaires; tout le 11ème quinquennat a piétiné, nous avons commencé à piétiner en 1972 et particulièrement après 1975 quand on a dû liquider un grand nombre de têtes de bétail».

Et de fait, on enregistre une décélération de la croissance de la production agricole depuis vingt ans, décélération qui s'est accentuée sur la période 1981-1985, dans le secteur collectif.[16] Certaines productions ont stagné et même diminué au cours de cette période, en particulier celle des céréales; et M. Ligatchev nous apprend incidemment que l'Ukraine qui contribuait à remplir les fonds céréaliers de l'Etat, y puise dorénavant plus de ressources qu'elle n'en fournit.[17]

Les responsables de l'agriculture peuvent-ils se targuer du moins, d'une amélioration après l'adoption du programme alimentaire :

Les résultats sont en effet meilleurs dans le secteur de l'élevage : M. Gorbatchev s'attribue un satisfecit en notant que la «tendance à la reprise de l'élevage» date de 1982; celle-ci peut en effet être associée aux décision prises alors dans «le programme alimentaire», si l'on en juge en particulier par le fort développement des cultures fourragères, et par le fait que les livraisons de viande à l'Etat ont été respectées depuis quatre ans.

Ce satisfecit ne peut cependant être étendu à l'ensemble de la production agricole et les résultats obtenus après l'adoption de ce programme apparaissent moins significatifs que la présentation de M. Nikonov sur les périodes 1981-1982 et 1983-1985 tendrait à le faire admettre, lorsqu'on constate qu'à une année de croissance — 1983 — succèdent deux années de stagnation (tableau I).

2-2 La *limitation des facteurs de production,* évoquée par certains, est un *faux problème,* et ne saurait être incriminée pour justifier ces faibles performances : c'est la deuxième constatation à laquelle aboutit M. Gorbatchev. L'agriculture a les moyens de faire mieux; outre un potentiel humain considérable, « elle possède un capital énorme », et les investissements qui lui sont octroyés sont « à la limite supérieure des besoins réels » (*), « l'agriculture a déjà trop perçu pour les résultats obtenus ». Il faut donc procéder à une redistribution des investissements destinés au complexe agro-industriel en faveur des industries en amont et en aval de la production agricole ainsi que de l'infrastructure rurale. Par ailleurs les ressources en terres et en eaux sont suffisantes et la progression des récoltes ne procédera pas d'une large extension des terres irriguées. Celle-ci continueront certes à augmenter et l'on en attend quelques effets. Mais le décret du 20 août 1986 porte un coup d'arrêt aux travaux de transfert d'une partie des cours d'eau du nord de l'Europe et de Sibérie, et devrait mettre fin à la vive polémique qu'avait suscitée ce projet.[18]

A la décharge des responsables de l'agriculture, cependant, celle-ci n'a guère reçu le soutien des autres secteurs. Les livraisons d'engrais, d'autres produits chimiques et d'équipements, n'ont pas été respectées; la qualité des produits ne correspond pas toujours aux besoins; M. Gorbatchev l'a reconnu lors d'une visite à l'Institut de recherche sur l'équipement agricole de Moscou : « Vous êtes en grande dette vis-à-vis du secteur agricole ».[19] Et dans ce domaine non plus, l'aspect quantitatif n'est pas prédominant : « Nous produisons pourtant plus de machines que le monde entier, le malheur est qu'elles s'usent rapidement et doivent être mises hors service. Vous fournissez aux fermiers un équipement de piètre qualité qui les laisse désappointés et les empêche de venir à bout de leur tâche ».

Ainsi encore les sols requièrent principalement des engrais phosphatés. Mais leur production augmente moins que celle des engrais azotés, et au cours des premiers mois de 1986, l'industrie des engrais s'est distinguée par un record de production de faible qualité.[20] Les « contrôles d'Etat » permettront-ils d'y remédier ? M. Gorbatchev a mis en garde les producteurs : une production de mauvaise qualité ne sera plus acceptée.

2-3 Le vrai problème, c'est l'usage qui est fait de ces ressources, telle est sa conclusion.

La décélération de la croissance de la productivité du travail s'est accentuée au cours des vingt dernières années. Les résultats ont été particulièrement décevants dans le dernier quinquennat. Malgré un accroissement non négligeable de la mécanisation du travail entre 1982 et 1985, la production par travailleur a pratiquement stagné en 1984-1985; l'observation des données sur les périodes 1981-1982 et 1983-1985 apparaît donc peu caractéristique de la situation, dans ce domaine également. Par ailleurs, malgré une tendance à l'amélioration du coefficient marginal de capital, celui-ci reste trop élevé.

* 25 à 30 % des investissements depuis 20 ans.

Enfin la chaîne des pertes, du champ au consommateur, est énorme. La presse fourmille d'exemples à ce propos; au 27ème congrès du Comité central, M. Gorbatchev les chiffrait à 20 % des disponibilités à la consommation, voire 30 % pour certains produits, et en janvier 1987, il rappelle que le volume des pertes reste un des aspects préoccupants de la situation agricole.

Si l'on ajoute les subventions aux prix, de l'ordre de 50 milliards de roubles soit 15 % du budget de l'Etat, on conçoit la charge que représente ce secteur pour l'économie soviétique.

Les résultats de 1986 peuvent pourtant leur donner quelques motifs de satisfaction : la récolte céréalière est la meilleure depuis 1978, la production agricole dans son ensemble a augmenté de 5,1 % et la productivité du travailleur de 6,9 %, alors que les ressources matérielles utilisées par rouble de production diminuaient de 2,8 %. Par ailleurs, mais est-ce vraiment un sujet de satisfaction pour tous, au cours du quinquennat la production des exploitations individuelles a augmenté davantage que la production collective, pour la première fois depuis des décennies.

Les responsables restent lucides et ne s'adonnent pas à l'autosatisfaction. « Ces chiffres ne disent pas encore que l'activité de ce très grand complexe économique qu'est l'APK a acquis la stabilité de la croissance qui est nécessaire; ils ne disent pas non plus que nous ayons appris à utiliser rationnellement les énormes moyens mis à disposition par l'Etat, ni à résoudre rapidement et sans pertes de temps, les problèmes qui se posent».

A la réunion du comité central du Parti du 23 janvier dernier, M.S. Gorbatchev posait «les questions essentielles auxquelles la réforme de l'économie doit faire face pour résoudre le problème agricole». Si l'on entrevoit quels sont «les handicaps à surmonter» (faible efficacité des ressources, pertes et gaspillages) et ce «à quoi il faut renoncer sans hésiter» (les mesures de type extensif) — reste sa dernière interrogation, qui n'est pas des moindres : «sur quoi faut-il se concentrer et que mettre à profit pour parvenir au but? ».

III - LA STRATEGIE DE LA REFORME

En même temps qu'une certaine continuité dans le processus engagé, la stratégie mise en œuvre pour venir à bout du problème alimentaire fait apparaître une forte volonté de changement. M. Gorbatchev n'hésite pas à invoquer les décisions fondamentales qui ont marqué, en mars 1921, le début de la NEP (nouvelle politique économique). En même temps la reconstitution est progressive et les solutions alternatives ne sont pas écartées. Cette stratégie s'articule principalement autour de trois axes.

3-1 - Des solutions technico-scientifiques : « les technologies intensives »

La nouvelle approche exige une intensification scientifique et technologique : nouvelles méthodes de culture, nouvelles techniques. La conception des «technologies intensives» n'est cependant pas totalement nouvelle, le programme alimentaire en fait état mais, dans les conditions d'une accélération du progrès scientifique et technique, leur utilisation devient «le cœur du système de gestion de l'APK». Au 27ème congrès du PC M. Gorbatchev en a fait «la clé du succès».

L'idée est de concentrer les forces et les moyens sur les facteurs qui garantissent les rendements les plus élevés, et la stabilité de la production. Pour ce faire, on établit des «systèmes scientifiques d'exploitation», par zones, qui mettent en balance les facteurs biologiques, techniques, économiques et sociaux et les coordonnent pour obtenir le maximum de production au moindre coût. On crée ainsi un cadre normatif à partir duquel se fait la gestion.[21] Il en a été construit un en Georgie dès 1982 et un système — étalon — est en cours d'élaboration dans le kraj de Stavropol. Par ailleurs, s'il s'agit de «recommandations», celles-ci sont en fait contraignantes pour les exploitants, le Gosagroprom faisant les arbitrages. Des contrats de partenariat peuvent par ailleurs être conclus par les exploitants avec les instituts scientifiques, qui en surveillent le bon usage.

La mise en œuvre de ces systèmes d'exploitation n'en est pas moins ambitieuse. Ils doivent faire face simultanément aux problèmes les plus aigus de l'agriculture soviétique : protection de la fertilité des sols, alors que la perte nette d'humus est estimée à 50 % et que l'acidité et la salination des sols augmentent; meilleur emploi des jachères dont les surfaces ont augmenté mais dont l'efficacité n'a pas crû en conséquence; révision fondamentale de la politique de bonification et une utilisation économe des eaux pour l'irrigation, recherche de méthodes de bonification non liées à l'eau ... pour ne citer que quelques-uns de ceux qu'énumère le président de l'académie des sciences agricoles A.A. Nikonov.

Par ailleurs l'extension des technologies intensives s'intègre dans le déroulement d'un programme de développement scientifique et technique fort ambitieux lui aussi; elle suppose en effet que soient fournis les moyens de production adéquats. Actuellement ces technologies sont concentrées sur les objectifs de production qui ont les retombées les plus fortes. Le Gosagroprom planifie, pour chaque république, les principaux produits agricoles qui seront cultivés selon ces technologies et des directives ont été données aux ministères concernés, pour y attribuer plus d'équipement et d'engrais, et ceux de la meilleure qualité. Car l'état des industries d'amont pose souvent problème : ainsi l'utilisation de la «technologie intensive» du chaulage est freinée par manque de chaux dans le pays, et elle ne pourra se développer qu'au rythme de l'industrie. En outre l'effet décroîtra au fur et à mesure que les technologies nouvelles s'appliqueront dans des conditions moins favorables.

Enfin — et ce n'est pas là le moindre handicap — ces technologies réclament «une discipline très stricte de la part du cultivateur : celui-ci doit être précis, bien informé, prendre en compte les particularités de chaque terrain, de la biologie, de la croissance des plantes ... réaliser les travaux en temps voulu». L'opération suppose donc, pour être menée à bonnes fins, que l'exploitation dispose de cadres qualifiés, et les responsables de l'opération le reconnaissent aisément, tous les cadres, loin de là, n'ont pas assimilé les nouvelles technologies. Un vaste programme de formation a été envisagé. Mais a-t-on les moyens de le mettre en place rapidement ?

Ainsi les technologies intensives préparent-elles surtout l'avenir. La bonne récolte céréalière de 1986 (210 millions de tonnes) serait pourtant imputable, en grande partie, à leur utilisation, qui aurait permis d'en accroître la production de 24 millions de tonnes.[22] Et d'ici 1990 on prévoit d'en étendre l'application sur cinquante millions d'hectares.

3-2 - La réorganisation du mécanisme économique de gestion

S'il est un domaine où la politique se veut novatrice, c'est celui des méthodes de gestion du complexe agro-industriel. C'est sur leur amélioration et leur renouvellement, que l'on compte principalement pour réaliser «le tournant radical du développement du secteur agricole».

Le processus est en marche depuis 1982, mais à une phase de restructuration, administrative principalement, en succède une autre qui privilégie les facteurs économiques. La portée des mesures qui ont été prises peut apparaître limitée, mais la démarche n'est pas figée et se développe dans trois directions principales.

● L'adoption d'une *structure horizontale* des organismes de gestion de l'APK a donné naissance, en 1982, à des organismes de coordination de tous les intervenants dans la filière alimentaire au niveau du district (RAPO) mais aussi de l'oblast (OAPO), de la république et du centre (comité d'état agro-alimentaire). Elle s'est prolongée, plus récemment, avec la création — expérimentale — de groupes de travail (brigades) «intégrées» qui rassemblent kolkhoz, services de réparation et de transport et représentants des usines de transformation. Cette restructuration vise à supprimer les barrières sectorielles, à briser la tutelle des ministères, mais aussi à limiter l'appareil bureaucratique; elle s'est traduite, en novembre 1985, par le regroupement à l'intérieur du «Gosagroprom», du comité d'état et des cinq ministères à vocation agricole, auxquels s'adjoignent les représentants des ministères et organismes liés à la production agricole.

L'idée est simple : on rassemble autour d'une même table tous les responsables de la production agricole et de son utilisation. Son application a cependant rencontré quelques difficultés. Le RAPO devait être le « maillon crucial » de cette organisation : il s'avérait en effet que c'est au niveau du district que les responsables sont le plus au fait des conditions concrètes de la production. Mais contrairement à sa vocation initiale il est devenu, le plus souvent, un nouvel intermédiaire administratif, incapable d'assumer sa tâche de coordination. Il n'a guère les moyens de faire respecter les engagements des services ministériels qui ne dépendent pas directement du Gosagroprom, et interfère trop souvent et à mauvais escient dans l'activité des exploitations, ce qui lui a valu un rappel à l'ordre sévère sur les limites de sa compétence : « Nombreux sont ceux qui veulent commander les directeurs des kolkhoz et sovkoz. Cela ne convient pas. Il ne faut pas croire que le président et les 40 ou 50 spécialistes du kolkhoz sachent, moins et plus mal, que les membres de l'appareil du RAPO de quoi ils doivent s'occuper et comment mener les affaires. Le principal organe de l'union agro-industrielle c'est le conseil du RAPO qui réunit les directeurs des exploitations et des services ministériels. Le président du RAPO, son appareil, sont les exécutants de la volonté du conseil ».[15]

En même temps, la tutelle politique, dont le plenum de mai avait souligné les excès, continue à s'exercer sur les RAPO : comment s'en étonner, le RAPO occupe généralement des locaux du comité exécutif de district dont le président est également celui du RAPO. Le développement des « brigades intégrées » et des combinats pourraient cependant leur faire une sérieuse concurrence : leurs structures sont en effet parallèles et M. Gorbatchev y est fort intéressé.

La création du Gosagroprom quant à elle a eu deux effets non négligeables : elle a facilité l'élimination de responsables gênants tel Zya Nurjev, président du comité d'Etat agro-industriel de 1982 à 1985, et fervent défenseur du projet de transfert des eaux, et permis la mise en place d'une nouvelle équipe; en même temps le personnel administratif a été considérablement réduit : 47 % du personnel des ministères dissous a été licencié. Mais le Gosagroprom reste un organisme lourd, et l'extension de ses responsabilités aux problèmes de planification, de financement, d'approvisionnement et de commerce extérieur, entame les compétences du Gosplan et des ministères concernés. Certains l'envisagent même comme « une vraie catastrophe ».

• Une *approche régionale* du problème agro-alimentaire : l'amorce d'une décentralisation ?

Les instances régionales (**) ont un rôle accru dans l'approvisionne-

(**) Comité exécutif de l'oblast ou du kraj (province), ou conseil des ministres des républiques autonomes et des républiques fédérées qui ne sont pas divisées en oblast.

ment de la population, principalement par trois voies :

• A partir de 1987, elles auront l'entière disposition des ressources en viande, lait et autres produits dégagés après versement à l'Etat des livraisons planifiées, et les plans de livraison seront fixes sur cinq ans. On évite ainsi de tomber dans le piège de voir réintégrer dans le plan l'effort accompli dans l'année. Ces produits pourront également faire l'objet d'échanges entre régions sur une base contractuelle, notamment par l'intermédiaire des coopératives de consommation. Mais en cas d'inexécution des plans de livraison à l'Etat, un montant équivalent sera retiré des ressources destinées à l'approvisionnement local pour le trimestre ou l'année suivants.

• Les instances régionales disposeront également d'une certaine marge de manœuvre au niveau des prix :

Pour diminuer les pertes de fruits et légumes, les antennes régionales du Gosagroprom auront le droit de modifier les prix de détail des produits périssables vendus dans les magasins de leur ressort, sur la base d'un fonds de régulation des prix saisonniers de gros et de détail dont la réglementation est à définir. Mais on espère aussi, par ce biais, casser les prix pratiqués sur le marché kolkhozien.

• Pour engager les exploitants agricoles à produire boissons, confitures, conserves et autres produits très recherchés par la population, ceux-ci seront autorisés à les vendre à des prix « avantageux » établis par les instances régionales, dans les magasins de leur ressort.

Par ailleurs, les plans d'achat de l'Etat, en particulier pour les céréales, devront être établis en fonction des « potentialités bioclimatiques régionales ». Ainsi les indicateurs d'objectifs devraient être désormais fondés sur les ressources disponibles dans les meilleures conditions géographiques et non plus à partir d'une vision normative bureaucratique. En même temps, pour inciter les exploitants à choisir les ensemencements qui correspondent aux besoins de l'Etat et aux conditions naturelles les meilleures, les organismes responsables de ces achats devront procéder à une différenciation des prix plus approfondie.

Ces instances auront donc à résoudre des problèmes d'ajustement auxquels elles sont peu préparées. Et ces mesures peuvent apparaître bien timides eu égard aux déficiences du système actuel des prix. Elles auront cependant une incidence sur la différenciation géographique des prix de gros, alors qu'il n'existe actuellement en URSS que trois zones de fixation de ces prix dans lesquelles l'on ne tient pas compte des spécificités de sols et climats. En arrivera-t-on à généraliser l'expérience — une de plus — qui était en cours dans le kraj de Stavropol, alors que M.S. Murakhovsky en était encore le secrétaire général du Parti : dans cette province en effet, les régions sont réparties en trois zones de prix et les exploitations en sept sous-groupes.

• *L'autonomie de gestion et l'autonomie financière* constituent les pierres angulaires de la réforme des exploitations agricoles.

Pour le directeur de l'institut économique de Moscou, M. Abalkin, l'orientation vers l'autonomie financière est la force motrice du changement; elle suppose en particulier que les décisions économiques soient prises par les chefs d'entreprise et non par les planificateurs et que le travail soit rémunéré en fonction du profit.[23]

Il y a des années pourtant que l'autonomie financière (khozraschet) est un des objectifs de la politique agricole, mais sans succès : les coûts de production croissants, les prix de vente inadéquats, les mauvaises conditions climatiques en sont en grande partie responsables. Il s'agit aujourd'hui de créer les conditions pour que l'intention soit réalisable et quelques mesures — modestes il est vrai — vont en ce sens. Ainsi le Gosagroprom et le comité d'état aux prix sont instamment appelés à contrôler les variations des prix des produits et services fournis à l'agriculture et à proposer, si nécessaire, la modification des prix d'achat de l'Etat.

On espère que, dès cette année, 23 % des kolkhoz et des sovkhoz auront trouvé leur équilibre financier. Quoiqu'il en soit, à partir de 1987, les deux tiers des exploitations d'Etat verseront une part de leurs bénéfices au budget (et le kolkhoz un impôt sur le revenu), selon des normes stables sur cinq ans, à partir d'une évaluation économique du sol, et de leur approvisionnement en ressources naturelles et en main-d'œuvre.

• L'autonomie de gestion qui devrait accompagner la contrainte de l'équilibre se traduit d'une façon générale par la volonté fortement affirmée de réduire la tutelle administrative et l'ingérence des organes du Parti et autres organisations d'Etat dans l'activité de l'exploitation. L'exemple des RAPOS montre cependant la difficulté de l'entreprise.

• Ainsi l'exploitation peut, en principe, produire « ce qu'elle veut, quand elle veut, comme elle l'entend ». Mais ce deuxième aspect de leur autonomie est encore plus théorique que réel. Elle reste soumise, en effet, aux trois contraintes — livraisons à l'Etat, limite d'investissement et allocation centralisée des principales ressources matérielles — qui lui sont imposées d'en haut. C'est à partir de ces contraintes qu'elle établit le plan de l'exploitation, qui est transmis à la hiérarchie supérieure et en redescend après ajustement sous forme obligatoire. De plus, le volume des livraisons à l'Etat ne doit pas être inférieur au niveau annuel moyen des cinq années précédentes. En somme, l'exploitation a l'initiative de produire plus, mieux, moins cher, dans la limite des ressources qui lui sont octroyées et de celles qu'elle pourra dégager par ses propres moyens.

Ce qu'on lui offre en compensation peut apparaître limité. La libre disposition d'une partie de sa production en est cependant l'aspect le plus incitatif; elle concerne dorénavant 30 % du volume planifié des livraisons de fruits et légumes (10 % de 1982 à 1986) ainsi que la production en sus du plan. Ces productions pourront être vendues directement sur le marché kolkhozien ou aux coopératives de consommation, à des prix « agréés », mais l'exploitation pourra également l'utiliser à son profit. La fixation de quotas de livraisons fermes sur cinq ans en accroît l'intérêt.

3-3 - *La mobilisation de la main-d'œuvre*

La mobilisation de la main-d'œuvre constitue le troisième volet de la réforme agricole; la réponse qui y sera faite et la modification des comportements qu'elle implique peuvent être considérées comme la clé de voûte du succès de l'entreprise.

C'est d'ailleurs le domaine dans lequel ont été prises, dès à présent, les dispositions les plus audacieuses mais en même temps les plus ambiguës. On en attend non seulement un effet économique — la solution du problème alimentaire — mais également le retour aux valeurs morales et familiales liées à une relation étroite avec la nature. La rémunération du travail en fonction du résultat final et la souplesse de l'organisation du travail constituent les deux atouts majeurs de cette mobilisation.

Mais pour qu'ils portent leurs pleins effets, on veut d'abord *redonner à l'agriculteur sa vraie place* :

« Que chaque champ, chaque parcelle de terrain... ait son maître » (Nikonov I/1987). Un an auparavant, V.S. Murakhovsky employait le même terme, « il faut travailler la terre en maître ». Et pour cela il faut rendre ses racines au paysan. Certains, tel V. Vassiliev, sont cependant pessimistes « le goût de la nature a été perdu, les campagnes sont déshumanisées, et la conscience a été remplacée par la contrainte », l'auteur songe-t-il au « mir », la solution est « de faire revivre le sentiment de la communauté » perdu en particulier avec « la création d'un revenu minimum dans les kolkhoz qui a développé l'égoïsme et l'individualisme ». « Grattez le russe, vous trouverez le paysan »; d'autres restent convaincus que cette affirmation de Lénine n'a pas perdu tout sens, et voient dans l'intérêt du cultivateur qui s'affaire du lever du jour à la nuit tombée, sur son « lopin », une raison d'avoir confiance.

Tout ceci suppose cependant que le travailleur soit payé en conséquence de ses efforts et trouve à employer ses revenus. Les formes traditionnelles d'encouragement — bonus, prime — sont toujours en vigueur. On notera que les livraisons en sus des quotas de produits céréaliers — toujours stratégiques — seront récompensées par la vente de biens relativement rares : voitures, équipement.

La rémunération du travail en fonction du résultat final et sur une base contractuelle est cependant le principal facteur de mobilisation de la main-d'œuvre et la souplesse de l'organisation du travail en est le corollaire. Les formes n'en sont pas vraiment nouvelles, mais elles reçoivent l'aval officiel pour se développer.

• Le contrat de groupe (kollektivnij podrjad) devrait être la panacée du système. Il est passé entre un groupe de travailleurs (le « collectif » ou la « brigade » sous contrat) et l'exploitation, pour l'accomplissement d'une tâche bien déterminée en fonction de laquelle le groupe est rémunéré. L'exploitation fournit les moyens, mais le groupe est totalement responsable de son exécution. Les modalités d'application de ces contrats sont variées; le contrat peut être passé avec des familles ou avec des individus. On parlera alors de contrat « sur une base familiale ou individuelle ». Il s'adresse le plus souvent à des cultivateurs auxquels l'exploitation fournit une terre et les moyens de la travailler, à charge pour eux de la faire fructifier comme ils l'entendent. Mais il peut aussi être conclu avec des éleveurs ou des mécaniciens, voire un atelier de réparation : le critère de base sera alors le nombre de tracteurs en bon état de marche au moment de la récolte. Tout dépassement de la tâche consignée dans le contrat donne lieu à un paiement en nature ou en espèces qui peut aller jusqu'au quart du surplus. Est-ce un leurre? L'application de ces contrats serait encore formelle. Si l'on en vient à bout, ils n'en pourraient pas moins transformer les comportements.

• Le contrat individuel de sous-traitance, avec les possesseurs de « lopins », se développe également avec succès depuis 1981. L'exploitation leur confie du jeune bétail, des veaux, des porcins à élever, à charge de les lui vendre une fois engraissés.

• Le contrat familial (semejnij podrjad) constitue un pas de plus dans la liberté d'entreprendre. Une famille se voit confier, par contrat avec une exploitation, la gestion d'une ferme (« la ferme familiale »).[24] Les terres, les bâtiments, le bétail appartiennent à l'exploitation et la famille vend sa production par l'intermédiaire de l'exploitation. Quoique très proche, par sa nature, des « brigades à base familiale », la ferme familiale s'en distingue par le fait qu'elle a un budget propre, qu'elle gère comme elle l'entend. Il n'y a pas de contrôle de sa comptabilité, non plus que du travail de chacun et de sa rémunération. Bien qu'encore peu nombreuses, les fermes familiales se seraient développées dans certaines régions.

On aborde là, cependant, un domaine essentiel pour apprécier les perspectives du processus de restructuration économique engagé, et tester jusqu'où veut et peut aller la réforme, au cours de la troisième phase qui devrait prendre place après 1990.

3-4 - L'approche du secteur privé

La situation du secteur agricole privé est un test souvent utilisé en Occident pour juger de l'efficacité relative du système socialiste d'agriculture, et ce n'est pas en vain qu'un auteur soviétique y voit « l'objet favori de la propagande bourgeoise ».[23] Il s'agit là, on le conçoit, d'un *secteur idéologiquement sensible*. Et si l'on arrive à le justifier par le fait que les facteurs de production demeurent propriété collective, les revenus qui en proviennent sont considérés par beaucoup, comme étant à la frontière de gains spéculatifs et facteurs d'inégalités. Par ailleurs, le risque d'un dérapage vers « l'esprit de petit propriétaire paysan » auquel se référait Lénine, est toujours appréhendé.

• Il n'en est pas moins reconnu « *utile* », et l'on note une attitude favorable du gouvernement à son égard. Parmi les réformes d'organisation du travail qui peuvent « améliorer l'approvisionnement de la population en utilisant au maximum les ressources locales », il y a en effet, à côté des kolkhoz et des sovkhoz, les jardins et vergers collectifs, les exploitations agricoles auxiliaires des entreprises industrielles[6], les exploitations auxiliaires privées (lopins), et « toutes doivent être développées ». Le secteur privé contribue en effet à sédentariser les gens et leur « donne le goût de la terre et du travail familial », dira V.S. Murakhovsky qui l'encourage « des deux mains ».

De plus il joue un rôle dans l'approvisionnement des villes et si l'on y ajoute que le secteur participe pour 30 % au moins à la production agricole totale du pays, qu'il fournit 18 à 27 % des revenus des agriculteurs et que sans cette contribution, ces revenus n'atteindraient que 45 à 55 % de ceux des travailleurs industriels, il apparaît non seulement « utile » mais *nécessaire*.

Faut-il voir cependant dans les déclarations officielles une attitude courante en temps de crise, ou comme certains le suggèrent, une crypto-décollectivisation; mais d'abord l'encourage-t-on vraiment ? La position des responsables est ambiguë : on favorise certes le développement des « lopins individuels » et si l'on inclut leur production dans le plan de l'exploitation, c'est en principe pour leur donner les facilités de l'accroître. Mais c'est là surtout un moyen de contrôle et d'intégration. Par ailleurs la vente directe des produits n'est pas encouragée et si les restaurants en coopérative privée s'y alimenteront (décret II 1987), le marché kolkhozien est « sous surveillance »[25]; il faut disposer d'un permis pour y vendre et pour l'obtenir, il faut être soi-même producteur. Les foires (jarmarka) qui jouissent d'un regain de succès ont un caractère ambigu, elles aussi : s'y côtoient les magasins d'état, coopératives de consommation, vendeurs isolés, mais elles dépendent de la municipalité et sont installées sur le lieu ou à proximité du marché kolkhozien; qui plus est, selon certaines informations de la presse, les prix qui y sont pratiqués sont proches des prix d'Etat. Enfin en autorisant les organes de l'Agroprom à jouer sur les prix de détail des produits vendus dans les coopératives de consommation, on tend à exercer un contrôle indirect sur les prix du marché kolkhozien.

• La *direction dans laquelle on s'engage est bien plutôt de rendre le secteur collectif attractif et compétitif* et de le hisser au niveau du privé. La rémunération du travail «collectif» en fonction du résultat final, la possibilité donnée à l'exploitation de vendre pour elle-même une part de sa production, la fixation de prix concurrentiels dans les coopératives de consommation, vont bien en ce sens.

Alors la ligne de démarcation entre les deux secteurs collectif et privé s'estompe-t-elle et la théorie de la convergence des systèmes trouverait-elle un champ d'application dans l'agriculture de l'URSS?

*

*   *

A court terme, la tactique est claire : tous les moyens sont bons pour débloquer la situation et il faut utiliser à fond les possibilités des secteurs collectif et privé.[26] Quelques éléments de cette tactique pourraient dégager des effets rapides.

Ainsi la diminution relative des ventes de produits agricoles au travers du circuit d'état, contribuera à réduire le poids des subventions, et en augmentant le volume des produits vendus sur le marché kolkhozien ou dans les coopératives de consommation, à des prix «agréés», à mi-chemin entre les prix du commerce d'état et ceux du marché, on augmente d'autant la masse globale payée par le consommateur. C'est une façon habile de rapprocher les prix réellement payés par les consommateurs des coûts alors qu'on ne prévoit pas de modification radicale des prix de détail dans l'immédiat.

Par ailleurs, une formation accélérée et le retour à la production de cadres administratifs «incités à se recycler» (le processus est en cours depuis plusieurs années) pourraient remédier à une des déficiences les plus graves de ce secteur, la faible qualification de la main-d'œuvre rurale.

Enfin si l'impact des technologies intensives sur les rendements céréaliers se confirmait, les besoins d'importation en seraient réduits d'autant avec toutes les conséquences favorables que cela implique pour la balance commerciale.

Les risques et les insuffisances ne sont pas non plus insignifiants.

«Des contradictions entre les intérêts individuels et ceux de l'Etat» sont inévitables, M. Gorbatchev en est conscient, et déjà des «signes inquiétants» se manifestent : «ici on planifie de diminuer la production de viande, là de lait ou de sarrazin ». Il espère cependant en venir à bout par des mesures économiques.

De même la « vérité des prix » réclamée par les réformateurs implique que les prix alimentaires prennent en compte l'utilisation de la terre et de l'eau, pratiquement gratuits et subissent la hausse des prix de l'énergie. Cependant le réajustement risque de peser lourd sur le consommateur. C'est pourquoi, il doit s'accompagner, en même temps que de mesures compensatoires pour les bas revenus, d'un large débat public. M. Gorbatchev en sortira-t-il gagnant et bénéficiera-t-il du soutien nécessaire pour poursuivre l'œuvre d'assainissement de l'économie qu'il a entreprise; « j'ai bien peur, écrit un lecteur de la *Gazette littéraire*, qu'en cas de renchérissement des produits, la population ne tourne le dos à la restructuration ». Par ailleurs, la refonte globale du système des prix ne devrait intervenir qu'en 1990. La procédure, longue et délicate, ne risque-t-elle pas alors de faire échec à l'efficacité des mesures d'ores et déjà introduites?

A plus long terme, un choix s'imposera. Comme le font remarquer les économistes réformateurs hongrois — et ils sont bien placés pour le faire — on ne peut pas rester longtemps dans un système à mi-chemin entre le plan et le marché, qui semble être la voie dans laquelle l'URSS s'engage en 1987. Si l'on veut éviter que le secteur d'Etat ne constitue un frein à l'expansion du secteur privé et ne l'asphyxie, il faut pousser la réforme. La réforme acquiert très vite sa propre dynamique. Le choix devra être fait dans les années 90.

NOTES BIOGRAPHIQUES

1. T.I. Zaslavskaja, *Izvestija*, 1985/1/6 et *Izvestija*, 18/4/1986.
2. Entretien de M.S. Gorbatchev avec M. Favo, secrétaire général du PC argentin, *Pravda*, 3/3/1987.
3. *Literaturnaja gazeta*, 1986/1/22.
« Il y a longtemps que les experts discutaient entre eux du fait que — tout en investissant des fonds énormes (dans l'agriculture) — nous étions toujours loin d'atteindre le but ».
4. Ch. Beaucourt, « L'arme alimentaire » dans « La drôle de crise : de Kaboul à Genève » (1979-1985). Ed. Fayard, Paris, 1986.
5. Et secrétaire du Parti du kraj de Stavropol' de 1970 à 1978. Région d'expériences agricoles.
6. Décret « O dal'nejchem soverchenstovanii ekonomiceskogo mekhanizma khozjajstvovanija v agropromychlennom komplekse strany ». *Pravda*, 29 mars 1986.
7. Décret « O neotlozhnykh merakh po povycheniju proizvoditel'nosti truda v sel'skom khozjajstve na osnove vnedrenija racional'nykh form ego organizacii i khozrasceta ». *Ekonomiceskaja gazeta*, n° 52, 1986/12.
8. « Ob individual'noj trudovoj dejatel'nosti ». Loi adoptée le 19/11/1986, *Pravda*, 20/11/1986.
9. *Pravda*, 27/3/1984.
10. On n'est pas peu surpris de lire que le débat a repris à propos de la reconstitution du réseau hydraulique de la Volga, et que, malgré les oppositions, la commission d'experts du Gosplan a opté pour la solution « extensive ». *Sovetskaja rossija*, 14/1/1987.
11. C. Beaucourt, « Les contrats céréaliers ont-ils un avenir ? » p. 48. Les contradictions entre l'intérêt financier et les objectifs stratégiques. *Economie prospective internationale*, 1985, n° 22.
12. V.P. Nikonov, Intervention à la réunion du comité central du PC. *Pravda*, 23/1/1987.
13. Vl. Treml', « Soviet foreign trade in foodstuffs ». *Soviet economy*, vol. 2, 1/3/1986.
14. *Vnechnjaja Torgovlja*, 1985 et 1922-1981.

M. Gorbatchev et l'agriculture

15. M.S. Gorbatchev, Intervention à la réunion du Comité central du PCUS. *Pravda*, 23/1/1987.
16. *Tableau I:* Les performances de l'agriculture — 1966-1986.
17. E.K. Ligatchev, *Pravda*, 23/1/1987.
18. Décret sur «l'arrêt des travaux de transfert d'une partie des cours d'eau du Nord et de Sibérie». *Pravda*, 20 août 1986.
19. *Pravda*, 4/11/1986.
20. *Ekon. gazeta*, 1986-2, n° 8, et *socialisticeskaja industrija*, 25/5/1986.
21. Les cartes technologiques sont utilisées pour établir le plan de l'exploitation.
22. A.A. Nikonov, président de l'académie des sciences agricoles. *Voprosy ekonomiki*, 1987/1, p. 78 et s.
23. *Planovoe khozjajstvo*, 1987-2.
24. «Ferma dlja semji». *Izvestija*, 17/1/1986.
25. A. Giroux, *Le Courrier des pays de l'Est*, novembre 1986, n° 312.
26. Décret «O merakh po povycheniju ustojcivosti zernovogo khozjajstva strany i uveliceniju khlebofu-razhnykh resursov v dvenatsatoj pjatiletke», *Pravda*, 6/8/1986.
Et décret sur le développement des collectivités de jardinage. *Izvestija*, 18/5/1985 et 7/6/1986.
Arrêté sur les mesures complémentaires à prendre pour développer la mécanisation de l'agriculture. *Trud*, 6/3/1987.
Autres sources
- Soviet economy, vol. II, n° 1, 1986 Panel on the soviet economic outlook.
- V.P. Gagnon, «Gorbatchev and the collective contract brigade». *Soviet studies*, 1987/1.
- K.E. Wadekin, «The private agricultural sector in the 1980's». *RFE*, 1985/8/2.
- V.I. Sidorenko, «Vazhnij istotchnik popolnenija prodovol'stvennogo fonda» (o razvitii litchnykh podsobnykh khozjajstv).
- RSEEA.
- G. Sokoloff, «En Gorbatchev, on ne peut que croire...» *Politique internationale*, 1986/87, n° 34.

Tableau
Les performances du secteur agricole

	Croissance par rapport à la moyenne quinquennale précédente						Croissance annuelle					
	1966-70	1971-75	1976-80	1981-85	1981-82	1983-85	1981	1982	1983	1984	1985	1986
A. Production agricole (1)												
1. - Totale	121	113	108,8	105,5	100,1	109,0	99	105	106,7	100	100	(3)
					(2)		97.4	102.8	109.1	108.9	109.1*	105,1
- Secteur collectif	126	117	113,7	105,3	—	—	98	106	106.7	100	100.9	
- Secteur privé	111	104	99	105,8	—	—	103	102.9	103.8	110	97.2	
2. Production végétale	122	109	109	103,4	—	—	—	—	—	—	—	—
- Production animale	120	117	108,5	107,9	—	—	—	—	—	—	—	—
B. Produits												
Céréales (4) (millions de tonnes)	167,6	181,5	205,0	180,3			(8) 158,2	186,8	192,2	172,6	191,7	(8) 210,0
Viande (poids abattu)	11,6	14,0	14,8	16,2			15,2	15,4	16,4	17,0	17,1	17,7
C. Productivité du travail (secteur collectif)	(6) 130	122	113	108	101	(6) 112	(7) 98	106	106,7	100,9	101,7	(7) 106,9
D. Capacités de production mises en service												
Engrais minéraux (5)		9,0	8,8	6,8							1,6	
Tracteurs (1.000 unités/an)		79,6	113,8	56,2							9,1	
Viande (1.000 tonnes/équipe)		4,1	3,1	1,8							0,2	

* Par rapport à la moyenne quinquennale 1976-1980.

Source:

(1) Narodnoe Khozjajstvo 1985, par rapport à la moyenne 1976-1980.
(2) V.P. Nikonov, Pravda 23/9.1987 et Narodnoe Khozjajstvo p. 42.
(3) Pravda 17/1.1987.
(4) Narodnoe Khozjajstvo 1985, p. 180.
(5) Ibid p. 259. Substances nutritives : millions de tonnes par an.
(6) Narodnoe Khozjajstvo p. 55 et 316.
(7) Croissance par rapport à l'année précédente, par travailleur annuel moyen.

Soviet Population, Manpower, Health, and Education Trends

Murray Feshbach

Introduction

In the remarkably active period in the USSR in economic, social, military and scientific areas since General Secretary Gorbachev acceded to the leading position of the Soviet state much attention — even unprecedented attention — has been paid to the social factors underlying the development of the Soviet society and polity. In his 27 January 1987 Party Plenum speech, Gorbachev called for a different approach in order to overcome the stagnation of the Brezhnev period. Moreover, according to him, socialism has not evolved as a concept beyond the level of the 30s and 40s. A different approach is obligatory, he declared. Virtually quoting the so-called Secret Report of the sociologist, Dr. Tatyana Zaslavskaya, he noted that the Soviet Union is now a different society; no longer will *administrativnyye mery* suffice or be appropriate to order people about. Policy became ossified, it became an anachronism. Policies in the late 50s and 1960 led to the elimination of co-operatives, according to Gorbachev, and led to the neglect of the social sector. « There emerged a sort of deafness to social issues. We see today what all this has led to ». Thus, « alcohol and drug abuse and a rise in crime (which) became indicators of the decline of social mores ».

Health problems in general, in addition to alcohol and drug abuse, have become urgent topics of many articles. The failure to overcome these problems may, in large part, have led to the resignations of two deputy ministers and the Minister of Health late last year. Given manpower constraints principally due to prior fertility decisions, the value of each person at the margin, and his or her health, becomes even more valuable.

While it is abundantly true that a certain amount of attention was paid by specialists to these issues even before Gorbachev's selection for the « front office » of the Soviet Union, noted both by a number of commentators and by Gorbachev himself, they are minor strokes in a much larger, intense canvas which Gorbachev now commands.

Ever since the results of the 1959 census of population became known, and especially after the 1970 census, which gave the leading authorities of the Soviet Union a systematic set of data without any demographic catastrophe in the interval between censuses, more attention has been paid to population issues.[1] From these comparative results, and the trends ever since, it became abundantly clear that the consequences of regional trends also needed to be addressed.

113

Fertility, mortality, morbidity, migration, nationality-linkages, educational attainment, degrees of urbanization, and so forth, became issues for the leadership.[2]

At the 27th Party Congress of 1986 the serious attention paid to population issues, mostly seen through the rubric of family-related issues, was clearly manifest. The 1971 Party Congress just noted the need to develop a scientific basis for forecasting the population. The 1976 Party Congress added the need to develop an «effective demographic policy». And the 1981 Congress, as noted earlier, witnessed the inclusion of at least 3 paragraphs of materials on population and health-related issues, plus others on education and manpower, in the (last) Accountability Report of General Secretary Brezhnev — a striking contrast to the previous limited attention to these issues. Moreover, as a follow-up to the Party Congress, a number of additional pro-natalist directives and decrees were issued with striking regional differential applications.

Demographic Trends

The overall population growth of the USSR has tended to range slightly below 1.0 percent per year over roughly a 20-year period partly due to overall declines in fertility, partly due to increases in mortality (and statistically negligible net in- or out-migration within the *overall* total population of the country).

Based on these legislative efforts, plus the anti-alcohol drive initiated in mid-1985, it appears that 1986 was the highest single year of growth for the RSFSR, for example, in the approximately 20 years since mortality began to increase throughout most of the Soviet Union (the low point being in 1964). For the USSR as a whole, the 2.9 million increase from 278.8 to 281.7 million persons between 1 January 1986 and 1 January 1987, respectively, represents the largest one-year net increase in the population since 1964 (at 3.0 million). (The lowest net increase in a single year took place in 1980 — a net increase of only 2.1 million persons.)

But some republics experienced much higher growth *rates* than others. Thus, in the southern tier of republics where the population is largely of Muslim origin, the yearly rates of population growth have been remarkably close to 3 percent per year — rates close to that of many less-developed countries. For example, during the year just passed (1986), the population of Tadzhikistan grew by 3.4 percent, of Uzbekistan by 2.8 percent, of Turkmenistan 2.5 percent, and the other 3 republics of Muslim origin, between 2.2 and 1.1. percent (the lowest being Kazakhstan, with a minority of Kazakhs among the total population of the republic). In contrast, despite the large net *absolute* increase in the Russian Republic, the annual *rate* of increase in the Republic's population amounted to only 0.8 percent; in the Ukraine it was 0.4 percent, and in Belorussia, the highest at 1.0 percent.[3]

As a consequence, the net growth of the population during 1986, in the 6 republics of Muslim origin — Azerbaydzhan, Kazakhstan, Kirgiziya, Tadzhikistan, Turkmenistan, Uzbekistan — amounted to approximately 1,220,000. In all, this figure comprised some 42 percent of the total net population growth of the Soviet Union. In the three Slavic republics — the RSFSR, the Ukraine, and Belorussia — with some 74 percent of the total population of the country, the net growth of the populations was slightly over 1,510,000. In all, then, the «Muslim» republics with one-quarter the population of the «Slavic» republics recorded four-fifths the net growth of the latter grouping.

A simple, and by definition, crude comparison, is that between the crude birth rates of the respective groupings. The crude birth rates in the three Slavic republics increased from 15.0 births to 16.5 births per 1,000 population in 1985 up to 15.5 to 17.1 births per 1,000 population in 1986. In contrast, among the four muslim republics for which 1986 data are available (excluding Azerbaydzhan and Turkmenistan), the range increased from 24.9 to 39.9 births per 1,000 population in 1985 up to 25.2 to 41.7 births per 1,000 population in 1986. Only because the base population in all 6 «Muslim» republics is so small is the impact of the differential fertilities still not overwhelming the net increase in the 3 Slavic republics.

Table 1
Birth rates, USSR and by republic: 1960-1986.

	1960	1970	1980	1985	1986
USSR	24.9	17.4	18.3	19.4	19.6
Slavic Republics					
RSFSR	23.2	14.6	15.9	16.5	17.1
Ukraine	20.5	15.2	14.8	15.0	15.5
Belorussia	24.4	16.2	16.0	16.5	17.0
Moldavia	29.3	19.4	20.0	21.9	22.7
Baltic Republics					
Estonia	16.6	15.8	15.0	15.4	(N/A)
Latvia	16.7	14.5	14.0	15.2	(N/A)
Lithuania	22.5	17.6	15.1	16.3	16.8
Transcaucasus					
Armenia	40.1	22.1	22.7	24.1	24.0
Azerbaydzhan	42.6	29.2	25.2	26.7	(N/A)
Georgia	24.7	19.2	17.7	18.7	(N/A)
Kazakhstan	37.2	23.4	23.8	24.9	25.2
Central Asia					
Kirgiziya	36.9	30.5	29.6	32.0	32.7
Tadzhikistan	33.5	34.8	37.0	39.9	41.7
Turkmenistan	42.4	35.2	34.3	36.0	(N/A)
Uzbekistan	39.8	33.6	33.8	37.2	37.3

N/A: Not available.

Source: Soviet official publications and plan fulfilment reports.

Nonetheless, O. Ata-Mirzayev, the head of the Population Labora-tory of the Tashkent State University, has estimated that Uzbekistan, with only 7 percent of the total population of the country, will contri-bute some 40 percent of the net growth of the entire population in the period 1979 to 2000, due largely to the fertility differential combined with the large (and growing) population base, and the higher mortality rates, especially due to the aging of the populations in the roughly-speaking, northern tier (of the Slavic republics).

Manpower
One of the major consequences of the fertility differentials in the past (especially the decline in crude birth rates and total fertility rates among the Slavic and Baltic peoples during the 1960s, as women attained higher levels of education, were urbanized, and joined the labour force)

has resulted in a demographic echo of major concern to the Soviet leadership. And this is one of the important factors underlying the drive to increase productivity — be it labour or capital — combined with the drive to accelerate scientific and technological progress. From an overall viewpoint, the net growth of the population aged 20 to 59 years of age grew, during 1970 to 1985, by 30 million persons; during 1986 to 2000, the same category will grow by only 6 millions, most of whom will reside in the southern tier. But the industrial plant, the military industrial complex, is located in the north, especially in the Moscow and Leningrad regions. To the degree that these peoples of the South do not tend to migrate from their traditional locations, then perforce the need to increase productivity is even more enhanced among the available work force.

Moreover, if one looks at the age distribution of the younger population within the country as a whole, or by republic, it can be seen that the regional differentials will continue to play an enormous role. Based on unpublished figures, it can be determined that the percent shares of the age group 0 to 14 years of age at the time of the January 1979 census of population — the prime working age group of 21 to 35 years of age at the turn of the century — will be about 21 to 22 percent of the Russian Republic and the Ukraine, 20 percent in Latvia, and over 41 percent in Uzbekistan.[4] To the extent that Uzbekistan is typical of the republics of Muslim origin, and assuming no large-scale migration from Central Asia, then the need for investment into the region is clear as is the necessity to improve productivity in the « north ».

Health

Simultaneously, as noted earlier, the health of each person at the margin becomes even more valuable given the reduction in numbers to one-fifth the net increase, and given that some 70 to 75 percent of the net industrial product is produced in the north, in the RSFSR and the Ukraine.

From the overall viewpoint of health measures, the report of a major improvement in the crude death rate for 1986 is certainly welcome. Whether the figure is correct, however, also needs to be determined.[5]

The crude death rate is a straightforward measure of the number of deaths in a country (or specific administrative-territorial unit) per 1,000 population (see Table 2). It does not adjust for changing age distributions over time, or within a country on a given date. For that the age-specific death rates need to be examined, and specifically the infant mortality figure. And finally, the life expectancy at birth figures also are subject to inquiry.

Table 2
Crude death rates, USSR and by republic: 1960-1986.

	1960	1970	1980	1985	1986
USSR	7.1	8.2	10.3	10.5	9.7
Slavic Republics					
RSFSR	7.4	8.7	11.0	11.3	10.3
Ukraine	6.9	8.9	11.4	12.1	11.0
Belorussia	6.6	7.6	9.9	10.6	9.6
Moldavia	6.4	7.4	10.2	11.2	9.7
Baltic Republics					
Estonia	10.5	11.1	12.3	12.6	(N/A)
Latvia	10.0	11.2	12.7	13.1	(N/A)
Lithuania	7.8	8.9	10.5	10.9	9.9
Transcaucasus					
Armenia	6.8	5.1	5.5	5.9	5.7
Azerbaydzhan	6.7	6.7	7.0	6.8	(N/A)
Georgia	6.5	7.3	8.6	8.8	(N/A)
Kazakhstan	6.6	6.0	8.0	8.0	7.3
Central Asia					
Kirgiziya	6.1	7.4	8.4	8.1	7.2
Tadzhikistan	5.1	6.4	8.0	7.0	6.7
Turkmenistan	6.5	6.6	8.3	8.1	(N/A)
Uzbekistan	6.0	5.5	7.4	7.2	7.0

N/A: Not available.

Source: Soviet official publications and plan fulfilment reports.

It is instructive to look at the trends in the crude death rate for the last two decades (with 1950 as an added reference point). From the table, it is readily apparent — and for the moment assuming that the rate for the country as a whole is basically correct — there had been a sharp decrease in the crude death rate between 1950 and 1964, from 9.7 to 6.9 deaths per 1,000 population (or 29 percent). From this point, however, until last year, there has been an almost inexorable increase. Thus, between the low point of 1964 and 1980, an increase of over 49 percent (10.3 divided by 6.9), a very slight decrease for two years, another two jumps to a postwar historic high of 10.8 in 1984 (an increase of 57 percent), and a decrease in the subsequent two years, to a level of 9.7 deaths per 1,000 — finally back to the 1950 level!

More precise measurement of mortality trends are provided by age-specific death rates. One of the major complaints in the West about Soviet statistics is either the complete lack of data on certain topics, or the cessation of publication when it would otherwise be embarrassing to continue to do so. Thus, Zaslavskaya, the renowned sociologist has written in *Pravda* about the lack of social statistics, and of the need for « administrative agencies (of the Soviet Union) to have complete, precise and truthful information about the situation as it exists in any sphere of social life, ... ».[6] Similarly, even V.G. Afanas'yev, the chief editor of *Pravda* and Chairman of the Board of the USSR Union of Journalists on 14 March 1987, noted that « Journalists were also poorly informed, after all, we do not yet have comprehensive social statistics ».[7] Thus, the Central Statistical Administration in apparent defence of its position of monopoly control of such statistics, has begun to publish much more in the realm of social statistics.[8]

Table 3

Age-specific death rates, USSR: 1969/70 to 1984/85

(Both sexes combined – number of deaths per 1,000 population of age group).

Age Group / Year	1969/70 (1)	1974/75* (2)	1975/76 (3)	1980/81 (4)	1984/85 (5)
0- 4	6.9	8.0*	8.7	8.1	7.7
5- 9	0.7	0.7	0.7	0.7	0.6
10-14	0.6	0.5	0.5	0.5	0.5
13-19	1.0	1.0	1.0	1.0	0.9
20-24	1.6	1.7	1.7	1.8	1.5
25-29	2.2	2.1	2.1	2.3	2.0
30-34	2.8	3.0	3.0	3.0	2.8
35-39	3.7	3.7	3.8	4.4	3.6
40-44	4.7	5.2	5.3	5.6	5.7
45-49	6.0	6.7	6.9	8.0	7.3
50-54	8.7	8.7	9.3	10.8	11.3
55-59	11.7	12.8*	13.4	13.9	15.1
60-64	18.0	18.3	18.9	20.6	20.4
65-69	27.5	27.9*	28.0	29.5	31.1
70 and over	75.7	75.2*	75.0	77.2	78.7

Source: 1969/70, 1974/75, 1980/81 and 1984/85 – *Vestnik statistiki,* No 12, December 1986, p. 71.

1975/76 – *Ibid.,* No 11, November 1977, p. 87.

* It is not known why the ASDR's for age groups 0-4, 55-59, 65-69 and 70 and over have been changed from previous publications of these rates.

TsSU has published in the December 1986 issue of *Vestnik statistiki,* the first set of data on age-specific death rates since 1976 — but only for both sexes combined; data by age and by sex have not been published since 1974. It is obvious from the table that conditions on the average

119

worsened for all age groups above ages 20-24 (inclusive), at least through 1980/81. I believe that the rates continued to increase until perhaps 1982/83, but the lack of data for the intervening years prevents any precise determination of the year-by-year trend. Improvement is notable at the younger ages (in 1984/85 compared with 1980/81) but the age-specific death rates for all age groups from 40-44 years and over, except the 45-49 years group, continue to increase according to these materials.

Infant mortality rates, that is the number of deaths per 1,000 live born children, have also reappeared. First released in *Ekonomicheskaya gazeta*, n° 43, 1987, p. 7, they are also the first data released by TsSU on this issue since 1975 (for the year 1974). According to the new figures, between 1983 and 1985 the rate increased from 25.3 to 26.0 deaths per 1,000 live born children. Several comments are necessary. Obviously, the first is that the increase, although not that much, still is the «wrong» direction. Second, is the question of the validity of these figures. Since the last reported figure previously was 27.9 in 1974, why did they not publish the figure for 1983 (at 25.3) if it were so low? Moreover, in June 1981, a leading Soviet spokesman noted at a press conference that the rate was about 30. The new figure for 1980 is 27.3[9] — a fairly large difference. More recently, *Pravda* in March 1987 published an article which contains information on the infant mortality rate in Surkhandar'inskaya oblast' of Uzbekistan. According to this source, the rate was 55 infant deaths per 1,000 live born children. If — and only if — this is typical of Central Asia, then the regional differentials must be enormous. In addition, the *Pravda* article noted that in Andizhan oblast', some 3 out of every 4 infant deaths have *not* been recorded.[10] One issue always is the lack of completeness. Another issue is a possible change in definition. And in this instance I suspect — but cannot prove — that there is a new definition which may exclude even more children from mortality figures (as well as births) who are counted as miscarriages or stillbirths. Thus, in the past, the Soviet definition excluded children who *lived* up to 6.99 days, but not 7.00 days, and who met 3 other criteria: less than 2,500 grammes in weight; less than 28 weeks in gestation; and less than 35 cm. in length. Perhaps these criteria no longer apply and if any child dies in the early neonatal period of up to 7 days they are excluded. This is not an unprecedented technique. In Romania, at the present time, if a child does not survive for 30 days, it counts neither as a birth or death. It remains for additional evidence to determine whether some variant of this procedure is applied also in the Soviet Union.

One of the important consequences of the omission of such deaths is the effect on the measurement of life expectancy at birth. Based upon the age-specific death rates by single year of age for a given year, life expectancy is a calculation based on the average number of additional years a person can be expected to live. If the rate for the 0-1 age group is understated or underestimated this has a significant impact on the overall measurement. Thus, I believe that the current figures for the Soviet Union — as low as I will demonstrate they are — are too high.

We have not had estimates of life expectancy in the Soviet Union published for any year later than 1971/72 until the publication last year of « comparable » figures.[11] The current figures, as published, are as follows (Table 4).

Table 4

Life expectancy at birth, USSR, total, male and female:
1926/27 – second half 1985/first half 1986
(Number of years).

Years	Total population	Males	Females
1926 (European USSR)	44	42	47
1938/39	47	44	50
1955/56	67	63	69
1958/59	69	64	72
1965/66	70	66	74
1971/72	70	64	74
1978/79	68	62	73
1983/84	68	63	73
1984/85	68	63	73
Second half 1985/ first half 1986	69	64	73

Source: All years, except 1965/66 – TsSU SSSR, *Narodnoye khozyaystvo SSSR v 1985 godu, statisticheskiy yezhegodnik,* Moscow, 1986, p. 547.
1965/66 – TsSU SSSR, *Naseleniye SSSR 1973,* Moscow, Statistika, 1975.

According to the figures in the table, the highest level of life expectancy for both sexes combined was attained in 1971/72. The dramatic improvement in 1984/85 only brings the Soviet Union up to the level of a quarter of a century earlier, in 1958/59. It appears as if no change took place between 1958/59 and 1971/72 for males, with some improvement for females. However, the table as reproduced here from the current official statistical yearbook is incomplete. *Glasnost'* has not yet led to incorporation of the figures for 1965/66, as previously published many times before the cut-off after 1971/72.

In the published estimates for 1965/66 — note that this two-year average figure is close to the date of the lowest crude death rate, as noted above, in 1964 — the combined life expectancy figure for 1965/66 was 70 years of age, with that for males at 66 and for females at 74.[12]

Thus, even though it appears from the latest table, cited above, that males were expected to live at most 64 years, the actual previous peak was two years greater. I have estimated that male life expectancy may have declined to a low of about 60 years by about 1980[13], or a decline of 6 full years. East Central Europe also has experienced some declines in life expectancy at birth, but much less so than in the Soviet Union. Thus, Peter Jozan of the Hungarian Central Statistical Office provided estimates which show a decline between 1970 and 1983 in Bulgaria of 0.7 years for males at birth (from 69.1 to 68.4); for Hungary, a decline of 1.2 years between 1970 and 1984 (from 66.8 to 65.6); and for Poland, a pattern of initial increase of 0.5 years between 1970 and 1982 (from 66.8 to 67.3) and a subsequent decline by 1983 to the initial level in 1970 (from 67.3 to 66.8).[14]

Jozan notes at the same time that the life expectancy of males at birth in Austria increased over roughly the same period, between 1970 and 1984, by 3.8 years (from 66.3 to 70.1 years) and in Sweden between 1970 and 1983, by 1.3 years (from 72.3 to 73.6).[15] A recent summary of European Economic Community figures for life expectancy of males at birth which notes that there is « bad news » for men — but only in comparison with the levels for females in the 12 nations of the Community — shows a range of 68.9 years for Portuguese males up to 73.0 years for Dutch males.[16] The countries of East Europe and the Soviet Union probably will not reach these levels for many years. As Dr. Jean-Claude Chesnais, of the French National Demographic Studies Institute, noted at a conference in late 1985, « No country has so puzzling mortality trends as (the) USSR. Even if the pace of mortality decline, namely for infants, seems to have been overestimated in the 1945-1965 period and if symmetrically the pace of deterioration is somewhat exaggerated since that time, there is clear evidence that mortality followed an unparalleled path, especially for males... ».[17]

Again regional disparities play an important role in mortality rates, in morbidity rates, in causes of death, in availability of medical services, and so forth. For example, the crude death rate for the country as a whole in 1985, as noted earlier, was 10.6 deaths per 1,000 persons. However, largely because of different age structures, the rate varied from a low of 5.9 in Armenia to 13.1 in Latvia.

Similarly other health measurements vary sharply between republics and, within republics, between rural and urban places. For example, one of the better indicators for Central Asian health patterns reveals that breast cancer in the country as a whole was 15.1 cases per 100,000 population, and in Turkmenistan, only 3.6 cases.[18] In other cases the rates for the Central Asian region are markedly worse. For example, Moscow City — even with a shortage now reported in the supply of medical personnel[19] — had 103.2 physicians for every 10,000 residents, whereas Frunze, the capital of Kirgiziya had 84.4, or about 20 physicians per 10,000 persons less than in Moscow. But within the republic the disparity between the capital city and all oblasts of the republic was much sharper. Thus, in 1982, with Frunze supplied at a rate of 81.6 physicians per 10,000 population, the four oblasts of the republic had rates of 20.3, 21.1, 23.0 and 29.0, roughly 25 to 35 percent the capital city rate.[20] Rates by cause-of-death follow the same pattern of wide disparity as in crude death rates.

In discussing issues of the retention of Islamic practices in Central Asia, the author of an article in *Pravda* noted that «there remains another much more critical (problem). I mean the problem of infant mortality, which continues to be high in the Central Asian republics, especially in rural areas, where medical services lag substantially in both quantitative and qualitative respects».[21] One of the consequences, linked to retention of religious traditions, has led to widespread utilization of folk healers, of mullahs who claim healing powers. The medical establishment has roundly condemned the rise in this phenomenon. Nonetheless, it is undoubtedly one of the consequences of the deterioration in delivery of medical services to the population.

On 18 September 1986, at a speech in Krasnoyarsk Kray, Gorbachev promised that «we are embarking upon a serious improvement of all our health services. You will soon have the documents and will learn about it».[22] Another promised innovation in the health field was the announcement in *Pravda* by a staff member of the Belorussian Ministry of Health that a State Committee on Health would be created.[23] Neither promise has yet been fulfilled, but they may well be in the near future if the level of attention to overall health, as well as to alcohol and drug abuse in particular, is symbolic of concern by the leadership. (On 15 August 1987, four months after the Colloquium, the central newspaper published a draft of a major decree on health.)

The most direct manifestation of such concern is the published 1987 budgetary allocation to health care and physical culture which shows an increase from the approved level of 17.5 billion rubles for 1986 up to 19.1 billion rubles planned for 1987.[24] While far short of the level of expenditures needed, the increase of some 9 percent is one of the highest increases in state budgetary allocations for the recent period. Nonetheless, at 4.3 percent of the entire State Budget (19.1 divided by 435.5 billion rubles), it remains far below the peak of 6.6 percent in the

123

early 1960s, a time when the crude death rate was some 50 percent below that at present.[25]

Education

The entire educational arena — institutions, system, policies and management — appears to be undergoing major changes at the present time. As one of the consequences of the changing size of cohorts coming out of the educational pipeline — particularly by republic — a number of changes have already taken place. Among the most important is that of emphasis on vocational technical training at the lower levels as part of the increased stress on production training, and in the diversion of students to vocational/technical schools rather than their continuing in the academically-oriented educational scheme.

Several major benefits, as well as costs, ensue from this policy. Among the two major benefits is the entry into the labour force of much larger numbers of workers: first, of females who do not continue on to higher educational institutions or serve in the armed forces, and of young males who are available for work sooner, if they are not conscripted because of medical or family reasons, or for the armed forces both sooner and longer. Thus, young males would serve now for two years on the average rather than for only 18 months (only for 12 months during much of the period after 1967 when the draft law was altered to draft 18 rather than 19 year olds) if college and university graduates, who enter as officers upon graduation from a higher educational institution (for the shorter period of time) are included. Moreover, many will become full-time workers upon discharge from active duty and thus will prolong their average length of working life. (The latter being one of the major motives, I believe, for the anti-alcohol drive and the attention to health issues at the present time.) However, there will be costs. And the costs deal with human capital formation. To the degree that many of the potential students do not pursue their education upon completion of active duty, there will be short-term benefits to the economy at the cost of long-term higher level human capital formation. The prior example under Khrushchev, in 1958, of requiring two years of work before entry into higher education proved to be a disaster in many ways, and was within a very few years thereafter abandoned as unworkable and unfortunate. Whether this will be fully replicated in the present scheme is doubtful but still possible.

Exactly what the guidelines are for higher and specialized secondary education in the educational reform process being undertaken at all levels, is not clear.

For example, on 1 June 1986, a « Draft Basic Guidelines for the Restructuring of Higher and Specialized Secondary Education in the

Country» was published in *Pravda*. However, TASS now reports that Guidelines on the Restructuring of Higher and Specialized Education have just been issued. It is not clear whether this is the final set of Guidelines, or whether another approach has been taken. It is not usual to have two sets of «guidelines», the second normally being a formal directive adopted on the basis of the original guidelines. Nonetheless, one of the most important points provided in the TASS report (of 20 March 1987) is that students will be expected to participate more fully in «socio-economic restructuring». I assume that means more formal production activities at the cost of classroom work. While this may be easier to effectuate in the physical and mathematical sciences, it remains to be seen how this will develop in other fields. The dependence on students also is a reflection of the need for additional manpower. The need to improve the quality of education, including expansion of the use of computers in and out of the classroom, is all part of the drive to implement the programme for «scientific and technological progress». The need for this development of a sort of «great leap forward» was underscored by Gorbachev at the 27th Party Congress where he noted that if the Soviet Union does not advance in the scientific and technological fields, it will virtually become a third-rate country. Perhaps hyperbolically stated, but the essence of his message.

Moreover, the «scientific/technical revolution», another rubric for restructuring of industry and of education, is necessary (according to Moscow World Service broadcasts in mid-March 1987) because «Soviet planning bodies are concerned about the fact that many jobs of the country's plants and factories remain unfilled. Solution is expected to be gained by the process of automation in all industries».[26]

In this very brief survey and summary of population, manpower, health and education issues, it can be seen that much more attention is being currently paid to the importance of related problems, to their interrelationship, and to the urgency, of finding solutions.

Notes

1. See my *Soviet Union: Population Trends and Dilemmas*, PRB, August 1982, Vol. 37, n° 2, Washington, DC.
2. See Murray Feshbach, «The Soviet Population Policy Debate: Actors and Issues», RAND, 1987, 86 pp.
3. Based on annual plan fulfilment reports, by republic. I am indebted to Ann Sheehy of Radio Liberty for supplying these republic publications.
4. See Table 7, in Murray Feshbach, «The Age Structure of Soviet Population: Preliminary Analysis of Unpublished Data», *Soviet Economy*, 1985, Vol. 1, n° 2, pp. 177-193, espec. p. 189.
5. A number of inquiries into the validity of the national income, foreign trade, and other figures have been published by Vanous, Hewett, and Hanson. I would also add the demographic and health figures.
6. *Pravda*, February 1987, pp. 2-3, espec. p. 3. This citation contains a clear hint that the data which we do have are NOT «complete, precise and truthful». One would hope that she elaborates on this theme in the future.

7. *Pravda,* 15 March 1987, p. 1.
8. This is not to gainsay that other organizations have not also participated in the *glasnost'* pattern of recent note. Thus, the Minister of Internal Affairs, Vlasov, has made a frank statement about the extent of registered drug addicts in the country. The precise source — perhaps the Ministry of Health — is not given for the latest publication of the number of people suffering from psychiatric diseases. See *Argumenty i fakty,* March 1987.
9. *Vestnik statistiki,* n° 12, December 1986, p. 71.
10. *Pravda,* 7 February 1987, p. 3.
11. Eg., see TsSU SSSR, *Narodnoye khozyaystvo SSSR v 1985 godu, statisticheskiy yezhegodnik,* Moscow, Finansy i statistika, 1986, p. 547, and *Vestnik statistiki,* n° 12, December 1986, p. 71.
12. TsSU SSSR, *Narodnoye khozyaystvo SSSR v 19-- godu, statisticheskiy yezhegodnik,* Moscow, Statistika, 19--.
13. Murray Feshbach, *The Soviet Union: op. cit.,* p. 34.
14. See Peter Jozan, « Recent Mortality Trends in Central-Eastern Europe », paper prepared for the Tenth US/Hungarian Economic Roundtable, Budapest, Hungary, 1-3 December 1986, p. 7. The report was originally prepared for the « Fourth Meeting of the United Nations/World Health Organization/ Committee for International Cooperation in National Research in Demography Network on Socio-Economic Differential Mortality in Industrialized Societies ».
15. *Ibid.*
16. *The Belgian Weekly Gazette,* 26 March 1987, p. 3.
17. Jean-Claude Chesnais, « Some Peculiarities of Eastern Europe and Soviet Union Population Trends ». Paper presented at the Third World Congress for Soviet and East European Studies, Washington DC, 30 October - 3 November 1985, p. 9.
18. R.D. Obramenko and V.P. Shchetinina, « K voprosu diagnostiki mestastazov raka molochnoy zhelezy », *Zdravookhraneniye Turkmenistana,* n° 5, May 1985, p. 19.
19. *Izvestiya,* 8 August 1986, p. 3, notes that there was a shortage of 9,000 physicians and 23,000 medical service personnel in the city.
20. TsSU Kirgizskoy SSR, *Narodnoye khozyaystvo, Kirgizskoy SSR v 1982 godu, statisticheskiy yez-hegodnik,* Frunze, 1983, pp. 188-189.
21. *Pravda,* 16 January 1987, p. 2.
22. Cited in FBIS, *Daily Report: Soviet Union,* 19 September 1986, p. R5.
23. *Pravda,* 25 December 1985, cited in BBC, *Summary of World Broadcasts, Soviet Union,* 4 January 1986, p. SU/8148/B/2.
24. *Pravda,* 18 November 1986, p. 3.
25. Also see the article by Christopher Davis in the forthcoming volume on the USSR economy, to be issued by the Joint Economic Committee, Congress of the United States, 1987.
26. BBC, *Summary of World Broadcasts, Part I, The USSR,* 25 March 1987, p. SU/8525/B/3.

Le secteur pétrolier de l'URSS

Serge Copelman

Une des bases fondamentales, et peut-être la plus importante de l'économie de l'URSS, est de toute évidence représentée par *le pétrole et l'industrie pétrolière.* Car, à la différence des autres secteurs industriels, celui du pétrole apporte à l'URSS non seulement la matière première pour ses besoins énergétiques et — en aval — la pétrochimie, mais représente surtout la principale source de devises dont ce grand pays a eu et aura toujours besoin.

Les problèmes posés ces dernières années par le pétrole sont multiples, avec de fortes incidences sur l'ensemble de l'économie soviétique dans la mesure où la baisse de la production et du prix du baril ainsi que la chute du dollar n'ont pu être compensées par les dirigeants de ce pays.

A tout ceci s'ajoute ces derniers temps un nouvel environnement politique, économique, social et international que M. Gorbatchev et son équipe (rajeunie) souhaitent créer.

On ne peut donc pas dissocier les problèmes liés au pétrole — tout comme ceux des autres industries — de ces récentes données que le nouveau dirigeant de l'URSS est en train d'essayer d'appliquer. D'autant plus que, d'ores et déjà, on constate quelques résultats qui peuvent être estimés comme positifs, même dans le secteur qui est traité ici.

1° - *La Production*

Le pétrole représente pour l'URSS, d'une part, la matière première nécessaire pour ses propres besoins énergétiques et pétrochimiques et, d'autre part, la principale source de devises, grâce à une massive exportation vers les pays occidentaux et même vers les pays frères. La preuve de l'importance de l'aspect « exportation » est représentée par le fait que 60 à 70 % des devises rentrées sont dues au pétrole (80 % environ étant le fait des produits énergétiques pris globalement).

Le graphique ci-après donne une bonne image de cette situation : (en Millions barils/jour).

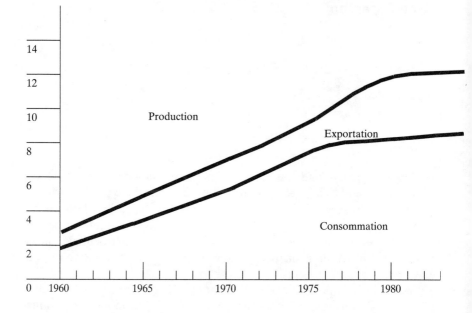

Les nombreux chocs et contre-chocs pétroliers que le monde a subis depuis 1973 ont eu des conséquences dans tous les pays, qu'ils soient producteurs ou importateurs, riches ou pauvres, industrialisés ou en voie de développement, membres ou non d'organisations comme l'OPEP, vendeurs ou non sur les marchés libres, ayant accepté et respecté ou non des quotas de production...

Toute cette situation a pour origine une forte augmentation du prix du baril mais, par la suite, et surtout ces dernières années, la chute de ce prix, bien qu'on assiste aujourd'hui à une certaine remontée. Ayant atteint 40 $ environ, il est descendu à un moment donné jusqu'à 10 $ et même 8 $ pour se situer début 1987 au niveau de 18 $. A cette situation fluctuante du prix du pétrole, s'est ajoutée d'abord une remontée spectaculaire du dollar qui a accusé, depuis 1985, une chute encore plus importante.

Tous les pays concernés ont essayé de trouver une solution afin de s'intégrer au mieux dans cette situation en recherchant la meilleure façon de survivre soit en tant que producteur-exportateur, soit en tant que consommateur-importateur.

Si certains pays ont réussi tant bien que mal à tirer leur épingle du jeu, l'URSS s'est vue confrontée à un élément négatif supplémentaire : la baisse de sa propre production du pétrole à laquelle s'est ajoutée

128

aussi l'obligation de continuer à subvenir aux besoins des pays frères comme la Pologne, la Roumanie, la Bulgarie, etc.

Voici donc l'URSS dans une situation extrêmement compliquée et complexe sur tous les plans liés au pétrole.

Ceci étant, l'Union Soviétique reste le deuxième producteur et consommateur mondial d'énergie prise globalement et, il faut le souligner, *le premier producteur de pétrole dans le monde.*

En 1984 sur 2,85 Gt, l'URSS en avait produit 613 Mt, c'est-à-dire 21,9 % de l'ensemble. En 1985, sur 2,8 Gt dans le monde, l'URSS n'avait plus produit que 594,5 Mt, à savoir 21,2 %.

Les volumes les plus importants, ont été :

(en Mt)

	1984	1985	1986
Monde communiste	745	734	763
dont : URSS	613	594,5	613
Chine	114	124,7	
Moyen Orient	587	537	
dont : Arabie Saoudite	233	175	
Iran	109	110	
Irak	60	70	
Amérique Latine	338	336	335
Afrique	253	258	237
Europe	186	194	192
Asie/Pacifique	158	161	
Amérique du Nord		575	562
dont les USA		491	480

Cette position de l'URSS date depuis longtemps et la progression de sa production de pétrole a été tout à fait exceptionnelle jusqu'au début des années 70 allant jusqu'à 17 % par an en moyenne entre 1955 et 1960.

Le niveau de production est devenu par la suite plus important, mais cette croissance s'est sensiblement ralentie entre 1975 et 1980 (5 % par an) pour subir ensuite une encore plus nette décélération avec une progression de moins de 1 % par an au début des années 80.

Le tableau ci-après contient les productions de pétrole en URSS de 1950 à 1986 (condensats de gaz inclus) :

La régression de la production s'explique actuellement surtout par le constant déplacement des sites de productions vers l'Est du pays, c'est-à-dire vers des régions de plus en plus éloignées des centres de consommation, avec des conditions de production et de transport de plus en plus difficiles et coûteuses.

(en Mt)

Années	Production réalisée	Production planifiée	Taux de croissance annuel (%)
1950	37,9	—	1950-55 = 13
1955	70,8	—	1955-60 = 17
1960	147,9	—	1960-65 = 11
1965	242,4	—	1965-70 = 7,9
1970	353	—	1970-75 = 5,7
1975	491	—	8,6
1976	519,7	520	5,8
1977	546	550	5,1
1978	571,4	575	4,7
1979	583,7	593	2,1
1980	604	620	3,4
1981	610	610	1,0
1982	614,7	614	0,7
1983	616,3	619	0,26
1984	612,7	628	−0,6
1985	594,5	—	−3,0
1986	(613)	(616)	—

La carte des gisements ci-jointe montre bien quels sont ces nouveaux sites par rapport aux anciens.

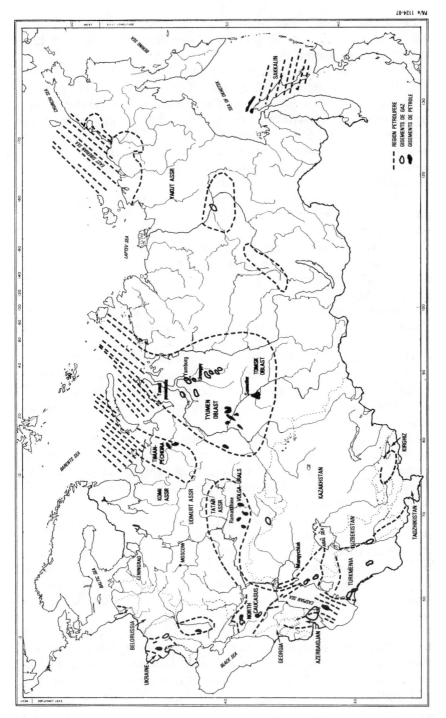

Les régions européennes Oural-Volga, Caucase, Caspienne, etc. produisaient en 1970 plus de 80 % du total pour descendre à 60 % en 1975 et à 35 % seulement en 1982.

Avant de parler de la baisse globale de production de l'URSS depuis 1983-1984, il est à noter que sa très importante production et sa position de premier producteur mondial sont le résultat de ses ressources très abondantes, d'investissements très massifs, auxquels s'ajoute une ténacité sans précédent, qui représentent autant d'éléments positifs. Ceux-ci se sont heurtés à des aspects négatifs comme de mauvais et vieux équipements techniques tout comme des méthodes de management qui n'étaient pas non plus à la pointe du progrès.

A ces derniers éléments s'ajoutent des conditions climatiques extrêmement difficiles et, dans leur ensemble, ce sont les aspects négatifs qui ont pris le dessus.

En effet, après avoir atteint le seuil de 400 Mt en 1972, la production soviétique est passée en 1983 à 616 Mt. C'est la première fois en 1984 que la production diminuait (de 0,6 %), chute qui a continué en 1985 marquant une baisse de 3 % pour arriver à 595 Mt. Ce recul de la production marquée au début du 12ᵉ Plan quinquennal constitue une circonstance aggravante aux difficultés qu'affronte généralement l'équipe de M. Gorbatchev. Cette affirmation reste valable malgré les résultats favorables de 1986, quand on a atteint de nouveau 613 Mt.

Les efforts à faire pour stabiliser la production au-dessus de 600 Mt ne faciliteront pas le choix des responsables soviétiques, ni entre exportation et demande intérieure, ni entre exportation vers l'Ouest ou vers les pays du CAEM.

Ces choix seraient encore plus difficiles si les conséquences de la catastrophe de Tchernobyl sur le programme électronucléaire conduisaient à freiner la substitution énergétique interne du nucléaire au pétrole, ou à essayer de passer le plus rapidement possible à une substitution du nucléaire et du pétrole par du gaz.

Le problème auquel est confrontée l'URSS aujourd'hui témoigne en fait des dangers d'une concentration excessive des exportations sur une seule catégorie de produits. Il ne faut pas oublier non plus que l'industrie du pétrole est affectée par la plupart des aspects qui caractérisent les autres secteurs industriels soviétiques, c'est-à-dire manque d'équipements de pointe, absence de technologie avancée et grands retards dans la productivité et l'efficacité.

Une des solutions trouvées pour résoudre en partie ces problèmes a été l'achat d'équipements occidentaux et une incitation permanente pour améliorer la productivité et les techniques déjà employées, auxquels s'ajoutent de massifs investissements dans ce secteur depuis 1951 et, surtout, depuis 1975.

Pour mieux fixer les idées, nous allons passer en revue les *principales régions pétrolières.*

Elles sont indiquées dans la carte jointe et présentent les caractéristiques suivantes :

A. *La Sibérie Occidentale :*

Bien qu'elle possède un des environnements les plus difficiles de la Terre, cette région produit 6 % du pétrole soviétique, ayant dépassé déjà depuis 1978 la région Volga-Oural et, depuis 1979, la production de l'Asie Centrale. Si en 1970 sa production a été de 31,4 Mt, elle est arrivée à 148 Mt en 1975 pour dépasser 312 Mt en 1980 et atteindre 353 Mt en 1982.

En novembre 1985, 15 puits y entraient en exploitation et en 1986 on en comptait 16 supplémentaires, tout spécialement dans la province de Tyumen, et ces derniers devaient produire à eux seuls plus de 9 Mt par an.

C'est surtout cette région qui est appelée à répondre aux Directives du Plan 1986-1990, comme on le verra plus loin.

B. *Volga-Oural*

Cette région, qui couvre 500.000 km^2 environ a produit généralement 25 % du pétrole soviétique. De 209 Mt en 1970, sa production atteint le sommet de 226 Mt en 1975 pour chuter ensuite à 191 Mt en 1980 et à 167 Mt en 1982. La majeure partie des puits sont en exploitation depuis 20 ou 30 ans, et les gisements facilement exploitables sont en cours d'épuisement. On y obtient de plus en plus d'huile mélangée avec de l'eau et, même avec des méthodes modernes, la part de cette région dans l'ensemble de l'URSS va continuer à baisser.

C. *Timan - Pechora (Komi)*

Il s'agit d'une région de 350.000 km^2 dans le nord-est de la partie européenne du pays. Deux étapes ont caractérisé le développement de ce bassin :

— entre 1930-1950, lorsqu'a été explorée la partie sud du Pechora pour n'y trouver que peu d'huile et de gaz.

— début des années 60, lorsqu'a commencé l'exploration des régions arctiques proches de la mer de Barents. Bien qu'assez riche en ressources pétrolières, son développement a été ralenti par l'environnement difficile et la trouvaille d'huiles lourdes et paraffiniques. Mais, malgré tout, cette région a fourni 7,6 Mt en 1970 pour produire 11 Mt en 1975, 18,5 Mt en 1980 et 20,3 Mt en 1982.

D. *Caucase du Nord*

Ce bassin, situé à l'ouest de la mer Caspienne, est en exploitation depuis plus de 60 ans.

C'est vers la fin des années 50 que la production a commencé à décliner et des puits ont fait l'objet de forages à grande profondeur afin d'en augmenter le rendement. Les résultats ont été de loin inférieurs aux efforts, car de 35 Mt en 1970, la production est arrivée à seulement 16,3 Mt en 1982. C'est toute cette région qui est caractérisée par une baisse très sensible de la production, c'est-à-dire même à l'est de la mer Caspienne.

E. *Transcaucase - Asie Centrale*

Ces deux régions s'étendent de la République de Géorgie à Azerbaijan dans les montagnes du Caucase, au sud de la Mer Caspienne vers la Turkménie et la République de l'Uzbekistan.

Les champs de Baku ont commencé à produire au 19e siècle et représentaient en 1900 50 % de la production mondiale de pétrole et en 1941 plus de 70 % de celle de l'Union Soviétique.

Cette région a vu sa production baisser pendant la seconde guerre mondiale; celle-ci a un peu augmenté jusqu'en 1966 quand elle représentait 8 % de la production soviétique.

Le bassin transcaucasien — situé de Baku vers la République de Géorgie — a vu sa production augmenter lentement jusque vers 1980.

Globalement, de plus de 50 Mt en 1970, après un sommet de 60 Mt en 1975, en 1982 la production n'y était que de 42 Mt environ.

F. *Autres régions*

L'Ukraine, la Biélorussie, la Baltique, etc. ont aussi accusé une nette baisse de la production, depuis 1970.

G. *Récapitulation*

Le tableau et graphique ci-dessous situent les régions par rapport à l'ensemble de la production (en Mt) :

(en Mt)

	1970	1982
Oural-Volga	209	167,7
Caucase du Nord	35	16,3
Sibérie Occidentale	31,4	352,9
Asie Centrale (inclus Kazakhstan)	30	28,1
Azerbaidjan	20,2	14,2
Ukraine	13,9	8,4
Komi	7,6	20,3
Biélorussie et Baltique	4,2	3
Autres (Sakhaline)	1,7	2,1
Total	353	613

PRODUCTION DE PETROLE PAR REGION (en millions barils/jour)

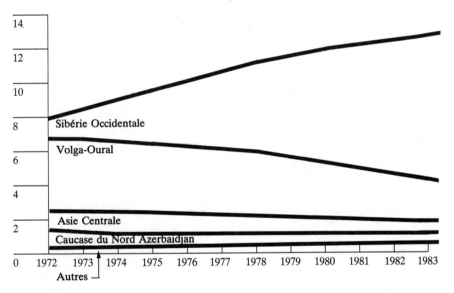

Il est à noter que depuis 1984, l'URSS ne publie plus de statistiques de production par région; on fait état seulement des tendances.

2° - *Le Commerce extérieur*
  a) *Exportations*
  En augmentation continue depuis 1958, c'est pour la première fois en 1985 que les exportations de pétrole de l'URSS ont diminué en valeur et en volume, comme on peut le voir dans le tableau ci-dessous :

	Total	Pays socialistes	CAEM	CAEM Europe	Ouest	PVD
Pétrole et produits pétroliers						
millions de roubles (1)	28.188	15.805	14.580	12.760	10.623	1.760
variations par rapport à 1984 en %	– 8,8	+ 1,9	+ 4,5	+ 5,5	– 21,7	– 3,1
millions de $ (2)	33.921	19.019	17.545	15.355	12.784	2.118
variations par rapport à 1984 en %	– 10,9	– 0,5	+ 2,0	+ 3,0	– 23,5	– 5,4
structure en %						
1984	100	50,2	45,2	39,1	43,9	5,9
1985	100	56,1	51,7	45,3	37,7	6,2
Volume estimé en millions de tonnes (4)						
1984	183,4	92,7	86,1	72,2	79,8	10,9
1985	168,5	91,8	84,9	70,5	64,5	12,2
1985/84	– 8,1	– 1,0	– 1,4	– 2,3	– 19,2	+ 11,9
Prix unitaire estimé en $/baril						
1984	28,4	28,2	27,4	28,3	28,7 (3)	28,1
1985	27,6	28,4	28,3	29,8	27,2 (3)	23,8

(1) La répartition par groupes de pays est faite d'après l'annuaire soviétique, rubriques par pays, le chiffre pour le Tiers-Monde étant résiduel donc moins précis.

(2) 1984 – 1 rouble = 1,23211 $; 1985 – 1 rouble = 1,20338 $ (chiffres ONU).

(3) Prix OPEP moyen pour 1984; prix moyen mondial pour 1985.

(4) Estimé à 7,3 barils pour 1 tonne.

Cette diminution des exportations se retrouve dans l'ensemble des résultats commerciaux de l'URSS qui ont rarement été aussi médiocres qu'en 1985.

Les ventes de pétrole vers l'Ouest ont été réduites et il est à souligner que, à l'exception de la Bulgarie et de la Roumanie, même les exportations vers les pays de l'Est ont été en nette régression.

Nous avons déjà évoqué l'importance du pétrole dans le commerce extérieur de l'URSS et les graves conséquences qu'ont eues les baisses de sa production, du prix du baril et du dollar.

La baisse du prix du pétrole — qui représente en moyenne 64 % des exportations en valeur de l'URSS vers l'Occident — a entraîné en 1986 un manque à gagner estimé à 7 G dollars correspondant à un tiers des revenus en devises.

En fait, l'URSS aurait livré quelque 15 Mt de moins qu'en 1984, alors que la demande de l'Europe de l'Ouest ne diminuait que de 2 à 3 Mt.

En ce qui concerne les *exportations vers les pays du CAEM européens et la Yougoslavie,* on doit rappeler ici qu'il s'agit, en fait, pour la plupart d'entre eux, d'une nette dépendance vis-à-vis de l'URSS.

Cette situation est due à la conjoncture mondiale qui a déterminé pendant 20 ans cette région à réduire, avec l'encouragement de l'URSS, la consommation de charbon au profit du pétrole et du gaz, pour arriver récemment à la nécessité de faire rapidement une nouvelle conversion afin de diminuer les besoins pétroliers. Grosso modo, de 2 Mt de pétrole importés en 1960, les achats en 1985 y ont atteint 90 Mt, l'URSS fournissant près de 66 Mt, soit 75 % environ des importations totales de ces pays.

Le tableau ci-dessous visualise l'évolution de cet état de fait entre 1980 et 1985 :

	Bulgarie	Hongrie	Pologne	RDA	Roumanie	Tchéco-slovaquie	Yougoslavie
Importations de pétrole brut (en millions de tonnes)							
1980	13,2*	8,3	16,3	21,9	16,0	19,3	10,2
1984	13,2*	8,8	13,6	23,2	13,5	17,2	9,7
1985	13,3*	8,6	13,7	23,8	13,9	17,3	8,5
dont en provenance d'URSS							
1980	12 *	7,5	13,1	19,0	1,5	18,8	4,8
1984	13 *	6,8	12,8*	17,1	1,5*	16,0*	0,5
1985	13 *	6,6*	12,9	15,7	1,9*	15,8*	...

* Estimations.

Il est à rappeler que ces importations ont été d'autant plus nécessaires pour l'ensemble de ces pays que, sauf la Roumanie et, dans une certaine mesure, la Yougoslavie et la Hongrie, les productions nationales sont extrêmement faibles.

En effet, en 1985, la Bulgarie a produit 0,15 Mt; la Hongrie 2,0 Mt; la Pologne 0,2-0,3 Mt; la R.D.A. pratiquement rien; la Roumanie 11,6 Mt (en baisse depuis 1980).

Au total dans la région, la production de pétrole couvre à peine le quart des besoins.

Il est à noter que l'évolution marquée tout au long des années 60 à 70 par un accroissement de la dépendance vis-à-vis de l'URSS, a été encouragée par des conditions de prix favorables, comme on peut le voir dans le tableau ci-après.

	Prix du marché mondial en dollars/baril	Prix CAEM dollars/baril (1)	Prix CAEM en % du prix mondial
1971	2,21	2,05	93
1978	12,70	11,39	90
1979	17,26	13,89	80
1980	30,22	14,01	46
1981	32,50	15,67	48
1982	34,00	21,91	64
1983	29,00	25,89	89
1984	28,20	27,28	97
1985	27,16	28,30	104

Les prix payés en dollar/baril sont ceux qui, en théorie, découlent de la moyenne des prix mondiaux des cinq dernières années.

Mais, depuis 1980, les prix soviétiques sont devenus de moins en moins avantageux et en 1985 supérieurs à ceux du marché mondial. A ce jour, ces pays n'ont pas profité du recul des prix pétroliers sur le marché mondial et il est probable que ce sera seulement en 1991 qu'ils en bénéficieront comme les pays occidentaux.

En plus, l'URSS a dû réduire le volume de ses exportations à partir de 1982 pour les situer à peu près à leur niveau de 1980. Il n'y a que la Pologne qui ait bénéficié d'un certain régime de faveur, lié aux graves problèmes de son redressement économique.

Le cas de la Roumanie est différent, car pratiquement indépendante de l'URSS avant 1980, elle a dû faire appel de plus en plus au pétrole soviétique et il n'est pas exclu que, déjà en 1987, elle en demande 3 ou même 5 Mt.

Toute cette dépendance pétrolière des pays frères constitue pour ceux-ci un grave problème dans la mesure où, sans même parler du prix payé par rapport au prix mondial, le paiement se fait en général en roubles convertibles ou parfois en devises fortes et, actuellement et à l'avenir, de plus en plus en produits de compensation, notamment équipements pétroliers et produits alimentaires.

Malgré tous les déboires rencontrés par l'URSS dans ses exportations vers l'Occident, il faut noter ici que ce pays a su s'adapter au mieux et très rapidement à la conjoncture de ces deux dernières années. L'URSS a fait en l'occurrence le nécessaire pour continuer à être présente sur le marché international, en suivant de très près l'évolution des prix pratiqués.

b) *Importations*

L'appel à des fournisseurs étrangers s'est traduit par des importations peu significatives par rapport à la production propre. Elles ont été de 6 Mt en 1980, 7 Mt en 1982, pour atteindre 14,3 Mt en 1984 et 13,3 Mt en 1985. Elles sont le fait beaucoup plus de nécessités d'ordre politique que de besoins énergétiques. Le principal fournisseur a été la Libye suivie de l'Irak, l'Arabie Saoudite et l'Iran.

Cet aspect de « bonnes relations » avec l'OPEP, et surtout avec l'Iran, se retrouve dans l'engagement pris par l'URSS de réduire ses exportations de pétrole vers l'Europe Occidentale de 420.000 t/mois pendant deux mois à partir du 1er septembre 1986. Ceci, afin d'aider l'OPEP à réussir dans sa politique des prix et des quotas, malgré le pressant besoin en devises de l'URSS qui aurait dû faire des efforts en vue d'exporter encore plus.

3° - *La consommation*

Nous avons déjà indiqué sur un graphique précédent la part de la consommation apparente de l'URSS par rapport à sa production et à ses exportations de pétrole.

Si la consommation pétrolière augmentait de 7 %/an environ jusqu'en 1975, le rythme moyen de croissance a été moins rapide depuis, se situant à 5,6 % environ par an.

Entre 1981 et 1985, la consommation soviétique a été celle indiquée dans le tableau suivant où nous avons inclus aussi, pour mieux fixer les idées, les tonnages aux Etats-Unis, en Europe Occidentale et dans le monde :

(en Mt)

	URSS	USA	Europe Ouest	Monde
1981	444,1	746,0	619,3	2.888,1
1982	448,5	705,5	590,8	2.803,7
1983	450,5	704,9	573,1	2.781,6
1984	440,7	726,8	577,4	2.823,0
1985	447,7	724,1	568,6	2.809,4

En 1985, l'URSS consomma 15,9 % du total mondial, tandis que les USA 25,8 % et l'Europe Occidentale 20,3 %.

Quelque 70 % de la consommation de pétrole se retrouve dans 3 secteurs de l'économie soviétique :
— énergie électrique ;
— transports ;
— industrie.

Le ralentissement de la croissance est dû particulièrement à des « économies d'énergie » qui représentent le résultat d'un effort volontariste pour réduire globalement la consommation par substitution. Nous allons revenir sur ce très important aspect dans le dernier chapitre de ce Rapport, mais d'ores et déjà nous soulignons que par « économies d'énergie » on entend en URSS :

— une amélioration sensible des rendements des champs pétroliers par une augmentation des performances et de la fiabilité des équipements et l'introduction de méthodes plus modernes d'exploitation.

— une réduction des consommations unitaires dans toutes les installations industrielles (raffinage, sidérurgie).

— un raffinage plus poussé, plus performant.

— une meilleure maîtrise des consommations domestiques (par exemple : introduction de compteurs dans les logements).

— des rendements meilleurs dans les transports.

— introduction de « l'heure d'été »

— une substitution de plus en plus importante du pétrole par d'autres matières énergétiques, plus particulièrement le gaz et le charbon.

Des résultats positifs ont déjà été enregistrés ; à titre d'exemple, la part du pétrole dans la consommation totale de combustible des centrales électriques qui était de 35 % en 1980 n'était plus que de 26 % environ en 1985.

Il est évident que le pétrole brut doit être transporté des champs d'où il est extrait aux lieux de consommation, qu'il s'agisse de raffineries ou d'exportation.

Ce *Transport* est réalisé plus particulièrement grâce à des réseaux d'oléoducs dont une partie est destinée aux produits raffinés. Plus de 90 % du brut est acheminé de cette manière sur 83 % de l'ensemble du réseau, le restant est utilisé pour le transport des produits raffinés.

Le développement des oléoducs a été spectaculaire ces dernières années, car de 4.000 km à la fin de la seconde guerre mondiale, ils étaient de plus de 76.000 km à la fin de l'année 1983.

Plus de la moitié de ce développement se situe entre 1970 et 1983 et 20.000 km environ — surtout représentés par des tuyaux de grands diamètres (1,020 et 1,220 m) ont été posés dans les dix premières années de cette période.

141

Depuis 1980, la construction de ce réseau a été ralentie suite, surtout, à la diminution de la production de pétrole. Il est à mentionner que, si en 1950-55, la distance moyenne du transport du pétrole était de 300 km, en 1980, celle-ci était de 1.850 km environ.

Pour les produits destinés à l'exportation, le transport est assuré par des navires pétroliers. Le poids en lourd (tonnage maximal qu'un navire peut normalement embarquer) de *la flotte sous pavillon soviétique* était en 1985 de 6,215 Mt, représentant 2,52 % du total mondial, en augmentation par rapport à 1979 quand il était de 5,875 Mt.

Il faut remarquer que le tonnage mondial a accusé une baisse très sensible entre 1979 et 1985, passant de 328 Mt à 246 Mt à la fin de la période.

Une très large partie de la consommation du pétrole brut en URSS est constituée par les produits raffinés destinés soit à une utilisation finale (essences, carburéacteurs, lubrifiants...), soit à des transformations dans l'industrie de la chimie, de la pétrochimie... (voir l'annexe « Quelques notions sur le pétrole »).

La première et principale transformation se fait dans les *raffineries* dont le nombre et la capacité ont considérablement augmenté dans les années 70.

Bien que l'URSS ne publie pas de statistiques relatives à la capacité de ses raffineries, on estime que, globalement, celle-ci est passée de 545 Mt en 1969 à plus de 607 Mt en 1984, tout en restant stable depuis. Dans la même période, la capacité de raffinage dans le monde était estimée à 3,970 Gt pour descendre à 3,60 Gt, la diminution la plus spectaculaire ayant été marquée en Europe de l'Ouest (de plus de 1 Gt à 0,7 Gt), celle des Etats-Unis ayant accusé aussi une baisse assez forte (de 875 Mt à 760 Mt).

En général, ce phénomène s'explique par une moindre consommation de pétrole, mais aussi par de nouvelles capacités installées au Moyen-Orient, en Afrique et, dans une certaine mesure, en URSS même.

Le principal problème rencontré dans l'industrie du raffinage est celui d'une trop faible capacité de « cracking catalytique » qui permet d'obtenir les produits raffinés les plus demandés avec un rendement et une qualité supérieurs à d'autres procédés.

En son absence, on obtient trop de produits dits « lourds », d'autant plus que le pétrole brut largement utilisé comme matière première est, à son tour, trop souvent, de qualité peu conforme aux résultats souhaités.

Les facteurs qui retardent une amélioration sont principalement :
— la vétusté des équipements en place ;
— la pénurie d'équipements soviétiques de très bon niveau, ce qui nécessite des achats en Occident, donc sortie de devises ;
— une demande encore élevée de produits lourds ;

— les difficultés de trouver des consommateurs de pétrole lourd pour obtenir en échange du pétrole plus léger.

Les autorités soviétiques, pleinement conscientes de cet état de fait, ont prévu de remédier à cette situation, en augmentant aussi la capacité de cracking, surtout dans le cadre du 11ᵉ Plan 1981-1985, sans beaucoup de succès.

4° - *Perspectives*

Nous venons de passer en revue la situation actuelle de l'industrie pétrolière de l'URSS en faisant référence, d'une part, à la nouvelle politique que M. Gorbatchev souhaite instaurer et, d'autre part, à un environnement spécifique au pétrole, qu'il soit soviétique ou mondial.

Il est bien évident que l'image qu'on a ainsi pu retenir n'est pas figée et le problème qui se pose est d'arriver à cerner son développement, au moins pour le proche avenir.

On constate que M. Gorbatchev et son équipe utilisent actuellement un langage nouveau, font preuve d'ouverture, souhaitent vivement une transparence dans toutes les actions... Autant d'aspects inédits qui ne demandent qu'à être concrétisés par des réalisations effectives, en commençant par un changement de la mentalité du peuple soviétique.

Pour l'instant, sans faire preuve de scepticisme ou de pessimisme, l'Occident est dans l'attente, et nous avons vu que de nombreuses questions se posent quant à la volonté réelle de changement et, dans l'affirmative, quant à la possibilité de le réaliser.

Tout en accueillant avec satisfaction les déclarations et les promesses ainsi que certaines actions des actuels dirigeants de l'URSS, il est certainement trop tôt pour en tirer une conclusion valable et ce n'est que dans un délai — probablement assez long — qu'on pourra en tirer une.

En ce qui concerne *le pétrole* celui-ci s'inscrit dans un contexte qui présente des caractéristiques et des incertitudes dans une très large mesure indépendantes d'une politique intérieure ou extérieure de l'URSS.

Malgré l'importance qu'il présente dans l'ensemble de l'économie de ce pays, il a été souvent dit ces dernières années que « l'augmentation de sa *production* n'est pas un but en soi ». Est-ce que c'était pour justifier dans une bonne mesure la baisse de la production des gisements, ou tout simplement la vérité ?

Quoi qu'il en soit, le nouveau Plan quinquennal prévoit d'abord une forte augmentation de l'industrie des constructions mécaniques et ne met plus l'accent principalement sur celle de la production de pétrole dans l'ensemble de l'énergie. Ceci pour plusieurs raisons :

— d'abord, parce que les gisements actuellement en exploitation sont soit en voie d'épuisement, soit de plus en plus difficiles à exploiter, ce qui entraîne un prix de revient très élevé;

— les nouveaux gisements exploitables sont très éloignés des centres de consommation et situés dans des régions avec un climat très rude;

— comme l'exploitation du gaz est plus facile et beaucoup plus maîtrisée du point de vue des techniques modernes, la substitution pétrole-gaz est devenue un objectif principal dans l'économie soviétique;

— les économies d'énergie seront de plus en plus poussées;

— aucun nouveau gisement géant n'ayant été découvert récemment, les nouvelles capacités de production proviendront désormais essentiellement de petits gisements dispersés, à faible productivité;

— le déclin des vieux champs des régions européennes dû, pour quelques-uns, aux dommages causés par l'utilisation de méthodes non adéquates;

— le nombre réduit de forages d'exploitation en mer;

— les coûts de production de plus en plus élevés (ils ont pratiquement doublé entre 1975 et 1980);

— le fait que l'essentiel des dépenses d'investissement ait été affecté au maintien du niveau de production, et non pas à son développement, le nombre de forages d'exploration étant très peu élevé.

Ceci étant, jusqu'en 1990 et même au-delà, c'est-à-dire jusqu'en l'an 2000, deux objectifs sont prioritaires:

— d'abord, un développement exceptionnel des champs de la Sibérie Occidentale, du Kazakhstan et du nord de la partie européenne de l'URSS.

La Sibérie Occidentale sera appelée à fournir vers 1990 les deux tiers de l'extraction globale du pétrole. Les dirigeants soviétiques ont pris conscience des défaillances qui ont caractérisé ce secteur ces derniers temps et ont prévu de rattraper dans les délais les plus brefs le retard qui en a résulté.

— ensuite, une modernisation des installations en place, aussi bien par l'introduction de nouveaux équipements d'origine soviétique, que, surtout, par l'adoption d'équipements automatisés et de méthodes modernes d'exploitation en provenance surtout de l'Occident.

Dans ces conditions, déjà en 1984, les prévisions faites pour l'année 1990 par différentes organisations spécialisées internationales et des experts, tablaient sur une production entre 540 et 620 Mt.

Le 12° Plan, lui, a comme *objectif* en 1990: 640 Mt, ce qui peut paraître très ambitieux vu les nombreux aspects défavorables qui caractérisent cette industrie. Bien sûr, par rapport aux réserves prouvées, cet objectif pourrait être atteint, car celles de l'URSS sont actuellement estimées à environ 8 Gt, ce qui correspond à 8,6 % des réserves mondiales (56 % se trouvant au Moyen-Orient, 12 % en Amérique Latine, 8 %

en Afrique, 5 % aux U.S.A. et moins de 4 % en Europe Occidentale). Encore, nous le répétons, faudra-t-il pouvoir exploiter réellement ces gisements.

En premier lieu, les Soviétiques devraient commencer à améliorer la technologie du forage, en augmentant aussi le nombre de puits. En Sibérie Occidentale, par exemple, ceux de prospection et d'exploration devront représenter vers la fin 1990 une profondeur totale de 14.000 km, c'est-à-dire le double de celle réalisée au cours du précédent Plan. Ceci serait à réaliser grâce à de nouvelles techniques — notamment des systèmes d'enregistrement et d'analyse des données sismiques — appliquées à quelque 5.000 gisements qui devraient être relevés, par une accélération du montage des appareils de forage (actuellement de 24 jours), par une nette amélioration des équipements (qui pèsent 70 % de plus que les équipements occidentaux), par une restructuration et modernisation des moyens de transports (qui représentent encore 35 % du coût des infrastructures) et, enfin, par une amélioration des cadences et du rythme de travail.

La situation dans *l'off-shore* est aussi très peu prometteuse. Les projets annoncés il y a peu d'années comme ceux de la mer de Barents, de la mer de Sakhaline et de la mer Caspienne ont été pratiquement abandonnés, toujours à cause des difficultés d'exploitation et du coût de celle-ci et suite à la décision ferme d'améliorer la productivité des champs existants en priorité.

Mais les projets pour l'exploration et l'exploitation des mers arctiques seront certainement repris dans un avenir pas trop éloigné, sans aucun doute en étroite coopération avec des entreprises occidentales.

Cet appel à une coopération avec l'Occident est, d'ores et déjà, retrouvé dans la recherche de technologies à la pointe du progrès qui devraient remplacer rapidement celles actuellement utilisées, sans oublier, bien sûr, les équipements.

Les Soviétiques sont très conscients du retard pris dans l'application de méthodes telles que, par exemple, la « récupération assistée » sur les gisements existants. C'est une préoccupation qui constitue actuellement une priorité, et dans le cadre d'une étroite collaboration avec les entreprises occidentales, la meilleure des méthodes est vivement recherchée.

Nous devons souligner que l'augmentation des investissements dans l'industrie pétrolière, afin d'atteindre les buts fixés à l'horizon 1990, est de 31 % par rapport au Plan précédent. Ce pourcentage doit être comparé avec le 7,6 % de la croissance de l'investissement global en capital fixe, le 30 % de la construction mécanique, 24 % de l'énergie électrique...

Un gros effort sera fait en matière *d'économies d'énergie*. Les prévisions d'ici 1990 prévoient, pour l'ensemble des énergies, des diminutions de l'ordre de 200 Mt équivalent pétrole, à comparer avec les 90 Mt du plan précédent. En fait, la consommation d'énergie par unité de revenu national doit baisser de 40 %, les économies d'énergie obtenues devant compenser l'augmentation des besoins globaux.

La consommation de pétrole devrait se situer en 1990 aux environs de 450 Mt, donc pratiquement du même ordre de grandeur qu'en 1985, quand elle a été de 447,7 Mt (certains experts estiment la consommation en 1990 autour de 500 Mt).

Nous avons déjà évoqué les facteurs qui vont concourir à une moindre consommation de pétrole, dont, aussi, le passage massif au gaz.

Toutes les mesures, destinées à maintenir la production soviétique à un niveau égal ou supérieur à 600 Mt par an et à maîtriser au maximum la consommation intérieure, auront aussi pour but de mieux cerner les exportations. Mais celles-ci ne devront plus constituer la priorité des priorités car, d'une part l'URSS va de plus en plus mettre l'accent sur le développement des exportations de gaz et, d'autre part, sur celui de produits ayant une valeur ajoutée, comme nous l'avons déjà souligné. De plus, pour des raisons politiques, Moscou s'est engagé début 1987 à réduire ses exportations (de 7 % ?), à la demande de l'Arabie Saoudite, et continuer ainsi à soutenir les actions de l'OPEP.

On s'attend donc à une baisse assez sensible des exportations de pétrole, mais, probablement, avec une restructuration des pays destinataires. Il se peut que les pays occidentaux en reçoivent plus et les pays en developpement moins, l'URSS gardant même la possibilité d'importer du brut des pays du Moyen-Orient grâce à des accords de compensation.

Quant aux problèmes posés par le *raffinage*, ceux-ci seront loin de voir une solution. Il n'est pas exclu qu'un programme de modernisation des raffineries soit commencé, mais en dehors des trois projets explicitement mentionnés dans le nouveau Plan (nouvelle raffinerie et unité d'huiles de base en Biélorussie, développement d'une raffinerie en Lituanie et la mise en service d'une autre unité en Turkménie), rien d'essentiel n'y est prévu. On se préoccupe malgré tout de mieux maîtriser les consommations d'énergie dans toutes les raffineries existantes, car les consommations unitaires sont extrêmement élevées.

Enfin, le réseau de *transport* par oléoducs ne fera pas l'objet d'une augmentation spectaculaire.

5° - Conclusion

Les perspectives ouvertes à l'industrie pétrolière en URSS ne semblent pas actuellement être les mêmes que pour d'autres secteurs industriels, en particulier pour ceux produisant des produits manufacturés. Maintenir le niveau de production de pétrole aux environs de 600 Mt par an sera dû plus particulièrement à des efforts concentrés en Sibérie Occidentale, mais les gains ainsi obtenus ne pourront pas compenser à 100 % les pertes constatées dans d'autres régions.

Pendant plusieurs années, l'URSS devra beaucoup investir afin d'adopter des techniques, des méthodes et des équipements occidentaux modernes, tout en appliquant des systèmes de gestion plus efficaces et plus productifs. Il ne faut pas oublier que les pertes en devises engendrées par le contexte des exportations du pétrole ont entraîné une détérioration de la trésorerie soviétique qui pourrait même pousser l'URSS à accroître ses emprunts auprès du système bancaire international. Car l'URSS ne pourra qu'augmenter ses achats en Occident pour résoudre dans l'immédiat les grands problèmes auxquels elle est confrontée, donc beaucoup plus des importations que des réformes.

Si les Soviétiques se sont bien rendus compte des dangers d'une concentration des exportations sur une seule catégorie de produits — le pétrole — on peut s'interroger et mettre en doute la possibilité du système soviétique à générer des ventes de biens manufacturés.

C'est surtout dans cet esprit qu'il faut se poser la question quant à la réelle concrétisation de la réforme économique dans un proche avenir, telle qu'envisagée par l'actuelle équipe au pouvoir.

De toute manière, pour réaliser ses objectifs, si l'URSS compte beaucoup sur ses propres moyens et potentialités, elle doit s'ouvrir de plus en plus à une coopération — surtout industrielle — avec les pays étrangers et plus particulièrement occidentaux, en s'intégrant ainsi dans le vieux concept de «division internationale du travail».

Et, bien évidemment, la réalisation des tâches confiées à l'industrie du pétrole sera étroitement liée au succès ou à l'échec de l'ensemble de la politique que M. Gorbatchev veut mettre en place.

Annexe

QUELQUES NOTIONS SUR LE PETROLE

A l'époque où les titans affrontaient les dieux, Prométhée déroba le feu du ciel pour en faire don aux humains. L'interprétation mythologique, très en avance sur son temps, comporte un fond de vérité. Le ciel, plus exactement le soleil, fournit l'énergie nécessaire à l'élaboration des végétaux à partir du gaz carbonique, de l'eau, des minéraux, et les calories dégagées par le feu de bois sont dues à la libération partielle de l'énergie enmagasinée. Beaucoup plus tard, l'homme a appris à tirer du feu l'énergie mécanique; commence alors la ruée vers tous les combustibles que la nature prévoyante a accumulés. Deux siècles durant le charbon fait la loi sur la terre, puis vient le tour du *pétrole*. Aujourd'hui, on est dans l'atome, et on peut dire que la maîtrise de cette énergie nouvelle, prise dans l'énergie propre des atomes, constitue un second bond prométhéen.

Le pétrole brut est un mélange complexe d'hydrocarbures gazeux, liquides et solides, formés de carbone et d'hydrogène, associés en proportions très variables. Après avoir subi un processus de formation durant plusieurs millions d'années, le pétrole se rencontre aujourd'hui au sein de roches poreuses, le plus généralement gréseuses ou calcaires, alternant avec des couches marneuses, imperméables.

Mais l'huile ainsi située dans les profondeurs de la terre n'a de valeur qu'au terme d'un long cycle ponctué d'opérations complexes qui sont:

A. *L'exploitation*; elle recouvre:
— les campagnes de prospection géologiques et géophysiques nécessaires au choix d'un périmètre de recherche et à la localisation des structures susceptibles de contenir du pétrole ou du gaz.
— les forages d'exploration, seul moyen de prouver qu'une structure contient effectivement des hydrocarbures et, dans ce cas, d'en évaluer les réserves. A terre, on utilise des engins de forage, et en mer, des plates-formes ou des navires spécialisés.

B. *La production*; elle recouvre:
— le développement des gisements dont les réserves récupérables sont estimées suffisantes pour représenter un intérêt commercial. Il consiste à mettre les installations nécessaires à l'exploitation.
— l'exploitation qui consiste à assurer la bonne marche des installations de production pendant toute la durée de vie du gisement. Elle peut comporter des opérations de récupération assistée, destinées à augmenter la part de pétrole obtenue par rapport à la quantité en place dans le gisement, tout comme le forage de nouveaux puits qui doivent remplacer ceux qui se détériorent ou s'épuisent.

C. *Les transports*, qui peuvent être maritimes ou terrestres.

D. *Les stockages*

E. *Le raffinage*, destiné à valoriser le pétrole brut. En effet, celui-ci est un mélange de nombreux hydrocarbures différents, accompagnés d'impuretés diverses et l'opération de raffinage a pour but de classer et de transformer ces hydrocarbures en éliminant des impuretés pour aboutir à des produits répondant à des besoins précis. Les cinq sortes d'opérations que représente le raffinage sont:

148

— la distillation ou le fractionnement;
— le craquage et le réformage;
— l'hydrodésulfuration;
— les traitements secondaires;
— les traitements finisseurs.
et permettent d'obtenir une large gamme de produits tant pétroliers que pétrochimiques.

On fabrique ainsi :
— les grands produits (carburants, carburéacteurs, gazoils et divers fuel-oils); des gaz liquéfiés (propane et butane), de l'isopentane, etc.;
— des produits non énergétiques comme des butènes, des trimères et tétramères de propylène, des solvants, des lubrifiants, des paraffines et cires et des bitumes routiers et industriels.

F. *La distribution* des produits finis, qui, en aval des raffineries, contient des stockages, des transports et des moyens de ventes à la clientèle.

Pour mémoire :
1 baril = 159 l = 0,14 t
1.000 b/j = 50.000 t/an
100.000 b/j = 5.000.000 t/an
1 t = 7,3 b environ
(selon densité du brut)

PRINCIPALES SOURCES

1. *Périodiques*
— Bulletin de l'industrie Pétrolière
— Business Eastern Europe
— Commerce et Coopération (Revue de la Chambre de Commerce Franco-Soviétique)
— Le Courrier des Pays de l'Est (mensuel édité par la « Documentation Française »)
— Eastern European Markets (édité par Financial Times)
— Current History
— The Brookings Review (édité par The Brookings Institution)
— Lettre d'information de la Chambre de Commerce Franco-Soviétique
— Le Figaro

— Le Monde, le Monde Diplomatique, Le Monde «Dossiers et Documents»
— Financial Times
— The Oil Daily
— Washington Post
— Etudes Soviétiques
— Oil and Gas journal
— Bulletin de l'Ambassade de France à Moscou

2. *Documents, Rapports, Etudes*
— CIA - Study on Soviet Oil Production, May 1986
— John P. Hardt - Oil Price Behaviour: Implications for The Soviet Union (Congressional Research Service - The Library of Congress)
— Philip Joseph (editor) - Capacité d'adaptation de l'URSS et des Pays d'Europe de l'Est aux technologies nouvelles (Colloque OTAN, Avril 1985)
— Intelligence Report on URSS (Rapport établi par le Bureau T. CFP de Washington)
— F. David et P. Malmartel - Les perspectives énergétiques et attitudes des Compagnies Pétrolières (TOTAL CFP-Direction Economique)
— Plan Econ Reports
— World Bank-Energy Forecasts
— France-URSS, un nouveau départ (L'exportation Magazine, Octobre 85)
— Gadon (J.L.) - Evolution récente de la conjoncture pétrolière de l'URSS (Institut Français du Pétrole, 1985)
— Gadon (J.L.) - La Politique énergétique de l'URSS - Bilan et Stratégies (Institut Français du Pétrole, juin 1986)
— Gadon (J.L.) - Perspectives pétrolières de l'URSS (Revue de l'Energie - n° 365/1984)
— Ed. A. Hewett - Energy Economics and Foreign Policy in the Soviet Union (The Brookings Institution, 1984)
— URSS - Le XIIe Quinquennat (Agence de Presse NOVOSTI-Moscou, 1986)
— M. Ryjkov - Sur les grandes options du Développement Economique et Social de l'URSS pour 1986-1990 et jusqu'à l'an 2000 (Agence de Presse Novosti-Moscou, 1986)
— M. Gorbatchev - Interventions au 27e Congrès du P.C.U.S.
— Bornstein (M) - «The Transfer of Western Technology to the USSR» (OECD-1985)
— Delemont (E) - «Le Pétrole» («Que sais-je» n° 158)
— Lamoureux (Chr. et autres) - «De la drôle de guerre à la drôle de crise» (Fayard, 1986)

- Lavigne (M) - « Economie internationale des pays socialistes » (Armand Collin, 1985)
- Sajus (L) - « Le Pétrole; Raffinage et Pétrochimie » (Armand Colin)
- TOTAL CFP - « Le Pétrole, le gaz et les autres énergies » (Mars 1986)
- USSR Energy Atlas (CIA, 1985)
- Oil and Gas 1987 (Financial Times International Year Book)
- World Outlook 1986 (The Economist Intelligence Unit)
- International Petroleum Encyclopedia 1985 et 1986

3. *Colloques, Conférences, Tables rondes*
- Le contrôle des exportations de haute technologie vers les Pays de l'Est (Centre de Recherches « Droit et Défense » - Université Paris V-Avril 1986)
- Les nouveaux Plans quinquennaux en Europe de l'Est (Centre Français du Commerce extérieur-Septembre 1986)
- Vienna East-West Conference, Juin 1986
- Entreprises conjointes (Association Internationale de Droit Economique-Université Catholique de Louvain-Novembre 1986)
- URSS : l'Ere de Gorbatchev (CEFRI, Janvier 1987)
- CISI Wharton Econometric Forecasting Associates
- DRI /Plan Econ - Paris et Londres, 1986
- Congrès International des Economistes de langue française (Budapest, Mai 1985).

The Soviet Gas Sector: Challenges Ahead

Arild Moe and Helge Ole Bergesen*

Introduction

The Soviet Gas Industry has been considered a success story in recent years. The rapid buildup and the overfulfillment of plan targets is the basis for this impression. The last time the Soviet gas industry was treated at this conference, Thane Gustafson contributed an analysis of the Soviet adaptation to technological pressures, using the oil and gas industries as a case.[1] The way the gas industry overcame the difficulties created by the pipeline-sanctions strengthened its image domestically and abroad. The industry has demonstrated more ingenuity and inventiveness than many older Soviet industries, thus in a way it started on « a new course » long before that became the order of the day. In our contribution we will try to assess how the sector has adapted and will adapt to new challenges both domestically and in the gas market.

Gas Reserves and Production

The USSR is the largest producer of natural gas in the world today, a position it has occupied since 1983 when it bypassed the United States.

The country has also, by far, the largest proven reserves of gas. The USSR has not published figures on their reserves later than as of January 1, 1981, but they are estimated to be about 42-48 trillion cubic meters[2], or more than 45 % of the world's total reserves.

Gas production started in the western parts of the country, and as late as 1976 the Ukraine was the biggest production region.[3] But from that point production shifted more and more to Western Siberia. In 1986, Western Siberia was responsible for 60 % of total Soviet production.

* The authors are grateful for suggestions and assistance from Javier Estrada and Rune Castberg.

Table 1
Soviet gas production 1963-1986 and plans 1965-2000
(Billion cubic meters).

	Actual	Plan	Annual growth (per cent)
1965	127.7	150	
1970	198.0	225- 240	9.2 (1966-70)
1975	289.3	300- 320	7.9 (1971-75)
1980	435.0	400- 435	8.5 (1976-80)
1981	465.0	458	6.9
1982	501.0	492	7.7
1983	535.7	529	7.0
1984	587.0	578	9.6
1985	643.0	630	9.5
1986	686.0	672	6.7
1987		712 ([1])	
1990		850 ([2])	5.4 (1987-90)
2000		1027-1156 ([3])	1.9-3.1 (1991-2000)

([1]) *Ekonomicheskaya Gazeta,* 48, 1986.
([2]) Revised plan targets for 1990, published in Ryzhkov's speech, *Pravda,* 19 June 1986.
([3]) Calculation based on *Sotsialisticheskaya Industriya,* 9 March 1986.

This table surely demonstrates an impressive growth. It should be remembered though, that the gas industry has been a «success story» only during the last ten years. Before that, the industry almost as a rule underfulfilled its annual production plans. The question now is if the industry can continue its expansion into the twelfth and thirteenth plan periods (1986-95).

Admittedly, the growth rates are lower than for the preceding periods, but nonetheless enormous volumes must be put on stream, net increments of 207 bcm in the period 1986-90 alone.

Planned production in fields outside Western Siberia seem to even out in the coming years, i.e. some fields are expanding but others are decreasing, so that total production outside the RSFSR is expected to increase by only 10-20 bcm, according to the Five-Year Plan. The upshot is that net increments to production must be provided by Western Siberia.

154

Regional distribution of Soviet gas production (bcm).

Production area	1975	1980	1984	1985	1986	Plan 1987	Plan 1990 [1]
USSR, total	289	435	587	643	686	712	850
RSFSR	115	254	413	462	503	535	650
Siberia	40	162	331	380	420	450	570
Tyumen	35.7	156	324	372	413	442	565
Urengoy	—	50	210	262 [2]	294 [3]		
Medvezhe	29.9	71	72	72	75		
Vyngapurovskoye	—	16	17	16	17		
Yamburg	—	—	—	—	4 [3]		200 [4]
Associated gas	—	12	19	21	23		
Other Siberian	4.1	6	7	7	7	8	
Urals	23	52	50	50	50	50	50
Volga	11	8	7	7	7	10	
North Caucasus	23	14	9	9	9	9	
Komi ASSR	18.5	17.5	16	16	16	16	
Outside RSFSR	174	181	174	181	183		200
Ukraine	68.7	52	43	43	43		
Azerbaydzhan	9.9	14.5	14	14	14		
Kazakhstan	5.2	5	5	5	7		15
Uzbekistan	37.2	39	37	37	35		
Turkmenistan	51.8	70.3	75	82	84		86

Main source: Soviet Geography, April 1986 and April 1987 (preliminary table).

(1) Materialy XXVII Syezda Kommunisticheskoy Partii Sovietskogo Soyuza, (Material from the 27th Party Congress), Politizdat, Moscow, 1986, p. 295 and 317; Plan targets in Ryzhkov's speech to the Supreme Soviet, Pravda, 19 June, 1986.

(2) There exist several differing assessments of the production level at Urengoy for 1985. OGJ, 26 May, 1986 gives the figure 270 bcm, whereas Soviet Geography announces 250 bcm. Our figure is midway, and makes the subtotals add up.

(3) FNI estimates.

(4) Sotsialisticheskaya Industriya, 24 September 1986.

The increments to production 1986-90 must, more precisely, come from two fields, Urengoy and Yamburg. During the 11th Five-Year Plan (1981-85), output from the Urengoy field increased by 200 bcm and it continued to increase by some 32 bcm in 1986 and will probably grow by at least 20 bcm in 1987. Some have argued that the field probably can yield even more, due to its enormous reserves and favourable geological characteristics. However, faster depletion could probably be to the detriment of the field's long term potential, a well-known problem in the Soviet oil industry. But if we assume that Urengoy reaches top level in 1987, Yamburg must take over. The development of this field has not, however, reached the stage Urengoy had attained in 1981. Originally production was scheduled to commence in 1986 with 36 bcm.[4] Indeed production was announced in September 1986[5], but apparently with very small volumes. Serious delays are regularly reported in the Soviet press. Technical problems are mostly related to the permafrost.[6] It can become difficult to expand production as soon and as rapidly as will be necessary if Urengoy levels out.

In addition there is uncertainty concerning the Medvezhe field. This field was scheduled to peak in 1987 at 70 bcm, but due to the problems at Yamburg new plans for exploration and investments are considered that will allow the field to stay at this level through 1989.[7] But such an effort could in itself divert resources needed at Yamburg and Urengoy if total inputs are not increased.

In Table 3 a scenario for future Soviet gas production is sketched. Developments outside Western Siberia are treated as a constant, fields with expanding production just compensating for fields with decreasing output. In the table the difference between total growth and the increase in West Siberian fields indicates the margin allowed for the fall in production from other fields in Western Siberia.

Table 3
Net increments to Soviet gas production 1981-2000
(bcm).

Year	Production low-high	Increase low-high	West-Siberian fields increasing
1981	465	30	31e Urengoy
1982	501	36	36e Urengoy
1983	536	35	39e Urengoy
1984	587	51	54e Urengoy
1985	643	43	50e Urengoy
1986	686	43	32e + 4e Urengoy + Yamburg
1987	725e	39	20 + 20 Urengoy + Yamburg
1988	764	39	40 Yamburg
1989	806	42	50 Yamburg
1990	850p	44	60 Yamburg
1991	866-877	16-27	Yamburg + Yamal
1992	883-904	17-27	Yamburg + Yamal
1993	900-932	17-28	Yamburg + Yamal
1994	917-962	17-29	Yamal
1995	934-992	18-30	Yamal
1996	952-1023	18-31	Yamal
1997	971-1057	18-32	Yamal
1998	989-1088	19-33	Yamal
1999	1008-1121	19-34	Yamal
2000	1027-1156g	19-35	Yamal

e = estimate   p = plan   g = official guidelines.
All historical figures are actual and future figures estimates, unless otherwise indicated.

In this scenario Urengoy levels out at 315 bcm in 1987 and Yamburg at approximately 220 bcm in 1993. At that time fields on the Yamal peninsula must be phased in. Plans for this area are still uncertain, but a production start from the Bovanenko field before 1990 has been announced as a «basic task for the industry».[8] By 1990 a new pipeline leading from Yamal over Torzhok to Uzhgorod on the Czech border should be ready to bring gas as far as Gryazovets[9], something that looks unrealistic today, but should not be ruled out, given the momentum in construction.

It is still too early to tell if the above-mentioned problems will curtail production growth in the Soviet gas industry. We do not know the plans for investments in the gas industry in the 12th Five-Year Plan, only the total growth rate for the energy sector, 35 per cent.[10] Judging from the experience of 1986, the oil industry's share of these investments may be growing. If this is true, the gas industry may have trouble obtaining sufficient investment capital, unless total energy investments are increased beyond the plan. This investment squeeze may lead to further emphasis on short term goals, such as production drilling, neglecting measures that ensure the longevity of the fields, such as exploration and maintenance. In other words: repeating the mistakes of the oil industry. Indeed, Gorbachev warned against this very tendency during his visit to Western Siberia in the autumn of 1985.[11] One could, of course, assume that this is a calculated strategy by Soviet planners. If the buildup continues into the early nineties (when the growth rate in gas production is scheduled to decrease, according to the guidelines for the economic development to year 2000), they could hope that there still will be time to shift resources to neglected areas. But we see no evidence of such calculations, and we find it more probable that problems are solved according to the priority of the day, which may indicate that there are problems ahead.

Costs in the Soviet Gas Industry

It is obvious that the geographical location of the gas reserves affects costs directly in at least two ways: the transport component in total costs of Soviet gas production has increased drastically, and costs will continue to rise as production moves northwards from the Urengoy field to Yamburg on the Taz peninsula and to the Yamal peninsula. On average Soviet gas in 1985 was transported more than 2300 km.[12] The most thorough analysis of Soviet cost estimates reports an average cost for extraction of 2.43 rubles per thousand cubic meters and 5.80 rubles for transportation. These costs are estimated to increase to 2.69 and 7.04 rubles respectively, in 1990.[13] (Dollar equivalents at exchange rate 68.92: 9.2 c, 22 c, 10.2 c, and 26.8 c per MMbtu.) In these cost estimates, the Soviet definition of factor cost is used, i.e. current operating costs plus 12 per cent of current capital investment. In Table 4 these costs are compared to the corresponding costs in the oil and coal industries.

Table 4
Estimated total costs (in roubles) per ton standard fuel equivalent (tsf).

	1981-85	1986-90
Gas	11.25	13.00
Oil	24.35	37.75
Coal	12.78	13.66

Source: Albina Tretyakova and Meredith Heinemeier: "Cost Estimates for the Soviet Gas Industry: 1970 to 1990", and corresponding volumes for the oil and coal industries, *CIR Staff Paper,* Washington, Bureau of the Census, 1986.

Domestic costs in the Soviet Union cannot easily be translated into foreign currency, even if this has been attempted several times in Western analyses. We have, therefore, deliberately chosen to leave the costs in the table in rubles. But we can safely state that the costs are very high, and increasingly so. But maybe just as interesting is the comparison of costs in the different fuel industries. The rising costs in the oil industry are staggering — this leaves gas in a, relatively speaking, more favourable position. Costs in the coal industry seem to be more stable. Indeed the tendency to rely more on open cast mining will tend to lower production costs. The bottleneck is transportation, where huge investments must be made, whether in railway capacity or high voltage transmission. In other words, if coal's role were to expand drastically, total costs would increase due to transportation. Gas, on the other hand, shows a fairly stable cost picture, even if production is expanding substantially.

Still, gas is becoming more costly, especially if costs in opening new fields and the construction of new pipelines are isolated. This must have some impact on decisions about future gas production. We believe that the awareness of costs is growing in the Soviet economy and that in the future a more rational strategy will be chosen, i.e. relying more on conservation rather than continuing the drive for increased production. However, the adjustments needed in the Soviet economy and in Soviet economic thinking will take time. In the meantime, let us say to the mid-nineties, it will be hard to avoid the old supply side strategy.

The question has been raised whether or not increased costs will affect export policy. It can be argued that since exports are marginal, compared to domestic consumption, marginal costs are the more relevant measure. But in the gas industry the expansion of production is mainly done for domestic purposes. The extra costs incurred because of export volumes are probably much lower than the average costs in the new fields, because of their size and economy of scale. This is very different from the oil industry, where the tendency is to develop smaller and smaller fields in more complicated environments, resulting in soaring marginal costs. Another important variable regarding costs and value assessments of gas exports is uncertain, too: the opportunity cost of imports for which the gas is paying (see below).

Gas Consumption in the USSR

When the gas industry of the USSR is discussed in the West, its external implications, i.e. exports, are usually the main interest. The domestic part is treated more as a residual. We will argue, though, that it is more realistic in many instances to interpret Soviet gas exports as secondary in importance, when compared to the domestic industry. This

159

Table 5
Gas consumption in the USSR per sector 1984.

	Bcm	Percent share	Growth 1983-84 %	Share of increment
Residential-Communal	64.3	13.9	6.4	15.3
of this to the population	23.0	5.0		
Industry	223.0	48.2	10.6	25.4
Of this:				
Chemical Industry	47.9	10.4	3.0	
Ferro-metallic	45.1	9.7	1.9	
Machine and metalworking	34.3	7.4	1.5	
Non ferro	8.4	1.8	0.0	
Construction materials	30.9	6.7	1.1	
Oil and gas industry	29.4	6.4		
Other industry	27.0	5.8		
Power stations	156.7	33.9	22.0	52.8
Other	18.8	4.0	2.7	6.5
Total	462.8	100.0	41.7	100.0

Source: Podgotovka i pererabotka gaza i gazovogo kondensata, 2, 1986. These data have been drawn to our attention by Matthew Sagers, see PlanEcon Report, 2, 1987.

relationship can be easily illustrated by the relative size of exports versus domestic consumption. In 1985 the USSR exported 12 per cent of its natural gas production, 5.4 per cent to Western markets.

The gas industry is the newcomer among Soviet fuel industries. Coal and oil are much older and have traditionally been the dominant fuels. In fact coal was the most important fuel until 1968. Gas has experienced a rapid development since the mid-fifties and in 1985 it became the most important fuel in domestic energy consumption measured in energy equivalents.

The distribution of gas consumption in the USSR is somewhat different from the structure in other industrialized countries. Households and the communal sector have a much lower share, and industry a correspondingly larger one. The share of gas used in power generation is also relatively high.

Still, in 1985 78.3 per cent of all living space was supplied with gas.[14] The number of gasified apartments increased by more than twenty million from 1975 to 1985, totalling 63.6 million that year.[15] According to the Soviet Gas Minister more than 80 per cent, 214 million of the population, already use gas in their homes (82 per cent in cities and 77 per cent in rural areas).[16] But to a large extent gas is used only for cooking. It should be kept in mind that heating in the cities is taken care of mainly by district heating (cogenerating power stations). This means that the ultimate potential for direct use of gas in households is smaller than in Western cities of comparable size.

As indicated in the table above, industry is also well penetrated by gas. In particular some industries have a very high gas share in their energy consumption: cast iron and open-hearth steel, 93 per cent; rolled steel, 50 per cent; steel pipes, almost 100 per cent; cement, 60 per cent; ammonia, over 85 per cent; methanol, 72 per cent; fire-proof material, almost 100 per cent (data for 1984).[17] Even if there still is a potential for more gas in Soviet industry, the growth in total gas consumption will be steeper outside the industrial sector.

In power generation the potential is still large. In 1980, 125 mt of mazut (heavy fuel oil) were burned in power stations, i.e. one third of total primary energy consumption in power stations. According to a Soviet analysis[18], at least half of this, 63 mt, could fairly easily be replaced with natural gas, since a large number of power stations are designed for dual use, oil and gas. They use gas in the summer when supplies are ample and oil in the winter when gas consumption elsewhere is peaking.

The bottleneck in changing them to gas on a year-round basis is the construction of distribution lines and gas storage facilities. The total capacity of gas storage in 1980 was only 5 per cent of total production. The underdevelopment of storage facilities reflects the initial understanding of natural gas as a supplementing fuel in sectors primarily fuelled by ample coal and oil. Dual use was considered cheaper than storage in evening out supply fluctuations.[19] If more storage capacity is created more oil and coal can be replaced. In addition to the substitution programme, the construction of new gas-fired power stations will continue to increase power generation's share of total gas consumption.

The question has been raised if it is possible to absorb the vast amounts of natural gas coming on stream in the years ahead. Our answer is that there is still much more oil and coal that can be replaced on a normal energy efficient basis. But in addition to this potential, we see signs that the Soviet authorities will embark on an even more radical substitution strategy, using gas for purposes that are deemed uneconomical in the West for price reasons, e.g. for transportation. Given the cost picture in Soviet fuel production and the reserve situation, this may still be a reasonable way to overcome supply problems. In addition, such a strategy can make it possible to maintain or even increase oil exports.

Soviet Interest in Gas Exports

Table 6 presents an overview of the present state of Soviet gas exports and estimates to the year 2000.

Table 6

Soviet gas exports 1982-2000 (bcm).

	1982	1983	1984	1985	1990	1995	2000
Total	60.6	64.2	68.8	75.8	105.9	123.3	132.6
Eastern Europe	32.7	35.6	36.8	41.1	52.0	64.0	72.5
CMEA-6	29.6	32.5	33.1	37.5	47.0	57.5	64.5
Yugoslavia	2.1	3.1	3.7	3.7	5.0	6.5	8.0
Western Europe via							
Czechoslovakia	**26.8**	**28.0**	**31.2**	**33.2**	**48.4**	**49.1**	**48.6**
Federal Republic							
of Germany*	10.3	11.1	13.5	13.5	19.5	20.7	20.7
France	4.1	4.1	6.0	7.4	12.0	12.0	12.0
Italy	9.3	8.5	7.7	8.3	12.0	13.0	12.0
Austria	3.1	4.3	4.0	4.5	4.5	3.0	3.5
Switzerland	—	—	—	—	0.4	0.4	0.4
Others	1.0	0.7	0.8	1.0	5.5	10.3	11.5
Greece	—	—	—	—	0.8	2.0	3.0
Turkey	—	—	—	—	3.0	6.0	6.0
Finland	1.0	0.7	0.8	1.0	1.7	2.3	2.5

* Including Berlin (West).

Sources: 1982-85: Calculated from *International Energy Statistical Review,* 27 January, 1987; 1990-2000: Own estimates based on contracts and scattered information.

As can be seen from Tables 6 and 7, revenues from gas exports have stagnated over the last years. Volumes will, however, rise until deliveries under the last round of contracts reach plateau level in the early nineties.

Table 7
Soviet hard currency revenue from gas exports
(mill. USD*).

	1982	1983	1984	1985
OECD-countries, total	3,757	3,267	3,827	3,900
Federal Republic of Germany				
[incl. Berlin (West)]	1,456	1,349	1,545	1,655
Italy	1,220	1,018	1,074	745
France	537	499	622	837
Austria	434	306	487	561
Finland**	106	95	99	102
Share of total exports to Western industrialized countries:				
	14.5%	12.3%	14.6%	17.5%

* Not all the gas is paid for in US dollars, however, and some of the fluctuations in income must be ascribed to changes in the exchange rate between dollars and European currencies.

** Finnish imports are not paid in hard currency, but are part of a clearing arrangement. The goods exported from Finland are of "hard currency" standard, however, and we therefore find it correct to include Finland in the hard currency group.

Calculated on the basis of *Vneshnyaya Torgovlya SSSR,* various years, adjusted for changes in the rouble/dollar exchange rate.

Soviet expectations concerning the development of their exports to a large extent correspond with general expectations about market developments in the West. The Soviets had additional reasons for hoping for a rapidly expanding gas market since their oil industry was in trouble. Oil exports had increased during the seventies and due to the price hikes on the world market the USSR gained windfall profits. In the early eighties production problems became imminent, and it was widely held that oil exports would have to decline at some point in the eighties. This, together with a positive outlook for gas, combined to form the conventional wisdom about Soviet energy exports from the early eighties, namely that gas would, within some years, replace oil as the major hard currency earner for the country.

The development so far has proved to be different on both accounts. True enough, Soviet oil production has been more or less flat since 1980. But still it has been possible to set aside larger volumes for

163

exports. This must be explained by the pivotal importance of oil in Soviet trade, necessitating a very strong priority for oil exports. At the same time, the development of the gas market has taken a gentler path than anticipated. Consequently, gas has not become the most important source of hard currency, but it constitutes a solid number two.

The figures above include only « ordinary » Soviet foreign trade. Additional hard currency is earned from exports of gold and, to some extent, arms. In this total picture the role of gas apparently is not so great. It must be kept in mind, however, that the alternatives are few. The USSR has not been successful in diversifying its exports. Gas is still promising, in terms of future potential, and it can be safely concluded that gas exports are treated very seriously by the Soviet leadership. It must be considered of utmost national significance to preserve the country's image as a reliable gas supplier and to work for larger market shares and penetration of new markets.

Soviet foreign trade will be treated elsewhere at this conference. In this context it suffices to say that there is no evidence that the commercial interests behind Soviet gas exports are decreasing, even if a more critical attitude towards technology imports is adopted and the burden of grain imports becomes cheaper because of the weak grain market and possible improvements in agricultural performance. The costs of maintaining or increasing oil exports are soaring, and any contribution to ease the pressure on oil would be welcome. But such a comparison is largely theoretical since, at present oil prices, both oil and gas exports are maximized. If oil prices started to climb rapidly, however, a comparison of costs and benefits of exporting the two fuels could possibly be undertaken in the new domestic economic environment. Earlier it has been suggested in Soviet economic debate that oil exports should be given priority over gas because oil fetches a higher price per calorific unit than gas does. We believe that the reserve situation and the cost picture would overcome this argument, if ever such a comparison were to be made.

Hence, the limitations on Soviet gas exports are not, and will not be, domestic considerations, but the market situation. The market situation is again composed of economic and political factors, both representing a challenge to Soviet exporters.

Political Considerations in Relation to Exports of Natural Gas

The commercial interests in gas exports have been described above. There has, however, been voiced opposition against excessive dependence on gas exports on a political basis.[20] The main argument seems to have been that growing exports automatically entailed reliance on imported Western technology. But more « nationalistic » concerns have also been indicated. Former Prime Minister Aleksei Kosygin was said to be opposed to selling the resources of the country off to capitalist countries.[21] From a military point of view it is obvious that reliance on NATO countries for important export outlets has negative aspects. The inflexibility of gas exports through pipelines could give a potential for some sort of political pressure if the dependence rose too high. This reasoning is a parallel to some of the concerns expressed on the Western side. The reports about such opposition are sparse, however, and it has certainly not gained much momentum, underlining the importance of the commercial motivation. The political obstacles for Soviet gas exports are therefore mainly to be found in the relationships with Western importing countries and the West as a whole.

A widely held goal for Soviet policy towards Western Europe is to tie these countries closer to the USSR.[22] Gas exports seem to be a perfect tool for achieving such a goal. The commitments and the long time-perspective of a gas contract pave the way for stable relationships between seller and buyer. In addition there is the potential for industrial imports from the countries taking gas, broadening the relations.

Another Soviet goal, which seems fairly obvious, is to use any opportunity to drive a wedge into the relationship between Western Europe and the United States. Again gas exports have been effective. Soviet exports to Western Europe, particularly the last round of contracts in the early eighties, created serious tensions within the Western alliance. The damage was, however, to a large extent self-inflicted. The political benefit to the USSR, in terms of intra-alliance tensions, must be regarded as a positive side-effect of the gas exports, rather than a prime motivation for them (the Soviets can hardly have foreseen this).

During the pipeline dispute imports of Soviet natural gas were criticized for several reasons. The most far reaching allegation was that increased imports from the USSR would make Western Europe vulnerable to Soviet political blackmail. By threatening to turn off the tap the USSR would be able to gain important political concessions.[23] This argument was disputed by the European countries, partly by pointing to the limited role Soviet gas would play in the overall energy picture, even if new contracts were signed.[24]

Another way of approaching the problem is to ask what risks the USSR would run if it were to use gas exports as a political weapon. An interruption of Soviet supplies would no doubt create problems in at least some markets. But the growing integration of the West European gas market in terms of infrastructure and swap-deals will make it all but impossible to single out specific countries for blackmail in the future. Consequently a number of important Western countries would be affected. Should such actions nevertheless be undertaken, the Soviet Union would be excluded as a serious supplier for a very long time. Given the economic significance of gas exports, it seems unlikely that the USSR would be willing to run such a risk. In our judgement a cut-off would only be likely in the wake of a military conflict. And in such a context cuts in gas supplies would be a minor problem.[25] This argument rests on the assumption that the Soviet Union does not become a clearly dominant supplier to the West European market, but retains a position as one of a group of important suppliers.

According to this reasoning the more gas the USSR exports, the more dependent it becomes on maintaining a reputation as a secure and stable supplier. An interesting corollary is that the country's dependence and vulnerability becomes a strength since it underlines its reliability as a supplier.

The country does have a reputation, however, for using energy exports to exert political pressure. In the late fifties and early sixties the country used cuts in oil deliveries as a political weapon against countries like Yugoslavia and Israel.[26] However, this was in a period when the country's oil exports were of only minor importance to the economy, indeed total Soviet foreign trade was much smaller than today. The markets affected were marginal and the economic costs very limited. In addition, reliability is even more important in gas trade than in international oil trade, due to the long term commitments and the inflexible infrastructure. (Energy has also been used as a political tool within the CMEA, but relations within the Eastern alliance are of a completely different nature from relations with hard currency countries, thus limiting the relevance of such examples in our context.)

Still, memories of actions taken by the Soviets 25-30 years ago, as well as the country's reputation for dumping oil, have haunted the Soviets since. They were, for instance, raised again by the IEA in 1982.[27] It seems fair to observe that Soviet exporters have worked hard over recent years to shed this reputation and to avoid any actions that can give reason for new suspicion.

However, this may be a fairly sophisticated way of reasoning within the Soviet system. Although it may be obvious to people dealing with Soviet exports, other parts of the bureaucracy may see the potential for political use and forget about the costs. An indication of this surfaced in the autumn of 1984, when a trade union official announced a Soviet fuel boycott of the United Kingdom, because of the ongoing miners strike. The statement was quickly denied by authoritative sources in Moscow, but the fact that such a statement passed through the censorship and probably through other bodies as well, indicates that the country's sensitivity in these questions is not universally perceived in the Soviet Union.[28] Consequently, the argument above that the Soviet Union will refrain from using gas as a political weapon because of its vulnerability in hard currency trade, rests on the assumption that questions concerning gas exports are treated by the competent foreign trade bodies.

Another question is to what extent the Soviet Union can and will use a strong position in the market to gain better commercial conditions. In this respect it is difficult to see that the country would behave in any other way than another supplier would in a similar position, except that in the real world it is difficult to discriminate between commercial and political pressure. In the case of the USSR, actions that would have been seen as commercial if performed by other exporters, will easily be interpreted as political, with the potential damage mentioned above. This is a problem Soviet gas exporters must take into consideration; it may reduce the country's leeway in the market, compared with other large exporters.

The Record

As indicated above, the general opinion among gas traders in Europe seems to be that the Soviet Union has become a professional and reliable member of «the gas family». However, there have been scattered reports about technical difficulties in gas deliveries. For example, in the winter of 1984-85 serious shortfalls allegedly occurred, particularly in deliveries to the Federal Republic and Austria. A short-fall of one third in the winter of 1981, due to compressor breakdown, is reported by Stern.[29] Confirmation of the actual size of the reductions is hard to come by, since the importers of Soviet gas do not reveal negative information about one supplier that could be used to strengthen the hand of other suppliers in ongoing or future negotiations. However, shortfalls in the winter season are understandable for the following reason: it seems that the Soviets have insufficient capacity to monitor the actual flow through the pipelines. One indication of this is that Ruhrgas had to build a station on the Czech-German border to measure content and volumes of the gas.[30] The problems are both within the Soviet Union and in the transit section through Czechoslovakia. Reports indicate that in cold periods valves are opened to a maximum, leading to reduced pressure and throughput at the end of the pipelines.[31] Our assessment of the pipeline capacity does not show any substantial overcapacity either in Uzhgorod at the Czech-Soviet border, or in the transit system through Czechoslovakia. As the winter 1984-85 was very cold, both in the USSR and in Eastern Europe, it is not really surprising that shortfalls occurred. With expansion of pipeline capacity already underway, a repetition of this is less likely, even if deliveries increase, because the relative overcapacity is also growing.

All in all, Soviet export capacity at the borderpoints to West Germany and Austria will amount to 60-70 bcm from 1989-90. This implies an overcapacity of some 12 to 20 bcm, compared with contracted export

167

volumes to West European countries served by these corridors at that time. An evaluation of this overcapacity raises several questions: how much overcapacity is needed for technical emergencies, how much is needed to cover daily fluctuations, how much is needed to cover flexibility in contracts? It is difficult to quantify, but taking all these factors into consideration may imply that the present overcapacity is not overwhelming, and certainly does not give room for large new contracts. But even if the *relative* overcapacity is small, significant *volumes* will be available when the above-mentioned factors do not strain the capacity. This implies that the Soviet Union will be well equipped to deliver additional volumes on a short-term or spot basis.

The Organization of Soviet Gas Exports

Most Soviet foreign trade organizations are regarded as having little influence outside their day-to-day dealings with foreign customers or suppliers. They have little or no influence on the producing ministries; institutionally most of them are subordinate to the Ministry of Foreign Trade. Indeed, this is a rather common concern in discussions about the problems of Soviet foreign trade. It is very hard, if not impossible, to channel reactions and demand from the markets abroad to the domestic factory. In addition to the institutional problem, the domestic producers have few incentives for accommodating the foreign trade demands that might reach them. Production for export may imply stricter controls on production without any reciprocal rewards. It may be easier and less risky for factory managers to stay away from exports and instead devote the production to the insatiable and less discriminating domestic demand. This is the reason why new institutional arrangements for foreign trade have been proposed, reducing the role of the foreign trade organizations and allowing more direct contacts between enterprises and the foreign markets.

Gas exports differ from the general picture in a number of ways. Gas in itself is not a sophisticated commodity. Just as for other raw materials, the contact between market and producer is not that important, except for delivery and, to some extent, composition. (Admittedly, there are also some special gases.) This is probably the main reason why gas, and indeed all raw material exports, are exempted from the foreign trade reform.[32]

However, Soyuzgazexport, the gas exports organization, from the outset faces the same problem in securing supplies from the producer, the Ministry of the Gas Industry (Mingazprom), as other foreign trade organizations. In connection with long-term gas contracts this is extremely important. Given the significance of gas exports, it is reasonable to expect that Soyuzgazexport has a strong say internally from the outset, but that may still not suffice to give the organization the relative autonomy and flexibility needed for efficient export marketing. But after many years of activity it now seems clear that the organization has achieved a relatively autonomous position within the Soviet system. There are several indications of this : a complicated floor-price and contract price system used to be part of Soviet gas contracts.[33] The purpose of this device was to stabilize revenues over time. It was widely held that this was a mechanism introduced for planning purposes by Gosplan, which is very much concerned with predictability. The concepts, if not really hampering Soviet sales efforts, served as a constant reminder of the peculiarities of the Soviet economic system, and made it difficult for Soyuzgazexport to gain acceptance as a « businesslike » actor in the gas market. It is therefore interesting to note that the concept has now been quietly abandoned. We see this as an indication of the prevalence of Soyuzgazexport's view over the traditional Gosplan stance.

Another important development is the reported flexibility in Soviet gas contracts, 20 per cent below and above the contracted yearly volume. Allegedly, this was a response to the flexibility introduced in the new Dutch contracts, but Soyuzgazexport claims that it introduced this measure first. Apparently, this flexibility is now extended to all Soviet contracts. In any case, this is also a factor that does not fit well into Soviet planning, but it shows readiness to adapt to the demands of the market.

Lastly, the behaviour of Soviet gas-sellers has made them acceptable as members of the exclusive « gas club » consisting of major traders in the West European gas market, a position a country like Algeria has not been able to achieve. Soyuzgazexport representatives behave professionally and with self-assurance, which is not always the case for Soviet foreign traders.

It has been argued, e.g. by Deputy Minister of Foreign Trade N. Osipov, that gas from the more costly fields should capture a higher price on the market.[34] This line of thinking, somewhat akin to the abandoned Norwegian argument for a premium price for the North Sea fields, shows that the commercial « Soyuzgazexport line » has not totally prevailed in Soviet thinking about gas exports. But this should hardly surprise us in a system where commerciality and market orientation are all but unknown concepts.

In theory Soyuzgazexport buys the gas from the Gas Ministry at the border. Basically the price, paid in rubles, is the same as for domestic consumers, but because the quality of the export gas is somewhat higher than usual, Soyuzgazexport has to add a premium. The gas is then sold abroad and the organization receives enough money to cover its expenses, as it operates on a so-called « khozrashchot », or self-financing basis.

Most of the money is channelled through the ordinary ways of the Soviet foreign trade system and finally ends up in the treasury to be allocated for foreign imports, or downpayment of loans.

So, formally, the gas export does not differ from other Soviet exports. But in reality there are important features that put gas trade in a special position. One is the sheer size: gas exports are one of the cornerstones of Soviet foreign trade, as mentioned earlier. But another important aspect is the alliance that has been built up between the producer, the Ministry of the Gas Industry (Mingazprom) and the seller (Soyuzgazexport).

As described above, the lack of contact between producer and seller constitutes a serious problem in Soviet foreign trade. In the gas industry, large-scale planning decisions is the major signal to make volumes of gas available for export. However, this may not always suffice to induce the producer to provide the internal « security of supply » that is necessary for the seller to become a reliable partner in the foreign markets.

What then are the incentives given to the gas industry? Obviously it is not the price. The ruble price paid to the ministry is largely irrelevant. We believe that the structure of the gas sales is more interesting. The typical reference in Soviet literature to the gas deals is that they are on « a compensation basis ».[35] This means that the sale of gas is closely related to imports of pipe and equipment to the gas industry. This view is clearly different from the perspective of the Western companies, who at least formally tend to view the gas deals separate from equipment exports, and try to avoid allegations of countertrade, which is a very negative concept in the free trade system. For the Soviets, countertrade, compensation, barter and other overlapping terms, i.e. linking exports and imports, have no negative connotations. On the contrary, they represent the normal forms of foreign trade. Theoretically, any actor in foreign trade would prefer export contracts with no strings attached, compared to deals involving countertrade, provided he can sell the same volumes for the same price in both cases. This also goes for the Soviet Union as long as we treat the country as one single, unified actor. But for any actor a deal involving countertrade may be more tempting than one that does not, when it allows larger volumes to be exported. And it seems fair to argue that Soviet gas exporters have used prospects of large scale industrial imports from the buyers of Soviet gas as a way to promote Soviet exports of gas.

These countertrade prospects have first and foremost involved large diameter pipe needed for adding additional pipeline capacity. But it has also encompassed equipment beyond the needs for exports.[36] It can safely be claimed that gas exports have played a major role in the development of the gas industry domestically. The exports have given the industry access to equipment that has benefitted the gas sector as a whole, and the foreign supplies have at times helped the gas industry avoid the recurrent bottlenecks in the Soviet production and supply system. Thus, the Soviet gas industry, unlike many other Soviet industries, has a strong self interest in exports.

As long as countertrade arrangements are used to obtain goods that the Soviets otherwise would have to buy for hard currency, the interest of the Soviet economy does not differ from that of the sub-actor, the gas industry. But since countertrade benefits the gas industry to such an extent, the industry easily develops its own institutional interest in using it for marketing of gas. And the question could be raised if this has not led to purchases of equipment that could have been supplied by domestic or East European manufacturers. The sharp turnaround in Soviet equipment production after the pipeline-sanctions suggests that there was an underutilized potential in Soviet industry. However, the tacit « alliance » between producer and seller is vital for Soviet gas exports and helps explain the progress the Soviets have made during the eighties in the European gas market.

The Structure of the Market

From the outset the international gas trade seemed to fit the Soviet economic system almost perfectly. The long-term, stable trade relations established by the contracts match the Soviet planning system almost perfectly, and certainly much better than most other forms of foreign trade. The traditional gas contracts are also advantageous to the USSR, because they can rather easily be linked with countertrade, for which the centralized Soviet system is well suited.

The market has, however, developed in a direction contrary to these basic Soviet needs and interests : more flexibility and repeated renegotiations are precisely the features of international trade that do not go well with Soviet economic planning. Still, we have seen a convincing Soviet performance in adapting to the market, something we attribute to the position of Soyuzgazexport. The question is now whether the USSR will lead the transformation of the market structure and take advantage of that, or if it will hold back to avoid a development that will increase the problems of adapting the trade to the internal Soviet structure. We will argue that the Soviet Union structurally is well equipped to offer short term and spot supplies. Using the extra capacity in the pipelines that is necessary for peak periods, to supply short term, could give the USSR a strong competitive edge. Moreover, by more use of short term and spot contracts, the Soviets could evade some of the obstacles to increased market shares in Germany, France, and Italy. The « 30 % limit » will probably not be used against supplies of this kind. The political obstacles against long term contracts with the USSR in some

171

new markets will also be less if the market has been growing used to spot or short term deliveries first.

Another positive aspect of short term marketing or spot sales for the Soviets is that a development in such a direction will tend to minimize offtake from regular contracts to the lower end of the flexibility range. Thus the market would be characterized by continuous competition, favouring suppliers with large flexibility.

On the other hand a development as described above would reduce the positive characteristics of gas trade for the Soviet system. Such a situation would be very different from the one originally envisaged for Soviet gas exports, namely as a stable currency earner. Even if a development in the direction of shorter term deals opens up advantages to the USSR, there are also substantial risks. The USSR could risk becoming something of a residual supplier or swing producer for political, as well as commercial reasons.

This would expose the Soviets to large fluctuations in gas prices and demand, which is clearly not in their interest. It can also make them more vulnerable to political opposition in the West, as it will be easier to reduce such short term supplies than to change commitments in long term contracts. We have no reason to doubt that Soviet gas dealers are well aware of these dangers.

Consequently, we believe that the USSR will be very wary of using spot deals and only use them when they do not compete with long term gas contracts. However, even if we do not see the Soviets leading the way in restructuring the market, they will be able to follow if such a development is forced upon them. But so far they are more comfortable with the present structure.[37]

Conclusion

This paper has treated both domestic and external aspects of the Soviet gas sector. Historically there has been a strong relationship between the two aspects. Imported equipment has played a significant role in the industry, whereas the relative ease with which the Soviets have made their offers in the European market, has been made possible by the huge build-up of the domestic industry. This relationship is in a way weaker today, with less dependence on imported technology, and with gas exports becoming a goal in themselves, not merely an extension of the domestic development of the industry.

The economic reforms announced so far have mainly been geared towards manufacturing industries and public consumption. Reforms affecting the extractive industries in general, and the gas industry in particular, have so far had a limited scope, changing the system of cost accounting in individual enterprises, or reorganizing the work force.[38] Important as such changes may be, they do not touch the really important and difficult problems facing the industry, namely the priorities between different fuel industries and conservation. The fuel industries constitute one of the pillars on which the present economic system is resting. Any «experiment» on a large scale cannot be allowed, because the negative consequences if a reform backfires will be too great. Hence the paradox: because of their importance, the fuel industries may become the object of serious reforms only at a late stage. The economic environment makes the gas industry follow a well trodden and dangerous path domestically.

The external part of the gas sector, the exporters, have been successful in exploiting the European gas market. They have skillfully adapted to prevailing trends in the market, and made themselves respected players. This position has probably been achieved through negotiating their position domestically as well. The market itself, however, looks less promising for the Soviets than it did only a few years ago. This negative development may ultimately also come to affect the relative independence of Soviet gas exporters. Time will show if they are able to retain their present position if they fail to come up with increased foreign currency revenues.

In the market itself the USSR has gained acceptance as a major and legitimate supplier of gas to the Continent. This does not mean that political disputes on the exact size of imports from the country are excluded, but that the main challenge now is of a commercial character.

NOTES

1. Thane Gustafson: «Soviet Adaptation to Technological Pressures: The Case of the Oil and Gas Sector, 1975-85», in Philip Joseph (ed): *Adaptability to New Technologies of the USSR and East European Countries*, NATO Colloquium, Brussels, 1985.
2. *BP Statistical Review of World Energy,* June 1986 and *International Petroleum Encyclopedia,* vol. 17, Tulsa, Pennwell Publishing Co., 1984, respectively.
3. Jonathan P. Stern: *Soviet Natural Gas Development to 1990,* Lexington, Lexington Books, 1980, p. 28.
4. See e.g. *Sovietskaya Rossia,* 13 March 1982. Before this there were plans to start production much earlier, see Thane Gustafson: *The Soviet Gas Campaign,* Santa Monica, Rand, 1983.
5. «V stroyu - Yamburg», *Sotsialisticheskaya Industriya,* 10 Sept. 1986.
6. See e. g. «Ispytyvayet Zapolyarye», *Sotsialisticheskaya Industriya,* 10 Sept. 1985.
7. «Dobychnye rezervy mestorozhdeniya Medvezhye», *Gazovaya Promyshlennost,* 6, 1986.
8. «Yamal: pervoocheredniye zadachi osvoeniya», *Gazovaya Promyshlennost,* 1, 1987.
9. «Osvoenya Yamala - kompleksnuyu nauchno-tekhnicheskuyu podgotovku», *Stroitelstvo Truboprovodov,* 1, 1987.
10. Ryzhkov's speech in *Pravda,* 19 June, 1986.
11. *Sotsialisticheskaya Industriya,* 9 Sept. 1985.
12. Viktor Chernomyrdin: «The Present State and Future Development of the USSR Gas Industry», paper presented at the 16th World Gas Conference, Munich, June 25, 1985.
13. Albina Tretyakova and Meredith Heinemeier: «Cost Estimates for the Soviet Gas Industry: 1970 to 1990», *CIR Staff Paper,* Washington, Bureau of the Census, 1986.
14. *Narodnoye Khozyaistvo 1985,* Moscow, Finansy i Statistika, p. 430.
15. Ibid.
16. Chernomyrdin, op. cit.
17. Ibid.
18. L.A. Melentyev and A.A. Makarov: *Energeticheski Kompleks* SSSR, Moscow, Ekonomika, 1983.

19. Matthew Sagers and Albina Tretyakova: «Constraints in Gas for Oil Substitution in the USSR: The Oil Refining Industry and Gas Storage», *Soviet Economy*, 1, 1986.
20. Bruce Parrott: «Soviet Foreign Policy, Internal Politics and Trade with the West», in B. Parrott (ed.): *Trade, Technology and Soviet-American Relations*, Bloomington, Indiana University Press, 1985, p. 48-49.
21. See a vivid account of this in Arkady Shevchenko: *Breaking with Moscow*, New York, Ballantine Books, 1985, p. 284.
22. See e.g. Angela Stent: «Economic Strategy» in Edvina Moreton and Gerald Segal (eds): *Soviet Strategy Towards Western Europe*, London, George Allen & Unwin, 1984.
23. For a broad discussion of the pipeline controversy and related topics, see *The Premises of East-West Commercial Relations*, A Workshop sponsored by the Committee on Foreign Relations, UnitedStates Senate, and Congressional Research Service, Library of Congress,1982
24. In a Soviet article, the same line of arguments are used, V. Klochek: «Vneshnyaya Torgovlya v 1983 godu», *Vneshnyaya Torgovlya*, 5, 1984.
25. See also the discussion in Jonathan P. Stern: *International Gas Trade in Europe*, London: Heinemann Educational Books, 1984, p. 59.
26. See Arthur Jay Klinghoffer, *The Soviet Union and International Oil Politics*, New York: Cambridge University Press, 1977. The issue is treated extensively in Jonathan P. Stern: *Soviet Oil and Gas Exports to the West: Commercial Transaction or Security Threat*, London, Gower, 1987.
27. *Natural Gas Prospects to 2000*, IEA, 1982, p. 22-23. The USSR is here together with OAPEC described as having used oil for political pressure. This warning is, however, not repeated in the most recent IEA gas study.
28. «Russia Embargoes Fuel to Britain», *The Times*, Oct. 31, 1984 and «Soviet Denies U.K. Energy Embargo», *International Herald Tribune*, Nov. 5, 1984.
29. Stern, 1984, op. cit.
30. E. Benke: «Der Ausbau der Erdgastransportsystems der MEGAL», *Erdoel-Erdgas*, 3, 1984.
31. Jonathan Stern, 1987, *op. cit.*, p. 55, ascribes the shortfalls to deliberate priorities by Gosplan for domestic, as opposed to foreign customers. We believe however that there is also an important element of lack of control here.
32. See «O merakh po korennomy sovershenstvovaniyu vneshneekonomicheskoy deyatelnosti», *Sotsialisticheskaya Industriya*, 23 Sept. 1986.
33. See e.g. Stern, 1984, op. cit.
34. N. Osipov: «Perspektivy Eksporta SSSR», *Vneshnyaya Torgovlya*, 2, 1985.
35. I.S. Bagramiyan and A.F. Shakai: *Kontrakt veka*, Moscow, Politizdat, 1984.
36. See Ed Hewett: «Near term prospects for the Soviet Gas Industry and Implications for Foreign Trade», Joint Economic Committee, U.S. Congress, Washington, 1982. Thane Gustafson: *The Soviet Gas Campaign*, Santa Monica, Rand, 1983; Gustafson, 1983; John B. Hannigan & Carl H. McMillan: *The Soviet - West European Energy Relationship: Implications of the Shift from Oil to Gas*, Ottawa, Carleton University Research Report, 1983.
37. For a broader discussion of Soviet gas exports to the West see Helge Ole Bergesen, Javier Estrada, Arild Moe and Anne Kristin Sydnes: *Natural Gas in Western Europe: Markets, Organisation, and Politics*, Forthcoming 1988, Frances Pinler (publishers), London.
38. See e.g. «Khozyaystvennaya Reforma - Osnova uskoreniya», *Gazovaya Promyshlennost*, 1, 1987.

Energy Policy in the USSR: A New Course?

Jochen Bethkenhagen

1. *Preliminary Remarks*

The subject of this analysis is Soviet energy policy under the new political leadership. Taking into consideration the results of the 27th Party Congress and of the 12th Five-Year Plan adopted in June 1986, we will examine, among other things, if, and which, changes of the trend are developing in Soviet energy policy. In this context we will have to assess in particular whether (a) there is a transition from a supply-oriented to a demand-oriented policy and whether (b) coal and nuclear energy will, within the next few years, partially replace oil as a fuel. This study will be focused on the coal and nuclear energy sectors because the energy sources oil and natural gas are the subject of two other papers during this colloquium.

2. *The Results of the 11th Five-Year Plan (1981-85)*

The results of the energy sector have by no means been encouraging during the 1981-85 Five-Year Plan.[1] The production targets were clearly missed for all energy sources, except for natural gas with an output exceeding the target (see also tables A1 to A4 at Annex).

The importance of natural gas in the generation of primary energy increased further. Its contribution to the output from domestic resources rose from approximately one quarter to one third. Although the nuclear energy proportion doubled to 2.5%, it remained insignificant in international comparison. Crude oil and coal lost importance although, with a proportion of 38%, oil continued to be the most important energy source of the Soviet Union.

Jochen Bethkenhagen

Table 1
Production of primary energy in the Soviet Union.
Target of the Five-Year Plan and actual output in 1985.

	Unit	Target	Actual	Difference	Actual output in % of target
Coal (net)	Mn tons	700	648	− 52	92.6
Crude oil	Mn tons	630	595	− 35	94.4
Natural gas	Bn m³	630	643	+ 13	102.1
Nuclear energy	Bn kWh	220	167	− 53	75.9
Hydropower	Bn kWh	230	215	− 15	93.5
Total (¹)	Mn tons of coal equivalent	2.323	2.232	− 91	96.1

(¹) Including wood, peat, shale.

Table 2
*Production of primary energy in the Soviet Union
(per cent).*

	Crude oil	Natural gas	Hard coal [1]	Brown coal [1]	Nuclear energy	Hydropower	Others
1980	44.0	26.4	19.6	3.4	1.2	3.1	2.1
1985	38.2	34.3	17.3	2.9	2.5	3.2	1.8
1990 [2]	34.1	38.0	16.0	2.7	4.8	3.0	1.5
1990 [3]	34.3	38.7	16.2	2.7	3.5	3.1	1.5

[1] Net output.
[2] According to five-year plan targets.
[3] Estimates.

The power station capacity of approximately 29,000 MW installed up to late 1985 clearly remained below the target of 39,000 MW, i.e. by approximately one quarter, which caused the Chairman of the Ministerial Council of the USSR, N.I. Ryzkhov, to utter straightforward criticism on the occasion of the 27th Party Congress of the CPSU: «In the course of the 11th Five-Year Plan period the USSR Ministry of the Power Industry fell short of its targets in starting up nuclear power plants, which created an additional demand for fossil fuels. Taking into account our country's strained fuel balance and the growing role of nuclear power generation, setbacks of this kind are impermissible in future».[2]

The chronic backlogs in the construction of nuclear power plants are largely due to deficiencies in planning and implementation of capital expenditures. Serious mistakes in the construction of the reactor plant «Atomasch» as well as in some nuclear power stations including, inter alia, the Chernobyl plant, have become known. Frequently the shortage of material, labour and transport resources prevents the timely completion of capacities.[3] In mid-1984 the Politburo was forced to adopt «additional measures for the improvement of reliability and safety of nuclear power stations». Moreover, a State Committee for Safety in the Nuclear Power Industry was created in 1983. Presumably, there are thus specific problems concerning both safety and costs in addition to the usual investment problems of the Soviet economy.[4] As a matter of fact, considerable overruns of expenditures planned for the construction of nuclear power stations are also typical in the West where they, too, frequently cause considerable delays in completion.

When considering overall primary energy production, it has to be said that the target has been missed by approximately 100 million tons of coal equivalent. A growth rate of only 2.6% was reached instead of an annual average of 3.6% as planned. Thus, productions growth has again slowed down.

Table 3
Primary energy production of the Soviet Union.
Annual average growth in %.

1971-1975	5.3
1976-1980	4.2
1981-1985	2.6
1986-1990 (Plan)	3.6

This result is unsatisfactory, especially since capital expenditures for the fuel industries (crude oil, natural gas, coal) were increased, i.e. by just over 50%, under the 11th Five-Year Plan as compared with the 10th Five-Year Plan. Accordingly, the share of the fuel industries in overall industrial investments rose from 21 to 27% (see Table A5 at Annex).

The above-average allocation of investment capital for an extension of fuel production may also be seen as support for the thesis that planners were disappointed by the outcome of their efforts regarding energy savings and, therefore, continued to advocate a supply-oriented energy policy. In the existing organizational framework conditions this appeared to be the safe choice.

3. *The 12th Five-Year Plan:*
Expedited Growth of Primary Energy Generation

This theory is also supported by the targets adopted by the Supreme Soviet in June 1986. These targets suggest that growth in the production of primary energy (fuels plus nuclear energy and hydropower) will still be clearly accelerated during the period from 1986 through 1990 (3.6% p.a.) in comparison to growth developments during the first half of the eighties (2.6% p.a.).

Table 4
Production of primary energy in the Soviet Union in 1985, 1986 and the 1990 target.

	Unit	Actual		Target		Growth 1990/85	
		1985	1986	1987	1990	Mn tons of coal equivalent	in %
Coal (net) [1]	mn tons	648	675	670	715	46	10.3
Coal (gross)	mn tons	726	751	744	795	46	9.5
Crude oil	mn tons	595	615	617	635	57	6.7
Natural gas	bn m^3	643	686	712	850	246	32.2
Nuclear energy [2]	bn kWh	167	162	184	390	74	133.5
Hydropower [2]	bn kWh	215	215	226	245	10	14.0
Others [3]	mn tons of coal equivalent	39	39	39	40	1	2.6
Total	mn tons of coal equivalent	2.232	2.330	2.372	2.666	434	19.4

[1] Estimated net production from 1986 through 1990 (90% of gross production).
[2] 1986 and 1987 estimates.
[3] Wood, peat, shale; 1986 and 1990 estimates.

180

Natural gas is to account for more than one half of production growth. In the event of the targets being achieved, natural gas would become the most important energy source of the Soviet Union and increase its share in production from 34 % (1985) to 37 % (see Table 2). Crude oil is to lose further importance and account for only one third of primary energy production by 1990 (1985 : 38 %).

3.1. *Chernobyl : Irritation but no Change of Course*

Apparently, the Chernobyl disaster has not affected planning for an extension of nuclear power stations. However, the chances for the implementation of the plan are meagre. Just two months after the accident the Supreme Soviet decided to increase generation of atomic power from 167 billion to 390 billion kWh within five years. Thus, the proportion of nuclear energy in overall power generation is to rise from 11 % in 1985 to 21 % by 1990 (Table A6 at Annex). In this way, nuclear energy would account for 6 % of overall primary energy production. This objective would imply an extension of nuclear power capacities by approximately 40,000 MW, which means that eight 1,000 MW reactors would have to be started up every year.[5] Chernobyl has, thus, not caused a change of policy but rather some short-term irritation.

Even after the Chernobyl disaster there are mainly three reasons for the Soviet Union to expand nuclear energy :
— Nuclear power stations can be constructed in the immediate vicinity of consumption centres. The high transport costs that would be connected with the expansion of fuel extraction in Siberia will be avoided.
— Currently, nuclear energy is considered to be the only type of energy that could safeguard the Soviet Union's self-sufficient energy supply in the long run.
— The close interdependence between the military and civil use of atomic energy.

The Soviets have always attributed the Chernobyl disaster to human error which is the reason why numerous managers, inter alia the Chairman of the State Committee for Safety in the Nuclear Power Industry, Kulov, and the Deputy Ministery in the Ministry of Power Engineering and Electrification, Shasharin, were dismissed. Moreover, the Politburo decided on the creation of a Ministry for Atomic Energy.[6]

From official Soviet statements[7], it appears that a sequence of serious operating errors, among others the disconnection of the emergency cooling unit, led to the accident and its serious consequences. Against this background no obligation was obviously felt to shut down the other nuclear power stations of the Chernobyl type (pressure tube or RBMK type reactors). By the end of 1985 a total of approximately 16,000 MW,

55 % of the Soviet nuclear power stations, were equipped with pressure tube reactors. The rapid start-up of the first two blocks of the Chernobyl power station, in November and December of 1986, also suggests that no specific changes have been made to the reactor design.

No accurate data regarding nuclear power generation are included in the 1986 plan fulfilment report. However, in comparison to 1985 a decline of only 3 % is being shown for the atomic power industry, which would be equivalent to a production of 162 billion kWh (1985: 167 bn kWh). In view of an average capacity of 26,000 MW p.a. this would, however, mean that the nuclear power stations were operating during 6,230 hours which is equivalent to 71 % of the maximum of the possible time of 8,760 hours p.a. On the whole, the production figure appears to be plausible when considering that:
— the other nuclear power stations were not switched off after the Chernobyl accident;
— the breakdown of the Chernobyl nuclear power station was largely offset by nuclear power stations that came on stream by the end of 1985; and
— load factors of over 75 % had already been reached by Soviet nuclear power stations earlier.[8]

In the short term the consequences of the accident with regard to power supply could thus be contained. The target of 1,605 bn kWh for overall power generation has only been slightly missed with an output of 1,599 bn kWh. However, low water levels have also contributed to the non-fulfilment of the plan by hampering power generation in hydro-power stations. If there have, nevertheless, been complaints in the Soviet press about bottlenecks in power supply during the winter months[9], such shortage was probably not due to inadequate supply but rather to too high demands.

On the other hand, the nuclear accident is likely to cause serious problems for the Soviet electricity industry in the long run:

(i) In 1986 only three new nuclear power blocks became operational: Kalinin, Zaporozska and Rovno (Table A7 at Annex). However, the net increase only amounted to 1,000 MW. If the five-year target is still to be reached, 10,000 MW will have to come on stream each year between 1987 and 1990. This is not likely to happen. Changes will probably be made in the design of new nuclear power stations in order to exclude manipulations of safety equipment such as those carried out by the personnel of the Chernobyl station. This will presumably result both in substantial delays in the completion of reactor blocks and in stricter quality controls during the construction of nuclear power stations. In view of such measures, a capacity increase by 20,000 MW to approximately 50,000 MW by 1990 would already have to be regarded as a success. It would be equivalent to an atomic power generation of approximately 280 bn kWh.

(ii) For the period from 1986 through 1990 the Five-Year Plan provides for the shutdown of old thermal power stations with an overall capacity of 15,000 MW.[10] These modernization measures can presumably not be realized. Even the outdated equipment is urgently needed to make up for at least part of the failures in the nuclear power sector.

There are two implications:
— The consumption of fuels will be higher than envisaged in power stations. If all power stations earmarked for shutdown remain operational, fuel consumption would rise to 20 million tons of oil equivalent p.a.
— The objective of clearly reducing specific fuel consumption in power stations per kWh generated would then hardly be met. Already during the 11th Five-Year Plan no progress was achieved in this respect. The consumption of 326 g of coal equivalent per kWh in 1985 was hardly much lower than that of 328 g of coal equivalent per kWh in 1980.[11]

(iii) The accident of the Chernobyl power station is likely to have frustrated for a long time the hopes of the Soviet power engineering industry to export nuclear power stations to countries outside the CMEA. In this regard it is also doubtful that the talks with China, Syria, Libya and Iraq concerning Soviet deliveries in the next few years will have positive results. Delays will have to be anticipated in agreed exports to the smaller CMEA countries. At the last CMEA meeting in Bucharest in November 1986 the common nuclear energy programme of the smaller countries was conspicuously revised: instead of the 37,000 MW initially planned for 1990, an output of 50,000 MW was adopted as the new target for the year 2000 (1986: approximately 8,000 MW).

Furthermore, three political aspects of the nuclear power station accident should be highlighted although, in the framework of this study, they can only be roughly outlined:
— A new course was introduced in the information policy concerning the accident. The political leadership in Moscow endeavoured not to cover up the accident but to provide domestic and foreign public opinion with information that was relatively open for Soviet conditions.
— The political reactions of the Soviet Union's allies were also noticeable. For instance, the head of the State Office for Nuclear Safety and Radiation Protection of the GDR, Sitzlack, stated in one of the first press releases after the accident: « The GDR has its own national and additional safety provisions ».[12] This could also be

183

interpreted as indirect criticism of the state of Soviet reactor safety technology.

— The Chernobyl accident has made it clear that in civil use of nuclear energy safety is indivisible and that there is an international community which is at risk. The Soviet Union and the other CMEA countries will continue to expand nuclear energy. By East-West cooperation the risks of nuclear energy could certainly be reduced. Existing obstacles in the field of technology transfer policy should, therefore, be reviewed critically as to whether they might eventually be counterproductive for the West.

3.2 *Coal: Go East*

According to the long-term Soviet energy programme, coal is to regain importance for energy supply by the year 2000. In order to reach the planned output of over 1 billion tons[13], reserves in the eastern part of the country are to be especially developed: they account for 73 % of overall Soviet resources (6,400 billion tons), a large part of which can be extracted by open-cast mining.

The long-term programme foresees two phases:

— Up to 1990 the « prerequisites for an intense increase of coal production during the following years » are to be created.
— In the nineties coal is to contribute above average to energy production.

The targets of the 12th Five-Year Plan largely reflect this long-term programme. Up to 1990 gross production is to rise to 795 million tons (net: 715 mn tons), which is still equivalent to below average growth. The proportion of coal in energy production will drop further (18 %; 1985: 20 %), provided the production of other energy sources is on schedule.

A boost in coal production during the 12th Five-Year Plan is to be achieved mainly in the eastern part of the country. Four-fifths of the planned production growth, amounting to approximately 70 million tons, are to be contributed by the three large coal districts of Kuznetsk, Ekibastuz and Kansk-Achinsk alone. Accordingly, the proportion of open-cast mining in overall coal production will also rise. It had already risen from 38 to 42 % during the 11th Five-Year Plan and is to reach approximately 46 % in 1990.

Table 5
Geographical distribution of Soviet coal production
(million metric tons of gross mine output).

	1980	1985	1990 (^{1})	Change 1990 over 1985
USSR	716	726	795	+ 69
Deep-mined	445	421	429	+ 8
Strip-mined	271	305	366	+ 61
Kuznetsk Basin	145	145	160	+ 15
Ekibastuz	67	81	96	+ 15
Kansk-Achinsk	28	41	65	+ 24
Donets Basin	204	197	193	− 4
Other	272	262	281	+ 19

(^{1}) Plan.

Source: Theodore Shabad: News Notes. In: Soviet Geography, April 1986, p. 266. – Energija. No. 12/1986, p. 2.

Soviet coal policy was for a long time dominated by the conflict between the two districts of Kuznetsk and Donets competing for investment capital. Such competition is being fought on the background of two concepts: coal in the *European part* of the Soviet Union has to be won mainly by *underground mining*, where the geological mining conditions are deteriorating, which causes relatively high capital expenditures and production costs. On the other hand, transport expenses are low since the deposits are in the vicinity of the large consumption centres; in the *eastern parts* of the country (Siberia, Central Asia), however, coal can largely be produced by *open-cast mining*. Production costs in open-cast mining are said to be on average about five times lower than in underground mining, labour productivity even ten times higher.[14] However, considerable transport problems are connected with the extension of open-cast mining. Representatives of the Siberian department of the Academy of Sciences in particular have repeatedly pointed out that, for instance, the coal mined in the Kuzbas can still be used economically at a distance of 2,000 km. They also frequently criticized the preference given to the Donets during the seventies.

The «eastern pressure group» has apparently won in this competition. Already in the long-term energy programme, Kuznetsk — as distinct from Donets — is explicitly mentioned in connection with the districts in which mining is to be extended and expedited within the next few years. In the draft directive Donets is also not mentioned, whereas «expedited development» of the coal basins of Kuznetsk, Ekibastuz and Kansk-Achinsk is expressly called for. This course was probably not

185

corrected at the Party Congress of the CPSU, even though a passage was included in the directive that technical conversion and reconstruction were to be « continued » in the Donbas.[16]

After a ten years' stagnation phase coal output in *Kuznetsk* is to be increased by approximately 10 % to 160 million tons by 1990. Already in 1985, 37 % of the coal was produced by open-cast mining there, and this proportion is to rise further (1990: 41 %). The resources that can be produced by open-cast mining (categories A, B and C1) allegedly amount to more than 11 billion tons, including 1.8 billion tons of coking coal. Kuznetsk coal is of very good quality: its thermal value is indicated to be 7,000 to 8,500 kcal/kg, and its ash (4 to 16 %) and sulphur (up to 1 %) contents are low.[17]

By the year 2000 Kuznetsk is to be developed into the largest coal district of the Soviet Union and to produce approximately 215 million tons of coal. This is said to amount to one fifth of the presumable overall output of the USSR.[18]

The largest production growth in absolute terms is to be reached by 1990 in the open-cast mining of *Kansk-Achinsk* (24 million tons).

The geological reserves in this district amount to approximately 600 billion tons, 100 billion tons of which are currently considered as suitable for economical mining. The Kansk-Achinsk lignite has a thermal value of 3,000 to 3,400 kcal/kg. Its sulphur content is relatively low (0.2 to 0.7 %); the lignite tends to self-ignite. The water content of 40 %, which is not high at all for lignite, renders mining difficult in winter.

The production growth envisaged for Kansk-Achinsk in the 12th Five-Year Plan approximately reflects the targets already disclosed in the Soviet press in 1983. At that time targets of 70 million tons for 1990 and 170 to 200 million tons for the year 2000 were mentioned.[19] Previous concepts, according to which a large thermal and energy complex (KATEK) could be established in Kansk-Achinsk on the basis of an annual output of 400 million tons, have thus been definitely abandoned. This is mainly due to four reasons[20]:

— The transmission of large amounts of electric current will not yet be cost-effective in the medium term due to high line losses even when using ultra-high voltage lines.
— The growing demand for electric power in the European part of the country is to be met to a major extent by nuclear power stations.
— For the liquefaction of lignite cost-effective process techniques are not yet available.
— Air pollution would be excessive: with an output of 400 million tons and a sulphur content of 0.5 %, emissions p.a. can be estimated at 3.2 million tons of SO_2 which is approximately the amount emitted in the CSSR in 1982.[21]

Instead of turning coal into electrical power and liquid products in large quantities in the immediate vicinity of the open-cast mines, there are new plans for the transport of coal by slurry-pipelines. The draft of the 12th Five-Year Plan, too, explicitly calls for «an intensive use of hydraulic pipeline transport for ores and coal». The construction of a 250 km long pipeline from the Kuzbas to Novosibirsk has, however, been considerably delayed. For the KATEK a project has been developed by the coal research institute at Kraznoyarsk according to which the pipeline transport of coal would be cost-effective in comparison with railroad transport. «For the future» it is planned to haul 110 to 120 million tons of ore concentrates and coal through pipelines[22], although previous experience has shown that a major technical use of pipeline transport cannot be expected before the nineties.

For a foreseeable period the bottleneck in the development of new deposits in Siberia will not be production but in transport and the creation of processing capacities in the immediate neighbourhood of the deposits. The continuous delays in the completion of the Beresovskoye No 1. power station (800 MW planned for 1984; final capacity 6,400 MW), which is to be provided with coal by open-cast mining at a distance of 14 km, is one example.

Similar problems also limit the potential for expansion in the Ekibastuz (Kazakhstan) coal district. Its reserves amount to approximately 10 billion tons. Currently the coal is produced exclusively by open-cast mining. Despite the low thermal value (4,200 kcal/kg) the coal is rated as hard coal in the USSR. Its ash content fluctuates substantially (22 to 55 %). Combustion is only possible with an ash content of up to 43 % so that upgrading (mixing) of the coal is necessary to a certain extent. Currently the coal is used in twenty power stations, inter alia some in the Urals and in western Siberia. Plans also foresee the construction of a fuel and energy complex (ETEK) at Ekibastuz. In the long term the output is to reach 120 to 135 million tons p.a., with the coal mainly to be consumed in four power stations of 4,000 MW each in the vicinity of the open-cast mines. Part of the electric power produced is to be transmitted by a 1,500 kV line from Ekibastuz to the centre (capacity: 6,000 MW).[23]

The 12th Five-Year Plan approximately corresponds to the long-term targets. By 1990 the output is to be boosted to 96 million tons. Problems are obviously caused by the combustion of coal in the 4,000 MW power station Ekibastuz which was completed in 1984 but has been producing below its capacity limit so far. During the period from 1986 through 1990 capacities of Ekibastuz 2 are to become operational and the construction of Ekibastuz 3 is to be expedited.

187

4. Plan Fulfilment in 1986 and Outlook

In 1986 the production of primary energy reached the highest growth rate (4.5 %) of the eighties. The decline in crude oil extraction was halted and an increment of 20 million tons was achieved. The natural gas industry surpassed the target of 672 billion m^3 by 14 bn m^3. The repercussions of the Chernobyl nuclear accident have (still) been kept within narrow limits. Atomic power generation fell slightly short of the pre-year result; overall power generation missed the target only slightly (by 0.4 %). The plan fulfilment report announces the completion of three nuclear power station blocks with pressurized water reactors at Kalinin, Rovno and Zaporozska (1,000 MW each). The planned start-up of two pressure tube reactors (Chernobyl and Ignalina) did not take place.

It is remarkable, however, that the long-lasting phase of stagnation in the coal industry appears to have been overcome. Already in 1985 output was increased by 14 million tons (gross). In 1986 the increase even amounted to 25 million tons, exceeding the target of 734 million tons by 17 million tons.

Presumably, in 1985 and 1986, measures that had been taken at the beginning of the eighties to overcome the chronic production problems in the coal industry started to show favourable effects. They included primarily a modernization programme for underground mines and measures for a rapid increase of open-cast production.[24]

The fuel industry — like the whole Soviet economy — appears to have substantial production reserves that can be mobilized by organizational and disciplinary measures within a short period of time. It is noteworthy, for example, that after the dismissal of both the oil and the coal ministers (in 1985) the respective industries reached high growth rates.

Currently it appears quite likely that the five-year plan targets for fuel production can be achieved. Capital expenditures for this industry have been considerably boosted during recent years and are also to expand above average during the 12th Five-Year Plan. By their overfulfilment of the targets in 1986, the coal and gas industries have produced a comfortable cushion for themselves, at least in 1987. This was made possible by the new planning guidelines. Previously, the results achieved were the basis for the targets of the subsequent year («achieved level approach»), which reduced the industries' interest in overfulfilling the plan. In future the annual plans are to be in line with the five-year plan so that the target of the previous year and not the actual result becomes the basis for the targets of the subsequent year.[25]

The new arrangement will have the following consequence: the 1987 target of 744 million tons for coal output — i.e. 10 million tons more than had been planned for 1986 — remains 7 million tons below the result achieved in 1986. However, the coal industry, too, was explicitly invited to submit counter-plans. Taking the actual 1986 figures as a yardstick, the targets for overall primary energy production represent a growth rate of only 1.7 %.

It cannot be expected, however, that the 1987 target and the five-year plan objective for power generation from nuclear energy will be met. Nuclear power was to account for 70 % (223 billion kWh) of the overall growth of power generation between 1986 and 1990 (315 billion kWh), whereas hydro-power was to account for only 10 %. Assuming half that growth rate for nuclear power, approximately 110 billion kWh would have to be provided additionally by thermal power stations. This would, however, require an additional amount of fuel in the order of 36 million tons of coal equivalent. It can by no means be excluded that at least part of it will be provided by an overfulfilment of the five-year plan targets by the gas and coal industries. But even if it will be possible to exceed the coal target by 1990, the growth in coal and nuclear energy production will not suffice to substitute for major supplies of oil.

5. *Supply-Oriented Policy (still?) has Priority*

In the field of energy production the targets of the 12th Five-Year Plan do not suggest any new course. However, the realization of the targets indicates some unexpected success, mainly in the coal industry. Despite considerable failures in nuclear power generation, the growth rate of primary energy production is likely to be relatively high (3.5 % p.a.). Energy supply will, thus, hardly be an obstacle to economic growth in the Soviet Union. On the other hand, substantial investment funds will be tied up by this « growth policy ».

By the relatively high growth targets for primary energy production and the above-average allocation of funds to the fuel sector the Soviet Union has indicated that it intends to continue its supply-oriented energy policy. This is astounding, especially since it has been emphasized time and again that the expenditures for energy savings measures are by one-half up to two-thirds lower than the costs of a corresponding growth of energy production.[26] If there has, nevertheless, been no change towards a demand-oriented energy policy, this may be due especially to the following reasons:

At least until the adoption of the 12th Five-Year Plan, Soviet planners utilized the — certainly realistic — assumption that in the Soviet economic system a supply-oriented strategy had better chances of materializing. Increases in production can be achieved by concentrating funds on only a few investment objectives. A strategy of saving energy, on the other hand, requires a multitude of decisions concerning R&D, capital expenditures and organizational changes that have to be taken primarily at decentralized levels. There were too few incentives for this approach in the Soviet Union's than existent economic mechanism (see also Tables A8 and A9 at Annex).

The «radical reform» of this economic mechanism as called for by Gorbachev is to largely overcome such shortfalls.[27] By greater application of indirect management methods and an orientation to profits, enterprises are to be motivated to make an economical use of inputs. However, whether this will lead to greater efforts to save energy is not at all certain. Saving successes can only be achieved if the economic leadership can make up its mind to increase energy prices drastically. However, this decisive prerequisite for a new course in Soviet energy policy is still missing.

Notes

1. See 1985 plan fulfilment report dated 26 January 1986.
2. See Pravda of 4 March 1986.
3. See for instance Izvestiya of 15 February 1982, Sozialisticheskaya Industriya of 10 February 1982 and Literaturnaya Ukraina of 27 March 1986.
4. «During recent years there has really been a rapid increase in capital expenditures for the construction of nuclear power stations. However, that is due to the fact that (after several accidents in US nuclear power stations) the safety requirements for nuclear power stations increased immensely and complex multistage protection systems were to be developed.»
N. Lopatin (Deputy Minister for Energetics and Electrification of the Soviet Union): Steps of Electrification. In: Soviet Exports. No. 2/1986, page 6.
5. Pravda of 5 March 1986.
6. Pravda of 20 July 1986.
7. USSR State Committe on the Utilization of Atomic Energy: The Accident at the Chernobyl Nuclear Power Plant and its Consequences. Information compiled for the IAEA Experts' Meeting, 25-29 August 1986, Vienna.
8. In 1986 the nuclear power stations of the Federal Republic of Germany reached a time output of 84 %. See «Elektrizitätswirtschaft» No. 4/1987, page 141.
9. Izvestiya of 10 November 1986, Pravda of 29 September 1986.
10. In the long-term energy programme of the USSR until the year 2000 (Energy Programme 2000) substantially higher capacities are indicated for substitution: until 1990: 55,000 up to 60,000 MW; until 2000: another 70,000 to 80,000 MW. See Ekonomicheskaya gazeta No. 12/1984 (supplement). Probably modernization projects are also included in the programme (target until 1990: 25,000 MW).
11. Narodnoe Chozjajstvo SSSR of 1985 g., page 156.
12. «Neues Deutschland» of 30 April 1986.
13. M.I. Shchadov (Minister of the Coal Industry of the USSR): Coal: Problems of Mining and Use. In: Energiya No. 12/1986, page 6.
14. M.I. Shchadov, loc. cit., page. 3.
15. A.A. Trofimuk, S.M. Nikolayev: Siberia. Geographical Contrasts, Mineral Resources and Problems of their Development. Novosibirsk 1982, page 15.
16. In Pravda of 17 December 1987 and at the 27 Party Congress of the CPSU the previous investment policy of the Coal Ministry was criticized. See: Theodore Shabad: New Notes. In: Soviet Geography, April 1986, page 267.
17. A.A. Trofimuk, S.M. Nikolayev, loc. cit., page 15. For the Kuznetsk boiler coal, however, clearly lower thermal values (approx. 5,500 kcal/kg) are being indicated. See Planovoe Chozyaystvo No. 7/1983, page 84.
18. M.I. Shchadov, loc. cit., page 6.
19. Ekonomicheskaya Industriya of 20 February 1986.

20. Sozialisticheskaya Industriya of 20 February 1986.
21. Assumed ash bond of the sulphur: 20 %. See « Air Pollution by SO_2 in the CSSR », Adapted by Jochen Bethkenhagen and Maria Lodahl, in : « Wochenbericht des DIW », No. 46/1986.
22. Sozialisticheskaya Industriya of 20 February 1986 and « Neues Deutschland » dated 8/9 February 1986.
23. N. Lopatin, loc. cit., page 6.
24. Jochen Bethkenhagen and Hermann Clement : « The Soviet Energy and Raw-Material Economy in the Eighties ». Oldenbourg 1985, page 66.
25. Pravda of 18 November 1986.
26. See Moskovskiye Novosti of 21 October 1984.
27. Economic Reforms in the USSR : State and Perspectives. Adapted by Ulrich Weissenburger and Heinrich Machowski, in : Wochenbericht des DIW No. 9/1987.

Table A1
Primary energy production in the USSR.
Trend and composition 1970 to 1990.

Year	Total		Share in %					
	M tonnes of coal equivalent	Change in % (1)	Oil	Gas	Coal (2)	Nuclear power	Hydro-electric power	Others (3)
1970	1236	4.9	40.9	19.1	32.0	0.2	3.3	4.3
1975	1596	5.3	44.0	21.6	27.9	0.5	2.6	3.4
1980	1959	4.2	44.0	26.4	23.1	1.2	3.1	2.1
1981	2003	2.2	43.5	27.7	22.0	1.4	3.1	2.4
1982	2052	2.5	42.7	29.0	21.8	1.6	2.8	2.1
1983	2102	2.4	41.9	30.3	21.2	1.7	2.8	2.0
1984	2169	3.2	40.4	32.2	20.3	2.2	3.1	1.8
1985	2232	2.9	38.2	34.3	20.2	2.5	3.2	1.8
1986	2330	4.4	37.8	35.0	20.2	2.3	3.1	1.7
1987 (4)	2372	1.8	37.2	35.7	19.7	2.6	3.1	1.6
1990 (4)	2666	3.6	34.1	38.0	18.6	4.8	3.0	1.5

(1) Compared with the previous year; 1970, 1975, 1980 and 1990: average annual increase in the preceding period (1966-70, 1971-75, 1976-80, 1986-90).

(2) Net production.
(3) Wood, peat, shale.
(4) Plan.

Source: Narodnoe Chozjajstvo SSSR; DIW Data Bank on CMEA Energy.

Primary energy production in the USSR.
1970 to 1990.

Year	Oil M.T.	Gas B.CBM	Coal [1] M.T.	Nuclear power B. kWh	Hydro-electric power, others [2] M.T. of coal equivalent	Total M.T. of coal equivalent
1970	353	198	577	8	94	1236
1971	377	212	592	8	95	1297
1972	400	221	604	11	97	1352
1973	429	236	615	16	96	1420
1974	459	261	631	22	93	1502
1975	491	289	645	24	96	1596
1976	520	321	654	29	92	1679
1977	546	346	663	42	99	1763
1978	572	372	664	45	101	1835
1979	586	407	658	55	106	1901
1980	603	435	653	73	103	1959
1981	609	465	638	86	109	2003
1982	613	501	647	96	100	2052
1983	616	536	642	110	102	2102
1984	613	587	636	142	106	2169
1985	595	643	648	167	110	2232
1986 [3]	615	686	675	162	110	2330
1987 [4]	617	712	670	184	114	2372
1990 [5]	635	850	715	390	121	2666

[1] Net production.
[2] Wood, peat, shale.
[3] Provisional figure.
[4] Plan and estimated.
[5] Plan.

Source: Narodnoe Chozjajstvo SSSR; DIW Data Bank on CMEA Energy.

Jochen Bethkenhagen

Table A3
*Coal production in the USSR 1970 to 1990
(million tonnes).*

Year	Gross production					Net production		
	Total	of which:		of which:		Total	of which:	
		Hard coal	Lignite	Deep mined	strip		Hard coal	Lignite
1970	624	476	148	457	167	577	433	144
1971	641	488	153	462	179	592	442	150
1972	655	499	156	465	190	604	451	153
1973	668	511	157	468	199	615	461	154
1974	685	524	161	472	213	631	474	157
1975	701	538	164	475	226	645	485	160
1976	712	548	164	480	232	654	494	160
1977	722	555	167	478	244	663	500	163
1978	724	557	167	470	254	664	501	163
1979	719	554	165	460	259	658	497	161
1980	716	553	163	445	271	653	493	160
1981	704	544	160	429	276	638	481	157
1982	718	555	163	432	286	647	488	159
1983	716	558	158	425	291	642	487	155
1984	712	556	158	418	294	638	487	151
1985	726	571	155	421	305	654	502	152
1986	751	592	159	419	315	675	520	155
1990 [1]	790	616	174	425	365	715	545	170

[1] Plan.

Source: Narodnoe Chozjajstvo SSSR: Theodore Shabad: News Notes, in: Soviet Geography, various years; DIW estimates.

194

Table A4
Soviet coal production:
net production as a share in gross production in per cent.

Year	Total	Hard coal	Lignite
1970	92.5	91.0	97.3
1971	92.4	90.6	98.0
1972	92.2	90.4	98.1
1973	92.1	90.2	98.1
1974	92.1	90.5	97.5
1975	92.0	90.1	97.6
1976	91.9	90.1	97.6
1977	91.8	90.1	97.6
1978	91.7	89.9	97.6
1979	91.5	89.7	97.6
1980	91.2	89.2	98.2
1981	90.6	88.4	98.1
1982	90.1	87.9	97.5
1983	89.7	87.3	98.1
1984	89.6	87.6	95.6
1985	90.1	87.9	98.1

Source: Narodnoe Chozjajstvo SSSR.

Table A5
Investments in the fuel industries in the USSR ([1]).

Period	In % of total industry investment				Investment per physical unit production increase in the fuel industries			
	Total	of which			Oil	Gas	Coal	Total([2])
		Oil	Gas	Coal				
1971-75	18	9	4	5	33	26	*	57
1976-80	21	12	5	5	33	14	123	29
1981-85	27	17	5	5	257	14	*	62
1984	27	16	6	5	*	56	307	326
1985	28	18	6	4	408	82	140	186

([1]) At 1984 prices.
([2]) RBL per tonnes of coal equivalent (* decrease in production). Periods of investments: see first column. Period of production: 1966-71, 1972-76, 1977-81, 1982-86, 1985, 1986.

Source: Narodnoe Chozjajstvo SSSR. DIW Data Bank on CMEA Energy.

Table A6
Share of nuclear energy in the Soviet Union's electricity output.

Year	Capacity		Production		Share of nuclear energy in	
	Total	of which: Nuclear power plants	Total	of which: Nuclear power plants	Capacity	Production
	in MW		in Billion kWh		in %	
1970	166150	1612	741	6	1.0	0.8
1975	217484	5546	1039	20	2.6	1.9
1976	228307	6975	1111	26	3.1	2.4
1977	237805	7975	1150	35	3.4	3.0
1978	245441	8975	1202	45	3.7	3.7
1979	255282	11385	1238	55	4.5	4.4
1980	266757	13425	1294	73	5.0	5.6
1981	276722	16305	1326	86	5.9	6.5
1982	285492	18305	1367	96	6.4	7.0
1983	293558	21805	1418	110	7.4	7.7
1984	303693	25245	1492	142	8.3	9.5
1985	312800	29245	1545	167	9.3	10.8
1986 ([1])	315000	30245	1599	162	9.6	10.1
1990 ([1])	380000	69000	1860	390	18.2	21.0

([1]) Planned or estimated.

Source: Energiya 4/85, p. 18; USSR Statistical Yearbooks; DIW Data Bank on CMEA Energy.

Table A7

Nuclear power plants in the USSR (as at December 1986).

Reactor name	Total capacity in MW	Reactor units in MW	Year of commissioning
1. Pressure-tube reactors			
Total	14453	(26 blocks)	
Obninsk	5	5	1954
Troitsk (Siberia)	600	6 × 100	1958/62
Beloyarskiy	900		
Beloyarskiy-1		100	1964
Beloyarskiy-2		200	1967
Bilibino	48		
Bilibino-1		12	1973
Bilibino-2		12	1975
Bilibino-3		12	1976
Bilibino-4		12	1976
Leningrad	4000		
Leningrad-1		1000	1973
Leningrad-2		1000	1975
Leningrad-3		1000	1979
Leningrad-4		1000	1980
Kursk	4000		
Kursk-1		1000	1976
Kursk-2		1000	1978
Kursk-3		1000	1983
Kursk-4		1000	1985
Chernobyl'	2000		
Chernobyl'-1		1000	1977
Chernobyl'-2		1000	1978
Smolensk	2000		
Smolensk-1		1000	1982
Smolensk-2		1000	1985
Ignalina-1	1500	1500	1983
2. Pressurised water reactors			
Total	15470	(23 blocks)	
Novovoronezhskiy	2525		
Novovoronezhskiy-1		210	1964/69
Novovoronezhskiy-2		365	1969
Novovoronezhskiy-3		440	1971
Novovoronezhskiy-4		440	1972
Novovoronezhskiy-5		1000	1980
Kola	1760		
Kola-1		440	1973
Kola-2		440	1975
Kola-3		440	1981
Kola-4		440	1984

Armenia	815		
(Metsamor)			
Armenia-1		405	1976
Armenia-2		410	1979
Rovno	1880		
Rovno-1		440	1980
Rovno-2		440	1981
Rovno-3		1000	1986
South Ukraine	2000		
(Konstantinovka)			
South Ukraine-1		1000	1982
South Ukraine-2		1000	1985
Zaporozh'ye	3000		
Zaporozh'ye-1		1000	1984
Zaporozh'ye-2		1000	1985
Zaporozh'ye-3		1000	1986
Kalinin	2000		
Kalinin-1		1000	1984
Kalinin-2		1000	1986
Ulyanovsk WK-50 ([1])		50	1965
Balakovo-1	1000	1000	1985
3. Fast Breeders			
Total	762	(3 blocks)	
Beloyarskiy (BN-600)		600	1980
Ulyanovsk BOR-60		12	1969
Shevchenko		([2]) 350	1973
USSR, total	30245	(52 blocks)	

([1]) Boiling water reactor.
([2]) Of which 200 MW is used for water desalination.

Sources: DIW Data Bank on CMEA Energy; Theodore Shabad: News Notes, in: Soviet Geography, no. 4/1986.

Table A8

Primary energy consumption in the USSR.
Trend and composition 1970 to 1985.

Year	Total [1]		Share in % [2]					
	M tonnes of coal equivalent	Change in % [3]	Oil	Gas	Coal	Nuclear power	Hydro-electric power [4]	Others [5]
1970	1084	4.8	34.4	21.7	35.1	0.3	3.6	4.8
1975	1377	4.9	37.8	24.1	30.9	0.6	2.7	3.9
1980	1650	3.7	38.8	27.5	26.5	1.5	3.3	2.5
1981	1679	1.8	38.6	28.5	25.2	1.7	3.3	2.8
1982	1729	3.0	37.6	30.2	25.1	1.8	2.9	2.5
1983	1779	2.9	36.6	31.7	24.5	2.0	2.9	2.4
1984	1858	4.4	35.0	33.6	23.5	2.5	3.2	2.1
1985	1927	3.7	33.4	35.6	22.9	2.9	3.2	2.0

[1] Including changes in stock.
[2] Excluding changes in stock.
[3] Compared with the previous year; 1970, 1975 and 1980: average annual increase in the preceding period (1966-70, 1971-75, 1976-80).
[4] Including net export of electricity.
[5] Wood, peat, shale.

Source: Narodnoe Chozjajstvo SSSR; DIW Data Bank on CMEA Energy.

Table A9
Economic growth and primary energy consumption in the USSR.
Average annual change in per cent.

	PEC	PNI	IP	Elasticities ([2]) PEC/PNI	PEC/IP
1975/70	4.9	5.7	7.4	0.86	0.66
1980/75	3.7	4.3	4.4	0.86	0.84
1985/80	3.2	3.6	3.7	0.89	0.86

([1]) PEC = Primary Energy Consumption; PNI = Produced National Income; IP = Industrial Production.
([2]) Ratio of growth rates.

Source: Narchoz SSSR; DIW Data Bank on CMEA Energy.

Soviet Water, Air, and Nature Preservation Problems of the Gorbachev Era and Beyond

Craig ZumBrunnen

1. Introduction

One of the seemingly inevitable consequences of developing an industrial economy is the emergence of serious environmental problems such as air and water pollution, wildlife and habitat destruction, accelerated soil erosion, deforestation, over-fishing, plus a myriad of resource use conflicts. At least as far back as the internationally publicized Lake Baykal water pollution cause célèbre in the 1960s the Soviet Union has admitted the existence of significant environmental problems.[1] A presumed Soviet ministry official writing under the pseudonym of Komarov penned a blistering attack on Soviet environmental problems which was published in Russian in Germany in 1978 and translated into English in 1980.[2] In 1983 Pryde provided the general Western scientific community with a concise overview of Soviet environmental problems.[3] In essence for nearly twenty years both Soviet and Western observers have been commenting on Soviet environmental problems.

Similar to the United States, the overall Soviet record of effectively coping with environmental problems is certainly less than stellar. While some significant improvements have been made as will be documented below, very major longterm problems exist and will not be easy for the Soviets to solve in ecologically beneficial ways. Included among these serious chronic problems are water quality and quantity, deforestation, soil erosion, wildlife and habitat protection, and to somewhat of a lesser extent air pollution. In sum these environmental problems loom large enough to pose signifiant impediments to Soviet efforts to maintain, let alone, accelerate economic growth. Gorbachev's emphasis on intensive rather than extensive growth clearly is designed to help alleviate, if not solve, some of the chronic environmental externalities associated with past deleterious Soviet approaches to natural resource exploration, evaluation, exploitation, and allocation.

Before exploring the current nature of Soviet environmental problems and prospects a brief historical retrospective seems warranted.

2. Overview of Soviet Conservation History

The systemic problems of various Soviet economic institutions and policies will be catalogued in a latter section. It is far too simplistic, however, simply to point the finger at Soviet economic institutions and policies as the root cause of all Soviet shortcomings with regard to environmental protection. One must also evaluate Soviet environmental problems from both historical and geographical perspectives.

At the time of the Bolshevik victory in the Civil War, the Soviet Union was clearly an underdeveloped country. Accordingly, it would seem to have been quite unlikely that much, if any, emphasis or awareness existed regarding environmental quality issues, except for the widespread problems of sanitation and water supply.[4] Surprisingly, however, even in the 1920's the neophyte Bolshevik government enacted a very considerable number of conservation related laws and decrees, many signed by Lenin.[5] During the late 1960's leading up to the centenary of Lenin's birth and on into the early 1970's, the Soviet press placed a great deal of emphasis on these signatures as testimony of both Lenin's stature as an early conservationist as well as concrete examples of the long standing commitment of the Soviet Union to environmental conservation and protection.[6]

Not surprisingly, as the early Soviet industrialization drive began in earnest, concerns over environmental protection and conservation took a back seat. This is quite understandable because most major environmental problems really only become manifest as a result of intensive industrial, urban, and agricultural development. The exigencies of the times and the efforts directed towards winning the Second World War clearly received appropriate priority over environmental matters. Without doing significant damage to historical accuracy, one may look to the Lake Baykal water pollution controversy in the early 1960's as the turning point in renewed Soviet consciousness and concern over environmental protection.[7] Shortly we will review the seemingly plethora of relevant Soviet conservation legislation over the last twenty years.

The second series of factors one must remain cognizant of when trying objectively to explore the Soviets' environmental management record is the Soviet Union's geography. Concisely, these geographical factors can be expressed as a series of inverse geographical distributions between the locations of resource supplies and resource needs. The most obvious and striking is the Soviet Union's water supply and demand patterns. Whereas the more densely populated and heavily industrialized western portions of the country account for approximately 80 percent of the industrial output, they contain only 24 percent of the USSR's fresh water resources. The arid southern regions are even more disadvantaged, constituting 27 percent of the territorial landmass, but receiving only 2 percent of the total fresh water.[8] This situation is quite unlike the American patterns (with the possible exception of the American southwest), where the major population and industrial bases are located in geographical environments with adequate moisture. This inverse locational pattern between supplies and demands also exists with regard to most mineral resources, iron ore being a notable exception with the huge Krivoy Rog deposits in the Ukraine and the Kursk Magnetic Anomaly (KMA) ores in southern European Russia. Siberia looms ever larger in its role as a supplier of energy resources to the entire country and for export. Compared with the United States, the Soviet Union's agricultural land base, while enormous in area, is not nearly as well endowed with regard to length of growing season and quantity and reliability of precipitation. As a further example, the harshness of much of the country's climate in the winter poses serious problems with such processes as the secondary treatment of industrial and municipal waste water. In essence, these various geographical relationships result in added development and transportation costs, productivity constraints, and ecological disruption problems in relatively fragile natural environments. Accordingly, even a total reformulation of Soviet economic institutions would not begin to solve some of the Soviet Union's geographically based environmental problems.

3. Institutions of the Command Economy and Environmental Protection

Other publications have focused on various theoretical and institutional shortcomings of the Soviet Union's economic system with regard to environmental quality and resource management.[9] The purpose here is simply to present a concise generic overview of some of the major institutional reasons for chronic Soviet environmental problems.

The argument has long been made by Soviet and other socialist theoreticians that the Soviet economic system possesses inherent advantages over Western market or mixed-market economic institutions in terms of preventing, or at least, coping effectively with various environmental problems. Simply stated, this argument is based on the theoretical functioning of a triad of Soviet (and socialist) institutions.[10]

The first of these postulated institutional arrangements is the lack of a private profit motive in natural resource usage. The natural tendency of private entrepreneurial behavior to generate social costs, defined as the divergence between private and total costs, is all too often correctly laid at the feet of the private profit motive.[11] Hence, the mere lack of a private profit motive is used as prima facie evidence of the environmental protection superiority of the Soviet system. An identical argument is commonly made with respect to the theoretical advantage of public or state owernship and control of natural resources in the Soviet Union. Supposedly, this property rights structure maximizes the general societal welfare rather than that of the private welfare of resource users and decisions makers (in the Western context, read: private resource owners). The final theoretical part of the triad is the central planning of

203

exploration, extraction, utilization and allocation of all raw material and biological resources.

As this paper and many of the works cited in it bear witness, these theoretical advantages have not yet empirically demonstrated their clear superiority over Western institutions in coping with and preventing environmental disruption. The unfortunate, but indisputable, fact is both Western and Soviet institutional responses have thus far functioned far from ideally with regard to environmental externality problems. Rather than trying to articulate a case for which system has been the «least worse», the objective here is to enumerate some of the most critical practical (and theoretical) problems in the day-to-day operation of Soviet economic institutions and behavior which have obviated the above postulated advantageous triad.

For brevity's sake, eight obstacles to environmental quality will be mentioned, many of which are unfortunately shared with the West, but some of which are different. All of these generic institutional problems are cited in a series of recent Soviet news accounts of the activities of the Commission on Environmental Protection and the Rational Utilization of Natural Resources under the Presidium of the USSR Council of Ministers formed in 1981.[12]

First, despite its pervasiveness in the Soviet Union and its strongly appealing theoretical advantages over decentralized, often conflicting, private resource decision-making; central planning is by no means a panacea. Real resource use conflicts, such as between hydropower generation and irrigation withdrawals, are not easily assumed away by central planning.[13] Any planning effort seems to suffer from three generic types of problems (1) lack of sufficient detail in plans, (2) imperfect plan coordination, and (3) inadequate and distorted information.

All of these imperfections are essentially innate to any form of planning. In the Soviet case, however, some of them are exacerbated by the general information flow structure of the Soviet economy. In contrast to market economies which are to a considerable degree coordinated by the horizontal flow of price information, the Soviet economy is coordinated by vertical flows of information and commands. As a result, harmful, yet potentially useful, waste products of one enterprise may simply be discarded into convenient waterways rather than being intercepted and made available as a valuable resource input to another complementary production process, even though the two enterprises might be located quite near each other geographically.

A third problem area involves the failure of regulations. Essentially, these failures can be grouped into three general types. First, as will be mentioned again in the next section on the Soviet environmental laws, their enforcement is often lax. In particular, the Soviet press over the past twenty years has published what amounts to a rather sad chronology of production enterprises being placed in production either without waste treatment facilities being completed or, at least, without the written approval of all three of the inspection services under the auspices of the USSR Ministries of Public Health, Fisheries, and Land Reclamation and Water Management. Second, while in theory quite stringent, the Soviet MPC's (maximum permitted concentrations) of pollutants are often poorly monitored and enforced. Third, the fines for pollution violators have been insignificantly small, difficult to assign, and commonly overturned on appeal.[14]

Fourth, some problems arise from the economic and environmental administrative apparatus. The most obvious one is the lack of clear administrative jurisdiction, overlapping jurisdictions, and duplication of administrative agencies and functions similar to the situation in the United States. Finally, as has all too commonly been true in the United States, the Soviet Union has exhibited a chronic propensity to underutilize and misallocate money originally earmarked for pollution control.[15]

Fifth, while the Soviet Union has produced some positive examples of nearly open citizenry protest and political opposition to water pollution problems, most notably the Lake Baykal pollution controversy[16], such environmentally positive political pressure has played a very minor role compared to the environmental movements of Western Europe, Japan, and the United States.[17]

Sixth, the physical causes of environmental disruption, of course, are the same in all industrial societies. Accordingly, all societies are materially advanced, constrained, and environmentally affected by the technologies they possess and use. The Soviet Union has produced some notable technological breakthroughs and improvements in water pollution abatement, for example.[18] Nonetheless, it is fair to say that the Soviet Union, in general, lags behind the West in both waste treatment technology and its implementation.

Seventh, much of the Soviet Union's chronic problems with environmental problems may be traced institutionally directly to its long term effective social preferences and its managerial incentive system. Simply stated, the USSR's leadership, especially since the rise of Stalinism, has pursued a relentless policy of rapid industrialization. Surrounded since its inception with essentially hostile foreign powers, such a policy seems to have been prudent for the Soviet government's survival. Nevertheless, the priority has long been on rapidly increasing production and not upon such « non-productive » activities as pollution abatement and nature protection in general. Second, this emphasis on ever expanding industrial and agricultural production led to the evolution of a managerial incentive system in which « plan fulfilment » or « over fulfilment » rather than environmental protection activities yielded the ubiquitously sought after bonuses and intangible rewards.[19]

The eighth and final factor to be noted has long been the irrational (i.e., essentially non-scarcity prices) Soviet resource pricing structure in which many resources, such as water, were treated as free goods. Hence, no one nor no ins titution which uses commodities without a fee has a strong incentive to use the resource prudently.

We will return later to discussions of changes underway from extensive to intensive economic growth strategies and reforms in natural resource pricing policies and their possible impacts on environmental problems. Similar to Western nations, as environmental problems began to manifest themselves, one of the key Soviet institutional responses was to promulgate a series of rules, laws, and regulations with the hoped for goal of alleviating environmental problems.

4. The Environmental Paper Chase: Environmental Protection Legislation

Over the last 30 years the Soviet Union has enacted a multitude of laws concerning nature conservation and natural resource utilization.[20] The Russian Republic (RSFSR) alone ratified at least 19 nature conservation executive decrees between 1956 and 1960, the most significant of which was the 1960 RSFSR Conservation Law.[21] All 15 Union Republics had major conservation laws on the books by 1963.[22] Recently, the Soviet Union published a compendium volume cataloguing major Soviet nature protection and resource management documents and legislation ratified from 1917 through 1985.[23] While not a complete listing of all such items, it is nonetheless interesting to note the relative number of documents cited by selected time periods. Seventeen items are listed for the period from 1917 through Lenin's death in 1924. From that time until the post-War year of 1948 only eight documents are listed. Including the two documents dated in 1948, only seven new documents are noted through the end of the 1950's. The increased Soviet concern with environmental matters is suggested by the 18 documents enumerated for the decade of the sixties, eleven of which were promulgated in 1968 and 1969. Clearly, the zenith in terms of Soviet legal activity regarding natural resources and environmental protection occurred in the 1970's with 47 separate documents listed. The first half of the eighties reveals somewhat of a slackened pace with seventeen major party and governmental documents enacted. It is not entirely accurate to assume that this recent reduction in the rate of legal codification reflects the resource management efficacy of previous legislation.

In general, and again on paper, Soviet environmental laws appear quite sound, yet there have been and continue to be significant problems for a variety of practical and theoretical reasons. For instance, many Soviet authors from a wide spectrum of disciplines continue to complain that the conservation laws are unsatisfactorily enforced, poorly prosecuted, appropriate restitution for environmental damages is infrequently ordered by the courts and/or enforcements agencies, and most laws and judicial decisions involve ineffective fines and administrative reprimands.[24] Industrial facilities have long been and still often are being operated without purifying installations being completed or working properly.[25] Zile[26] claims that, at least until the beginning of the seventies, the various new laws included little truly meaningful innovation over previously existing laws, that All-Union and Republic laws were often in conflict, and that the various environmental laws apparently had failed to incorporate adequately the non-interference (among uses and users) principle into the planning process. This latter, so-called, « departmental approach », is a very real obstacle to the comprehensive processing and/or pollution control treatment of Soviet industrial and agricultural waste products. This myriad of interbranch waste processing and disposal conflicts has recently led to the call for the creation of an interbranch scientific and technical complex, tentatively named the « Secondary Resources and the Comprehensive Utilization of Raw Materials », under the joint auspices of the USSR State Committee for Science and Technology and the USSR State Committee for Material and Technical Supply.[27]

At the same time, the impression that legal enforcement is totally lacking should not be given. For instance, the Soviet press has reported on a number of cases over the past several years where industrial enterprises have been required to cease their operations due to pollution violations.[28] Fines and criminal sentences for pollution violations and fish and animal poaching are commonly mentioned in the Soviet press.[29] Many of these same sources complain about the overworked employees and understaffing of various regulatory agencies, and again, the all too common ineffectiveness of fines and legal sanctions to prevent pollution or poaching.

This latter point seems implicit in the continuing concerns of the Politburo with the report of the USSR State Committee on Hydrometeorology and the Environment on the country's effort to protect the natural environment against pollution.[30] Directive after directive seems to be issued designed to ameliorate or prevent pollution. Z.N. Nuriyev, Vice-Chairman of the USSR Council of Ministers, appears to have made major critical remarks on the observance of environmental protection and rational utilization of natural resources legislation at the 11th

USSR Supreme Soviet in July of 1985.[31] Finally, additional proposals for improving legislation for strengthening Soviet environmental protection are scheduled to be introduced during the third quarter of 1987.[32]

5. An Overview of Major Problem Areas and Management Successes : Chronic Water Quality Problems

For nearly fifteen years now some of my own research efforts have documented a multitude of chronic Soviet water quality problems as well as some of their successes in reducing these pollution problems.[33] Figure I which follows includes the locations of the places and geographical features cited in the remaining sections of this paper. Over the past couple of decades the Soviet press and technical journals have printed a large number of water pollution accounts.[34] These written stories indicate that serious chronic water pollution problems still exist along the Baltic, Black, and Azov Sea coasts and within the Ural-Volga-Caspian Basin, the Ob'Irtysh-Tom' river system, Lake Baykal, the Yenisey-Angara system, the Dnepr Basin, the Dnestr Basin, the Severskiy Donets and Don river systems, the Aral Sea Basin, lakes and rivers in Central European Russia, various rivers draining the heavily industrialized Ural Mountains, lakes and rivers within the Baltic Republics and Karelia, the Kuban' Basin, and various waterways in Transcaucasia.[35]

Space here does not allow for a full descriptive accounting of even a handful of these case studies; however, a few highlights are worth mentioning. First, the pollution problems at Lake Baykal still remain unsolved after 25 years of argument and debate.[36] Lakes Ladoga and Onega in Karelia, and Imandra in the Kola Peninsula are still plagued by effluents of the chemical and pulp and paper industries.[37] Planning errors in a flood protection project seem to be creating a veritable cesspool at the mouth of the Neva River.[38] Ten years after plans were announced for eliminating pollution along the Baltic Sea coast and other waterways within the Baltic Republics chronic problems persist and the quantity of discharged effluents has actually increased.[39] Pollution from offshore drilling operations, however, in the Baltic, Black and Azov seas has diminished.[40] Coastal pollution and groundwater contamination by industrial wastes remain unsolved in Crimea.[41] Salinity levels continue to increase and the « productive biomass » of the Azov Sea to decline as a result of both pollution and insufficient river inflow.[42] An effluent dam burst at the Stebnik potassium fertilizer plant in L'vov Oblast' on September 15, 1983, which sent some 4.5 million cubic meters of very saline brine surging down the Dnestr River resulting in a massive fish kill and reeking other types of ecological damage.[43] The water supplies of several cities of L'vov, Ivano-Frankovsk, Chernovtsy,

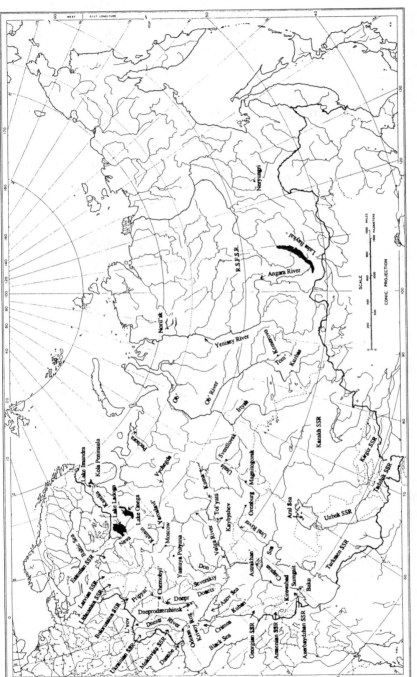

FIGURE I. Map of Place Names Cited in Text.

Khmel'nitskiy, Ternopol', and Odessa oblasts in the Ukraine and in certain areas of the Moldavian Republic were contaminated.[44] Follow-up reports provided details of the criminal investigation into the incident as well as updates on the improving quality of the water supplies within the Dnestr Basin.[45] A resolution calling for the cessation of pollution in the Caspian remains far from fulfilled, especially in the vicinities of Baku, Sumgait, and Kirovabad.[46] While many problem areas still exist along the Volga and Kama Rivers, the Volga's quality near the cities of Kalinin, Yaroslavl', Tol'yatti, Kuybyshev, and Astrakhan', and the Ural's quality near Orenburg, and Magnitogorsk are reported to have improved in recent years.[47] In Sverdlovsk Oblast' in the heavily indus-trialized Ural Mountains 90 percent of industries are now purported to have recycled industrial water supply systems and 82 percent of the waste water is reputed to be undergoing treatment prior to discharge.[48] Major pollution control efforts are reported to be progressing well in the Tom' River Basin of the heavily industrialized Kuznetsk Basin of West Siberia.[49]

Finally, the most spectacular recent Soviet pollution problems, of course, are associated with the Chernobyl' nuclear accident. The Pripyat' and Dnepr rivers have been threatened with radioactive waste as have the land resources in the surrounding area. While the accounts of the Chernobyl' event continue to be published, the late Shabad has published an extremely useful 23 page summary document on the geo-graphical and environmental aspects of the accident up through early autumn of 1986.[50] Only time will tell how serious the long term environ-mental effects of this event really are.

Table 1 presents time series data on newly installed capacity of both water and air pollution facilities. The data for waste water treatment capacities are ambiguous. On the one hand, the data indicate an unfor-tunate downward trend over time. On the other hand, these data may still reflect an overall improvement in waste water treatment as more and more enterprises and municipalities are equipped with such treat-ment installations, and hence, a sort of « sewage treatment capacity saturation » process may well be underway. Then, too, the widespread Soviet introduction of closed-cycle industrial water supply systems (see Table 2) helps to lower the need for additional sewage treatment capa-city.

Table 1

Newly installed capacity for the prevention of water and air pollution.

	1976-80	1981-85	1985
Installations for Purifying Waste Water, in millions of m³/day	36.9	26.8	4.0
Water Recycling Systems, in millions of m³/day	121.7	122.1	29.1
Installations for Catching and Rendering Harmless Harmful Substances from Exhaust Gases, in millions of m³/hour of gas	172.4	200.0	35.6

Source: Narodnoye Khozyaystvo SSSR v 1985 g., Moscow: "Finansy i Statistika", 1986, p. 387.

Again, the data from Table 2 included in the next section require some clarification. Overall there has been a marked increase in the capacity of such systems between 1982 and 1985 of 15.3 percent or 32.5 cubic kilometers per year. Overall the recirculating systems represent approximately the entire annual flow of the Volga River at its mouth. As a share of the total industrial water demand, however, the trend is flat. In general, the Transcaucasus region and Central Asia lag behind the rest of the country. Given the general water supply problems of these regions this is perplexing. The dramatically reduced share supplied by such systems in Lithuania appears to result both from a modest absolute decrease in the capacity of such systems and a presumably relatively large increase in industrial water demand in the republic. Nonetheless, the installed capacities of water recirculating systems in the major industrialized republics, such as Belorussia, the RSFSR, and the Ukraine, is rather impressive.

Water Quantity Problems

Implicit in Table 2 below are the general problems of water supply in the Soviet Union. Without the recycled industrial water supply systems shown in Table 2, the consumptive water demand for Soviet industries would be nearly 150 percent higher. In his forthcoming book Tolmazin amply documents the severity and geography of Soviet agricultural, industrial, and municipal water supply problems, for the country as a whole, but especially for the Ukraine.[51] He carefully documents many of the major ecologically deleterious consequences of the proposed Danube water diversion scheme. Table 3 lists aggregate, presumably consumptive, water demand for selected years from 1980 through 1985 by the three broad sectors of water usage. Somewhat surprising is the declining demand for irrigation water. Apparently this may reflect more rational irrigation practices.

Table 2
Volume of circulating and reused water by Union Republics.

Region	Total, in Km³				Proportion of Total Industrial Water Demand Satisfied by Recycled Water, in Percentage Terms			
	1982	1983	1984	1985	1982	1983	1984	1985
USSR	211.9	226.1	237.4	244.4	68	69	70	69
Moldavian SSR	3.0	3.1	3.2	3.2	93	93	93	93
Armenian SSR	1.9	1.8	2.2	2.3	78	77	81	82
Belorussian SSR	6.5	6.6	6.7	7.0	79	79	80	81
Ukrainian SSR	52.8	54.3	58.0	59.5	77	76	78	78
RSFSR	128.9	138.0	141.8	145.7	68	70	72	70
Kazakh SSR	7.9	9.7	10.5	11.5	55	58	56	60
Lithuanian SSR	2.8	2.9	3.1	2.9	91	88	64	57
Latvian SSR	0.4	0.4	0.5	0.5	53	54	55	56
Tadzhik SSR	0.2	0.3	0.5	0.6	25	39	47	53
Uzbek SSR	3.8	4.9	6.5	6.5	38	45	52	49
Kirgiz SSR	0.2	0.3	0.4	0.4	26	32	38	39
Azerbaydzhan SSR	1.3	1.6	1.7	1.8	33	37	38	38
Georgian SSR	0.9	0.9	0.9	1.0	30	34	34	37
Estonian SSR	0.9	0.9	0.9	0.9	23	23	24	26
Turkmen SSR	0.4	0.4	0.5	0.6	21	21	19	21

Source: Narodnoye Khozyaystvo SSSR v 1985 g., Moscow: "Finansy i Statistika", 1986, p. 385.

As indicated early in this paper the Soviet Union does not have a very good match between regions of abundant water supply and regions possessing high demand. This has long been recognized as a problem and, of course, is the geographical reason behind the long discussed and debated plans to divert copious volumes of water from the Vychegda and Pechora rivers of the European North into the Volga-Kama-Caspian Basin and through the Volga-Don Canal into the Sea of Azov. The Danube-Dnepr Canal is another such project in the southern European USSR. A similar massive project to reverse a significant portion of the flow of the Ob'-Irtysh system into the Aral Sea Basin has also been long planned. One of the most significant ecologically positive decisions of the Gorbachev era has been the recent outright cancellation of both the Vychegda-Pechora and the Ob'-Irtysh projects.[52] While the decision to cancel the Central Asian river diversion project seems to have been very sound both economically and ecologically, it seems highly likely to be laden with overtones of Great Russian chauvinism from the perspective of water starved Central Asians. Academicians, scientists, private citizens, and writers all played active roles in this debate, most opposed to the large-scale diversisons. In cancelling these projects on utilizing existing regional water resources more efficiently and economically rather than on the massive scale and prohibitively costly diversion schemes.[53]

Table 3
Demand for fresh water.

	Cubic Kilometers			In Percentage		
	1980	1983	1985	1980	1983	1985
Total	288	278	282	100	100	100
In which number:						
For Irrigation and Agri-cultural Water Supply	161	153	150	56	55	53
For Industrial Needs (Including Agricultural Production)	105	101	107	36	36	38
For Municipal and Domestic Needs	22	24	25	8	9	9

Source: Narodnoye Khozyaystvo SSSR v 1985 g., Moscow: "Finansy i Statistika", 1986, p. 384.

Surrounding the recent chapters in the river diversion debate has been a very positive (i.e., critical) reassessment of the value of large-scale, and often environmentally harmful, economic development projects. For example, ecological considerations and better cost accounting approaches have been posing practically lethal threats to large water dams and reservoir impoundment projects.[54]

In the last analysis, Gorbachev and his planners and their successors for decades into the future will be faced with the sobering and stark reality of severe regional water supply problems over much of the most developed portions of the Soviet Union. These problems already are functioning and in the future will even more function, as a tenacious geographical break on continued economic development for both industry and agriculture. In fact, water supply rather than water pollution may be the more intractable natural resource problem.

Air Pollution Problems and Prevention

The relative contribution of various sources of air pollution in the Soviet Union differs significantly compared to those of the United States. The explanation is very straightforward. Motorized vehicles rule the highways and their noxious gases pollute the atmospheres of major American cities whereas industrial smokestacks rather than automobiles perform the same dirty job in the Soviet Union. Unfortunately, vehicle emissions are becoming a major source of air contamination in several Soviet cities.[55]

On July 11, 1985, the Presidium of the USSR Supreme Soviet issued a decree charging the USSR State Committee on Hydrometeorology and the Environment's State Inspectorate with various functions in monitoring the protection of the atmosphere.[56] As of 1983 air quality was being monitored in nearly 500 Soviet cities. Dust, sulfur dioxide, and hydrogen sulfide emissions were reported to have been either stabilized or reduced in almost 70 percent of these cities. All newly constructed industrial facilities were being outfitted with highly efficient gas scrubbers and dust traps. Nonetheless, air-pollution abatement was judged as being far from adequate. For example, in 1982 such abatement equipment was found to be ineffective or inoperable, at the following percentage of industrial facilities managed by the stated ministries: 17 percent in the USSR Ministry of Petroleum-Refining and Petrochemical Industry, 25 percent in the USSR Ministry of Ferrous Metallurgy, 25 percent in the USSR Ministry of Mineral Fertilizer Production, 27 percent in the USSR Ministry of Nonferrous Metallurgy, and 40 percent in the USSR Ministry of Power and Electrification. The atmospheres of the cities of Noril'sk, Kemerovo, and Dneprodzerzhinsk were singled out by Z. Nuriyev, Chairman of the Commission on En-

214

vironmental Protection and the National Utilization of Natural Resources under the Presidium of the USSR Council of Ministers, as being particularly problematic.[57] In 1985 Lev Tolstoy's estate-museum at Yasnaya Polyana was still being polluted by the gaseous emissions of the Azot Chemical plant after years of repeated efforts and decrees to protect the estate dating back to 1921.[58] Ash and slag have been accumulating in the vicinities of various Kazakhstan and other power plants.[59] New urban nodes along the BAM (Baykal-Amur-Mainline) are being inundated with fly ash from the burning of high-ash Neryungri coals.[60] Overall, industrial smokestacks pollute the air of nearly all major Soviet industrial cities. The most positive improvement in urban air quality has been the shift away from coal and oil towards natural gas for electricity generation and space-heating within major urban areas. Many cities in the Transcaucasus, Central Asia, and especially Siberia are plagued by chronic winter temperature inversions generated by the persistent Siberian high pressure cell. Coal and wood burning for winter space heating in these cities creates serious air quality problems.

Table 4

Interception and neutralization of harmful substances being discharged from stationary sources of air pollution by Union Republics.

Region	Quantity of Harmful Substances Intercepted and Neutralized by Gas and Particulate Interception Structures and Installations, in millions of metric tons				Percent of Total Quantity of Harmful Substances Being Discharged which were Intercepted and Rendered Harmless			
	1982	1983	1984	1985	1982	1983	1984	1985
USSR	197.1	200.8	205.9	209.3	75	75	76	76
Estonian SSR	8.3	8.9	8.6	8.5	92	93	93	93
Kirgiz SSR	0.9	1.0	1.0	1.1	80	82	82	83
Moldavian SSR	2.3	2.3	2.2	2.2	82	82	82	82
Kazakh SSR	21.4	23.8	25.4	27.9	83	83	82	82
Tadzhik SSR	0.5	0.5	0.5	0.5	77	78	79	80
Lithuanian SSR	1.5	1.5	1.5	1.5	76	77	77	77
RSFSR	118.4	119.1	123.1	123.6	74	74	76	76
Armenian SSR	0.8	0.8	0.8	0.7	77	77	76	74
Ukrainian SSR	34.9	34.6	34.1	34.8	73	73	73	74
Latvian SSR	0.5	0.5	0.5	0.5	66	69	70	71
Belorussian SSR	3.2	3.3	3.6	3.2	68	69	71	68
Uzbek SSR	2.8	2.8	2.8	2.9	65	64	65	65
Georgian SSR	0.6	0.6	0.6	0.6	51	55	52	55
Azerbaydzhan SSR	0.8	0.9	0.9	1.0	45	48	50	53
Turkmen SSR	0.2	0.2	0.3	0.3	31	32	34	30

In 1985 the volume of intercepted harmful substances increased by more than 15 million metric tons or by 8% compared with 1980.

Despite increased industrial production, as a result of the implementation of atmospheric protection measures, the quantity of harmful substances being discarded into the atmosphere decreased by 5% over the 1981-1985 period.

Source: Narodnoye Khozyaystvo SSSR v 1985 g., Moscow: "Finansy i Statistika", 1986, p. 386.

Table 4 summarizes recent Soviet efforts to trap and render harmless the particulate and gaseous emissions generated by stationary sources of air contamination. As one can see the percentage of these substances intercepted has been essentially constant from 1982 through 1985 at about 75 percent. Turkmenia again rates last in terms of its air pollution abattement record, instead of being next to last as it is with regard to recirculating industrial water systems, Estonia ranks first in air pollution abatement. Similar to the industrial water systems, the sheer size of the RSFSR makes it practically determine the average percentage of abatement. As Table 4 notes, despite industrial growth the quantity of substances still escaping into the atmosphere decreased by 5 percent between 1981 and 1985. Casual empiricism while visiting many Soviet cities over the past nearly two decades makes this writer rather dubious about the accuracy of the empirical data used to compile Table 4. The suspicion is that the Soviet record with regard to air pollution abatement is overstated by this table. The skies of Moscow, Kiev, and Leningrad are very likely to represent a breath of fresh air compared to those of cities in the heavily industrialized Donbas, Kuzbas, and Urals! A multitude of published complaints about the quality of air pollution abatement equipment lends further credence to the assessment that the Soviets have much work yet remaining to make their skies blue.[61]

Nature Preservation

The final topic to be discussed here is the recent Soviet record with respect to nature preservation. The Soviet Union has three categories of land areas under preserved or reserved status: State Nature Preserves called *zapovedniki*, National Nature Parks, and Hunting Preserves. The category of National Nature Parks is a quite new and positive ecological and recreational concept in the Soviet Union. The *zapovednik* system predates the revolution with the 1912 establishment of the Lagodekhskiy *zapovednik* located in the Georgian Republic. Also, the large Barguzin *zapovednik* along the shores of Lake Baykal was formed in 1916.[62] While the status of such nature reserves has vacillated both in number and area over the years, clearly as Table 5 indicates the territorial extent of these nature protection units has increased dramatically over the past decade. In fact, the total area more than doubled between 1975 and 1985. Implicit in Table 5 is the fact that the more recent Soviet additions to their reserved lands have encompassed significantly larger areas. For example, the Yugan reserve created in 1982, the Olekmin reserve created in 1984, and the Central Siberian reserve created in 1985 cover 648,636 hectares, 847,102 hectares and 972,017 hectares, respectively. The largest current unit is the Taymyr preserve created in 1979 out of 1,348,316 hectares in the northern part of central Siberia. All four of these large preserves are located in the RSFSR.[63] Obviously, the larger the areal extent of a given *zapovednik* the more ecologically intact it may remain.

Table 5
Nature preserves (zapovedniki), *hunting reserves and national nature parks.*

	1975	1980	1984	1985
Number of Nature Preserves and Hunting Reserves	120	135	147	150
Their Area in 1,000s of hectares	8,683	11,060	14,814	17,549
Number of National Nature Parks	3	7	12	13
Their Area in 1,000s of hectares	178	411	752	788

Source: Narodnoye Khozyaystvo SSSR v 1985 g., Moscow: "Finansy i Statistika", 1986, p. 383.

In April 1981 a resolution of the USSR Gosplan and the USSR State Committee on Science and Technology affirmed the status of the *zapovednik* system.[64] In 1983 a detailed description of the climates, soils, landscapes, vegetation, and animals of each reserve was published.[65] The stated indispensable conditions for a Soviet *zapovednik* are the prohibition of any activity which would be disturbing to the natural complexes of the protected territories except for the conducting of scientific research, including the continuous monitoring of important natural objects.[66] This objective was clearly not universally observed during the exigencies of World War II, for example, when oil was discovered and pumped on the territory of the Zhiguli Nature Preserve near Kuybyshev. During a 1983 scientific fieldtrip to the Central Chernozem Nature Preserve near Kursk as a guest of the Moscow Institute of Geography, this author was able to observe various types of scientific research being conducted on the preserve. Clearly, the management of this preserve was guided more by a multi-use perspective rather than a pure « ecological or wilderness » preservation perspective.

In cooperation with the UNESCO « Man and Biosphere » program a number of Soviet *zapovedniki* have been transferred at the present time into the category of biospheres with the purpose and goal of helping to protect the genetic fund of both floral and faunal species.[68] The Soviets appear to be quite active participants in this program. Overall, the recent Soviet efforts and trends in this area of nature protection seem quite sincere and positive.

6. Expenditures and Investment in Environmental Protection

Recent Soviet industrial expenditures for environmental protection and the rational use of natural resources are summarized in Tables 6 and 7 which follow. Table 6 lists 1985 industrial expenditures for such uses by republic and grouped into four macro regions. Again, of course, the average All-Union percentage increase from 1980 to 1985 is heavily biased by the RSFSR's figure. Two of the three Baltic republics have shown significant increases over the five-year period. Except for basically agricultural Moldavia, the industrial heartland republics of the RSFSR, the Ukraine, and Belorussia fit the national trend for increased expenditures. In Transcaucasia, Armenia and Azerbaydzhan lag the national average significantly, while Georgia ranks second only to Lithuania. Interestingly enough Turkmenia stands out as the only Central Asian republic that has demonstrated a level of increased expenditures exceeding the national average. Considering that Turkmenia ranked lowest in the data displayed in Tables 2 and 4, this augmented level of industrial expenditures for environmental protection within the republic seems clearly understandable and warranted.

Table 6

Expenditure of basic funds by industries for environmental protection and rational use of natural resources by Union Republics in 1985 (at end of the year).

Region	In Millions of Rubles	1985 as % of 1980
USSR	20,970	150
Estonian SSR	150	126
Latvian SSR	95	163
Lithuanian SSR	175	198
RSFSR	14,066	151
Ukrainian SSR	3,757	155
Belorussian SSR	517	143
Moldavian SSR	110	126
Armenian SSR	133	126
Azerbaydzhan SSR	185	126
Georgian SSR	119	190
Kazakh SSR	1,115	142
Kirgiz SSR	55	128
Tadzhik SSR	50	144
Turkmen SSR	56	187
Uzbek SSR	387	134

Source: Narodnoye Khozyaystvo SSSR v 1985 g., Moscow: "Finansy i Statistika", 1986, p. 388.

Trends in state capital investment in measures designed to protect the environment and make more rational use of resources presented in Table 7 are somewhat troubling. The steep upward trend from the 1971-75 plan period to the 1976-80 plan period was reversed absolutely with regard to both water and air resources capital investments for the 1981-85 period. The fraction of overall total expenditures in areas other than air and water resources, however, grew from 14.2 percent in the 1976-80 plan period to 19.2 percent in the 1981-85 period. Perhaps this trend away from simply air and water resources is positive, but unlikely. It seems the evidence and data for water and air resource problems presented earlier in this paper would warrant increased rather than the decreased absolute levels of capital investments in air and water resources as shown in Table 7. N.I. Ryzhkov claims, however, that implementation of various planned scientific and technical measures during the 12th Five-Year Plan in the field of resource conservation will result in a 28.6 billion ruble savings in the unit cost of industrial production as compared against 16.3 billion rubles in the 11th Five-Year Plan.[69] In summary, despite a plethora of decrees, resolutions, and publications exhorting more efforts in the area of environmental protection, it seems that these levels of capital investment are too low. At the same time, however, one must clearly interpret this as yet another example of the Soviet Union's increasingly severe problems with scarce investment capital.

Table 7

State capital investment in measures for nature protection and rational use of natural resources

(in constant prices; millions of rubles).

	1971-75	1976-80	1981-85	1985
Measures for Nature Protection and Rational Use of Natural Resources	7,291	10,824	11,120	2,486
In which number: For Protection and Rational Use of Water Resources	5,411	8,338	8,087	1,683
For Atmospheric Protection	725	950	899	234

The total sum of expenditures for nature protection and rational use of natural resources (including outlays in the forestry economy) amounted to about 43 billion rubles in the 1981-85 period, of which more than 9.5 billion rubles were expended in 1985.

Source: Narodnoye Khozyaystvo SSSR v 1985 g., Moscow: "Finansy i Statistika", 1986, p. 387.

7. Summary and Conclusions

This short overview paper of some of the Soviet Union's environmental problems leaves much omitted. Problems such as over-fishing and the destruction of spawning beds, timber harvesting practices and replanting rates, land reclamation and irrigation, soil erosion and salinization, biocide usage, wildlife preservation and habitat destruction and poaching have unfortunately, but necessarily, been excluded. All of these amongst a host of other environmental and resource problems are indeed major issues which deserve serious attention by the Soviet regime.

A brief exploration of the final version of the Communist Party Program and Party Statutes of the 27th CPSU Congress may provide a few hints as to the vision the Gorbachev leadership has for addressing these various environmental problems now and into the future. Four quotations from the final version of the Party Program[70] seem most germane:

Scientific and technical progress should be aimed at a radical improvement in the utilization of natural resources, raw and other materials, fuel and energy at all stages — from the extraction and comprehensive processing of raw materials to the production and use of the final product. It is necessary to accelerate the pace of lowering the materials-intensiveness, metal-intensiveness and energy-intensiveness of the national income. Resource conservation will become a decisive source of satisfying the growth of the national economy's requirements for fuel, energy, and raw and other materials.

A top-priority task is to improve the correlation among capital investments in the resource-extracting, processing and consuming branches and to carry out a redistribution of money in favor of branches that ensure the acceleration of scientific and technical progress.

The system of levers and incentives is called upon to provide real advantages to labor collectives that achieve successes in the acceleration of scientific and technical progress, produce the best output, and increase the profitability of production.

Price formation must be improved, so that prices will more accurately reflect the level of socially necessary outlays, as well as the quality of products and services, and will more actively stimulate scientific and technical progress, resource conservation,...

All four of these quotes pertain to much broader Soviet environmental and natural resource management questions than have been discussed in this paper. Nonetheless, they are all relevant to the four problem areas which have been addressed: water quality, water quantity, air quality, and nature preservation. The first quotation describes

221

Gorbachev's rational goal of achieving economic growth through intensive (i.e., more efficient use of resource inputs) as opposed to extensive means (i.e., an emphasis on the growth of inputs). In fact, the Soviets have little choice but to try to actively pursue such strategies as natural resource scarcities in terms of absolute availability, quality, and costs are becoming ever more evident for a large number of industrial raw materials, including for the purposes here water supplies for industry and agriculture.

The second and third quotes speak in very general terms of economic incentive levers designed to induce both workers and economic managers of the economy to make investment decisions which facilitate this intensive growth strategy.

The final quote on price formation seems crucial to any hoped for Soviet successes in addressing their myriad of natural resource management problems. Article 15 of the 1970 Soviet Water Law specifically stated that water use was to be free. Nonetheless, a potentially very hopeful event occurred as of January 1, 1982, when water use charges were introduced everywhere in the USSR for water taken from « water resource systems » by industrial enterprises.[71] Water charges for irrigation use have been and are being experimented with again today. Then, too, a number of proposals for effluent discharge charges have been proposed.[72] The USSR State Planning Committee has received a number of practical proposals for improving plan indices related to environmental protection and rational natural resource utilization. At least up to 1983 the only ecological expense figured into the unit cost of the output of Soviet industries was the above noted water consumed from water-intake systems. The mining industry now at least has to take into account outlays for land recultivation in its unit costs.[73]

A joint decision by Gosplan, the USSR State Construction Committee, and the Presidium of the Academy of Sciences led to the articulation and enactment in October 1983 of « Temporary Standard Rules for Determining the Economic Effectiveness of the Implementation of Environmental Protection Measures and Evaluating the Economic Damage Done to the National Economy by Pollution of the Natural Environment ».[74] The guiding principle of these rules is a benefit-cost analysis of the cost of environmental protection measures against the magnitude of the environmental pollution damage which they would prevent. These are all very positive recent developments, but still leave much to be articulated in terms of truly comprehensive and effective ecologic-economic planning indices.

Thus, it seems quite unlikely that environmental concerns and problems are about to fade into the background of the consciousness of either the Soviet populace or leadership as evidenced, for example, by the pervasive environmental concerns voiced at recent Soviet writers' congresses.[75] It seems as though environmental concerns are being used by the Gorbachev leadership as a vehicle for allowing, if not indeed encouraging, the expression of pent-up criticisms of bureaucratic mismanagement and corruption. In the process a quasi-democratic dialogue critical of the Soviet Union's management of the environment is being heard within wide circles in Soviet society. Furthermore, the Guidelines for the 12th Five-Year Plan provide a general laundry list of environmental protection and rational resource use goals.[76] In his political report to the 27th Party Congress General Secretary Gorbachev stated:

A firm rule must be established to which the over-consumption of resources is disadvantageous and economizing receives a tangible reward

and that:

More resolute economic, legal and educational measures are necessary here. All of us living today are accountable for nature to our descendants and to history.[77]

He has correctly set out the tasks and hopefully this paper provides some insight into the sheer magnitude and immense difficulties and obstacles which current and future environmental problems pose for Gorbachev and his citizens being able to achieve their desired goals of sustained high levels of economic growth and well-being. Environmental protection measures are only an interim, yet perhaps necessary, stage on the way towards the lofty, but unfortunately unattainable, goal of a waste-free technological society.

Notes

1. Craig ZumBrunnen, «The Lake Baikal Controversy: A Pollution Threat or a Turning Point in Soviet Environmental Consciousness?», Chapter 6 in *Environmental Deterioration in the Soviet Union and Eastern Europe*, edited by Ivan Volgyes, New York: Praeger Publishers, 1974, pp. 80-122.
2. Boris Komarov (pseudonym.), *Unichtozheniye prirody: Obostreniye ekologicheskogo krizisa v SSSR*, Frankfurt am Main: Possev Verlag, 1978 and *Destruction of Nature in the Soviet Union*, White Plains, New York: M.E. Sharpe, 1980.
3. Philip R. Pryde, «The 'Decade of the Environment' in the USSR», *Science*, Vol. 220, No. 4594 (April 15, 1983), pp. 74-79.
4. Craig ZumBrunnen, *The Geography of Water Pollution in the Soviet Union*, Ph.D. dissertation, University of California at Berkeley, 1973, pp. 279-358.
5. *Ibid.*, pp. 111-114.
6. *Ibid.*, pp. 111-114.
7. Craig ZumBrunnen, «The Lake Baikal Controversy: A Pollution Threat or a Turning Point in Soviet Environmental Consciousness?», *op.cit.*, pp. 80-122.
8. B. Babich, V. Lozanskiy, and A. Kuzin, «The Conservation and Rational Utilization of Water Resources Is a Major Economic Problem», *Current Digest of the Soviet Press* (hereafter, *CDSP*), Vol. 32, No. 41 (November 12, 1980), p. 1., translated from *Planovoye khozyaystvo*, No. 8 (August 1980), pp. 97-102.
9. Marshall Goldman: *The Spoils of Progress: Environmental Pollution in the Soviet Union*, Cambridge: MIT Press, 1972, pp. 43-75; ZumBrunnen, *The Geography of Water Pollution in the Soviet Union, op. cit.*, pp. 129-192. Craig ZumBrunnen, «A Review of Soviet Water Quality Management Theory and Practice», Chapter 13 in *Geographical Studies on the Soviet Union: Essays in Honor of Chauncy D. Harris*, edited by George J. Demko and Roland J. Fuchs, Chicago: University of Chicago, Department of Geography, Research Paper No. 211, 1984, pp. 261-294.

10. For example, see: Oskar Lange and Fred Taylor, *On the Economic Theory of Socialism*, New York: McGraw-Hill, 1964, pp. 103-108.
11. For a critique of the theory and practice of private enterprise, see: William K. Kapp, *The Social Costs of Private Enterprise, 1971 edition*, New York: Schocken Books, 1971.
12. For example, see: *Izvestiya*, July 29, 1983, p. 3; *Izvestiya*, Sept. 10, 1983, p. 3; *Kommunist*, No. 15, October 1983, pp. 80-89; *Izvestiya*, Nov. 2, 1983, p. 2; *Ekonomicheskaya Gazeta*, No. 16, April 1984, p. 17; *Izvestiya*, June 16, 1984, p. 3; *Izvestiya*, July 14, 1984, p. 2; *Izvestiya*, Sept. 22, 1984, p. 2; *Pravda*, July 3 1985, p. 3; *Izvestiya*, July 3, 1985, pp. 2-3; *Izvestiya*, August 10, 1985, p. 3; *Literaturnaya Gazeta*, Oct. 29, 1986, pp. 1, 10.
13. For example, see: discussion of such issues in Victor Mote and Craig ZumBrunnen, « Anthropogenic Environmental Alteration of the Sea of Azov », *Soviet Geography: Review & Translation*, Vol. 18, No. 10 (Dec. 1977), pp. 744-759.
14. ZumBrunnen, « A Review of Soviet Water Quality Management Theory and Practice », op. cit., pp. 270-279.
15. *Ibid.*, pp. 279-281.
16. For example, see ZumBrunnen, « The Lake Baikal Controversy: A Pollution Threat or a Turning Point in Soviet Environmental Consciousness? », op. cit., pp. 80-122.
17. Donald R. Kelley, Kenneth R. Stunkel, and Richard R. Wescott, *The Economic Superpowers and the Environment: The United States, the Soviet Union and Japan*, San Francisco: W.H. Freeman & Co., 1976, various pages.
18. ZumBrunnen, « A Review of Soviet Water Quality Management Theory and Practice », *op. cit.*, pp. 267-270.
19. *Ibid*, 281-283.
20. V.M. Blinova, ed., *Okhrana priroda: sbornik normativnykh aktov*, Moscow: Yuridicheskaya literatura, 1971.
21. « Russian Republic Law: On Conservation in the Russian Republic », *CDSP*, Vol. 12, No. 44 (November 30, 1960), pp. 3-5.
22. Zigurds, L. Zile, « Kolbasov's *Legislation on Water Use in the USSR* from the Perspective of Recent Trends in Soviet Law », in *Water Law in the Soviet Union*, ed. Irving K. Fox, Madison: The University of Wisconsin Press, 1971, p. 83.
23. A.M. Geleyeva and M.L. Kurok, eds., *Ob okhrane okruzhayushchey sredy: Sbornik dokumentov partii i pravitel'stba, 1917-1985, gg.*, Moscow: Izdatel'stvo politicheskoy literatury, 1986, 415 pages.
24. For example, see: A.L. Yashin, « Moral'nyy dolg nashego pokeleniya », *Priroda*, No. 7, (July 1965), pp. 56-57; T. Sushkov, « Pravovaya okhrana priroda », *Sovetskoye gosudarstvo i pravo* (May 1969), pp. 3-10; G. Filimonov, « Problems and Opinions: Protecting the Environment », *CDSP*, Vol. 30, No. 34 (September 20, 1978), p. 18; « Plenary Session of USSR Supreme Court », *CDSP*, Vol. 38, No. 3 (February 19, 1986), p. 18; Craig ZumBrunnen, « A Review of Soviet Water Quality Management Theory and Practice », Chapter 13 in *Geographical Studies on the Soviet Union: Essays in Honor of Chauncy D. Harris, op. cit.*, pp. 266-273.
25. For numerous such examples, see Goldman, *Spoils of Progress, op. cit.*, various pages; ZumBrunnen, *The Geography of Water Pollution in the Soviet Union, op. cit.*, various pages; ZumBrunnen, « A Review of Soviet Water Quality Management Theory and Practice », *op. cit.*, pp. 266-272 and accompanying footnotes; Yu. Khrenov, « The USSR Supreme Soviet Between Sessions: Who Is Indebted to Nature », *CDSP*, Vol. 37, No. 23 (July 3, 1985), p. 22.
26. Zile, « Kolbasov's *Legislation on Water Use in the USSR* from the Perspective of Recent Trends in Soviet Law », *op. cit.*, pp. 78-79.
27. *Pravda and Izvestiya*, March 5, 1986, pp. 4-5.
28. For example, see: *Izvestiya*, August 9, 1983, p. 2, for a discussion of sanctions imposed on industrial firms along the Tom' River in Kemerovo Oblast'.
29. For examples, see: *Izvestiya*, December 4, 1985, p. 6; *Pravda*, December 18, 1986, p. 6; *Izvestiya*, October 7, 1984, p. 2; *Izvestiya*, July 27, 1984, p. 6; *Izvestiya*, July 14, 1984, p. 3; *Izvestiya*, June 3, 1984, p. 3; *Pravda*, October 21, 1983, p. 3; and *Izvestiya*, October 29, 1984, p. 6.
30. « In the Politburo of the CPSU Central Committee », *CDSP*, Vol. 38, No. 13 (March 30, 1986), pp. 19-20.
31. *Izvestiya*, July 4, 1985, p. 1.
32. *Vedomosti Verkhovnogo Soveta SSSR*, No. 37 [2371], September 10, 1986, Item 782, pp. 729-736.
33. ZumBrunnen, *The Geography of Water Pollution in the Soviet Union, op. cit.*, pp. 1-776; ZumBrunnen, « Institutional Reasons for Soviet Water Pollution Problems », *Proceedings of the Association of American Geographers*, Vol. 6 (April 1974), pp. 105-108; ZumBrunnen, « A Spatial and Quantitative Estimate of the Water Pollution Generating Potential of the Soviet Union: A First Approximation », Discussion Paper No. 40, Department of Geography, The Ohio State University, December 1973, pp. 1-58; ZumBrunnen, « The Lake Baikal Controversy: A Pollution Threat or a Turning Point in Soviet Environmental Consciousness? », *op. cit.*, pp. 80-122; ZumBrunnen, « Water Pollution in the Black and Azov Seas », Chapter 2 in *Environmental Misuse in the Soviet Union*, edited by Frederick Singleton, New York; Praeger Publishers, 1976, pp. 33-59; ZumBrunnen, « Water Pollution », Chapter 5 in *The Ukraine within the U.S.S.R.*, edited by I.S. Koropeckyj, New York: Praeger Publishers, 1977, pp. 109-134; Mote and ZumBrunnen, « Anthropogenic Environmental Alteration of the Sea of Azov », *op. cit.*, pp. 744-759; ZumBrunnen, « VNDIVO and Ukrainian Water Quality Management », *The Annals of the Ukrainian Academy of Arts and Sciences of the United States*, Vol. 13, Nos. 35-36 (1973-

1977), pp. 116-143; ZumBrunnen, «An Estimate of the Impact of Recent Soviet Industrial and Urban Growth upon Surface Water Quality», in *Soviet Resource Management and the Environment*, edited by W.A. Douglas Jackson, Columbus, Ohio: AAASS Press, 1978, pp. 83-104; and ZumBrunnen, «A Review of Soviet Water Quality Management Theory and Practice», *op. cit.*, pp. 257-294.
34. For a sample listing of such published accounts, see: ZumBrunnen, «A Review of Soviet Water Quality Management Theory and Practice», *op. cit.*, footnote number 36, pp. 267-269.
35. For recent pollution accounts, see: *Literaturnaya Gazeta*, May 25, 1983, p. 15; *Izvestiya*, July 29, 1983, p. 3; *Ekonomicheskaya Gazeta*, No. 30, July 1983, p. 9; *Izvestiya*, August 9, 1983, p. 2; *Pravda*, August 27, 1983, p. 3; *Izvestiya*, October 27, 1983, p. 6; *Zarya Vostoka*, November 22, 1983, pp. 1-3; *Izvestiya*, December 31, 1983, p. 3; *Izvestiya*, January 5, 1984, p. 3; *Izvestiya*, January 16, 1984, p. 3; *Pravda*, January 21, 1984, p. 1; *Pravda*, March 11, 1984, p. 3; *Izvestiya*, March 26, 1984, p 6; *Izvestiya*, April 17, 1984, p. 3; *Pravda*, April 29, 1984, p. 6; *Pravda*, May 21, 1984, p. 7; *Izvestiya*, July 1, 1984, p. 2; *Izvestiya*, July 14, 1984, p. 2; *Sovetskaya Kultura*, January 28, 1984, p. 6; *Pravda*, December 28, 1984, p. 3; *Izvestiya*, January 12, 1985, p. 3; *Izvestiya*, March 6, 1985, p. 2; *Izvestiya*, March 9, 1985, p. 3; *Izvestiya*, June 8, 1985, p. 2; *Izvestiya*, June 27, 1985, p. 6; *Pravda*, January 11, 1985, p. 3; *Pravda*, January 12, 1986, p. 3; *Izvestiya*, February 17, 1986, pp. 3 et 6; *Izvestiya*, March 5, 1986, pp. 4-5; *Izvestiya*, June 20, 1986, p. 7; and *Pravda*, December 28, 1986, p. 2.
36. For example, see: *Pravda*, Dec. 28, 1984, p. 3; *Pravda*, Jan. 11, 1986, p. 3; *Pravda*, Jan. 12, 1986, p. 3; *Izvestiya*, Feb. 17, 1986, pp. 3, 6; *Pravda*, Dec. 26, 1986, p. 2.
37. *Literaturnaya Gazeta*, May 25, 1983, p. 15; *Pravda*, March 11, 1984, p. 3; and *Izvestiya*, Jan. 12, 1985, p. 3.
38. For example, see: *Pravda*, May 21, 1984, p. 7; *Literaturnaya Gazeta*, October 29, 1986, p. 11; and *Izvestiya*, January 11, 1987, p. 3.
39. *Izvestiya*, March 26, 1984, p. 6; and *Izvestiya*, June 20, 1986, p. 7.
40. *Izvestiya*, July 14, 1984, p. 2.
41. *Pravda*, August 27, 1983, p. 3; *Izvestiya*, July 14, 1984, p. 2; and *Izvestiya*, March 9, 1985, p. 3.
42. For example, see: Mote and ZumBrunnen, «Anthropogenic Environmental Alteration of the Sea of Azov», *op. cit.*, pp. 744-759; and *Izvestiya*, January 16, 1984, p. 3.
43. *Izvestiya*, October 27, 1983, p. 6.
44. *Izvestiya*, June 27, 1985, p. 6.
45. *Izvestiya*, July 1, 1984, p. 2; and *Izvestiya*, April 17, 1984, p. 3.
46. *Izvestiya*, June 8, 1985, p. 2.
47. *Izvestiya*, April 17, 1984, p. 3; and *Pravda*, April 29, 1984, p. 6.
48. *Ekonomicheskaya Gazeta*, No. 30, July 1983, p. 9.
49. *Izvestiya*, August 9, 1983, p. 24.
50. Theodore Shabad, «Geographical Aspects of the Chernobyl' Nuclear Accident», *Soviet Geography*, Vol. 27, No. 7 (September 1986), pp. 504-526.
51. David Tolmazin, *Ukrainian Water Resource Problems*, Edmonton: University of Alberta, forthcoming, 1987.
52. For example, see: *Pravda*, February 17, 1984, p. 3; *Izvestiya*, June 22, 1984, p. 2; *Sovetskaya Rossiya*, August 29, 1984, p. 3; *Pravda vostoka*, January 9, 1985, p. 1; *Sovetskaya Kirgiziya*, April 5, 1985, p. 2; *Pravda*, October 23, 1985, p. 3; *Sovetskaya Rossiya*, December 20, 1985, p. 3; *Sovetskaya Rossiya*, January 3, 1986, p. 3; *Pravda*, February 10, 1986, p. 2; *Pravda*, February 12, 1986, p. 3; *Pravda*, February 12, 1986, p. 3; *Izvestiya*, August 22, 1986, p. 3; *Literaturnaya Gazeta*, September 3, 1986, p. 10; *Literaturnaya Gazeta*, October 29, 1986, pp. 1, 10; and *Pravda*, November 15, 1986, pp. 1-2.
53. *Pravda*, August 16, 1986, p. 1; and Pravda and Izvestiya, August 20, 1986, p. 1.
54. *Sotsialisticheskaya Industriya*, October 12, 1983, p. 4; *Pravda*, October 10, 1983, p. 1; *Sovestkaya Rossiya*, May 4, 1984, p. 3; *Izvestiya*, August 11, 1984, p. 1; *Izvestiya*, October 20, 1984, p. 2; *Literaturnaya Gazeta*, September 3, 1986, p. 10; *Literaturnaya Gazeta*, October 29, 1986, pp. 1, 10; *Izvestiya*, November 30, 1986, p. 2; and *Pravda*, December 1, 1986, p. 2.
55. *Pravda*, July 3, 1985, p. 3.
56. *Izvestiya*, November 29, 1985, p. 3.
57. *Kommunist*, No. 15, October 1983, pp. 80-89.
58. *Sovestkaya Rossiya*, July 9, 1985, p. 4.
59. *Izvestiya*, May 28, 1984, p. 2.
60. *Izvestiya*, October 7, 1984, p. 2.
61. For example, see: *Kommunist*, No. 15, October 1983, pp. 80-89; and *Pravda*, July 3, 1985, p. 3.
62. Geleyeva and Kurok, eds, *Ob okhrane okruzhayushchey sredy: Sbornik dokumentov partii i pravitel'stva, 1917-1985 gg.*, op. cit., pp. 403-407.
63. *Ibid.*, p. 406.
64. *Ibid.*, p. 403.
65. A.M. Borodin and E.E. Syroyechkobskiy, eds., *Zapovedniki SSSR*, Moscow: Lesnaya promyshlenost'*, 1983.
66. Geleyeva and Kurok, eds., *Ob okhrane okruzhayushchey sredy: Sbornik dokumentov partii i pravitel' stba*, 1917-1985, op. cit., pp. 403.
67. Personal inspection by author during IGU Pre-Congress fieldtrip in 1976.
68. Geleyeva and Kurok, eds., *Ob okhrane okruzhayushchey sredy: Sbornik dokumentov partii i pravitel'stba, 1917-1985 gg.*, op. cit., pp. 403.

69. *Pravda*, June 19, 1986, pp. 1-5.
70. «Proletarians of All Countries Unite!: THE PROGRAM OF THE COMMUNIST PARTY OF THE SOVIET UNION (NEW VERSION). - Adopted by the 27th *CPSU* Congress», *CDSP*, Special Supplement, December 1986, pp. 8-12.
71. *Ekonomicheskaya Gazeta*, No. 2, January 1982, p. 2.
72. ZumBrunnen, «A Review of Soviet Water Quality Management Theory and Practice», *op. cit.*, pp. 284-292.
73. *Pravda*, November 14, 1983, p. 7.
74. *Ekonomicheskaya Gazeta*, No. 16, April 1983, p. 17.
75. For translated coverage of these writers' congresses, see: *CDSP*, Vol. 37, No. 52 (January 22, 1986), pp. 1-9; *CDSP*, Vol. 38, No. 31 (September 3, 1986), pp. 8-10; and *CDSP*, Vol. 38, No. 32 (September 10, 1986), pp. 8-10.
76. *Pravda*, November 9, 1985, pp. 1-6.
77. *Pravda*, February 26, 1986, pp. 2-10.

Bibliography

B. Babich, V. Lozanskiy, and A. Kuzin, «The Conservation and Rational Utilization of Water Resources Is a Major Economic Problem», *Current Digest of the Soviet Press* (hereafter, CDSP), Vol. 32, No. 41 (November 12, 1980), p. 1, translated from *Planovoye Khozyaystvo*, No. 8 (August 1980), pp. 97-102.

V.M. Blinova, ed., *Okhrana priroda: sbornik normativnykh aktov*, Moscow: Yurudicheskaya literatura, 1971.

A.M. Borodin and E.E. Syroyechkobskiy, eds., *Zapovedniki SSSR*, Moscow: Lesnaya promyshlennost', 1983.

CDSP, Vol. 37, No. 52 (January 22, 1986), pp. 1-9.

CDSP, Vol. 38, No. 31 (September 3, 1986), pp. 8-10.

CDSP, Vol. 38, No. 32 (September 10, 1986), pp. 8-10.

Ekonomicheskaya Gazeta, various issues, see footnotes.

G. Filimonov, «Problems and Opinions: Protecting the Environment», *CDSP*, Vol. 30, No. 34 (September 20, 1978), p. 18.

A.M. Geleyeva and M. L. Kurok, eds., *Ob okhrane okruzhayushchey sredy: Sbornik dokumentov partii i pravitel'stva, 1917-1985, gg.*, Moscow: Izdatel'stvo politicheskoy literatury, 1986.

Marshall Goldman, *The Spoils of Progress: Environmental Pollution in the Soviet Union*, Cambridge, MIT Press, 1972.

«In the Politburo of the CPSU Central Committee», *CDSP*, Vol. 38, No. 13 (March 30, 1986), pp. 19-20.

Izvestiya, various issues, see footnotes.

William K. Kapp, *The Social Costs of Private Enterprise*, 1971 edition, New York: Schocken Books, 1971.

Donald R. Kelley, Kenneth R. Stunkel, and Richard R. Wescott, *The Economic Superpowers and the Environment: The United States, the Soviet Union and Japan*, San Francisco: W.H. Freeman & Co, 1976.

Yu. Khrenov, « The USSR Supreme Soviet Between Sessions : Who Is Indebted to Nature », *CDSP*, Vol. 37, No. 23 (July 23, 1985), p. 22.

Boris Komarov (pseudonym.), *Unichtozheniye prirody: Obostreniye ekologicheskogo krizisa v SSSR*, Frankfurt am Main : Possev Verlag, 1978 and *Destruction of Nature in the Soviet Union*, White Plains, New York : M.E. Sharpe, 1980.

Kommunist, various issues, see footnotes.

Oskar Lange and Fred Taylor, *On the Economic Theory of Socialism*, New York : McGraw-Hill, 1964.

Literaturnaya Gazeta, various issues, see footnotes.

Victor Mote and Craig ZumBrunnen, « Anthropogenic Environmental Alteration of the Sea of Azov », *Soviet Geography: Review & Translation*, Vol. 18, No. 10 (Dec. 1977), pp. 744-759.

« Plenary Session of USSR Supreme Court », *CDSP*, Vol. 38, No. 3 (February 19, 1986), p. 18.

Pravda, various issues, see footnotes.

Pravda Vostoka, various issues, see footnotes.

« Proletarians of All Countries Unite ! : The program of the Communist Party of the Soviet Union (new version). Adopted by the 27th CPSU Congress », *CDSP, Special Supplement*, December 1986, pp. 8-12.

Philip R. Pryde, « The 'Decade of the Environment' in the USSR », *Science*, Vol. 220, No. 4594 (April 15, 1983), pp. 74-79.

Russian Republic Law : On Conservation in the Russian Republic », *CDSP*, Vol. 12, No. 44 (November 30, 1960), pp. 3-5.

Theodore Shabad, « Geographical Aspects of the Chernobyl' Nuclear Accident », *Soviet Geography*, Vol. 27, No. 7 (September 1986), pp. 504-526.

Sotsialisticheskaya Industriya, October 12, 1983, p. 4.

Sovetskaya Kirgiziya, April 5, 1985, p. 2.

Sovetskaya Kultura, January 28, 1984, p. 6.

Sovetskaya Rossiya, August 29, 1984, p. 3.

T. Sushkov, « Pravovaya okhrana priroda », *Sovetskoye gosudarstvo i pravo* (May 1969), pp. 3-10.

David Tolmazin, *Ukrainian Water Resource Problems*, Edmonton: University of Alberta, forthcoming 1987.

Vedomosti Verkhovnogo Soveta SSSR, No. 37 (2371), September 10, 1986, Item 782, pp. 729-736.

A.L. Yashin, « Moral'nyy dolg nashego pokeleniya », *Priroda*, No. 7 (July 1965), pp. 56-57.

Zigurds L. Zile, « Kolbasov's Legislation on Water Use in the USSR from the Perspective of Recent Trends in Soviet Law », in *Water Law in the Soviet Union*, ed. Irving K. Fox, Madison: The University of Wisconsin Press, 1971, pp. 75-90.

Zarya vostoka, November 22, 1983, pp. 1-3.

Craig ZumBrunnen, *The Geography of Water Pollution in the Soviet Union*, Ph.D. dissertation, University of California at Berkeley, 1973.

Craig ZumBrunnen, « A Spatial and Quantitative Estimate of the Water Pollution Generating Potential of the Soviet Union: A First Approximation », Discussion Paper No. 40, Department of Geography, The Ohio State University. December 1973, pp. 1-58.

Craig ZumBrunnen, « Institutional Reasons for Soviet Water Pollution Problems », *Proceedings of the Association of American Geographers*, Vol. 6 (April 1974), pp. 105-108.

Craig ZumBrunnen, « The Lake Baikal Controversy: A Pollution Threat or a Turning Point in Soviet Environmental Consciousness? », Chapter 6 in *Environmental Deterioration in the Soviet Union and Eastern Europe*, edited by Ivan Volgyes, New York: Praeger Publishers, 1974, pp. 80-122.

Craig ZumBrunnen, « Water Pollution in the Black and Azov Seas », Chapter 2 in *Environmental Misuse in the Soviet Union*, edited by Frederick Singleton, New York: Praeger Publishers, 1976, pp. 33-59.

Craig ZumBrunnen: « Water Pollution », Chapter 5 in *The Ukraine within the U.S.S.R.*, edited by I.S. Koropeckyj, New York: Praeger Publishers, 1977, pp. 109-134.

Craig ZumBrunnen: « VNDIVO and Ukrainian Water Quality Management », *The Annals of the Ukrainian Academy of Arts and Sciences of the United States*, Vol. 13, Nos. 35-36 (1973-1977), pp. 116-143.

Craig ZumBrunnen, « An Estimate of the Impact of Recent Soviet Industrial and Urban Growth upon Surface Water Quality », in *Soviet Resource Management and the Environment*, edited by W.A. Douglas Jackson, Colombus, Ohio: AAASS Press, 1978, pp. 83-104.

Craig ZumBrunnen, « A Review of Soviet Water Quality Management Theory and Practice », Chapter 13 in *Geographical Studies on the Soviet Union: Essays in Honor of Chauncy D. Harris*, edited by George J. Demko and Roland J. Fuchs, Chicago: University of Chicago, Department of Geography, Research Paper No 211, 1984, pp. 261-294.

The Problems of Industrial Modernisation in the USSR

Boris Rumer

Introduction

Industrial modernization has been proclaimed to be the main goal of the economic program of the new Soviet leadership. It has been almost two years since Gorbachev's selection to the post of the General Secretary — a substantial amount of time in our rapidly changing world. So far, the Soviet leader has succeeded in liberalizing somewhat the spiritual life of Soviet society. However, the main political and economic institutions of the Soviet system have remained untouched. Despite all his early promises, Gorbachev's behavior in the economic sphere has been very cautious and extremely inconsistent. For example, it is hard to understand how industrial enterprises can be transferred to the system of self-financing without a radical solution to the problem of prices, supplies, inevitable bankruptcies of enterprises and resulting unemployment. The rationale behind such seemingly contradictory measures as more rigid centralization and greater rights for enterprises is also unclear. One can cite many other paradoxical examples of recent steps made by the new Soviet leaders in the economic sphere. It appears that they do not have a well thought out economic program. Instead, they realize the immediate necessity to put an end to the process of transformation of the Soviet economy into a Third World-type economy and, most of all, to avoid the loss of the status of a military superpower. Prompted by this fear, the leaders of the Soviet Union have planned to carry out a radical modernization of industry or, in other words, to reindustrialize the Soviet economy. In terms of its ambition and scale, this plan is reminiscent of Stalin's plan of industrialization. As is well known, the latter remained unfulfilled. How realistic is Gorbachev's plan for reindustrialization?

The Meaning of Industrial Modernization

The planned program of industrial modernization provides for mass reconstruction of enterprises and replacement of obsolete capital. According to the plan, fixed capital replacement rates will double by 1990 (from 3% in 1985 to 6% in 1990).[1] Old equipment should be replaced with the most modern machinery designed to meet the highest technological standards in the world. Implementation of this program requires enormous investment in upgrading of existing capacities and acquisition of new technologies.

The 12th Five-Year Plan provides for an increase in investment in industry, primarily heavy industry, at the expense of consumption. According to Gorbachev, the focus of investment policy will shift from «expansion of industrial fixed capital to its modernization».[2] The plan also contains a program for a radical modernization of the machine-building sector which, by comparison with the previous five-year plan period, will receive 80% more investment. The emphasis here is advanced technology. Tbe prospects for obtaining new technology from the West are not very encouraging due to a number of political and economic reasons, among which the reduction in Soviet hard currency reserves is very important. It is unclear whether Gorbachev's foreign policy initiatives will pay off in the form of Western credits and equipment. Therefore a large-scale program of industrial modernization such as proposed by Gorbachev and his associates, must rely primarily on the domestic machine-building base.

Thus, important decisions, which at the planning stage constitute the basis for industrial modernization, have been made. But what are the real conditions for their implementation? Does the investment situation in the Soviet industry make it possible to allocate investment to upgrading of existing capacities? Will this much larger amount of investment be used effectively? Is there a strong enough base that could absorb it? Can we expect the machine-building sector to accomplish the tasks facing it?

Reallocation of Investment from Construction of New to Upgrading of Existing Capacities

Giving priority to investment in upgrading of existing capacities (not construction of new ones, as was done during the eleven preceding five-year plan periods) is the fundamental precondition for the implementation of the modernization program. In his report to the 27th Party Congress Prime Minister Nikolay Ryzhkov stated that « a characteristic feature of the new five-year plan is the emphasis on technological rearmament and reconstruction of existing production. The share of capital investment allocated to this purpose will increase from 37% in 1985 to 50% in 1990. In those branches and regions where capital has become especially obsolete, this number will be even higher.[3]

The course toward priority for investment in upgrading of existing capacities and, accordingly, reduction of the share of new construction, was adopted by the Soviet leadership in the early 70's. But despite the decisions of the 24th, 25th and 26th Party Congresses, despite the persisting calls to channel the flow of investment into reconstruction and modernization, the share of new construction remained 60% in 1985.[4] Whereas in the previous five-year plan period (1981-85), based on published statistics, the share of reconstruction and modernization grew by six percentage points (from 31. 6% to 37. 5%), the current five-year plan provides for a thirteen-percentage-point increase.⁵ Achieving this number will require enormous changes in the entire investment sphere of the economy. But, first of all, how accurate is the picture reflected in official Soviet statistics?

One of the most sophisticated specialists in the area of investment statistics, Delez Palterovich of the Institute of Economics of the Soviet Academy of Sciences, hinted in November 1986 that enterprises falsify information concerning investment in modernization. They report construction of new capacities as modernization and reconstruction.[6] Therefore, it is likely that the official Soviet indications of the share of investment in modernization are higher than the reality.

It should be noted that the Soviet leaders appear to be sensitive to this issue. Perhaps they understand the futility of their efforts. A meeting took place in December 1986 at the Central Committee where the leadership — M. Gorbachev, N. Ryzhkov, Ye. Ligachev and L. Zaykov — together with the heads of industrial ministries, discussed the economic results of 1986 and measures that need to be taken in order to guarantee the fulfillment of the 1987 plan. One of the issue repeatedly emphasized by the participants of the meeting was that «the bulk of capital investment should be chanelled not to the construction of new capacities but to reconstruction and modernization of existing enterprises».[7]

But this direction of the investment policy met with opposition of Soviet scholars. The December 1986 issue of the leading economic journal *Voprosy Ekonomiki* contained an article written by a recognized authority in the field of investment planning, Lyudmila Smyshlyayeva. She referred to the proposal to increase significantly the share of investment allocated to reconstruction and modernization as inappropriate.[8] Another prominent expert, L. Braginskiy, wrote in October 1986 in the Party's principal ideological journal *Kommunist* that «a sharp counterposing of two basic trends in capital investment — reconstruction and new construction — is economically unfounded».[9]

In the pre-Gorbachev years Soviet experts refrained from criticizing the investment policy of the leadership. But today, in the period of openness, or «glasnost», some economists feel brave enough to speak out on the subject.

Thus, the disagreement of leading economic scholars with the leadership's policy of sharp reallocation of investment has been established. Do these and other experts object to the preferential funding of modernization and reduction in the enormous volume of investment in new construction? In principle, they agree that this step is justified and even necessary. Objections are raised to the proportion, speed and scale of the implementation of such an ambitious economic plan without adequate preparations. Reading between the lines, we can see that the experts see little possibility of achieving by 1990 the planned targets for capital stock renovation on the basis of a qualitatively new technology. Few believe in the success of the reconstruction and modernization campaign in the conditions in which it is being conducted.

This attitude is reflected not only in scholarly publications, but in the practice of economic planning. The Gosplan and the ministries were mandated by a government decree in 1985 to develop plans for modernization and reconstruction by individual branches. But by the end of 1986 almost nothing had been done to prepare those plans.[10] A similar situation existed at the beginning of the previous, 11th Five-Year Plan period. Writing in 1981, the deputy chief of the Department of Capital Investment of Gosplan, A. Stepun, admitted that the ministries did not work out long-term plans for technological re-equipment on the basis of new technology in time for the 11th Five-Year Plan period.[11]

Since then we have witnessed a rejuvenation in the leadership of the economy which is now managed by better educated and more dynamic technocrats. But, the wheels of this most important economic program continue to spin in one place.

Gorbachev's team inherited from Brezhnev's an idealized, one-sided approach to modernization of industrial enterprises. They see its implementation in the concrete conditions of the Soviet economy.

In an ideal situation the major portion of capital investment is allocated to the acquisition of new equipment and a minor part of it to reconstruction of buildings and other structures. Therefore, as a result of modernization and reconstruction, one unit of added capacity should consume much less capital than as a result of new construction. But in reality most enterprises built after the war and, especially before the war, require a radical reconstruction which is now often more expensive than new construction. It should be noted that many enterprises are located in urban areas and do not have reserve land for territorial expansion.

Proponents of rapid and comprehensive reconstruction and modernization remain undeterred by the lack of success. They attribute it to shortcomings in the work of ministries, enterprises, or individual failures of various officials and continue to advocate this policy.

However, there are more objective reasons responsible for the lack of success of this program. The reason for the failure is that the economy's investement sphere was totally unprepared for such a large-scale program. The corresponding scientific, design, planning and machine-building bases were not re-oriented or prepared. The construction industry was not reorganized, nor was it equipped to engage in renovations. Finally, no-one established the kind of material stimulation which would compensate for running the risk of not fulfilling the production plan, with all the material consequences resulting therefrom.[12]

The latter constitutes a very significant problem. Gosplan does not reduce output targets when it prepares plans for reconstruction and modernization. Indeed, it raises them. There are limits to the ability of an enterprise to function under the conditions of reconstruction when its machinery and various items of equipment are being replaced. At least a partial slowdown of production is unavoidable. However, in practice enterprises are expected to carry out reconstruction without stopping production, the planned targets for which are not lowered. If their work absolutely must be stopped, permission to do so is sought from the highest authorities. It is very difficult, and practically impossible, to carry out a quick and thorough reconstruction and modernization and combine it with continuity of production. The choice is clear: either the plan has to remain unfulfilled or reconstruction has to be stretched out*.[13] Gosplan pressures the ministries which, in turn, pressure enterprises to achieve both plan targets and quick reconstruction. But, instead of rebuilding the old structures and replacing old equipment, new shops are being built adjacent to the old ones which, in essence, is construction of new capacities. This work is then reported to the central authorities as reconstruction and modernization. Enterprises simply do not have any choice.

Those who are at the top of the economic planning apparatus are not capable of dealing with the trade-off between accelerated replacement of capital stock and output growth. At any given moment they cannot accept a decline in industrial production because day-to-day interests have always been given top priority by the Soviet leadership. The inability to take a temporary setback for the sake of a long-term advance has been an inherent feature of the Soviet system. This is also one of the fundamental reasons why the program of industrial modernization has made little progress. But even in an ideal situation it would have been impossible to introduce, within the first years of the current five-year plan period, changes so deep that they would affect the entire process of investment in industry. It would entail re-directing the process with a 70 year history and an enormous amount of inertia.

"The Revolutionary Mission of Machine-Building"

That was precisely the term used by Lev Zaykov who is now one of the most important members of the Politburo. Zaykov is responsible for Soviet industry and for the plan of development of the machine-building sector in 1986-90. « Without a powerful and far-reaching qualitative leap in machine-building the country cannot guarantee the fulfillment of the

---

* Soviet planning officials even have a special term for it-« crawling reconstruction. »

plan» said Zaykov in August 1986. This leap should result in 80%-95% of Soviet machine-building output reaching the «world standard».[14] Speaking at a meeting in the Central Committee, Zaykov used the term «the *highest* world standard» (emphasis added).[15] This is the most important goal of the machine-building program entailed in the 12th Five-Year Plan, its «most important economic and political task»[16], the key to successful modernization of industry.

In 1986 Vladimir Fal'tsman published the results of his study of quality control statistics supplied by government organizations and information concerning the international standing of Soviet-produced equipment collected by foreign trade organizations.[17] Based on Fal'tsman's analysis, one must conclude that the share of Soviet machine-building output that meets the world standard is so small that, in order to raise it to the 80%-95% mark, it will be necessary to replace two-thirds of the total machine-building output in the current five-year plan period. It is hard to imagine that any Soviet expert seriously believes in the feasibility of this task.

Soviet leaders are adopting emergency measures aimed at reaching the targets set by the plan for the machine-building sector. Lev Zaykov declared in November 1986 that «the machine-building complex has been given everything that our economy has. Construction and development of a number of enterprises of other industries has been stopped. In a word, it has been given the maximum».[18] In 1986 alone investment in machine-building has risen dramatically. In the machine-tool industry, which is considered the key branch for the entire machine-building sector, investment rose by 46% over the 1985 level.[19] But will the machine-building sector be able to digest this sudden enormous injection of investment? Has enough of construction industry's capacity been allocated to meet the demands of the machine-building sector? Are machine-building plants prepared to carry out such an enormous task?

The plan for the introduction of fixed capital in machine-building was fulfilled only by 77% in 1986.[20] Thus, even under the most favorable, even extraordinary conditions, the program for completed investment in machine-building remained unfulfilled by 23%. It should be noted that fixed capital introduced in 1986 was created as a result of appropriations made in previous years when the level of investment was much lower. Nonetheless, the results fell short of the plan target by a large amount.

This happened in a situation where the level of investment activity in other industrial sectors had been lowered and resources had been focussed on machine-building. What can we expect in the latter years of the current five-year plan period when enormous investment, authorized in 1986, will have to be spent on the actual project of reconstruction, modernization and new construction? By that time the consequences of the slowdown in other sectors mentioned by Zaykov will be felt. The situation in those industries is bound to deteriorate and it will boomerang to machine-building.

Such serious violations of investment balance in the Soviet economy cannot go unpunished. Khrushchev's maneuver in the late 1950's that entailed a sharp re-allocation of investment to the chemical industry, was very similar to the current machine-building program. It had very serious unforeseen consequences for the entire Soviet economy. In his assessment of the results of Khrushchev's action a leading specialist on investment planning in the Soviet Union, Victor Krasovskiy, warned that « the investment ship cannot change its course sharply ».[21]

Zaykov, Silayev and other members of the top industrial leadership understand that the construction industry is not ready for the implementation of this ambitious investment program. They see the solution to this problem in charging enterprises with the task of carrying out a large portion of reconstruction on their own. Zaykov told a meeting of machine-building plant managers that « it is necessary to develop construction by means of enterprises' own construction brigades »*.[22] But shifting the burden of very complex and labor-consuming reconstruction work onto the shoulders of enterprises will not save the situation. The majority of enterprises have small construction brigades which lack the necessary equipment. It is not surprising that, despite persistent demands to increase machine-building enterprises' own construction activity, little progress has been made toward this goal. Published data for 1986 reflect an unsatisfactory situation in this sphere in a number of branches of the machine-building sector.[23]

Already in the first year of the 12th Five-Year Plan period the targets were not reached. Statistics for 1986 indicate that the output plan was fulfilled in only six out of sixteen reported categories of machine-building production. Out of these six, three targets were reached only in monetary terms. In the conditions of hidden inflation which drives the prices of machine-building products upward, this information does not appear reliable. According to the statistical report for 1986, « the investment process has not experienced any significant changes. Dispersion of capital investment has not been overcome; the plan for putting fixed capital into production has not been fulfilled ».[24] The plan for construction in industry has not been fulfilled either. At the same time capital expenditures on reconstruction and modernization increased by 17% over the 1985 level, or by 5.7 billion roubles.[25] Thus, a significant shift of resources to upgrading of existing enterprises occured in 1986. But the machine-building and construction industries have been unable to absorb this investment.

* Khozyaystvennyy sposob.

Apparently, the targets for the machine-building sector established in the five-year plan have not been translated into concrete tasks for enterprises. Ministries have lowered the original goals set by the plan. For example, the five-year plan has directed the machine-tool industry to raise the share of forging and stamping machinery that meets world standards to 86% of its output of such equipment by 1990. But the chief administration in the Ministry of Machine-Tool Industry responsible for the production of this equipment has reduced this number to 62%. It should be noted that this type of equipment is very important for modernization of both the civilian and defense industry. Perhaps Gorbachev's anger toward the ministries can be explained by their passive resistance to the unrealistic plans of the Party leadership. The ministries are fully aware of the real capabilities of their enterprises.

Automation — the Key Concept of Modernization

The concrete implementation of modernization of industry consists of greater automation. Prime Minister Nikolay Ryzhkov told the 27th Party Congress that « the characteristic feature of automation in the 12th Five-Year Plan is fast development of robots and flexible automated production lines (GAP*) which guarantee high productivity. The number of industrial robots will increase threefold.[26] Let us see how realistic these plans are.

In the course of the 11th Five-Year Plan period the output of industrial robots more than doubled and reached the 15,000 unit mark in 1985.[27] This, certainly, illustrates the quantitative achievement. But does this growth in production of sophisticated equipment meet the real needs of the Soviet machine-building sector? A recent study showed that in 1985 in most branches of the machine-building sector the demand for advanced metal-cutting equipment did not exceed 30% of the total demand for this type of equipment.[28]

Regardless of whether it can be adapted in the workplace, machine-building enterprises are under pressure to order new and expensive equipment. Often it is against their own interest to do so. Unsatisfactory application of robot technology is often a result of mandated introduction under poorly prepared conditions. Sometimes it is carried out to comply with a government decree; to enhance enterprises' prestige; or as a demonstration of efforts to upgrade the production process for the purpose of impressing higher authorities. Ultimately, the policy of forced introduction results in isolation of advanced technology, whatever enterprise adopts it. Information on enterprises of the machine-building sector indicates that there is little enthusiasm for — and in many cases

---

* «Gibkoye Avtomatizirovannoye Proizvodstvo» — Flexible Automated Production Line.

passive resistance to — the introduction of numerically controlled machine tools and machining centers, robots, etc.[29]

According to one authoritative Soviet expert, development and introduction of robots was not based on economic reasoning. The slogan « robotization is the answer to all problems » was put forward and more than 20 ministries responded with a campaign to promote industrial robots. Most participating branches of industry lacked the necessary resources and experience. The robots that they developed and built ended up being too expensive and one-tenth as reliable as the best robots in the world market. Moreover, these robots were used to automate old machines and technologies.[30] These are the achievements of the robotization campaign in the Soviet industry at the start of the 12th Five-Year Plan period.

The most ambitious task of the planned automation of industrial production is the creation and introduction of GAPs-flexible automated production lines. These constitute flexible systems of equipment working in a coordinated fashion following a single program and encompassing all stages of the technological process. In other words, these are production lines without people. What is the status of this program, which, according to Prime Minister Ryzhkov, will be developing rapidly in the 12th Five-Year Plan period?

Let us turn for an answer to one of the leading experts in the field of automation of industrial production in the USSR, the Chairman of the Committee for Automation of the National Scientific-Technological Society, Professor L. Volchkevich. He thinks that « many entreprises base their actions on the future promise of GAPs, but more so on their ambitions and sentiments produced by the atmosphere of excitement surrounding this issue. They try to acquire GAPs now or plan to do so in the near future. What can this « mass movement » and haste lead to? It is worth thinking about it seriously before it's too late ».[31]

Volchkevich described the unreliability and ineffectiveness of GAP components and whether « in these conditions it is necessary to hurry with a mass campaign. Obviously, not. What should be done then? Only science can answer this question. But so far it has not provided answers to questions of where and how to build the first GAPs ».[32]

The foremost Soviet theoretician in the field of GAPs, Academician Lev Koshkin, is no more optimistic than Professor Volchkevich. He wrote that « progress beyond separate components of future GAPs has not been achieved ». In his estimate, development of GAPs will require an investment of 35 billion roubles, but « so far there cannot even be any mention of returns from (investment in) GAPs ».[33]

Thus, Prime Minister Ryzhkov's optimism for flexible automated production lines is not supported by the opinion of Soviet scientists.

Professor Volchkevich used the following metaphor to describe the current state of affairs in his field : «(We are) as far away from production lines without people as we are from the stars».[34]

Research and Development

Gorbachev and his associates understand that modernization of industry is impossible unless the entire system of research and development is reorganized radically. They have taken a number of steps in that direction. One of the most important measures was an attempt to break departmental barriers standing in the way of integration of research. The function of development of new technology is split among many branches of machine-building. This leads to dispersion of responsibility among various ministries whose own self-interests are often mutually exclusive and obstruct mobilization of resources and acceleration of development of advanced technology.

To overcome these obstacles new Interbranch Scientific-Technological Complexes (MNTK*) have been created. These include both basic research institutions from the Academy of Sciences system and applied institutes and laboratories subordinated to ministries. The result of this innovation is envisaged as a research conglomerate focused on a single research task and guided by a powerful brains trust. Its functions include the entire R&D process from fundamental research to making and testing samples of new products. Thus, in addition to their research component, MNTKs must include testing and design bureaus and substantial production facilities.

In industry this highly intensive R&D process must be matched by a greater capacity to absorb new technology. This requires creation of testing and experimental facilities and special shops and services for putting new technologies into production. Lev Zaykov told a meeting of enterprise managers in Leningrad that such shops and services «must constitute at least 7%-10% of production capacity of every — I repeat — every enterprise».[35]

By the start of the 12th Five-Year Plan period less than half of research organizations in the Soviet Union had testing and experimental facilities. For the machine-building sector the figure was only 47%.[36] It is not surprising, then, that the results of many research programs recommended for production remain unused because they cannot be tested.

Efforts devoted to the innovation process have spread to the psychological sphere. Deputy Prime Minister and the Chairman of the Bureau for Machine-Building Ivan Silayev claims that «in order to make goods that meet the world standard it is first of all necessary to eradicate the

* MNTK — Mezhotraslevoy Nauchno-Technicheskiy Kompleks.

syndrome of inability to search the forward edge which is deeply rooted in the minds of many». According to Silayev, «breaking the psychological barrier is the biggest obstacle standing in the way of modern production».[37]

Zaykov's statement that expansion of the research and development sphere must be carried out «as we go along» is not an accident. This means that the level of production should not be reduced. The fact that an enterprise has set aside 7%-10% of its capacities for testing and experiments does not mean that its plan targets will be reduced accordingly.

A similar approach has been taken in the creation of MNTKs: member-institutions remain dependent on their original branch ministries for finances, investment and other resources.[38] The dualism of the concept of MNTK leaves member-institutions in the jurisdiction of branch ministries which control resource allocation, yet takes them outside the ministerial system. From the practical point of view, the idea of the Interbranch Scientific-Technological Complex is stillborn. The ministry is primarily responsible for the fulfillment of its plan. There can be little doubt that it will give top priority to this goal when it comes to distributing resources allocated to it. Half-measures such as MNTKs reflect the lack of decisiveness typical of the Gorbachev administration's approach to the management of the economy.

This can be best illustrated by a recent exchange between a leading scholar in the field of machine-building Academician Yuriy Nesterikhin and a director of a large enterprise. In his reply to Nesterikhin's question why the enterprise management would not put into production the results of scientists' research, the director said: «Do you know what plan targets I have? They are approximately 50% higher than my capacities. Everything is getting done on overtime and in (the atmosphere of) assault (on the plan). What am I to do with new technology? Nobody will reduce my plan targets. Look, virtually every enterprise is trying to fulfill the plan for production and fails to fulfill the plan for new technology. That is because the former means a 33% bonus for the personnel, while the latter — only 8%. And as long as the government does not reduce our production plan targets in proportion to the (plan for new technology) or allocate additional capacities for it, I am sorry, but I cannot do anything».[39]

Creation of testing and experimental facilities at a large number of enterprises, that would meet the high standards set in the process of research and development of modern equipment, is a highly ambitious goal which cannot be achieved in one five-year plan period.

It is also doubtful that Soviet designers will be able to get rid of their «syndrome of inability» which has formed in the course of several generations. The problem here is not with the undeserved inferiority complex of individual designers. The entire Soviet corps of engineers and designers in industry in general, and in machine-building in particular, is becoming increasingly incompetent. For example, a survey conducted in a large design bureau of a leading machine-building plant showed that only 20% of designers were capable of designing a simple part on their own; and only 5% could design a simple machine. This survey also has established that only one-fifth of those listed as designers can carry out very simple professional tasks. As one Soviet specialist in the field of machine design observed, « a mass-produced 'designer' incapable of solving serious problems is the central figure in today's designer corps ».[40]

This is not by any means a complete examination of the full range of problems facing the machine-building sector in the Soviet Union. But even the few issues that have been mentioned here, make quite clear the gap between the reality and the plan of industrial modernization.

Cuts in Defense Spending — an Opportunity for Modernization of Civilian Machine-Building

Some Western analysts have expressed a view that Gorbachev and his associates, pursuing the goal of industrial modernization, will switch resources from defense machine-building to civilian machine-building.[41] There is no doubt that such measures would improve prospects for the upgrading of the civilian sector. But since information concerning separate planning of defense and civilian machine-building is not available, we can only discuss this possibility on a purely hypothetical level and based on past experience. If we look at the proportion of investment allocated to the machine-building industry in the twelve five-year plan periods, three sharp increases become obvious: in the two pre-war five-year plan periods, particulary starting in the mid-1930's when new armament programs were developed in anticipation of conflict with Nazi Germany; in the two post-Khrushchev five-year plan periods (1966-70 and 1971-75), particulary in the first half of the 1970's, when there was also explosive growth in armaments production; and the new rise that began in the current five-year plan period.

Proportion of investment allocated to machine-building as a percentage of industrial investment in Soviet industry as a whole.[42]

	Five-year plan periods												
	1	2	3	war	4	5	6	7	8	9	10	11	12
Machine-Building Allocation %	18.1	29.5	33.5	34.4	16.4	12.9	12.1	15.4	19.8	22.5	22.2	24.6	30

We might naturally wonder about the role of the defense sector of the machine-building industry in decisions concerning investment in machine-building. According to Gorbachev's speech on June 11, 1985, investment in the civilian sector of the machine-building industry amounted to about 5% of the total volume of productive investment in the economy in the 11th Five-Year Plan period.[43] By combining this figure with Soviet statistics on productive investment in the machine-building industry as a whole[44], it was possible to determine that the share of the defense sector in total investment in the machine-building industry was no less than 57% in the first half of the eighties.

Does the 12th Five-Year Plan provide for any growth in investment in the defense sector of the machine-building industry? This question can be answered only on the basis of isolated statements that occasionally appear in the Soviet press. Gorbachev offers the most authoritative pronouncements on the subject. In his May 1985 speech in Leningrad the General Secretary likened the current goals of the Soviet economy to its goals on the eve of World War II, when « it was felt that the threat to the socialist state was increasing », and preparations for war were under way.[45] Thus, it appears that the ratio between investment in defense machine-building and civilian machine-building will not change in favor of the latter.

There is considerable evidence which suggests that the level of investment activity in the machine-building sector of the Soviet economy is closely and strongly tied to the development of new armaments programs. This connection can be traced throughout the three post-Stalin decades — 1956-65, 1966-75, and 1976-85. The average annual rate of growth in investment in machine-building was 9% in the first period; 12% in 1966-75; and 3.5%-4% in 1976-85.[46] It appears that the trends in investment dynamics are paralleled by trends in the development of the armaments program. The 1976-85 slump in the investment in the machine-building was likely to affect the defense sector as well.

It is plausible that investment and armaments programs followed the scenario outlined below. Rapid growth of investment in machine-building in 1966-75 resulted in a marked increase in productive capacities in the defense sector of the machine-building industry. Allowing 4-5 years for construction, research, development, testing, etc.*, the effect of the accelerated growth in investment in the 1966-75 period extended on through the entire 1976-85 period, though not thereafter. The sharp slowdown in the growth of investment throughout the latter period must have extended to the defense sector as well.

The decline in the level of investment activity in the 1976-85 period also explains the slower growth and slower rate of replacement of fixed

* Author's estimate.

assets in the defense sector of the machine-building industry. It also led to a sharp drop in the rate of introduction of new productive capacities and upgrading of existing capacities in the latter half of the 1980's. Growth in armaments production and the development of new systems is far more difficult, if not altogether impossible, under such conditions. This is the real reason why plans now call for a doubling of investment in machine-building.

The military-industrial complex, whose representatives (Ivan Silayev, Nikolay Talyzin, Lev Voronin, and others) are now occupying key positions in Soviet economic planning, has left a decisive imprint on the 12th Five-Year Plan. Declarations calling for an acceleration in techno-logical progress in machine-building as a means of promoting economic growth seem little more than a smokescreen that conceals the dominant trend of expansion and modernization of productive capacities in the defense industry.

Conclusion

Rejuvenation of the Soviet economy is an economic and political task. Its implementation depends on real liberalization and introduction of market elements which is bound to produce changes in the political system as well. Even under the most favorable conditions it is a long-term process. In his January speech Gorbachev emphasized that changes in the political system are out of the question.[47] This diminishes the possibility of any major economic reform taking place in the foreseeable future. By the same token, industrial modernization in general is a long-term process even if it is stimulated by a large infusion of investment. But modernization of the defense industry is of immediate importance and cannot be postponed.

In the same January 1987 speech to the Plenum of the Central Committee Gorbachev said: «It is very important for us, members of the Central Committee, to be realistic».[48] Being realistic one should admit that the program of modernization of Soviet industry mandated by the 12th Five-Year Plan does not stand on a solid foundation. But it is unclear why the Soviet leaders cannot understand this. And, if they do, how could they adopt such a plan?

One should not overlook the old Stalinist approach to management which presumes that the greatest returns will be brought by the greatest demands and pressure. It worked in the period of industrialization. But at what price? Is the Soviet society ready to pay the price today and can the regime force another such deal upon it?

Notes

1. Quoted in Lyudmila Smyshlyayeva, « Sovershenstvovaniye Struktury Kapital'nykh Vlozheniy i Os-novnykh Fondov », *Voprosy Ekonomiki,* No. 12, 1986, p. 133.
2. Mikhail Gorbachev, « Politicheskiy Doklad Tsentral'nogo Komiteta KPSS XXVII S'yezdu Kom-munisticheskoy Partii Sovetskogo Soyuza », in *XXVII S'yezd Kommunisticheskoy Partii Sovetskogo Soyuza,* V. 1, Moscow, *Politizdat,* 1986, p. 46.
3. Nikolay Ryzhkov, « Ob Osnovnykh Napravleniyakh Ekonomicheskogo i Sotsial'nogo Razvitiya SSSR na 1986-1990 Gody i na Period do 2000 Goda », in *XXVII S'yezd Kommunisticheskoy Partii,* V. 2, Moscow, *Politizdat,* 1986, p. 20.
4. *Narodnoye Khozyaystvo SSSR v 1985 q.* , Moscow, *Finansy i Statistika,* 1986, p. 52.
5. Ibid.
6. Delez Palterovich, « Proizvodstvennyy Apparat i Intensifikatsiya », *Voprosy Ekonomiki,* No. 11, 1986, p. 40.
7. *Pravda,* December 26, 1986, p. 1.
8. Lyudmila Smyshlyayeva, « Sovershenstvovaniye Struktury », *Voprosy Ekonomiki,* No. 12, 1986, p. 137.
9. L. Braginskiy, « Nauchno-Tekhnicheskiy Progress i Voprosy Rekonstruktsii », *Kommunist,* No. 15, 1986, p. 38.
10. Lyudmila Smyshlyayeva, « Sovershenstvovaniye Struktury », p. 137.
11. A. Stepun, « On the Rational Direction of Capital Investment in the Eleventh Five-Year Plan », *Planovoye Khozyaystvo,* No. 10, 1981, p. 36.
12. Boris Rumer, *Investment and Reindustrialization in the Soviet Economy,* Westview, Boulder, Co, 1984, p. 36. — L. Braginskiy, *Nauchno-Tekhnicheskiy Progress i Voprosy rekonstruktsii,* p. 40.
13. A. Tsygichko, « Vyvod iz Ekspluatatsii Ustarevshikh Sredstv Truda », *Planovoye Khozyaystvo,* No. 4, 1985, p. 88.
14. *Izvestiya,* August 9, 1986, p. 2.
15. *Izvestiya,* August 9, 1986, p. 2.
16. *Izvestiya,* August 9, 1986, p. 2.
17. Vladimir Fal'tsman « Prioritety Tekhnicheskoy Rekonstruktsii Mashinostroyeniya », *Voprosy Ekonomiki,* No. 6, 1986, p. 55.
18. Lev Zaykov, « Korennyye Zadachi Mashinostroiteley », *Ekonomicheskaya Gazeta,* No. 47, November 1986.
19. *Stanki i Instrument,* No. 2, 1986, p. 3.
20. *Izvestiya,* January 19, 1986, p. 2.
21. Viktor Krasovskiy, *Problemy Ekonomiki Kapital'nykh Vlozheniy,* Moscow, *Ekonomika,* 1967, p.
22. Lev Zaykov, « Korennyye Zadachi », p. 4.
23. *Izvestiya,* January 19, 1987, p. 2.
24. *Izvestiya,* January 19, 1987, p. 2.
25. *Izvestiya,* January 19, 1987, p. 1; *Narodnoye Khozyaystvo SSSR v 1985 q.* , p. 52.
26. Nikolay Ryzhkov, « Ob Osnovnykh Napravleniyakh », p. 20.
27. *Narodnoye Khozyaystvo SSSR v 1985 q.* , p. 132.
28. B. Bal'mont, « Sovershenstvovaniye Sistemy Raspredeleniya i Ispol'zovaniya Metalloobrabatyv-ayushchego Oborudovaniya », *Planovoye Khozyaystvo,* No. 7, 1985, pp. 6-7.
29. Ibid.; G. Kulagin, « O Nekotorykh Usloviyakh Intensifikatsii Mashinostroyeniya », *Planovoye Khozyaystvo,* No. 7, 1985, p. 25; « Robot Nachinayet i Proigryvayet », *Sotsialisticheskaya Industriya,* June 8, 1986.
30. « Roboty dlya Galochki », *Sovetskaya Rossiya,* May 29, 1986.
31. L. Volchkevich, « Roboty i Ekonomika », *Trud,* April 4, 1986.
32. Ibid.
33. « Roboty dlya Galochki », *Sovetskaya Rossiya,* May 29, 1986.
34. L. Volchkevich, « Roboty i Ekonomika », *Trud,* April 4, 1986.
35. Lev Zaykov, « Korennyye Zadachi », p. 4.
36. V. Zhamin, « Intensifikatsiya Nauki », *Ekonomicheskiye Nauki,* No. 4, 1985, p. 31.
37. I. Silayev, « Mashinostroyeniy — Osnova Rekonstruktsii », *Sotsialisticheskaya Industriya,* June 24, 1986.
38. B. Konovalov, Interview with Academician Yu. Nesterikhin, *Izvestiya,* June 30, 1986.
39. Ibid.
40. *EKO,* No. 6, 1986, pp. 129, 131.
41. Jan Vanous, « The Soviet Trade Crisis: Choose Tractors or Tanks », *The Washington Post,* August 17, 1986, p. c1.
42. *Kapital'noye Stroitel'stvo v SSSR,* Moscow, *Gosstatizdat,* 1961, p. 66; *Narodnoye Khozyaystvo SSSR v 1984 q.,* p. 338; *Narodnoye Khozyaystvo SSSR v 1965 q.,* p. 534; Bob Legget, « Soviet Investment Policy: The Key to Gorbachev's Program for Revitalizing the Soviet Economy » (forthcoming).
43. Mikhail Gorbachev, « Korennoy Vopros Ekonomicheskoy Politiki », report read to the meeting of the Central Committee, June 11, 1985, Moscow, *Politicheskaya Literatura,* 1985, p. 13.
44. *Narodnoye Khozyaystvo SSSR v 1984 q.,* p. 377.
45. *Kommunist,* No. 8, 1985, p. 26.

46. *Kapital'noye Stroitel'stvo v SSSR*, p. 68; *Narodnoye Khozyaystvo SSSR v 1967 q.*, p. 508; *Narodnoye Khozyaystvo SSSR v 1977 q.*, p. 354; *Narodnoye Khozyaystvo SSSR v 1980 q.*, p. 338; *Narodnoye Khozyaystvo SSSR v 1984 q.*, p. 381.
47. «Doklad M. S. Gorbacheva», p. 16.
48. «Doklad M. S. Gorbacheva na Plenume TsK KPSS», *Soviet Media Daily Digest*, Radio Liberty, January 28, 1987, p. 14.

Industrial Modernisation and Defense in the Soviet Union

Richard F. Kaufman*

1. Introduction

This paper examines General Secretary Mikhail Gorbachev's initiatives to modernize industry from the perspective of the interactions and trade-offs between the civilian and defense sectors. It begins with a discussion of the problem of declining capital productivity and the plans to improve performance through greater investment and advances in technology, especially computer and related technologies. Secondly, the effects of the defense burden on capital productivity are considered. Finally, an attempt is made to assess the role of the military in the modernization program, and to make some judgments about future prospects.

2. Modernization: The Capital Factor

Current Soviet economic policy is intended to improve efficiency and arrest the long term slowdown of growth. To achieve these ends, Gorbachev has adopted a two-track strategy. For the short term, steps are being taken to reduce alcoholism, absenteeism, corruption, and incompetency in order to increase worker productivity. These actions include organizational and high level personnel changes and address what Gorbachev terms the « human factor ».

The more far-reaching actions concern efforts to upgrade the country's plant and equipment. These constitute the modernization program. In the past, Soviet leaders set goals for economic « intensification ». Gorbachev goes further than those who preceded him and has announced as his goal « the structural transformation of the economy ». To accomplish this, Gorbachev has proposed an 80 percent increase in capital investment in civilian machine-building in 1986-1990 over 1981-1985, accelerated rates of replacement and improvement of the nation's capital stock, stricter quality control, and efforts to speed up scientific and technological progress. The modernization measures are intended to increase capital productivity and to address what may be termed the « capital factor ».

* The views expressed in this paper are those of the author and not necessarily of the Members of the Joint Economic Committee.

The problem of declining productivity and its effects on economic growth can be seen in Table 1. The slowdown in the growth of the gross national product roughly corresponds with the deterioration of total factor productivity. The latter increased slightly in the late 1960's but declined throughout the 1970's and the first half of the 1980's. However, a breakdown of labor and capital productivity shows that labor productivity (output per work hour) has increased steadily since 1965, and at a rate equivalent to some Western industrialized countries, including the United States. After rising at a 3 percent rate in 1966-1970, labor productivity growth slowed to an average annual rate of about 1.2 percent. It declined at a 2.2 percent rate in 1966-1970 and by nearly twice that rate for most of the period since 1970.

These trends are even more pronounced in the industrial sector. Table 2 compares the growth of industrial output with productivity. Total factor productivity has been declining since the late 1960's, but again capital productivity is the culprit.

What accounts for the negative trends? Of the factors that one can point to, the investment famine of the late 1970's and early 1980's deserves special mention. Soviet leaders, in an effort to increase industrial efficiency and the quality of manufactured goods for the 10th Five-Year Plan (1976-1980), decided to reduce by about 50 percent the planned growth of new fixed investment. The idea was that, with a slower rate of investment, there would be less tautness in the plan,

Table 1
USSR: growth of GNP and factor productivity.
(Average Annual Percentage Change).

	1966-1970	1971-1975	1976-1980	1981	1982	1983	1984	1985	Preliminary 1986
Gross National Product	5.1	3.0	2.3	1.4	2.6	3.2	1.4	1.1	4.2
Total Factor Productivity	0.9	-1.1	-1.1	-1.6	-0.4	0.3	-1.3	-1.4	1.7
Workhour Productivity	3.0	1.3	1.1	0.5	1.6	2.5	0.9	0.7	3.6
Capital Productivity	-2.2	-4.6	-4.3	-4.7	-3.4	-2.9	-4.6	-4.5	-1.2
Land Productivity	5.0	2.9	2.5	1.5	2.7	3.1	1.5	1.8	4.2

Source: CIA-DIA, 1987.

Labor productivity has grown more or less steadily while the declines on the capital side are greater for industrial production than for the overall economy.

Not surprisingly, high capital output ratios reflect the low capital productivity and the fact that more and more capital has been required to produce a unit of output. As Table 3 shows, capital-output ratios have gotten progressively worse since 1965.

The Soviet leadership seems painfully aware not only of the aged and largely obsolescent capital stock, but also of the relative backwardness of industrial technology. One would not want to denigrate Soviet industrial achievements or ignore the advances in many areas of civilian and military technology. Indeed, there is a substantial amount of technology transfer from the Soviet Union to the West (J. Kiser, E. Rivin). Nevertheless, evidence is strong that in most areas Soviet industrial technology lags behind the West. A leading study published in 1977 concluded there was no evidence that the technological gap between the USSR and the West had been substantially reduced in the previous 15-20 years (R. Amann, et al., p. 66).

Table 2

USSR: growth of industrial output and factor productivity.
(Average Annual Percentage Change).

	1966-1970	1971-1975	1976-1980	1981	1982	1983	1984	1985	Preliminary 1986
Industrial Production	6.2	5.5	2.7	1.3	0.8	2.7	2.6	2.7	3.6
Total Factor Productivity	-0.2	-0.2	-1.9	-3.0	-3.2	-1.1	-1.1	-0.9	-0.2
Workhour Productivity	3.1	3.9	1.3	0.6	0.0	2.2	2.1	2.2	3.1
Capital Productivity	-2.3	-3.0	-4.7	-6.1	-5.9	-4.0	-3.9	-3.7	-2.4

Source: CIA-DIA, 1987.

Table 3

USSR: incremental capital-output ratios.

Period	Industry
1951-1955	1.3
1956-1960	1.4
1961-1965	2.1
1966-1970	2.1
1971-1975	2.7
1976-1980	5.8
1981-1985	8.7

Source: Noren, 1986.

resources would be used more efficiently, and there would be greater productivity (G. Schroeder). However, the strategy backfired. There was a marked decline in industrial production during this period, along with sharp downturns in productivity and capital output ratios. Soviet industry very likely has still not recovered from the inadequate investment and the running down of the capital stock.

Abel Aganbegyan, who for years has been urging modernization of the machine-building industries, now speaks openly of the «economic stagnation» of the past 10-15 years (Aganbegyan 1987). Gorbachev himself has been publicizing Soviet industrial and technical shortcomings in an effort to win support for his program. In his Khaborovsk speech, he spoke of the serious mistakes when «in our scientific and technical policy, in many branches we oriented ourselves to the average technical level, to the repetition of the same decisions, and incorporated old equipment in our new designs for new enterprises». In words reminiscent of John F. Kennedy, Gorbachev assured his audience that, in this Five-Year-Plan, «we will get machine-building moving at a fast clip». But, he went on to say, the results would not be felt for 2-4 years (Gorbachev 1986).

In addition to sharply increasing investment in civilian machine-building, the modernization program emphasizes greater production of technologically advanced equipment. N. I. Ryzhkov discussed economic intensification in his report to the party congress on the 1986-1990 plan. He lamented the lags in the «assimilation of progressive technologies», and called for greater automation of production. Automation, he said, is grounded in electronic computer technology, robotics, and flexible automated production facilities, all of which need more rapid development and application (Ryzhkov 1986).

Large increases are planned for the production of computer equipment, including personal computers, instrumentation equipment, robots, numerically controlled machine tools, and machining centers. Greater spending for «science» and the establishment of inter-branch scientific and technical complexes are intended to promote the development of new technologies, and their incorporation into the industrial base (CIA-DIA 1987, pp. 17, 22).

Again, existing Soviet capabilities should not be discounted. For example, the Soviet currently manufacture a full range of computer systems, including microprocessors, minicomputers, mainframes, and fifth generation machines. They have achieved a form of self-sufficiency in production and management, and there has been substantial integration with CEMA computer industries (Goodman, p. 18).

Nevertheless, there are shortfalls between the computer systems and related technologies of the Soviet Union on the one hand, and those of the West on the other. It is believed that Western industries have advantages in volume of production, reliability, and quality for a wide range of hardware and software products. S. E. Goodman estimates Western leads of 2-16 years (Goodman, p. 41). The U.S. intelligence community estimates U.S. leads of 7-12 years for major categories of advanced manufacturing technologies: microprocessors, computer-operated machine tools, minicomputers, mainframes, supercomputers, software, and flexible manufacturing systems. (Leads are the estimated times required for the Soviets to achieve series production similar to U.S. series production today) (CIA-DIA 1987, p. 5).

It is noteworthy that all these computer-related technologies have military as well as civilian applications. They are essential not only in the automated manufacture of military and civilian products, but are also embedded in many of the products themselves in the form of microelectronics.

3. *The Defense Burden and Productivity*

The sustained, high defense burden has probably contributed to Soviet lags in technology. Soviet defense spending as a share of GNP, in current prices, is estimated to have risen from 12-14 percent in 1970 to about 15-17 percent in 1982, although the real growth in defense activities is believed to have been the same as economic output during this period.

Whether viewed in constant or current terms, the Soviet defense burden is very large, twice or somewhat more than twice the size of the U.S. defense burden. It is often presumed that large defense burdens constrain growth because of the opportunity costs of using scarce resources in relatively nonproductive ways. Another hypothesis, with implications for the modernization program, is that defense spending contributes to the retardation of industrial development and technology.

There have been several efforts to estimate the effects of Soviet defense spending on civilian industry and technology. One such effort measures the distribution of final demand for machinery production among consumer durables, producer durables, and military durables. Using a residual methodology to estimate military durables after deducting known uses from total machinery production, it is found that the military share increased from 19 percent in 1965 to 33-37 percent in 1985. During the same period, the share of final demand for producer durables fell from 70 percent to 47 percent. Although there are many uncertainties in this methodology, the analysis supports the view that defense has been crowding out the civilian industrial component of investment (Bond and Levine).

253

Using a more sophisticated approach, another researcher believes it is possible to identify the effect of defense spending on capital productivity. S. Cohn combined the official Soviet input-output table estimates of a Soviet scholar, and the residual method to derive demand for the output of three high-technology machinery sectors important to technological advances: precision instruments, transportation equipment, and electronics and unspecified machinery. Cohn found that for the three machinery sectors, military durables absorbed 44, 46, and 77 percent of production in 1972 and similar proportions in 1977. He concludes that defense production has been the principal beneficiary of technological progress, at the expense of investment (Cohn 1986).

Other approaches compare the growth and shares of civilian and military machinery output. The CIA has estimated that from 1965 to 1978 civilian machinery output grew faster than military machinery output. The trend reversed in the late 1970's when military output increased « resulting in a slowdown in civilian machinery growth » (JEC 1982, p. 255).

The CIA has also estimated that Soviet weapons procurement absorbs about one-third of the output of the machine-building sector (CIA 1986, p. 2). Presumably the CIA's estimates are based on the building block methodology. Private researchers have made similar findings and conclude that the slower growth of the machinery component of the capital stock impedes modernization and contributes to low growth of capital and productivity (Levine, p. 160).

Using published statistics for the Soviet machinery ministries, the DIA has estimated that 60 percent of machinery production is provided by the nine ministries considered to be primarily involved in defense production, and that the share has been increasing (DIA). It is acknowledged that ministry data contain an unknown margin of error in that substantial amounts of civilian goods are produced in the defense ministries. At the same time, the civilian machinery ministries provide defense goods such as trucks, cars, and instruments directly to the military, and components to the defense ministries.

Nevertheless, the findings are consistent with those of the CIA and others who observe that defense receives a disproportionately large share of industrial and high-technology production.

4. *Interactions and Trade-Offs*

A key set of issues concerns how modernization of the civilian industry might affect defense and how defense activities might affect modernization. With regard to Gorbachev's intentions, there are at least three possibilities. The first is that modernization is a smokescreen for a new military buildup. One expert concludes that the planned large increase in machinery investment and production is intended primarily to modernize the defense industry so it can respond to the U.S. Strategic Defense Initiative (SDI) (Rumer). However, the slowdown in military procurement spending rates of civilian goods in defense firms, the transfer of a number of top defense industry managers to civilian industry, and the diffusion of priorities in the national plan (Becker, pp. 49-50) suggest that, for the time being, any new military buildup is unlikely. There is no evidence so far that Gorbachev has changed defense spending policy, or that increased investment is primarily targeted for the defense sector.

Two other possible explanations seem more plausible : that modernization is a policy for a fundamental shift of resources from defense to the civilian sector, and, alternatively, that it is intended as a pause in defense production only until civilian industry has been retooled.

It is clear that the military would like to think they will benefit from modernization directly and indirectly. A long-standing principle of the Soviet system is that a strong industrial base is necessary for defense, and that principle has driven economic policy. One military official, Major General Vasykov, writing in the October 1985 issue of *Kommunist vooruzhennykh sil,* identified « fundamentally new instruments, computer-controlled machine-tools, robot equipment, and the latest generation computers », as requirements for serial production of modern weapons (JEC 1986, p. 50). The new weapons of the 1990's are expected to require more sophisticated guidance, sensor, computer, and communications systems based on advanced microelectronics, design, fabrication, and testing capabilities. Military leaders are aware of the relative inferiority of Soviet military technology and the inadequacies of the defense industrial base.

U.S. intelligence experts believe the military will be the ultimate beneficiary of successful modernization and that the military supports it for that reason (ibid). Under this view, the military understands that improvements will ease resource constraints and set the stage for more rapid military modernization.

The U.S. intelligence community's approach is to ask whether the machinery sector can meet the resource requirements needed for industrial modernization. Four areas of increased resource demands have been identified : factory capacity, basic materials, intermediate products, and labor. The Soviet military is thought to be well positioned in the short term to accommodate the demands of modernization for machinery resources. The expansion and upgrading of defense plants in the past decade means that most of the production capacity to support military procurement until the early 1990's is already in place (CIA-DIA 1987, pp. 29-30).

Table 4
USSR: Military-civil competition for resources.

Resource	Need in Civilian MBMW Sector for Modernization	Availability of Outside of MBMW Sector	Transferability from Military to Civilian MBMW	Comment
Materials				
Basic/Raw:				
Energy	Medium	High	High	
Intermediate:				
Chemical feed stock	High	Medium	Med-High	
Engineering fibers	High	Low-Med	High	
Micro-electronics	High	Low	High	
Specialty steel	Med-High	High	Med-High	
Aluminium	Med-High	High	High	In very short supply in both sectors

Conventional:				
Electric motors	Med-High	Low	Med-High	
Diesel engines	Med-High	Low	Med-High	
Advanced:				
Engineering plastics	High	Low-Med	High	
Micro-processors	High	Low-Med	High	
Composites	Medium	Low-Med	Medium	
Micro-electronic components	High	Low	Medium	In short supply
Manpower				
Skilled:				
Computer programmers	High	Low-Med	High	Shortage exists throughout economy
Electronics technicians	High	Low-Med	High	
Software engineers	High	Low-Med	High	
Researchers	Med-High	Med-High	Medium	
Machinists	Medium	Low-Med	High	
Industrial engineers	Medium	Low-Med	High	
Unskilled:				
Laborers	Low-Med	High	High	

Source: CIA-DIA, 1986.

257

The CIA and DIA report that the Soviets will move forward with *most* of the military modernization that the intelligence community has projected for the next few years. But they conclude that some new weapons could be delayed because of competing demands for basic materials, intermediate goods, and skilled labor (CIA-DIA 1986, p. 23). Table 4 indicates where the intelligence agencies think shortages and competition for resources between civilian industries and the military might occur. For example, there are shortages of microelectronics and computer programmers and high needs for both in the machinery sector (MBMW) for modernization. The transferability of both from the military to MBMW is also high. Will such resources be diverted from military to civilian uses for Gorbachev's modernization program, and if so what would that signify about the basic system of priorities?

The real test of Gorbachev's program will be in the longer term. The Soviets will have to tool up for the next generation of weapons in the late 1980's or early 1990's. The demand for new investment for defense plant and equipment will rise in this period. If as a result of modernization there is greater production of advanced equipment and substantially improved productivity, both civilian and military demands for machinery output could, in theory, be satisfied. If modernization does not succeed, choices would have to be made about cutting back on modernization or postponing major defense initiatives. The CIA-DIA assessment is that, despite some expected improvement in Soviet economic performance over the next few years, it is doubtful that sufficient progress can be made in improving the level of technology and reversing productivity trends to achieve faster growth in the 1990's (CIA-DIA 1987, p. 26).

Yet, it is possible that, measured against their own present levels of technology rather than those of the West, there will be substantial progress. Moreover, the CIA and DIA may be underestimating the output potential of existing capacity and over-emphasizing resource constraints. For example, it seems unlikely that shortages of skilled workers will slow modernization except for the brief periods it might take for retraining. There also may be a tendency among Western analysts generally to underestimate the potential effects of major increases in investment on industrial performance.

The intelligence agencies are probably correct that not enough progress will be made in the next few years to avoid civilian-military trade-offs in the allocation of resources. When competing demands become serious enough, the modernization program could come to a halt or be drastically scaled back if military procurement is not kept in check. It is hard to envisage real progress in modernization and increased military procurement occurring at the same time. Soviet leaders may be constrained from derailing the modernization program by the knowledge that the military would not be able to close the military technology gap with the United States in the near or medium term even if more resources were allocated to defense. Over the longer term, unless the defense burden is substantially reduced, it will continue to limit technological advances and act as a counterweight to modernization efforts.

These judgments are based in part on the increasing difficulties faced by military procurement and the institutional constraints on innovation. The Soviet Union has lagged behind the U.S. in military technology for many years. It has compensated for this deficiency mainly by a «brute force» procurement strategy of overwhelming the opposition with numerical superiority in the case of conventional weapons, and very large weapons such as land based missiles (which lacked accuracy) in the case of strategic offensive weapons. This overstates the matter somewhat because there are some examples of state of the art technology in deployed systems, and the Soviets have had successes in using lower levels of technology to field effective weapons. As a rule, the Soviets have been forced to play the role of copiers and adapters of U.S. military technology. Numerous studies by the CIA and the U.S. Defense Department document Soviet lags (JEC 1976, p. 54; JEC 1977, p. 40; DOD 1980, p. 82; DOD 16, Chapter II).

Soviet military procurement has favored simple designs and a development process that minimizes risk. The more simple weapons produced often possess good combat capabilities. They are also often limited to a single military mission and have relatively short service lives. As a result, they are more difficult and costly to maintain (CIA 1986, p. 23).

In 1982, N. V. Ogarkov published a booklet criticizing his colleagues in the military for moving too slowly in the exploitation of new technology. Military doctrine now attaches great importance to the application of microcircuitry and other advanced technologies (Odum, p. 7). The trend is toward fewer weapons that are sophisticated, multipurpose, and more costly. But defense production will continue to be hampered by lags in support industries such as those producing machine tools and computers, and deficiencies in computers and microelectronics themselves.

While the rates of technical change and capital turnover are accelerating in the West, the Soviets tend to keep machine tools in production past their obsolescence. There are significant and apparently increasing flows of technology between defense and civilian industry and, of course, defense has been given the highest priority in terms of the quantity and quality of resources. But this has not been sufficient for defense production facilities to keep up with Western levels of technological advancement. If changes are not made, institutional barriers, such as secrecy and excessive compartmentation, the absence of an environment in which innovation is encouraged, and a system that impedes scientific-industrial interaction, will continue to hold down the development of manufacturing technologies.

5. *Conclusions*

Declining capital productivity has held back the growth of the Soviet economy and is symptomatic of technological backwardness. To deal with this problem, Gorbachev has proposed huge increases in investment in civilian machine-building, and an ambitious program of replacement and improvement of the nation's capital stock. The question is whether this effort can succeed despite the burden that defense spending places on the economy, in particular the effects of military procurement on machinery production.

The disproportionate defense burden is not the only likely cause of technological backwardness. Other important factors include the inadequacy of incentives for the introduction of new technology into production, the lack of effective consumer demand for new products, and deficiencies in the organization of research and development. Given the state of economics and the available information, there is no way to assign weights to the various causal factors. The unusually high level of the Soviet defense burden, and the priority it has received in allocating scarce resources needed for advanced technology, suggests that it should be considered a major contributing cause.

Over the next few years, the Soviet leadership will have to make difficult choices about civilian modernization and new increases in defense spending as the military tools up for the next generation of weapons. Soviet civilian and military technology lag behind the United States, especially in key areas of manufacturing technologies, and the lags have grown in recent years. Even if there is little or no growth in military procurement, there is virtually no chance that the Soviets can catch up with Western military technology in the foreseeable future. Substantial increases in military procurement would probably spell the end of modernization if it does not fail for other reasons.

References

Abel Aganbegyan, Interview, Budapest Television Service, FBIS-SOV-87-046, Vol. III, N° 046, 10 March 1987.

R. Amann, J. M. Cooper, and R. W. Davies (eds.) *The Technological level of Soviet Industry,* New Haven, Yale University Press, 1977.

Abraham S. Becker, *Soviet Central Decisionmaking and Economic Growth, A Summing Up,* R-3349-AF, The Rand Corporation, Santa Monica, California, 1986.

Central Intelligence Agency (CIA), *The Soviet Weapons Industry: An Overview,* 1986.

Central Intelligence Agency-Defense Intelligence Agency (CIA-DIA), *The Soviet Economy Under a New Leader,* 1986.

Central Intelligence Agency - Defense Intelligence Agency (CIA-DIA), *Gorbachev's Modernization : A Status Report,* 1987.

Stanley Cohn, « Measuring the Impact of Soviet Defense Spending on Technology », in Thomas Lucid, Judith Reppy, George Staller (eds.), *The Economic Consequences of Military Spending in the United States and the Soviet Union,* Cornell University, Peace Studies Program, 1986.

Stanley Cohn, « Sources of Low Productivity in Soviet Capital Investment », in JEC 1982.

Defense Intelligence Agency (DIA), *Level and Trend of the Gross Value of Output in the Soviet Defense Machinery Ministries,* 1979.

Department of Defense (DOD), *The FY 1981 Department of Defense Program for Research, Development and Acquisition,* 1980.

Department of Defense (DOD), *« The FY 1987 Department of Defense Program for Research, Development, and Acquisition »,* 1986.

Mikhail Gorbachev, Speech in Khaborovsk, July 31, 1986, *The Current Digest of the Soviet Press,* Vol. XXXVIII, N° 31, September 3, 1986.

Joint Economic Committee (JEC), Hearings, *Allocation of Resources in the Soviet Union and China - 1976,* Part 2, Washington, D.C., Government Printing Office, 1976.

Joint Economic Committee (JEC) Hearings, *Allocation of Resources in the Soviet Union and China - 1977,* Part 3, Washington D.C., Government Printing, Office 1977.

Joint Economic Committee (JEC) Hearings, *Allocation of Resources in the Soviet Union and China - 1981,* Part 7, Washington, D.C., Government Printing Office, 1982.

Joint Economic Committee (JEC) Hearings, *Allocation of Resources in the Soviet Union and China - 1985,* Part 11, Washington D.C., Government Printing Office, 1986.

Joint Economic Committee (JEC) *Soviet Economy in the 1980's: Problems and Prospects,* Part I, Washington, D.C., Government Printing Office, 1982.

John W. Kiser, III, « Technology: We Can Learn a Lot from the Soviets », *Washington Post,* August 14, 1983.

Herbert S. Levine, « Possible Causes of the Deterioration of Soviet Productivity Growth in the Period 1976-1980 », in JEC 1982.

James Noren, « Soviet Investment Strategy Under Gorbachev », paper presented at the 18th National Convention of the American Association for the Advancement of Slavic Studies. New Orleans. November 1986.

W. E. Odum, « Soviet Force Posture: Dilemmas and Directions », *Problems of Communism,* July/ August 1985.

Eugene I. Rivin, « Soviet R&D - The Benefits for U.S. Industry », *Mechanical Engineering,* April 1983.

Boris Rumer, « Soviet Military Spending », *Christian Science Monitor,* September 24, 1986.

N. I. Ryzhkov, « On the Basic Guidelines for the Economic and Social Development of the U.S.S.R. in 1986-1990 and in the Period up to the Year 2000 », *The Current Digest of the Soviet Press,* Vol. XXXVIII, N° 12, April 23, 1986.

Gertrude Schroeder, « The Slowdown in Soviet Industry, 1976-1982 », *Soviet Economy,* Vol. 1, January-March, 1985.

Soviet Economic Cooperation with CMEA Countries – A Breakthrough for Industrial Cooperation?

Fredrik Pitzner-Jørgensen

Introduction

Economic cooperation between the Soviet Union and the rest of the CMEA countries is carried out mainly by plan coordination and specialisation programmes.

Since 1975, coordinated Five-Year Plans have been worked out supported by the Complex Programme of 1971, the Long-Term Sectorial Target Programmes of 1978 and 1979, and recently the Complex Programme for Scientific-Technical Progress of 1985.

It can be stated without many details that plan coordination in its present form contains a number of weaknesses. The branch ministries and similar intermediate bodies — not the producing enterprises — take part in bilateral trade coordination negotiations. This may be an advantage from a central management point of view, but it certainly does not promote direct contact between the enterprises.

It is difficult to judge precisely the lack of results of plan coordination efforts. But a crude conclusion may be drawn: the much advocated plan coordination, intended to contain an element of mutual influence of the countries on each other's economic planning, has never been very efficient. In practice, the CMEA countries have been able to accomplish no more than a very weak coordination of mutual trade plans. Some traded goods have been coordinated in physical terms (mostly raw materials), leaving prices to the formula agreed upon, and making contract prices in intra-CMEA trade follow a yearly gliding average of world market prices of the previous five years. Other goods have been coordinated in value terms, leaving physical amounts to be decided after price fixing.

An attempt to influence economic development more strongly has been made by means of a conscious division of labour, termed «Specialisation and Cooperation of Production».

The term «Specialisation» in this context covers production sharing within the CMEA, whereby the countries involved agree to a division among themselves of limited production programmes, allowing each country the status of being specialised in part of the production programme in question.

A specialisation agreement leaves no intra-CMEA competition.

Specialisation agreements often contain a «Production Cooperation» element. This covers a number of industrial cooperation forms, and may constitute a convenient supplement to specialisation, as it allows the countries to make large-scale sub-supplier agreements in connection with final goods specialisation.

« Specialisation and Cooperation » is an important instrument in CMEA economic cooperation. It has, however, had only very limited effect on economic development and economic structure of the member countries. Only some 15 per cent of intra-CMEA trade is covered by specialisation agreements, and the percentage of national gross production of course is much smaller. Moreover, specialisation agreements to a certain extent have only consolidated already existing trade patterns. Significant results have been reached only in some newer industries, where no single country appears to have been able to prove in advance any serious damage from the specialisation proposals of the partners to its own, well-established industrial interests.

All in all, Specialisation and Cooperation may have cemented a number of regional monopoly producers within narrow product ranges. Clearly, the goal of accelerating economic development through integration of production of the member countries cannot be reached this way.

Through the conclusion of Specialisation and Cooperation agreements between enterprises and economic organisations of different CMEA countries, a contact network has been woven. With about 120 multilateral Specialisation and Cooperation agreements and maybe more than 1,000 bilateral ones in force, several thousands of companies are in more or less direct contact with partners in other CMEA countries. The majority of these agreements have been concluded within the machinery industries and the chemical industry.

A very dedicated attempt to unite forces in CMEA economic cooperation may lie in the establishment of so-called international economic organisations. These are limited in number — about 60 — but they represent a rather high degree of international commitment from the participating countries.

A few forerunners were created in the fifties and sixties, but only after the Complex Programme of 1971 was this cooperation instrument activated on a larger scale.

Two sorts of international economic organisations have come into existence: interstate economic organisations and international production organisations.

Interstate economic organisations are intended to improve coordination of member states' activities in connection with certain parts of their economic and scientific-technical cooperation. The limitations on the activities of interstate economic organisations are strict: they are consultant and coordination organisations only, with no production activity. However, this principle has been broken in a number of instances.

The international production organisations are meant to have their own business activity. Some of these do possess the means of production which they utilise. Others have corporation status without possessing their own means of production, and still others do not even rate as corporations.

It seems justifiable to conclude from the above statements that plan coordination in its present form has lost much of its impetus. Great programmes alone cannot do the job of enhancing economic development of the CMEA countries.

Also, the Specialisation and Production Cooperation instrument has been disappointing, when judged from an economic growth point of view.

Finally, the international economic organisations, representing a high degree of international commitment, are limited in number. Only some of them are directly involved in production, and they are strictly limited in their business possibilities.

The crucial point, of course, is whether the CMEA can create a new division of labour and thereby give support to further economic growth. In the minds of many CMEA economists there is no doubt: industrial cooperation must be developed, and direct links between companies and other economic organisations all over the territory of the CMEA must be created.

This matter will be discussed in the following sections. Initially (Section 2) two alternative models of industrial cooperation are shown. Direct links are then described in some detail (Section 3). The room for manoeuvre through direct international links between companies must depend upon the position of the companies in their national environment. This point is taken up in Section 4. Finally, Section 5 contains some conclusions regarding prospects of CMEA industrial cooperation.

2. Two Alternative Models of Intra-CMEA Industrial Cooperation

Using a certain amount of simplification, each country of the CMEA may be described in terms of the traditional Centre-Periphery Model. The State planning commission acts as the Centre, and the companies and other economic organisations together form the Periphery.

The functioning of the national economy in short derives from the interaction of the two levels of decision-making mentioned. In the « classical » centrally planned economy, the Periphery supplies information to the Centre about production possibilities and input needs. The Centre carries out an aggregation and communicates back the results to the Periphery. After a small number of interactions between Centre and Periphery, a feasible — and hopefully in some respect optimal — plan is identified. The Centre names the plan targets, and the Periphery starts production, deliveries, etc.

Whether this interaction is initiated by the Centre or by the Periphery is of minor importance here. Also, the problem of inducing the Periphery not to cheat about their production functions is not the main concern here, although this too has to do with economic growth in a planned economy. The critical point is that business links, i.e. the contacts, contracts, etc., are tied for the fulfilment of the plan targets only, not for the purpose of the enterprises involved. In this way links between producers and consumers of industrial goods are becoming of secondary importance, and any non-fulfilment of delivery plans is punished in a very mild way. But this in turn undermines the «more important» production plans.

An economy, where production programmes of all industries are in principle governed by the Centre, has been termed a «Command Economy».

In a Command Economy, the Centre maximises an exogeneously defined optimality criterion, limited by known restrictions on input (available resources) and on output (production capacities) (Pitzner-Jørgensen 1986: 139). The optimality criterion may consist of a set of relative utilities of the industries of the economy. These relative utilities must be defined by the Centre during very early stages of the planning process. The production programme that leads to maximum combined utility is then chosen as the optimal plan. Under normal conditions, it is possible to calculate from the maximisation the set of optimal prices of all inputs and outputs in the economy.

The value added of each enterprise is determined by the central plan, as both production levels and prices are issued by the Centre. The plan, together with the technological state of the enterprises and the specific rules for retention of profits, decides whether the individual enterprise will become either a net contributor to, or a net recipient from, the rest of the economy — or in a special case be in exact balance with its environment.

The net contribution from the enterprise to the rest of the economy works like a variable taxation or subsidy. Thus, the Centre acts as a redistributor of what could be termed surplus value added.

So much for the Command Economy.

Alternatively, production programmes could be decided upon independently by the enterprises, maximising their own utility, be it net profits, sales, prestige, etc. In this case, the limits to the enterprises' growth are set by the possibilities of mutual exploitation. In an extreme case, the limits to the success of one enterprise within a limited period of time is set by the bankruptcy of all partner enterprises exactly at the end of that period. In practice, of course, such a situation is seldom seen. Generally speaking, mutual net transfers between enterprises here depend on direct agreements alone.

An economy with practically no directive central influence on Periphery activity plans will, in what follows, be referred to as a « Market Economy », stressing the primacy of Enterprise-to-Enterprise interaction over Enterprise-to-Centre relations.

In short, the Command Economy is characterised by centrally determined net transfers between enterprises, whereas in the Market Economy each enterprise is pursuing its own goals, its net financial position being determined by its direct interaction with other enterprises.

In the Market Economy, the enterprise operates at a profit not by virtue of subsidies from the Centre, but by a favourable combination of input and output prices, production volume and technology. In the case of failure, the enterprise must reorganise or go bankrupt. It will have only itself to blame, because the Centre does not play any active role in production.

Thus, inter-enterprise links do mean a lot more in the Market Economy than in the Command Economy. These links must be direct, because the Centre is unable to act as an intermediate link. The links may range from trade contracts of shorter or longer duration, over production cooperation of a more binding form, to maximum commitment through direct investments, mergers and takeovers. « Direct Links » certainly is a broad concept — but it belongs to the Market Economy, not the Command Economy.

Do member-countries of the CMEA belong to the Command Economy or to the Market Economy? The answer probably is a mixed one: some of the more tightly planned countries clearly fall into the definition of the Command Economy, but a few member countries are on their way towards the Market Economy.

Probably CMEA Cooperation today can be well described as a double Command Economy, with producers subordinated in the national context to national plan commissions and in the intra-CMEA context to the combined set of national plan commissions.

Direct Links in a Market Economy are restricted by net transfer agreements between enterprises only, i.e. by their mutual trade agreements. Enterprises will be free to decide on their own production programmes, trading partners, and prices. In international trade, this presupposes convertibility of the currencies involved.

Actual CMEA cooperation is characterised by politically set prices and bilateral trade balancing in these prices. There is no supra-national Centre and hence no supra-national redistribution. But the balancing in certain agreed prices equals net transfers in any *different* price system.

The whole CMEA can hardly be expected to jump from the Command Economy into the Market Economy in one great leap forward. This leads to a number of questions. Will the CMEA countries enter a transitional period? Can the central economic administrations manage to lift selectively the above-mentioned restrictions? Has the transitional period started already — where and how?

3. Recent Development of Direct Links Between Enterprises of Different CMEA Countries

Neither State managed trade nor Specialisation and Cooperation in its CMEA shape count as Market Economy phenomena. State managed trade surely is very far from that model, and Specialisation and Cooperation - though bearing the seeds of Direct Links between enterprises in a Market Economy - in itself is no real Market Economy phenomenon either.

This is seen when judging specific specialisation measures. Analyses of these with regard to specialisation criteria do indicate quite clearly that Command Economy is still the game of the day. (Pitzner-Jørgensen 1983: 43-46).

The crudest specialisation criterion is the attempt to create large-scale production of goods. International competition between CMEA countries is seen as a waste of resources in « parallel production ». National branch ministries are all interested in protection from the threat of parallel producers in brother countries. They would like simply to concentrate the largest possible production share in their own hands. And this may be agreed upon by rival countries, likewise attempting to secure this particular production on their territory - provided that the first country is willing to give up another piece of the cake: specialisation status in some other goods.

This specialisation is made with only slight consideration of relative production costs, and therefore indeed counts as an exogeneous, centrally determined criterion.

Economic efficiency is not taken into account in specialisation agreements, but there is a certain amount of discussion about technical efficiency of different candidate specialised producers for the goods in question. Unfortunately, different choices of technical characteristics give different orders of precedence of the producers. If, as a Solomonic solution, a combination of technical characteristics is used as the specialisation criterion, still the weights of the characteristics are disputable. Moreover, the use of given technical characteristics as a specialisation criterion still does not secure economically optimal specialisation.

Attempts to use still other criteria for specialisation have been made, one of which deserves mention. All interested countries are asked to rank a number of productions by export profitability, defined as the ratio of export value to production costs. Typically, numbers a little above unity result from such calculations. These figures, calculated for a specific set of productions in all possible countries, are then deflated by the countries' sums of export profitabilities. Specialisation can be decided upon from the deflated figures giving the specialised status to the country with the highest profitability as regards a specific production.

Of course, the problem with all these criteria is that prices — both national and intra-CMEA — are fixed by the central planners — not by the enterprises. So the latter still depend on the former.

Although Specialisation and Cooperation efforts belong to the Command Economy, they have sparked off a number of international economic organisations. Until 1985 the number of such organisations totalled only 50, but recently there have been signs showing willingness from the CMEA countries to raise that number.

These international economic organisations are interesting from a Market Economy point of view, because they represent points of common interest between the participating CMEA countries, which cannot be satisfied by weak Specialisation and Cooperation only. Some of the international organisations are given wide independence and, it may be asserted, the limitations of CMEA cooperation are being tested here, influencing future development of the CMEA economic institutions.

In connection with possible signs of a Market Economy, those inter-state economic organisations dealing with coordination only are of little interest. It might be worthwhile, however, to take a closer look at the other half, i.e. the international production organisations. These split into three forms : joint firms having their own production activity; joint corporations, one step above the firms, having both production and coordination tasks; and comradeships, resembling most of all some sort of business club.

The first joint firm within the CMEA was the Polish-Hungarian coal waste firm « Haldex », organized in 1959, producing building materials from by-products of coal mining; the second one — the 1964 Bulgarian-Hungarian « Intransmash », producing and marketing internal factory transport systems; and the third one — the 1966 multilateral firm « Medunion » selling medical equipment.

« Haldex » was formed as a joint firm on a share basis; « Intransmash », although a corporation, works as a coordinator only between its two national members. The « Medunion » is an even weaker construction, an international comradeship, i. e. lacking corporation status.

In 1972, just after the first Complex Programme, a bilateral joint company, the cotton works « Druzba » in Zawierce, Poland, was set up between Poland and the GDR. These two countries in 1973 formed the

« Interport » harbour facilities cooperation, based in Szczecin, Poland. The GDR took part in still another pair of concerns, the partner being the USSR: the « Assofoto » (Moscow, 1973) for common planning within the photographic industry, and the « Domokhim » (Moscow, 1974), for combined planning of chemical industry problems connected to household consumption.

At the same time, four multilateral joint corporations were formed: the « Interatominstrument » (Warsaw, 1972): research, production and sales of nuclear power station equipment; the « Intertekstilmash » (Moscow, 1973) with cooperation in textile machinery as its field of work; the « Interatomenergo » (Moscow, 1973): nuclear equipment, training of specialists, etc, and the « Interkhimvolokno » (Bucarest, 1974): chemical fibres.

The multilateral joint corporations were designed to work on a profit-and-loss and self-financing basis, just as the bilateral ones and the joint firms. But only « Interatominstrument » was succesful — since 1978 this one has been self-financing.

In the second half of the seventies, no multilateral joint corporations were established. Instead, a number of multilateral economic comradeships were organized. This of course marks a set-back for the development of joint firms. Only one multilateral joint firm was established, namely the « Interlichter » (Budapest, 1978), a shipping enterprise mainly employed on the river Danube, but also serving freight lines between Danube ports and India and Vietnam.

During the years 1979-1981, a new wave of bilateral joint firms shot up, many of which were planned to improve the extracting industries. Following the « Erdenet » (USSR-Mongolia, in Mongolia, 1973): copper and molybdenum; and the « Mongolsovtsvetmet » (USSR-Mongolia, Ulan Bator 1973): gold and feldspar; this new wave consisted of firms like « Mongolbolgarmetall », « Mongolczechoslovakmetall », « Haldex-Ostrava » (Czechoslovakia-Hungary) and « Vietsovpetro » (Vietnam-USSR), (Vorotnikov 1986: 80-81).

In October 1985, two Soviet-Bulgarian science and production corporations were established in the field of robots and manufacturing systems. In each case, the partners joining forces are one Soviet and one Bulgarian corporation. The two joint corporations have at their disposal certain funds of both convertible currencies and CMEA transferable roubles. Both are operated by five-year plans and annual plans. The general managers of the joint corporations have the right to negotiate prices and to conclude contracts. Final goods prices must still follow the CMEA price formula, but input prices can be negotiated freely, the only limitation being that total value of inputs must not exceed total value of the final goods in the production of which they are consumed. This way the joint corporations cannot deviate their prices from the general CMEA formula. Still, there is some room for flexibility.

Also in 1985, the Soviet-Czechoslovak joint corporation « Robot » was established. The purpose of this corporation is to develop industrial robots and flexible production systems. In addition, « Robot » assists the other CMEA countries in questions of Specialisation and Cooperation.

At the end of 1985, it was decided at government level to supplement the « Robot » by the multilateral corporation « Interrobot », the task of which will be to create a multilateral cooperation in the field of robots (Abolikhina 1986 : 57-61).

According to CMEA information, a number of new joint firms are under way. The USSR and Bulgaria are setting up a joint firm producing electronics for automobiles, and the USSR and Poland have recently signed government agreements about the establishment of no less than five joint firms (Abolikhina : ibid. and Vorotnikov : ibid.).

4. National Economic Mechanisms

The institutional framework of the individual CMEA countries is a mixture of planning and incentive mechanisms. The following *table* attempts to combine information about all details without losing the general view.

The table gives a gloomy picture of the institutional barriers between the present state of affairs and the Market Economy, where there will be no directive planning and where the importance of officially set prices will diminish considerably.

The picture does not cover all of the institutions of the CMEA countries. It shows, however, that centrally determined plans, prices, etc. will prevent most of the countries from advancing decisively towards a Market Economy state of affairs.

Quite recently, the Soviet Union has issued new rules of management on economic and scientific-technical cooperation with the Socialist Countries (Ekonomiceskja Gazeta No. 4, 1987 : 5-6). The sheer length of that document tells a lot about the matter. There may be small relaxations of central control with the enterprises, but all the trouble is in vain, as long as the Centre keeps involved in setting up plans and communicating them to the enterprises in the form of directives.

Table
Institutional frameworks in the CMEA countries, 1986.

Institutions	Country Codes:									
	BUL	CUB	CZE	GDR	HUN	MON	POL	RUM	SOV	VIE
Directive planning	X		X	X		X			X	X
Economic incentives	X	X			X		X			
Official prices for certain goods	X	X	X	X	X	X	X		X	X
Regulatory prices for certain goods	X		X				X	X		
Free prices for certain goods			NO	NO						
Sales taxes depending on price level		X	X	X						
Sales taxes used as price formation instrument										X
Profit tax	X			X	X	X	X			
Asset tax	X		X		X		X			
Wage fund tax on fund increases				X			X			
Wage fund tax on fund value					X		X			
Planned distribution of profits			X	X		X			X	
Variable taxation on surplus profits						X			X	
Independent bank credit policy	X				X		X			
Competition among bank credit demanders	X				X					
Competition among banks					X					
Companies able to influence state plans	X									
Development fund depending on profits	X	X	X	X	X	X	X		X	
No wage fund formation at company level			X	X	X	X	X			X
Incentive fund formation at company level			X	X	X		X			X
Enlarged rights in foreign trade to companies	X			X	X		X			
Retention rights of export income to companies										
— for new export purposes			X	X			X			
— for import structure change purposes	X				X				X	

Source: Bautina, 1986: 157-174.

5. Conclusions

Evidently, each of the great Complex Programmes of the CMEA has been followed by a number of new economic organisations. If the latest Complex Programme for Scientific-Technical Progress stays viable, the mushrooming of new joint firms etc. will probably continue, and perhaps even accelerate.

The limit to the viability of the Programme almost certainly rests with the ability of the CMEA to institutionalise economic independence of joint firms.

This is equal to reviving competition on CMEA territory. One can hardly imagine any competition *between* enterprises belonging to different CMEA countries without at least the same degree of independence *inside* each country.

Specialisation and Cooperation within the CMEA today rests on highly political prices. The existing network of business contacts therefore is endangered, if intra-CMEA trading prices are freed from political intervention.

But in the present situation, plan coordination still governs prices and deliveries between CMEA countries. Direct Links really do not exist.

References

Abolikhina, G.: Razvitie form naučno-proizvodstvennogo sotrudničestva (Development of Forms of Scientific-Production Cooperation), *Ekonomičeskoje Sotrudničestvo Stran-Členov SEV,* No. 11/1986, pp. 57-61. (Moscow).

Bautina, N.V.: Plan i samostojatelnost v khozjajstvennykh mekhanizmakh stran-členov SEV (Plan and Independence in Economic Mechanisms of the Member-Countries of the CMEA), *Ekonomika i organizatsija promyshlennogo proizvodstva,* No. 9/1986, pp. 157-194 (Novosibirsk).

Ekonomičeskaja Gazeta, No. 4, 1987, pp. 5-6: «O merakh po sovershenstvovaniju upravlenija ekonomičeskim i naučno-tekhničeskim sotrudničestvom s sotsialističeskimi stranami» Postanovlenie Tsentralnogo Komiteta KPSS i Soveta Ministrov SSSR (Measures to Perfectioning Management of Economic and Scientific-Technical Cooperation with Socialist Countries, Decree-Law of the Central Committee of the KPSS and the USSR Council of Ministers). (Moscow).

Pitzner-Jørgensen, F.: *Comecon-samarbejdet — modeller for praktisk planlaegning for et system af økonomier* (The CMEA Cooperation — Models for Practical Planning for a System of Economies), (Ph. D. thesis), Institute of Economics, University of Copenhagen, 1986.

Pitzner-Jørgensen, F.: *Specialisering og Kooperation i Comecon* (Specialisation and Cooperation in the CMEA), The South Jutland University Centre, Esbjerg 1983.

Vorotnikov. V.: Sovmestnye khozjajstvennye organizacii (Joint Economic Organisations), *Ekonomičeskoje Sotrudničestvo Stran-Členov SEV, No. 8/1986, pp. 79-85. (Moscow).*

Soviet Trade with the Industrialised West

Daniel Franklin

While Leonid Brezhnev was still alive, a Soviet planner contemplating the strength of his country's foreign-trade position could have been forgiven for reaching some rather complacent conclusions.

My country, he might have said, is big and self-sufficient in most natural resources, so its dependance on foreign trade is relatively small. Its imports are equivalent to little more than a tenth of national income (according to the Soviet statistical yearbook, and ignoring exchange-rate complications); this is in line with the share of that other giant, the United States (and compares with Britain's import-share of nearly a quarter). Unlike America, though, over half of the Soviet Union's trade is with a « sheltered » area, Comecon, with its guaranteed markets and comparatively stable prices. In trade with the West, there had been a great piece of luck : thanks to OPEC, the oil on which the Soviet Union has relied for some two-thirds of hard-currency exports soared in value in the 1970s, with the result that the country could buy more from the West without too much effort, and without running up the sort of hard-currency debt that crippled Poland. There seemed every chance that this luck would last.

As for the system for conducting foreign trade set up by Stalin, it provided shelter from potentially devastating Western competition without noticeably harming Soviet exports to the West. In return for Soviet protectionism against the West there were no « retaliatory » restrictions on Soviet oil deliveries to Western markets (the West seemed prepared to buy just about as much of the stuff as the Russians could supply), and the main barrier to selling more Soviet manufactured goods was the self-inflicted one of poor quality. On the whole, our hypothetical planner might have argued, the Soviet Union's protectionist foreign-trade system was working well.

This comfortable picture has been shattered by two things : the oil price came crashing down, and Mikhail Gorbachev came crashing in. The collapse of the oil price not only knocked a big hole in the Soviet Union's main source of hard currency, making it necessary to look for other hard-currency exports as a replacement for oil; it also laid bare an embarrassing weakness. The Soviet Union has been exposed as a super-power with the sort of « one-crop » export structure more commonly associated with a Third-World economy. Cheaper oil has therefore reinforced the sense of urgency in Gorbachev's drive to turn his country into an economic superpower as well as a military one.

Part of that drive involves recognising the damaging effects of having cushioned Soviet industry from international competition for so long. For all the stability it offers, the Council for Mutual Economic Assistance (to give Comecon its full name) has also aptly been dubbed the Council for Mutual Economic Inefficiency. If Soviet industry is to compete with the West, Soviet foreign trade has to become more flexible, and more open. Gorbachev knows this, and his response has been to set about introducing the most far-reaching reform of the Soviet foreign-trade system since Lenin's day.

The sudden change in the oil price, together with Gorbachev's reform of the trading system, make this a time of exceptional upheaval in Soviet trade with the industrialised West, a time for uncomfortable questions to replace the comfortable old Soviet assumptions. How damaging for the Soviet Union is the fall in the oil price? How far will the foreign-trade reform go? Will it work? Above all, is what Gorbachev has in mind fundamental change in Soviet trade policy with the West, or merely a tactical shift? These are the main questions addressed in this paper.

The Reverse Oil Shock

The Soviet Union has come to rely increasingly on energy exports, especially oil, in its trade with the West. This has happened partly because of the enormous windfall gains from the OPEC price rises of the 1970s. Between 1975 and 1980, as the tables below show, the volume of Soviet oil deliveries to the West rose by only a quarter, but the value of these sales increased more than threefold. The share of oil and gas together in total Soviet exports to OECD countries rose from under a half in 1975 to nearly four-fifths in the early 1980s.

Table 1
Soviet exports to OECD countries
($ billion).

	1975	1980	1981	1982	1983	1984	1985
Total	8.56	24.82	24.36	26.20	26.66	26.38	22.34
of which:							
Oil	3.98	14.43	14.32	16.66	17.56	16.69	12.72
Gas	0.26	2.84	4.08	3.76	3.27	3.84	3.89
Oil & Gas as % of total	49	70	76	78	78	78	74

Source: Jochen Bethkenhagen, "Oil prices and their impact", paper presented to The Economist/Girozentrale conference, "East-West Trade Under Gorbachev", December 1986.

It is easy to see why the sudden drop in the price of oil last year was potentially devastating for the Soviet Union. Taking the 1985 level of oil

Table 2
Volume of Soviet oil exports to OECD countries
(oil & oil products, mbd).

1975	1980	1981	1982	1983	1984	1985
0.96	1.21	1.08	1.33	1.50	1.58	1.31

Source: As for Table 1

sales to the West as a base, every dollar off the price of a barrel of oil costs the Soviet Union $0.5 billion in lost revenue over a year. In the latter part of 1985, Urals crude was selling on the spot market at about $27 per barrel; by the middle of 1986 the price had dropped to about $11 per barrel.

The price of gas is pegged to that of oil, and would eventually come down by a corresponding amount. To make matters worse, the sharp depreciation of the dollar was also adversely affecting the Soviet Union's terms of trade, since the country receives mainly dollars for its energy-dominated exports but pays mainly in other currencies for its imports from the West, the bulk of which come from Europe and Japan.[1]

Taking these developments for oil, gas and the dollar together (and assuming an average oil price for 1986 of $15 per barrel), Western analysts reckoned the Soviet loss of buying-power compared with 1985 could be in the order of $8 billion, equivalent to more than a third of the country's exports to the West in 1985. Soviet planners have several options available to compensate for this loss, but there are problems with all of them.

One possibility is simply to *sell more oil*. This might be called the «traditional planners' response»: if the oil isn't bringing in enough money, just open the tap wider. The trouble is that the Soviet Union is less flush with the stuff than it used to be. For the first time since the war, oil output actually fell in 1984 and again in 1985 (which helps explain why oil deliveries to the West also fell in those two years), though there was a recovery in 1986, when output rose by 3 % and was almost back to its 1983 peak. Deliveries to other Comecon countries, which account for about half of total Soviet oil exports, cannot be cut much further without the risk of a political reaction in those countries. True, there is enormous scope in the Soviet Union to save wasteful consumption of oil, or to substitute other fuels in electricity production, but these potential gains will be slow in coming. The Chernobyl disaster, which has put a strain on energy supplies and further delayed the nuclear-power programme, has not helped.

Table 3

Soviet production of oil and gas

	1980	1981	1982	1983	1984	1985	1986
Oil (m tonnes)	603	609	613	616	613	595	615
Gas (bn cu m)	435	465	501	536	587	643	686

Sources : Narodnoye Khozyaystro SSSR v 1985, p. 157; *Pravda*, 18th January 1987.

What about *selling more gas?* Here the problem is certainly not supply, since output has been soaring up at the rate of about 7 % a year in the 1980s. But gas is a less flexible commodity than oil : storage and transport are more difficult, and it is generally sold on long-term contracts. Above all, demand for Soviet gas in the West has been limited (partly because, after the pipeline controversy, Western countries have looked to other sources of supply), and is unlikely to rise sharply. So gas will at best be only a partial substitute for oil.

Planners would dearly love to *increase sales of manufactured goods* to bridge the oil gap. The reasons for their conspicuous lack of success with this in the past are well known : poor quality of Soviet products, insufficient incentives for Soviet enterprises and foreign-trade organisations (FTOs), lack of marketing expertise. No sudden change for the better can be expected — certainly not the sort that could make a significant contribution to hard-currency exports, since Soviet sales of manufactured goods start from such a low base. In the short term, two other options for raising extra hard currency fast are more promising : *bigger gold sales* (the Russians have plenty of it to sell), and *bigger borrowing* (their credit rating remains excellent). However, planners have to worry about the effect on the gold price of any substantial increase in sales, and for political reasons they have in the past been conservative borrowers.

The oil price shock has created an immediate difficulty in terms of lost hard-currency revenue. Looking farther ahead, it is clear that the Soviet Union is likely to face an export revenue problem even if the oil eventually returns to something like its 1985 level. A recent study by Jonathan Stern[2] ventures a rough quantification of the problem.

Stern predicts that Soviet oil production will stay at about 600 m tonnes for the rest of the 1980s, after which it will decline, first slowly, then steeply in the mid to late 1990s. He reckons oil exports to the West could drop to some 40 m tonnes a year (0.8 mbd) by the mid-1990s and 25 m tonnes by the end of the century, only partly offset by an increase in gas sales to the West from 30 billion cubic metres in 1985 to some 50 bcm in the mid-1990s and 60-70 bcm by the end of the century.

Assuming the world oil price recovers to $25 per barrel in the 1990s, Soviet hard-currency earnings from oil and gas would be down on their 1985 level (excluding inflation) by some $2 billion a year in the mid-1990s and by about $3 billion a year by the end of the century. As Stern is the first to admit, there are an awful lot of «ifs» in such calculations. But it is reasonable to reckon that Soviet planners are having to work with broadly similar assumptions.

The Adjustement in 1986

How has the Soviet Union coped so far with the oil shock? The short answer is: quite well. According to the United Nations Economic Commission for Europe[3], Soviet imports from the West in the first nine months of 1986 roughly stagnated in dollar terms, but fell by 17 % in volume, compared with the same period in 1985 (see Table 4). Even this degree of stability, however, was achieved at a considerable cost. As might have been expected, planners used a combination of the options mentioned above to soften the blow.

Table 4

Soviet trade with the West

(percentage change over same period of previous year).

	Soviet Exports		Soviet Imports	
	Value (^{1})	Volume	Value (^{1})	Volume
1982	5	10	3	2
1983	− 3	7	−4	2
1984	3	7	−2	5
1985	−12	−8	−2	− 1
1986 (Jan-Sep)	− 7	17	−1	−17

Note:

(^{1}) In US dollars.

Source: ECE, Economic Survey of Europe in 1986-1987.

Soviet exports to the West were down by 7 % in value in the first nine months of last year, a smaller drop than might have been expected, and there was a 17% increase in the volume of these exports. Although, according to the ECE's survey, the price of Soviet crude oil exported to the West fell by some 46 %, and that of oil products by some 39 %, there was a lag in the impact of oil price falls on gas prices. In addition, the Soviet Union managed to boost the quantity of its energy deliveries to the West by about a fifth in this period, partly thanks to the recovery in domestic energy production. There were also signs of a big effort to promote Soviet exports of manufactured goods: exports to the West of

« engineering products »[4] increased about 16 % in the first nine months of 1986, with sales of motor vehicles growing particularly fast, though this category still represented a mere 2 % of total Soviet exports to the West.

Despite this deployment of extra resources, the Soviet trade deficit with the West tripled from $ 1.2 billion in the first nine months of 1985 to $ 3.5 billion in the first nine months of last year, according to Soviet statistics.[5] This was partly offset by an estimated $ 1 billion rise in arms exports to the Third World (though it is not clear how, and how quickly, such sales are actually paid for). Soviet gold sales are reported to have increased from their 1985 level of some $ 2.5 billion. The heavier borrowing from Western banks, which began in 1985, continued (see Table 5); between January 1985 and September 1986, Soviet net liabilities vis-à-vis BIS reporting banks increased by $ 6.3 billion[6]. Western estimates of Soviet net hard-currency debt vary considerably, but it seems that (partly fuelled by the effect of the dollar's depreciation on the non-dollar part of the debt) it may have risen by about $ 8 billion last year, to a total of $ 22-$ 24 billion.[7]

Table 5
Medium- and long-term funds raised on international financial markets
($ billion).

1982	1983	1984	1985	1986
0.2	0.1	0.9	1.5	1.8

Source : As for Table 4.

More important than the overall totals of trade with the West is the structure of that trade. In this respect the Soviet Union had one great piece of luck in 1986: at last it had a decent grain harvest. At last, too, the Russians released grain output figures, after a long silence. The official plan report gives last year's grain harvest as 210.1 m tonnes, compared with 191.7 m tonnes in 1985 (itself a substantial improvement on the disastrous harvest in 1984) and an average for 1981-85 of 180.3 m tonnes. This saved imports worth over $ 2 billion last year, leaving more room for the imports of machinery and equipment that the Soviet Union so badly needs.

Soviet Import Policy

It is worth remembering that Gorbachev is by no means relying exclusively on Western technology in his drive to modernise the Soviet economy. Within the Soviet Union there are people who argue, with some justification, that « addition » to Western technology has in fact had the damaging side effect of discouraging innovation at home. Gorbachev's economic reforms are partly aimed at improving the links between research and production. He is clearly hoping for more innovative dynamism from his own factories.

At the same time, Mr Gorbachev is also putting pressure on his Comecon partners to supply better-quality goods in return for deliveries of Soviet raw materials — goods which in some cases can take the place of products until now imported from the West. Official figures point to a steadily increasing share of socialist countries in Soviet foreign trade since 1981, and a steadily decreasing share of Western market economies (see Table 6). However, these figures have to be treated with more than a pinch of salt: they reflect the fact that prices in Comecon trade have been rising, while dollar prices (converted into roubles at the official exchange rate) have fallen. This may lead to a very misleading picture of the real trend in the flows of trade.

Table 6

Regional distribution of Soviet trade turnover
(exports plus imports as % of total exports plus imports).

	1979	1980	1981	1982	1983	1984	1985	1986 (¹)
Socialist countries	56.1	53.7	52.8	54.3	56.0	57.5	61.1	67.0
Developed capitalist countries	32.1	33.6	32.2	31.6	30.1	29.3	26.7	22.6
Developing countries	11.8	12.7	15.0	14.1	13.9	13.2	12.2	10.3

Note:

(¹) The figure of 67% for socialist countries is given in the 1986 plan report; the other two figures for that year are estimated on the basis of trade returns for the first nine months.

Sources: Statisticheskiy Yezhegodnik Stran-Chlenov SEV, various years; Economist Intelligence Unit, "Country Report: USSR", No. 1, 1987; Pravda, 18th January 1987.

Then there is the security dimension. The Soviet Union has been stung by grain and pipeline embargoes, and by the West's strategic export controls. Mr Gorbachev is too much of a realist to believe that complete self-sufficiency for the socialist countries in all areas of high technology is an achieveable goal. But he certainly wants to reduce his country's vulnerability to any future Western embargoes.

With all these caveats, there is no doubt that Western technology is crucial to Gorbachev's plans — and its importance may grow if, as many people expect, Soviet factories fail to meet their ambitious targets for the production of new machinery. At least in part, his efforts to improve relations with Western Europe are to be explained by the desire to secure better access to the technology West European companies can supply. A prominent Polish dissident commented recently that « modern Western technology is more important for the Soviet Union than Poland is »; even allowing for a little colourful Polish exaggeration, the point is vividly made.

What sort of technology is Gorbachev most interested in buying from the West? His import priorities are changing along with Soviet investment policy as a whole. The emphasis is no longer on building new factories, but on modernising existing ones : in the current Five-Year Plan, the aim is to increase the share of total investment taken by equipment for modernisation from a third to a half. Accordingly, in trade with the West there is now less enthusiasm for the mega-projects that used to be so fashionable with Soviet planners, but keen interest in machinery and technology that can enhance efficiency at existing plants. The Russians are looking West for anything that can help them reduce material inputs or save energy. The new watchwords are modernisation, automation, computerisation.

This shift in emphasis is important for Soviet planners as they consider the narrower room for manoeuvre as a result of cheaper oil. Unless the price of oil recovers far more strongly than it already has, there is unlikely to be much growth in the overall volume of Soviet imports from the West; indeed, these imports may even shrink somewhat. Within the total, however, a change in structure can be expected (see Table 7): planners will want the share of manufactures (especially machinery and transport equipment, SITC 7) to rise at the expense of other categories (notably grain, harvests permitting).

Table 7
Structure of Soviet imports from the West, 1985.

Category (one-digit SITC section)	% Share
Primary products (0-2, 4)	23.5
of which:	
Food (O)	20.2
Crude materials (2)	2.3
Fuels (3)	0.9
Manufactures (5-8)	74.1
of which:	
Chemicals (5)	10.6
Semi-finished industrial goods (6)	24.8
Machinery & transport equipment (7)	29.7
Miscellaneous manufactures (8)	8.9

Source: ECE, *Economic Bulletin for Europe*, Vol. 38, 1986.

The trend will be for hard currency to be viewed in much the same way as other resources for which supply has become less abundant in recent years: the priority will be to use it more efficiently. In June 1985, in his speech to a conference on science and technology, Gorbachev complained that: «Not everything is thought through in planning purchases. Sometimes they are not linked with plans for capital construction. Ministries and departments, eagerly defending their requirements for the acquisition of imported technology, do not devote sufficient attention to the sites where the capacities are being created for the use of imported equipment.» Hence, in part, the pressure to reform the Soviet foreign-trade system, so that both the selection and assimilation of technology from the West can be improved.

Further pressure to reform the organisation of foreign trade comes from the need to diversify exports to hard-currency markets. In order to obtain the modernising technology he wants in the current five-year period, Gorbachev will probably be prepared to increase Soviet borrowing from the West considerably. But the borrowing cannot go on indefinitely, nor will Gorbachev want to let Soviet debt rise to the point where Western economic levers begin to work. If energy prices stay low, and if painful import cuts (some time in the early 1990s?) are to be avoided, Gorbachev knows he has to increase non-energy exports to hard-currency markets. He is therefore giving his country's rusty foreign-trade system a long-overdue overhaul.

Reform of the Foreign-Trade System

The traditional Soviet trading system, under which almost all imports and exports were channelled through a few specialised FTOs under the Ministry of Foreign Trade, had two great advantages: it protected the Soviet economy from unwanted foreign competition, and it was fairly efficient at handling the relatively simple bulk commodities which make up much of Soviet exports. Its main disadvantages were that it acted as an excessively rigid barrier between end-users and suppliers, and it was inefficient at handling the more complicated array of equipment which is becoming increasingly important in Soviet trade. Gorbachev is trying to make the system more flexible by:

— Granting foreign-trade rights to over 20 ministries and nearly 70 large enterprises, from the beginning of this year.[8] Overall responsibility for foreign trade is vested in a new organisation called the State Commission for Foreign Economic Relations. The newly enfranchised ministries and enterprises can deal directly with foreign partners through their own foreign-trade arms — branch FTOs in the case of the ministries, «*firmy*» in the case of enterprises — and have limited rights to retain some of the hard currency earned from exports. It seems that purchases are still supposed to fall within the plan, so the freedom of the newly enfranchised ministries and enterprises is less than total.

— Allowing joint ventures with foreign equity participation on Soviet soil.

Several points should be borne in mind when discussing these changes. (i) They are designed for Soviet trade with all countries, including Comecon partners, not just trade with the West. (ii) While the reforms are revolutionary for the Soviet Union, they are not revolutionary for the communist world as a whole — the Soviet Union is merely following the example set by several East European countries years ago. (iii) The state's monopoly of foreign trade is not being broken; it is merely the near-monopoly of the Ministry of Foreign Trade which is being eroded. (iv) Commodities such as oil, gas and timber will continue to be handled by FTOs, so the devolution of trading rights will at first affect only a very small proportion of Soviet hard-currency exports (Western analysts put the figure at about 6 %, though of course it is Gorbachev's hope that this share will grow); the share of Soviet imports that could be handled by the newly enfranchised ministries and enterprises is potentially much bigger.

The immediate effect of the changes has been to cause a lot of confusion. Many Soviet officials do not seem to know exactly who is responsible for what anymore. When asked, FTOs tend to say that they still control all the things they did before (well, they would, wouldn't they). In the case of countertrade transactions there are increased problems of co-ordinating sales and purchases from different ministries. It is one thing formally to grant enterprises wider powers to help direct contacts with foreign partners, it is another for the Soviet bureaucracy to allow these contacts to happen readily by granting the necessary visas and travel permits. Perhaps the biggest difficulty for enterprises who have got foreign-trade rights is the shortage of trained personnel who can make the most of the new opportunities.

All these are teething troubles which can no doubt be overcome. With time, the new system should bring a number of benefits: less bureaucracy, speedier negotiations by avoiding the middlemen at the FTOs, more exposure for Soviet managers to Western business techniques and expectations. But there are also deeper problems which are likely to limit the effect of the changes. Part of the trouble is the pattern which is becoming maddeningly familiar to Gorbachev: well-intentioned measures decreed at the top of the hierarchy get watered down or ignored in the middle and lower ranks.

Take joint ventures. At the time of writing, the law on joint ventures has yet to be approved by the Supreme Soviet, but it is fairly clear what the main provisions will be.[9] They are, in the main, restrictive. The

Soviet partner must have at least a 51 % share in any joint venture, with profits to be shared in proportion to the initial capital contribution. Hard-currency expenditure, including payment of profits, has to be covered by hard-currency exports. Net profits are taxed at 30 % (with a two-year grace period), and profits repatriated to the West are subject to a further 20 % tax, though the Finance Ministry may grant special concessions in individual cases. Soviet law governs the running of the enterprise, including working conditions. The managing director must be Soviet. Materials from Soviet enterprises have to be bought through FTOs or enterprises licenced to conduct foreign trade. Transport and insurance must be arranged through Soviet organisations, while hard currency must be kept at the Soviet Foreign Trade Bank.

The idea of senior officials was to keep the provisions of the legislation deliberately broad, leaving individual companies room to work out arrangements to suit their needs. But all the instincts of the people actually drafting the legislation was to insert restrictions. Clashes of interest between the Soviet and Western side are bound to arise — over control of the joint enterprise, hiring and firing of staff, and not least over the repatriation of profits. The Soviet side is interested in acquiring capital and technology, and in expanding exports; Western partners do not want to create competition for themselves in their own markets, but they do want to sell to the Soviet Union and get a decent hard-currency return on their investment. According to the deputy minister of foreign trade, the Soviet Union has set out proposals for about 100 joint ventures (most of them in the machine-building sector and light industry), of which 30 are the subject of serious discussion.[10] Not surprisingly, Western companies have so far shown a lot of interest, but even more scepticism, about joint ventures. A senior Finnish business representative said privately that the first Finnish-Soviet company, set up at the time of the Ryzhkov visit to Finland this year, was a « Potemkim joint venture », and that Finnish businessmen were extremely wary of the conditions being laid down for joint ventures. At the same time, Finnish businessmen are clearly taking the possibilities extremely seriously: in March, they staged a high-profile conference in London on the theme of opportunities for Anglo-Finnish co-operation in the Soviet Union. This sort of dual thinking about joint ventures — scepticism mixed with a flurry of activity — seems to be typical of most Western countries. Businessmen have no illusions about the practical difficulties involved in setting up joint companies and making them work, but many feel they cannot afford to ignore this form of business if they want to gain or maintain a foothold in the Soviet market.

Do the Russians themselves have illusions about joint ventures? Soviet officials who seem to believe that these are the answer to many of their problems are likely to be disappointed — just as the Hungarians, Romanians and Bulgarians were disappointed before them. The East European experience with joint ventures, which dates from the early 1970s, is instructive. Hungary, with over 70 joint ventures, has been the most successful in attracting Western partners. But most of these are small (and some certainly fall into the «Potemkin» category): the total amount of foreign investment in these companies by the end of 1986 was little more than $100 m.[11] While the concerns of these countries at first centred on how to cope with the expected influx of Western firms, the worry soon became how to revise the joint-venture legislation so that it was more attractive to potential Western partners. Several adjustments in their joint-venture laws have been made. It is more than likely that the Soviet Union will go through a similar experience.

As for the devolution of trading rights to ministries and large enterprises, this may do more for the efficiency of Soviet importing than for the promotion of Soviet exports. In practice, centralised control over import decisions and the allocation of hard currency is likely to remain strong; even so, closer contacts between Soviet enterprises and Western partners should be a help. But the changes will have little or no impact on one of the main obstacles to improved export performance: the lack of effective incentives to sell to the West. Merely allowing enterprises to have direct contacts and sign contracts with foreign firms will not by itself make it more attractive to compete in hard Western markets rather than offloading their products on the soft domestic one.

Again, the East European experience is worth noting. It shows that decentralising the foreign-trade system, while still keeping the domestic economy sheltered from foreign competition, is not enough to stimulate export growth. Despite reforms to the foreign-trade system, Eastern Europe's share of total OECD imports has remained stubbornly below 2%. Clearly, Gorbachev's foreign-trade reforms will not by themselves make the Soviet Union more competitive in the West. Improved Soviet export performance for manufactured goods will depend above all on the extent of the Gorbachev reforms for the Soviet economy as a whole. For Soviet industry to become much more competitive in the West it has to be exposed to much more competition, both at home and from abroad. Will Gorbachev allow loss-making factories to go bust? Will enterprises have to compete at home for customers and be allowed to pick between suppliers (a reform which would open the way for joint ventures with Western firms to operate outside the plan)? Will price reform help to reduce the rigid barrier between foreign and domestic markets? Unless the reform at home is far more radical than the change-resisters would like it to be, the changes in the foreign-trade system will at best do a little to relieve Soviet problems in trade with the West; they will not solve them.

How Open Can They Get?

It would be wrong, however, to belittle the importance of the foreign-trade reforms under Gorbachev. They are a step, albeit a tentative one, in the direction of more intricate Soviet involvement in international trade. Contacts with Western partners will widen, and reach farther down the Soviet hierarchy. Despite the difficulties, joint ventures should gradually create closer relationships between Soviet and Western enterprises. Because the Soviet Union will want better access to Western markets to expand its exports of manufactured goods, it has opened a serious dialogue with the EEC, and is interested in joining the GATT and the IMF. All these things suggest not short-term thinking, but a long-term strategy of greater integration in world trade.

The strategy has political implications, of course. If certain sectors of Soviet industry do begin to compete more vigorously on Western markets, they are likely to come up against Western protectionism. To overcome this, Gorbachev will have to be on friendly terms with the West. Similarly, better relations with the West are likely to mean more relaxed application of CoCom strategic controls (witness the relaxation of controls with China after the improvement in Sino-American relations), and hence more access to advanced technology.

It is true that Gorbachev has so far gone only a small way towards making the Soviet economy more ópen. Despite the reforms, the foreign-trade sector remains largely isolated from the domestic economy. If, as argued here, the results turn out to be not particularly impressive, he may well face a hard choice a few years from now: to turn back, or to press ahead in a more determined fashion. Until then, Soviet trade with the West under Gorbachev will be characterised by a lot of upheaval but little or no growth: to use the fashionable jargon, it is a time of *perestroika («restructuring»)* without *uskorenie («acceleration»)*.

Notes

1. Compared with its value against the ECU in December 1985, the dollar had depreciated by 16 % by December 1986 and by 22 % by April 1987.
2. Jonathan Stern, *Soviet Oil and Gas Exports to the West,* Gower, 1987.
3. ECE, *Economic Survey of Europe in 1986-1987,* New York, 1987 (pre-publication text). These ECE figures are based on Western trade returns. Soviet trade figures show a slightly different picture, though the trends are the same: see «Soviet foreign trade performance during the first nine months of 1986: coping with a 15 % deterioration in non-socialist terms of trade», PlanEcon Report, Volume III Number 1, January 1987.
4. For the definition of «engineering products», see EEC, op. cit., p. 310.

5. PlanEcon Report, loc. cit.
6. ECE, op. cit., p. 314.
7. See, for example, *Neue Zürcher Zeitung,* 20th March 1987.
8. For a list of the newly enfranchised ministries and enterprises, see *East European Markets,* 14th November 1986.
9. A description of these provisions, and of the Soviet foreign-trade reform generally, is given by Philip Hanson in *Radio Liberty Reasearch,* 19th March 1987.
10. Jochen Bethkenhagen, «Strukturveränderungen durch Joint Ventures?», *Industrie und Handels-Revue,* March 1987.
11. «Joint Ventures in Eastern Europe and China», *Radio Free Europe Research,* 30th January 1987.

Soviet Strategy in Restructuring Trade with the Third World

Giovanni Graziani*

Is the Third World losing importance from an economic point of view in the eyes of the Soviet leadership? The declared objective of concentrating upon domestic difficulties through economic reforms, the relaunching of intra-CMEA integration via the «Comprehensive Programme of Scientific and Technological Progress to the Year 2000» and finally certain measures apparently tailored to suit the relations with the industrialized West — the reform of the foreign trade system and the new legislation on joint ventures in the USSR — all seem to leave the developing countries out of the picture.

Gone are the times when the USSR expressed all-out support for national liberation revolutions and substantial economic aid was offered to new friendly regimes. Today the peoples that were once under colonial rule at best receive «profound sympathy for their aspirations» (CPSU Programme presented to the 27th Party Congress), while much stress is being laid on the need of friendly states to develop «mainly through their own efforts».

The burden represented by the massive economic aid extended to some developing countries coopted in the CMEA, like Cuba and Vietnam, and by the increasing assistance to Nicaragua meets with growing criticism among the more developed community partners. The refusal to admit Mozambique into the CMEA seems to reflect the same kind of mood (Wiles 1982). However, this new attitude should be taken more as a sign of mounting dissatisfaction with the present state of affairs than as determination to substantially reduce these ties. Rather, the need to reorganize the Soviet-Third World trade structure has become the centre of a lively debate and, given the authority of the people involved, it will undoubtedly bring about changes in the future.

My aim is not to elaborate on these Soviet contributions, extensively documented elsewhere (Valkeiner 1986), but to analyse, in the light of these new attitudes, the possible features of such a reorganization, given recent trends and the constraints imposed by the Soviet domestic economy and the world market.

Stagnant Trade

The sluggishness of trade with developing countries (LDCs — excluding those that the USSR identifies as «socialist») is a matter of growing concern to the Soviet Union. Both its share in total trade and the growth rates show a tendency to decline steadily. Although a word of

* This paper is part of a research project financed by the Italian National Research Council (CNR).

caution should be expressed on the different direction of prices inside and outside the CMEA, the analysis of Soviet foreign trade distribution seems to point to an inward intra-socialist market tendency, with increasingly smaller roles played by both the industrialized West and the LDCs.

The LDCs share in Soviet exports has steadily declined since 1982, with a parallel drop in Soviet imports as from 1983. In 1985 the shares were roughly the same as in 1975 — 13 and 11% respectively (Graziani 1984c, updated).

Trade with the Third World has been steadily decelerating since the beginning of the 1970s. The only exception was Soviet exports to LDCs in 1976-80, which increased their growth rates in contrast to a decline of the latter in all other directions. And troubles also started in the most recent five-year period in 1982, with just a slight pick-up of the growth rate of imports in 1983. In this period even absolute values declined; twice for exports ('85 and '86) and twice again for imports ('82 and '86).

A Strongly Political Orientation

We can look at the same phenomenon in another way. If we reconstruct from the Soviet foreign trade yearbook trade with all LDCs identified by countries of origin or destination, including the LDCs that are considered socialist, we can see that the share of the latter with respect to the total has grown in the last quinquennium both as regards exports (up to 69%) and imports (up to 55%) (Table 1). The share taken by CMEA LDCs (39%) is particularly impressive, Cuba alone accounting for roughly a quarter of total trade.

On the other hand the share of non-socialist LDCs has declined steadily: down to 31% on the export side and to 45% on the import side (albeit with a small pick-up in 1983). Performance in exports to non-socialist LDCs is all the more disappointing if one considers that a growing share of the total (up to 9%) was earmarked for friendly «countries with a socialist orientation» — the share of the latter on the import side being much lower and stagnant. Afghanistan leads the way among these countries.

So far we have excluded the residual which can be calculated from Soviet trade statistics with non-socialist LDCs and which is not specified by countries of origin or destination. In the case of imports, the value is very low (between 1 and 3% of total reported trade) and corresponds very likely to some partners not listed in the Soviet foreign trade yearbook, but which are usually accounted for by international agencies (Hong Kong, Gabon, Kenya, Reunion, Jamaica, Mauritius, Dominican Republic and others, all together not more than 100 million $ a year), plus some strategic materials from the identified countries. Our results would not be substantially affected by including the import residual in our calculations.

On the contrary, the value of the unidentified residual in Soviet exports is much larger, ranging in the quinquennium between 41 and 51% of total reported exports to LDCs (Table 1). Western experts generally agree now that most of it corresponds to Soviet shipments of weapons (which, however, should not be limited to these figures), while a lesser part concerns strategic materials and other trade partners (Graziani 1984c). By including it in our calculations the share of exports to non-socialist LDCs would obviously be higher, but would still show a downward trend in this period (from 55 to 48%).

Summing up in the period under consideration: a) Soviet trade with all LDCs has shown a tendency to become more politically oriented; b) considering only civilian trade, this political trait is more evident on the export than on the import side. Even if we include the export residual, the share of non-socialist LDCs in 1985 is less than half of total exports to all developing countries and has been decreasing every single year, except 1982 (where the big increase in the sale of arms presumably more than compensated for the decline in civilian trade).

Soviet Attemps at Reorienting Trade

The emphasis increasingly placed by Soviet experts on economic rationality in international relations and the greater interest in capitalist-oriented rich LDCs and wider regional diversification, certainly cry for a different distribution of trade among developing countries. In this perspective, the present situation can only appear to be a burdensome legacy of the past.

Although no signs of change are evident from the statistics concerning the distribution of trade among these large regional groupings, something is on the move *inside* them.

An attempt at rationalization is going on inside CMEA where Cuba, Mongolia and Vietnam are induced to specialize in the production of primary commodities and/or light industrial goods utilising local raw materials, and their excessively USSR-centred trade is being reconsidered by both sides (Graziani 1984a, 1985).

More important for our purpose are the trends occurring inside the differentiated category of non-socialist developing countries (from now on quoted as LDCs). Here, although trade retains in the 1980s its traditional feature of concentration — the first ten partners amounting to more than three-quarters of the total identified trade, with India, the top partner, taking one quarter by itself — the concentration index tends nevertheless to decline up to 1984, both for exports and for imports (as from 1982), while a slight pick-up occurs in 1985 (Table 2).

Some diversification has thus apparently occurred in recent times within trade identified by countries of origin and destination. Furthermore, the USSR has been trading on and off in the 1980s with at least another 41 countries that are not indicated in her foreign trade yearbook, but report to international agencies. Here Hong Kong leads the way, her trade turnover running at some 60-70 million US $ on average every year.

There are, however, some other aspects which tend to contradict Soviet strategy. Let us distinguish the LDCs by economic criteria.

If we make a classification *by income category,* it appears that the USSR tends to export relatively more towards low-income countries and to import relatively more from high-income LDCs (Table 2).

Secondly, in periods of normal market conditions, where the export revenues of rich (mostly oil producing) partners are plentiful, the USSR tends to export relatively more towards them. When in 1982-83 the balance of payments problems started depressing richer LDCs imports, their share of Soviet exports correspondingly declined. This trend follows almost exactly the annual trend of OPEC countries, share in Soviet exports since they account for the greater part of higher income LDCs trading with the USSR. Their share of total identified Soviet exports to LDCs went up to 40% until 1982 and then steadily declined to 16% in 1985 (Table 3). Note that the share of the lowest income economies has always been rather large (more than one third). Since 1983 it has become the largest and is still growing.

The picture looks rather different on the import side. Here the higher income countries have always obtained a greater share than the other two categories put together (58% in 1985). The share of OPEC in high income countries has been growing from less than a quarter in 1981 to well over one half in 1985 (compare Tables 2 and 3), one of the reasons being the growing Soviet imports of oil for re-export (see below).

Analysing LDCs *by major export category* one can see that major petroleum exporters have been increasing their share (the largest one) of Soviet exports up to 1982, but this has gradually been cut back since then. The negligible importance of major exporters of manufactures (NICs) is also noticeable. Out of the six major NICs only Argentina, Brazil and Singapore appear in Soviet statistics. Even if we add Hong Kong, the share would still be minimal. No trade is conducted with South Korea and Taiwan for political reasons. NICs seem to be tough markets for Soviet exports, more so if we consider that the USSR sells mostly raw materials and intermediate products to them.

The NICs share seems to be much larger in Soviet identified imports. However, in this case, the USSR receives mostly foodstuffs (from Argentina and Brazil), Singapore being the only identified NIC which delivers on average a relatively larger volume of manufactured products. The latter constitute also the major import item from Hong Kong.

The Trade Balance Predicament

Problems arising from such a skewed direction of trade are complicated by the question of trade balances.

Here one should distinguish between the total reported balance — which is positive and has been running between 1.2 and 4.8 billion US $ in the 1980s — and the balance with the sum of identified LDCs — a negative one, accounting between 1.5 and 3.5 billion US $ — (Table 10). Keeping in mind what we previously said about the overall export residual, the most logical explanation is that the surplus is obtained mostly via military equipment sales, while the deficit occurs in civilian trade (Graziani 1984c). Indirect confirmation of such an explanation comes from the fact that this surplus in total reported trade starts occurring just at the beginning of the 1960s, the period of the first Soviet « offensive » in the Third World.

The negative balance with the sum of the identified LDCs is the result of various components, which should be classified according to the modes of settlements.

Officially, the USSR has a clearing account with only seven LDCs, to which CMEA LDCs, Yugoslavia and probably various « socialist-oriented countries » should be added. With a few exceptions (i.e. Egypt) the general tendency has been for the Soviet Union to run a surplus with this type of country.

India is a case apart. Until 1982 the USSR had a structural deficit with its top LDC partner, largely due to its inadequacy in meeting Indian advanced capital goods requirements. The deficit turned into a surplus only because Soviet imports were scaled down, following India's refusal to buy more Soviet equipment compared to oil and intermediate products.

On the contrary, the Soviet Union generally runs a deficit with the countries which are supposed to pay in convertible currencies.

If one looks at the LDCs classified by economic criteria, the Soviet Union tends to have a deficit with richer countries, with OPEC and NICs, while she tends to run a surplus with poorer countries — and the surplus tends to be higher with friendlier countries.

A rigid distinction cannot be made between a convertible currency settlements area — where more and more barter-like arrangements take place — and a clearing area — where some hard currency deals nevertheless occur. As a consequence a precise calculation of Soviet convertible currency receipts from the Third World is hardly possible. However, broadly speaking, one could reasonably argue that the USSR has to pay in convertible currencies most of her civilian trade deficit, while presumably her civilian trade surplus (which is much lower) either is not settled in convertible currencies or is not paid at all (this is probably the case of some friendly countries). How much of the surplus due to military equipment is paid in convertible currencies is a matter open to speculation. Since 1982, many OPEC countries have preferred oil for arms barter deals as they did not have any more reserves to use for this end anyway. One reasonable guess is that these high military sales carry with them the usual low interest long-term credits which will either be repaid in kind sometime in the future or will not be repaid at all.

A Classical North-South Trade Structure

The USSR has always seen the Third World in a markedly traditional way: as a source of food and raw materials and as an outlet for its manufactures.

If we look at identified Soviet imports between 1970 and 1984, the share of food and raw materials has even increased from 85 to 88% (although in 1981 it had reached a peak of 91%) (Table 4). Correspondingly the share of manufactures went down in the same period from 15 to 12%, although recovering in the 1980s from a low 9% in 1981.

The opposite is taking place on the Soviet export side. Here manufactures, both civilian and military, have always dominated the scene, although their importance seems to have decreased from 1970 (78%) to 1981 (65%), with a recovery by 1984 (75%). These results are obtained by comparing Tables 4 and 1. One will note on the contrary that civilian manufactures constitute less than half of the identified trade (Table 4). In a nutshell this trade pattern reveals all the problems facing Soviet decision-makers and the possible direction of change. We shall review them by groups of commodities, starting from the import side.

Soviet Quest for Food and Raw Materials

The increasing share of food and raw materials in Soviet imports challenges the conventional view of the USSR as a self-sufficient country, not needing substantial inputs from abroad.

As one can easily gather from Table 4, foodstuffs are the largest component of this category. They jumped from 50% in 1970 to 71% in 1984 (from a high of 74% in 1981), as an evident expression of: a) the difficulties of Soviet agriculture; b) growing domestic consumption; c) a redirection of supplies after the US embargo on grain.

A further inspection of the data in the same table reveals that while in 1981 cereals constituted almost one third of total foodstuffs imports, in 1984 they had decreased to less than one sixth. The high level of food imports was thus increasingly due to other items, tropical products among others. This trend seems in line both with the Food Programme and the current FYP, which call for self-sufficiency in basic grains, for continued imports of coarse grain and expansion of imports of tropical products and non-cereal food. The policy of further diversification of consumer demand actually implemented can only accelerate this process. All in all food imports will continue to rise. But this does not mean that they will necessarily increase as a share of total imports. If prices remain slack, the share might fail to rise.

Apart from food, two other groups of raw materials have shown a slight tendency to rise in the 1980s: fuel, which will be dealt with separately, and the «ores, metals and crude fertilizers» group. The latter is very revealing about growing Soviet import dependency on often strategic minerals and metals (Table 5). One should remember that tungsten, cobalt and bauxite, for example, are used in the production of metals for the armaments industry. Apart from the raw materials which the Soviet Union does not have, or does not have in sufficient quantities, the Soviet mineral industry seems to be plagued by increasing costs of extraction and the decreasing mineral content of its ores.

As I have already indicated elsewhere (Graziani 1984c) this situation has led Soviet policy-makers to develop an import strategy which corresponds to two basic rationales:

a) as a compensation of domestic shortages;

b) as a less costly alternative to local extraction.

An example of the first type of rationale is bauxite, critical for the Soviet aluminium industry: Guinea, Jamaica and India are the most important suppliers.

The case of phosphates can be viewed as an example of the second type of rationale. Although the USSR is the second world producer and a slight net exporter, it is importing increasing quantities of phosphates especially from Morocco.

Soviet policy concerning raw materials and commodities takes a variety of forms. Current trade is cleared in convertible currencies, when other forms of payment are impracticable — Jamaican bauxite is a case in point. However, barter deals are preferred. Recent examples include Peruvian minerals, Mozambique non-ferrous metal concentrates, Indian bauxite, Zambian cobalt and Sudanese cotton.

Like all big industrial powers the USSR also has a long term strategy to guarantee reliable sources of supply, through economic assistance tied to specific projects. Such are the cases of the older product buyback agreements concerning Moroccan phosphates and Guinean bauxite, or the more recent ones concerning Congolese poly-metallic ores and Afghan nitrogenous fertilizers.

Finally, in the longer term, one should not forget the multivariate

activity of Soviet teams in cooperation with several LDCs for the pros-
pecting and exploration of all kinds of raw materials in Africa, Asia and
Latin America.

The Oil Imbroglio

A discussion of the impact of declining oil prices on Soviet trade
generally centres on its relations with the West. This is all too natural,
since roughly 80% of total earnings from Soviet exports to the West
come from fuels and these constitute the bulk of total export revenues in
convertible currencies necessary to purchase the technology, equipment
and foodstuffs the USSR needs (Graziani 1986a). Sometimes it emphasizes the consequences this may entail for its CMEA and East European
partners, which, with the exception of Romania, depend almost completely on Soviet fuel shipments and are increasingly asked to invest in
the exploitation of Soviet deposits (Graziani 1982, 1983, 1984b).

But there is in fact a third aspect to this oil imbroglio which should
not be underestimated. Oil, and to a lesser extent gas, are an important
part of Soviet policy towards the Third World.

In recent years, growing amounts of petrol have been sold not only to
CMEA and other socialist LDCs, but also to non-socialist developing
countries like India, Brazil, Afghanistan and Ethiopia (with India by far
taking the lead).

Fuels, surprisingly, also account for an increasing share of imports
from LDCs (Table 4), even though the USSR is the largest world
producer of both fuels and the largest world exporter of natural gas,
while being the second one for oil.

Gas has been imported for quite a time. In fact, until 1973, the USSR
was a net importer of it. Iran (until 1980) and Afghanistan provide gas
through pipelines to Soviet regions close to the respective borders,
consequently freeing corresponding volumes of natural gas produced in
the USSR for domestic use and for export towards Europe. The USSR
has been gaining in terms of reduced investment in transport facilities,
apart from the prices paid, which the two countries sometimes claimed
were lower than those on the world market.

With the end of Iranian gas deliveries after the Islamic revolution and
the Afghan gas shipments running at some 2.3 billion cm a year, the rise
in fuel imports was composed entirely of oil. From 1981 to 1984 quantities and values of crude oil never stopped growing, involving up to
more than 3 billion US $ in the last year. This tendency was only
interrupted by a decline in 1985 and soon resumed its course in 1986
(Table 6).

The rise in imports was accompanied by a growing diversification of
sources of supply not only among traditional trade partners, but also

among new ones, like Saudi Arabia (although most of its shipments seem to be made on behalf of Syria and Iraq in return for Soviet arms).

Unlike natural gas, imported crude oil is intended exclusively for reexport, mainly to Western Europe, but also to Yugoslavia and Romania.

What is remarkable is that the rise in imports coincides with the crash in world oil prices and the consequent need for the USSR to channel growing quantities of its oil to convertible currencies markets in order to increase or to stabilize its exports earnings. In the 1980s, oil imports amounted to between 1/6 and 1/4 of Soviet oil exports to OECD countries.

Up to 1984 Soviet imports of oil contributed to the expansion of export revenues from the West, while over the period 1985-86 they prevented the same from falling even further. In fact, neither additional sales of gas and gold, nor increased borrowing — in addition to domestic measures like energy conservation and substitution of oil by other sources of energy — can be a complete panacea in periods of rapidly falling prices. The example of 1985 and 1986 has shown it clearly, notwithstanding the fact that in 1986 Soviet oil production recovered, after a year and a half of continuous decline.

The option could be now to step up production intensively. But in my opinion this course will not be chosen for the time being, although moderate increases of production can be expected.

Apart from all the other measures already implemented and cited above, imports will probably continue. The main reason for them is not domestic shortage, but growing costs of extraction. It's cheaper for the USSR to import from oil producing countries than to rely on increasingly costly investments in remote areas. Especially if, as seems to be the case in the 1980s, the USSR sells military and civilian equipment at increasingly favourable terms of trade in exchange for oil.

Summing up, if oil prices remain low, the USSR will be forced to continue importing oil, given its convertible currency constraint and CMEA countries' requirements. Meanwhile it tries to keep on good terms with OPEC countries. Already in 1986 the Soviet Union showed some restraint in its sales to the West, while in January 1987 it agreed to back OPEC export cuts by reducing its own to a certain extent. The recent establishment of diplomatic relations with Oman and UAE seem to go in the same direction.

The Redeployment of Production Lines to the South

A field of mutual interest seems to be opening up in Soviet-Third World relations. Soviet specialists are speaking more and more openly about the possibility of a « redeployment » of some production lines

297

from the USSR to LDCs (Ivanov 1986). Manufactured goods imports, namely industrial consumer goods, are indicated as the privileged object of this policy which seems to correspond to the long-proclaimed demand of LDCs to have a larger share of manufactures exports towards the Soviet Union.

In reality this redeployment is viewed in the USSR as part of the structural policy aiming at rationalizing international economic relations. Consumer goods is a sector in which the Soviet Union is traditionally a net importer (mainly from Eastern Europe, then from the West) and it is bound to grow in importance due to the measures adopted all through the 1980s in order to better the living conditions of the population.

The USSR might be seriously considering the LDCs as a possible source of such goods for two main reasons. The LDCs enjoy a comparative advantage in their production, since they can offer them at much lower costs and do not suffer from labour scarcity, which is plaguing the Soviet economy. Relocation of some labour-intensive production lines abroad seems all too rational.

The second reason is the favourable international situation. Tariff and especially non-tariff restrictions are being increasingly applied by the West to many types of consumer goods imports which, consequently, remain in need of an outlet.

Whatever happens in the future, recent experience is nothing to boast about. If we take the whole group of manufactures as a share of Soviet imports from the LDCs, it has even diminished from 15% in 1970 to 12% in 1984 (Table 4). There was, however, a slight and steady pick-up since the beginning of the 1980s (3%). But the movement of relative prices might be at the origin of such weak changes.

An analysis of the market shares of some commodity groups indicates more precisely where the area of specialization lies (Table 8). Textile yarn and fabrics stand out as the strong sector of this trade. Almost one fourth of total Soviet imports comes from the LDCs, although the share used to be higher (29%) in 1970. Imports are extremely concentrated. Roughly half of cotton fabrics come from India, with some others coming from Pakistan, Egypt, Syria and Iraq. In many cases this is the outcome of various forms of cooperation, either of the product-buy-back type or of the «conversion deal» type. An example of the latter being the exchange of Soviet raw cotton for Indian textiles produced with the former.

Clothing (9%) has always grown through the years. Apart from the countries already cited, we can recall the increase in imports of Thai garments after the US embargo or the recent offers to Indonesia. Both commodity groups figure very high in Soviet imports from Hong Kong.

Lastly, machinery and equipment coming from LDCs doesn't even account for 1% of the Soviet market. The bulk of imports are concentrated on India. 14% of Soviet imports from this Asian country in 1985 consisted of this commodity group. Some of them may be items produced under Western licence or in co-production with Western firms. Such is the case of Rank Xerox photocopiers, assembled by the Indian firm Modi. Others, like electronics components and software, are delivered on a subcontracting basis, starting from technology and equipment supplied by the USSR.

All in all, past experience is however still disappointing: in 1985 the share of manufactures in total Soviet imports was over 20% with only six LDCs — India, Pakistan, Syria, Egypt, Lebanon, Cyprus — the two latter accounting for a negligible fraction of Soviet trade.

Signs of change are nevertheless discernible. Many recent agreements include an increase in the share of manufactures imports, while barter deals do not exclude LDCs industrial consumer goods (e.g. Peruvian footwear as part of repayment of an earlier debt for past Soviet military equipment).

Are we going to experience a surge of the share of manufactures in Soviet imports from LDCs? In the short-medium term this may take place. Until their terms of trade with raw materials and commodities show a favourable trend, the growing absolute volume and value of manufactures import will be also accompanied by an increasing share in total imports of the same.

Soviet Machinery and Equipment:
The Difficult Breakthrough into Southern Markets

One of the main features of the current FYP is the emphasis put onto the engineering branch, which should develop at a much faster rate than industry at large. To this end, the volume of investment intended for machinery and equipment will double in comparison to the period 1981-85. The avowed intention of Soviet planners is to make the exchange of these goods the most dynamic sector of foreign trade. The recent reform of the foreign trade system and the right extended to some 20 ministries and 70 large enterprises to act directly on foreign markets and retain a large part of the profits in convertible currencies, should be seen in this context, since those associations account for a large share of machinery trade.

The aim of Soviet decision-makers is to restructure Soviet exports towards the West so as to sell more manufactured products as a share of total exports. However, apart from some traditional bright spots (cars, chemicals) this might be pure wishful thinking in the medium term. More machinery and equipment should thus be available for export in

299

other directions: could that mean the long-awaited breakthrough into LDCs markets?

Let us look first at the experience of the last fifteen years. Civilian machinery and transport equipment has lost in importance from 1970 to 1984 as a share of Soviet exports to LDCs (from 53% to 32%) (Table 4). However, from the Soviet point of view, the LDCs are an important outlet accounting for roughly one fourth of its total exports of machinery, almost fully regaining in 1984 the old 1970 position (Table 7).

In fact, these results are very disappointing. On average, more than one third of the machinery and transport equipment sold to LDCs has been delivered within the framework of projects built with the technical assistance of the USSR. This ratio in 1985 is even higher than 70% for countries like Iran, Nigeria, Pakistan, Algeria, South Yemen, Bangladesh, Congo and Tunisia. We must not forget here that the share of Soviet aid that goes into industry is over three quarters of the total and it consists of goods and not financial loans (Klochek 1986). As a consequence, only a minor part of machinery and equipment is sold in normal commercial deals, where Western equipment is preferred to Soviet.

I have already dealt at length with the causes of this failure — low technical level, lack of adaptation to local conditions, inadequacy of product specifications, marketing, after-sales services, maintenance, repair, stocks of spare parts — which have often aroused complaints from several LDCs. Lack of motivation on the part of Soviet FTO have done the rest. Finally, the more industrialized LDCs can produce some of the basic machinery and equipment themselves and therefore don't need Soviet products (Graziani 1984c).

The USSR is in fact suffering from increasing competition from them, both in LDCs markets and in the Western markets, in the whole manufacturing sector. Table 9 shows clearly that in the only two instances in which the USSR increased its shares in the LDCs market (chemicals and passenger road vehicles), the LDCs fared better, while it lost in the whole group « machinery and equipment » against a gain for the LDCs. The trends repeat themselves almost identically on Western markets, where the USSR cannot even claim the same type of barriers encountered by many industrial consumer goods sold by the six East European countries (Graziani 1986b).

Will the new boost given to domestic production in the engineering sector and the new international standards required for most of its products allow a breakthrough in Third World markets? Paradoxically, the quest for efficiency and profits in convertible currencies would suggest avoiding Southern markets for the time being, since even richer LDCs are now plagued with balance of payments difficulties due to the fall of oil prices, the slackness of other commodities' prices and the debt service burden. It seems plausible that exports to LDCs may increase on one condition: that the favourable credit terms available in the past do not come to an end, but rather are enlarged, while all kinds of cooperation agreements, barter-like arrangements and other new ways are set in motion.

As for the latter, the USSR is increasingly tying the delivery of its machinery to the purchase of further quantities of commodities supplied by its structural creditors. Such is the case of Argentina, which has seen its new five-year grain agreement subordinated to the acceptance of Soviet equipment for hydroelectric plants. A protocol issued at the end of 1985 indicates the minimum and growing amount of Soviet machinery that Argentina is obliged to purchase every year up to 1990. Obviously the Soviet Union does not refrain from straight barter: e.g. the deal of Energomachexport with the city council of Mendoza (Argentina) where 17 trolley-buses were exchanged in 1984 against foodstuffs produced in that province (Foreign Trade 1986).

If the finished product cannot be sold directly, a stage of its production can be delocalized. This is used, for instance, in the transport industry. Soviet tractors are assembled or coproduced in Pakistan, India and Afghanistan. Assembly of Niva cars, tractors and road construction equipment is being negotiated with Argentina, while equipment for hydroelectric stations is being produced in the same country with Soviet technology. Finally, Tractoroexport is developing special models of tractors with Bolivian and Mexican partners (Ivanov 1986).

When a developing country would not even accept that, resort has been made to trilateral deals. Typical of this procedure is the sale to Jamaica of tractors assembled in Canada and serviced by the same.

There are finally two forms of cooperation which are increasingly seen as promoters of machinery exports. The first is tripartite industrial cooperation (TIC), where a Western partner provides advanced technology, the USSR basic and intermediate equipment, and the recipient LDC labour and other resources. This seems to be one of the most dynamic forms of Soviet-West trade. The share of TIC contracts with respect to the total number of Soviet industrial cooperation contracts with the West has grown from 5% in 1981 to more than 8% in 1985, covering most of the industrial sectors. By 1982 Soviet FTOs had entered into TIC with over 200 firms from 25 Western countries in more than forty LDCs (UNCTAD 1985).

The second form is cooperation in third countries with the most advanced LDCs. One of the recent and most important examples of these ventures is the Capanda Dam Project in Angola, a 1 billion US $ hydroelectric power plant and irrigation complex, where the USSR is supplying four 130 megawatt turbines, Brazil the technology and construction, and Angola the labour. Portuguese capital is supposed to be involved in the deal as well (Countertrade and Barter Quarterly 1985). Then there are the joint ventures with Indian state and private firms, which are spreading all over the Third World and have even been included in the long-term agreement on the main guidelines of cooperation for 1985-2000. Both participation on a par and as a sub-contractor for the USSR are foreseen.

A Brighter Spot: Military Equipment

Overall unidentified residual in Soviet exports to LDCs is generally taken as a rough indicator of arms sales to the same. To arrive at a precise calculation of the value and quantity of this trade is an almost impossible task, given the secrecy surrounding such a matter (as is also the case in the West). Although it is not in the scope of this paper, let me point out from a methodological point of view some of the reasons why overall residual does not coincide with arms sales to the Third World.

As previously stated, a minor part of it includes strategic materials and exports to other countries not reported in the Soviet foreign trade yearbook.

However, other military equipment may be included in: a) the intra-country commodity residual (i.e. the value of exports to the individual countries not identified by commodities); b) the machinery and equipment sub-residual (i.e. the value of this commodity group not identified by individual items), when this is not included in (a); c) the identified machinery and transport equipment (e.g. aircraft and transport equipment); d) sales which do not appear altogether in the yearbook.

Presumably then overall unidentified residual understates Soviet arms sales to the Third World. Whatever the absolute value, the overall residual gives a good indication of trends in arms sales. As Table 1 clearly shows, its share in total exports to LDCs has always been enormous in the 1980s and has steadily grown from 41% in 1981 to 51% in 1984, while 1985 appears to have been a black year (only 44%!) and 1986 shows a recovery.

Apart from India, the main recipients of arms seem to have been Middle Eastern countries like Iraq and Syria, together with Libya. The USSR might soon start, nevertheless, experiencing the burden of such deliveries. Some of the countries involved do not have any more the convertible currencies necessary to pay for them while their oil shipments are very likely a repayment of past arms deliveries. As a consequence, they tend to rely on long-term credits on the part of the Soviet Union. The decline of sales in 1985 might be interpreted in this sense.

Moreover quite a few experts and planners are perhaps starting to think that the scarce strategic materials involved in producing arms would be better used in other sectors of the economy (Plan-Econ Report 1986).

Another option would be to sell the technology and not the finished product. Such seems to be the case of more industrialized LDCs like India, which has bought in 1980 the licence to manufacture the MIG-23 fighter and the T-72 battletank (Mehrotra 1985) while the transfer of technologies for the new MIG-27 and its further versions (MIG-29 and 31) is being considered.

Prospects of Restructuring

The following are reasonable expectations on future trends and considerations on Soviet strategy.

1) The LDCs are becoming more important for the USSR than they used to be. On the Soviet demand side more raw materials and consumer goods will be required, while on the supply side a large volume of machinery and equipment will be available for sale in those markets.

The international economic situation is particularly conducive to an enlargement of Soviet trade with the Third World. Oil and non-fuel commodities' slack prices, declining export revenues and heavy debt servicing of the majority of LDCs, finally growing protectionism in the West, all seem to work in the direction of making LDCs particularly open to Soviet offers of barter-like deals, even when inferior technological goods or higher prices are involved (Graziani 1986c). The benefit for the USSR should be increased by the windfall gains accruing from the bettering of its terms of trade due to the different trends in prices of manufactures and raw materials.

2) The more pragmatic and rational approach to international economic relations should imply a relatively larger volume of trade with richer countries and NICs, while entailing stricter terms with other partners. Such a reorientation of trade would proceed hand in hand with the current diversification of commercial relations, without forgetting to deal with the painful question of balances.

3) The trade structure should not witness dramatic changes, due also to the effect of international prices.

Soviet exports to LDCs will continue to be dominated by machinery and transport equipment, although the ratio between civilian and military items may change in the future. There may also be a drop in the oil share if the present situation doesn't change. Something new may happen on the import side. Here the value of industrial consumer goods should substantially rise. (Soviet manpower shortage and the structural adjustment under way provide an economic rationale for it.) Their share could increase, if it is not offset by corresponding rises in raw materials imports.

This trade structure seems to be sufficiently in line with the development model now advocated by many Soviet specialists for the Third World, i.e. not based any more on forced industrialization, but on raw materials, agriculture and light industry.

4) All in all, a rather complementary trade pattern will very likely continue to prevail, based as it is on a manufactures-for-raw materials and consumer goods-exchange. What appears is still an inter-branch type specialization, hardly giving signs of more progressive intra-industry trade. As we have seen, although areas of competition do exist, they are for the moment very limited, unlike those characterising Eastern Europe-LDCs relations (Lavigne 1986).

5) However, the new dynamic elements emerging from the preceding analysis show a Soviet « revealed » theoretical approach to trade with the Third World which is not any more the old pure « vent for surplus » approach, when excess production was intended for export in order to pay for imports which could not be produced at home. Both the export side (some enterprises producing expressly for exports) and particularly the import side (imports of consumer goods which are relatively less costly) reveal a new « comparative advantage approach » towards the LDCs more similar to that of the other industrialized nations of the world.

References

Countertrade and Barter Quarterly, 1985, Spring.

Foreign Trade, 1986, n. 3.

Graziani G., 1982, *Comecon, domination et dépendances,* Paris, Maspero.

Graziani G., 1983, « La dépendance énergétique de l'Europe orientale vis-à-vis de l'URSS: 1945-1981 », *Revue d'Etudes comparatives Est-Ouest,* vol. 14, n. 2, pp. 37-60.

Graziani G., 1984a, « Des multinationales à l'Est? », *Revue d'économie industrielle,* n. 28, 2e trimestre, pp. 36-58.

Graziani G., 1984b, « Les mouvements de capital au sein du Comecon », *Economies et Sociétés,* Cahiers de l'ISMEA, n. G 40, pp. 45-77 (translated as « Capital movements within the CMEA », *Soviet and Eastern European Foreign Trade,* Spring 1986, vol. XXII, n. 1, pp. 19-50.

Graziani G., 1984c, « Commercial Relations Between Developing Countries and the USSR », paper presented to the 1st annual meeting of the Italian Association for the Study of Comparative Economic Systems (AISSEC), Turin, Oct. (forthcoming in *Cambridge Journal of Economics*).

Graziani G., 1985, « The Non-European Members of Comecon: a Model for Developing Countries? », paper presented to the 3rd World-Congress of Soviet and East European Studies, Washington, D.C., Oct. 30-Nov. 4 (forthcoming in Kanet R. E. (ed.), *The Soviet Union and the Third World: from Breznev to Gorbachev,* Cambridge University Press).

Graziani G., 1986a, « Energy in Soviet-West European Relations », paper presented to the international colloquium « Les marchés internationaux de l'énergie », Grenoble, 4-6 March, (now published in Ayoub A. and Percebois J. (eds.). *Pétrole: marchés et stratégies,* Paris, Economica, 1987), pp. 302-320.

Graziani G., 1986b, « The E.E.C. Versus the East: Competition and Complementarity », paper presented to the IXth International Colloquium on the World Economy, Modena, 14-16 June.

Graziani G., 1986c, « Soviet Prices in Trade with the Third World », paper presented to the 3rd annual meeting of AISSEC, Siena, 17-18 October.

Ivanov, I.D., 1986, « The Soviet Union in a Changing Global Economic Setting: the prospects for trade oriented growth », UNCTAD/ST/TSC/4, 25 April.

Klochek V., Alexeyev A., Tretyukhin N., 1985, *Soviet Foreign Trade: Today and Tomorrow,* Moscow, Progress, Publishers, 278 p.

Lavigne M. (ed.), 1986, *Les relations Est-Sud dans l'économie mondiale,* Paris, Economica, 346 p.

Mehrotra S., 1985, « The Political Economy of Indo-Soviet Relations », in Cassen R. (ed.), *Soviet Interests in the Third World,* London, The Royal Institute of International Affairs, SAGE Publications, p. 220-240.

PlanEcon Report, 1986, vol. II, No. 14, 7 April.

UNCTAD, 1985, « Trends and Policies in Trade and Economic Cooperation Among Countries Having Different Economic and Social Systems », TD/B/1063, 17 July.

Valkeiner E.K., 1986, « Revolutionary Change in the Third World: Recent Soviet Reassessments », *World Politics,* Vol. XXXVIII n. 3, April, p. 415-434.

Wiles P. (ed.) 1982, *The New Communist Third World,* London and Canberra, Croom Helm, 392 p.

Table 1

Distribution of Soviet identified trade with all developing countries: a systemic classification (percentage shares of the total).

	1981	1982	1983	1984	1985	1986 (Jan.-Sept)
Exports to:						
Socialist LDCs	59.0	59.8	63.7	56.8	68.7	74.8
of which:						
CMEA LDCs	35.5	36.6	38.2	38.4	39.0	46.0
Other socialist	23.5	23.2	25.5	28.4	29.7	28.8
Non-socialist LDCs	41.0	40.2	36.3	33.2	31.3	25.2
of which:						
Countries with socialist orientation	6.0	5.8	7.2	8.8	8.7	10.1
Imports from:						
Socialist LDCs	42.3	49.8	47.0	51.1	55.5	65.3
of which:						
CMEA LDCs	18.7	24.8	25.0	27.1	28.3	37.1
Other socialist	23.6	25.0	22.0	24.0	27.2	28.2
Non-socialist LDCs	57.7	50.2	53.0	48.9	44.5	34.7
of which:						
Countries with socialist orientation	2.7	2.4	2.4	2.2	2.2	2.2
Memo item:						
Unidentified trade as a share of total reported trade with non-socialist LDCs						
Exports	40.6	46.2	48.7	50.7	43.7	49.6
Imports	1.8	2.1	2.8	1.4	1.2	2.0

Source: Calculated from *Vneshniaia Torgovlia SSSR v... g.*, various years.

Note: CMEA LDCs = Mongolia, Cuba and Vietnam. Other socialist LDCs = Laos, Kampuchea, Ch:na, North Korea and Yugoslavia. Countries with socialist orientation = Afghanistan, Angola, Ethiopia, Mozambique, Nicaragua and PDR Yemen.

Table 2

Distribution of Soviet identified trade with the LDCs classified according to economic criteria and share of first ten partners (percentage of the total).

	Exports					Imports				
	1981	1982	1983	1984	1985	1981	1982	1983	1984	1985
By income category										
Above 1,500 US $	40.7	45.9	34.2	24.8	23.1	57.7	56.8	64.9	62.9	57.8
Between 500 and 1,500 US $	23.4	19.4	24.0	23.3	23.4	16.7	11.8	11.0	12.0	14.0
Below 500 US $	35.8	34.7	41.8	51.9	53.5	25.6	31.4	24.1	25.1	28.2
By major export category										
"Major petroleum exporters"	43.6	45.8	38.8	26.2	23.7	16.8	26.5	32.9	37.9	34.2
Major exporters of manufactures	1.9	4.4	2.9	2.7	2.7	39.0	26.2	27.2	22.6	22.4
Other	54.5	49.8	58.3	71.1	73.6	44.2	47.3	39.9	39.5	43.4
Share of first 10 partners in total identified trade with LDCs (in percentage)	78.4	78.0	73.7	71.1	74.0	83.7	86.9	84.5	78.9	80.5

Source: Calculated from *Vneshniaia Torgovlia SSSR v... g.,* various years.

Note: Major petroleum exporters = OPEC + Mexico, Syria, Angola and Congo. Major exporters of manufactures = Argentina, Brazil and Singapore.

307

Table 3
Soviet trade with OPEC countries.

	1981	1982	1983	1984	1985	1986 (Jan-Sept)
OPEC share of Soviet imports from identified LDCs (in %)	13.1	21.5	29.4	34.7	31.4	30.4
Annual growth rates of Soviet imports from OPEC (in %)	20.3	40.3	42.0	14.6	10.7	–18.8 (over Jan-Sept 1985)
OPEC share of Soviet exports to identified LDCs (in %)	35.9	40.5	31.7	18.7	15.9	11.9
Annual growth rates of Soviet exports to OPEC (in %)	47.5	19.0	–25.0	–46.2	–16.9	–24.2 (over Jan-Sept 1985)
Soviet share of OPEC exports (in %)	0.1	0.1	0.2	0.2	1.5	
Soviet share of OPEC imports (in %)	1.7	2.1	1.8	1.1	1.1	
OPEC share of total identified Soviet exports (in %)	3.4	3.8	2.7	1.5	1.3	0.8
OPEC share of total identified Soviet imports (in %)	1.9	2.5	3.5	4.0	3.4	2.5

Source: Calculated from *Vneshniaia Torgovlia SSSR v...g,* and *U.N.,* Monthly Bulletin of Statistics, various years.

Table 4
Trade structure of the USSR with the LDCs (% shares by commodity group-identified trade).

SITC	Soviet Exports			Soviet Imports		
	1970	1981	1984	1970	1981	1984
Food & raw materials (0 to 4 plus (67 + 68))	36.5	58.7	51.5	84.8	90.7	87.9
Manufactured goods (5 to 8 less (67 + 68))	63.5	41.3	48.5	15.2	9.3	12.1
of which:						
All food items (0 + 1 + 22 + 4)	13.0	10.4	6.7	49.9	73.7	71.5
Cereals (041 + 045)	2.8	2.7	1.6	2.2	23.8	11.2
Agricultural raw materials (2 – 22 – 27 – 28)	5.0	7.3	4.6	23.6	7.4	5.9
Ores, metals & crude fertil. (27 + 28 + 67 + 68)	9.7	9.0	8.6	9.3	5.1	5.5
Fuels (3)	8.8	32.0	31.6	2.0	4.4	5.0
Chemicals (5)	2.8	4.4	3.8	1.3	1.1	1.6
Machinery & equipment (7)	53.3	32.6	31.8	0.1	0.6	1.9
Other manufactured goods (6 + 8) less (67 + 68)	7.4	4.3	12.9	13.8	7.6	8.6

Source: Calculated from *U.N.*, Monthly Bulletin of Statistics, various years.

Table 5
Soviet import dependency in selected minerals and metals.

Commodity	Net Imports as a Percentage of Consumption		Principal Sources
	1980	1984	
Antimony	19	6	Yugoslavia
Barite	51	49	Bulgaria, North Korea, Yugoslavia
Bauxite & Alumina	55	48	Greece, Guinea, Hungary, India, Jamaica, Yugoslavia
Bismuth	—	71	Japan, Netherlands, Peru, Romania
Cobalt	10	47	Cuba
Fluorspar	50	53	China, Kenya, Mexico, Mongolia, Thailand
Magnesite	—	14	North Korea
Mica	10	13	India
Molybdenum	—	15	Mongolia
Silver	3	24	Switzerland, United Kingdom
Tin	21	30	Malaysia, Singapore, United Kingdom
Tungsten	12	43	China, Mongolia
Zinc	6	4	Australia, Finland, Mexico, Peru, Poland

Source: Mining Annual Review 1980 and 1984.

Table 6

Estimated Soviet imports of oil for re-export (in millions of US dollars).

	1981	1982	1983	1984	1985	1986 (Jan-Sept)
Algeria	—	—	1	158	287	147
Iraq	1	20	515	820	662	427
Iran	601	207	472	258	135	16
Libya	502	1,550	1,364	1,390	1,048	816
Saudi Arabia	—	—	211	358	452	138
Syria	91	169	189	112	105	84
Angola	2	5	4	4	3	4
PDR Yemen	6	5	4	4	6	4
Total	1,203	1,956	2,760	3,104	2,698	1,636
Growth rates in nominal terms (in %)		+62.6	+41.1	+12.5	-13.1	-13.7 (over Jan-Sept 1985)
Estimated growth rates in physical terms (in %)		+58.0	+53.4	+18.6	-13.1	+43.4 (over Jan-Sept 1985)

Source: Estimates based on Vneshniaia Torgovlia SSSR v…g., various years, *Vneshniaia Torgovlia*, No. 12, 1986 and on average annual price of oil published in U.N., Monthly Bulletin of Statistics, various years. The latter can only be considered a proxy for deflating growth rates in nominal terms. In fact, exporting countries trade oil at various prices, especially in the case of barter-like arrangements. Moreover, in periods of rapidly changing prices, even quarterly average export prices may be inadequate.

Table 7
*Share of the developing countries in Soviet exports of manufactures
(by commodity groups – in %).*

Commodity Group	1970	1981	1984
Chemicals (SITC 5)	11.1	15.1	13.1
Machinery & transport equipment (SITC 7)	24.3	19.0	24.0
Other manufactured goods (SITC 6 + 8)	10.9	9.0	25.3

Source: Estimated from *Vneshniaia Torgovlia SSSR v...g.* and *U.N.*, Monthly Bulletin of Statistics, various years.

Table 8
*LDCs market shares in trade of manufactures with the USSR
(LDCs exports to the USSR as a % of Soviet total imports for each commodity group).*

	1970	1981	1984
Chemicals (SITC 5)	2.9	2.5	3.5
Machinery & transport equipment (SITC 7)	—	0.3	0.7
Other manufactured goods (SITC 6 + 8)	8.1	6.9	7.3
of which:			
Textile yarn and fabrics (SITC 65)	29.3	20.3	24.5
Clothing (SITC 84)	4.7	7.2	9.0

Source: Calculated from *U.N.*, Monthly Bulletin of Statistics, various years.

Table 9

Market shares of the developing countries and of the USSR in the manufacture imports of the industrialized West and of the LDCs, by Main Commodity Groups of Manufactures.

Markets	Commodity Groups	Chemical Products SITC 5		Machinery & Transport Equipment SITC 7		of which: Passenger Road Vehicles & Their Parts		Other Manufactured Goods SITC 6 + 8		of which: Iron and Steel SITC 67		Non Ferrous Metals SITC 68	
	Year	LDCs	USSR	LDCs	USSR	LDCs	USSR	LDCs	USSR	LDCs	USSR	LDCs	USSR
Developed market-economy countries	1970	3.6	0.5	1.3	0.2	0.1	0.1	11.6	0.8	2.3	1.1	30.7	2.8
	1981	4.5	0.9	5.3	0.2	0.9	0.5	16.4	0.1	6.1	0.4	21.1	1.9
	1984	4.9	1.1	8.6	0.2	1.1	0.3	20.3	0.1	9.9	0.5	21.6	...
Developing countries	1970	8.1	0.9	3.3	4.7	3.6	1.6	15.9	1.8	8.2	3.9	23.1	2.8
	1981	13.0	1.2	8.8	2.0	10.9	1.0	21.6	0.5	11.2	1.6	32.3	...
	1984	15.2	1.3	10.9	2.9	12.3	2.1	25.0	1.9	18.2	1.6	28.2	...

Source: Calculated from *U.N.*, Monthly Bulletin of Statistics, various issues.

Table 10
Unspecified residual in Soviet exports to LDCs and balance of trade.

	1980	1981	1982	1983	1984	1985	1986 (Jan-Sept)
Unspecified residual in Soviet exports to LDCs:							
a) in millions of foreign trade roubles	3,085.9	3,520.1	4,703.4	5,125.0	5,540.4	4,194.6	2,977.4
Annual growth rates %		14.1	33.6	9.0	8.1	−24.3	+15.7
							over Jan-Sept 1985
b) in millions of US dollars	4,728	4,893	6,476	6,898	6,793	5,009	4,175
Annual growth rates %		3.5	32.4	6.5	−1.5	−26.3	+39.3
							over Jan-Sept 1985
Share of residual in total exports to LDCs (in %)	44.7	40.6	46.2	48.7	50.7	43.7	49.6
Balance with the LDCs (reported total)	R. 1,777.7 $ 2,740	892.0 1,240	3,477.1 4,788	3,349.0 4,508	3,393.5 4,161	1,976.7 2,361	2,186.0 3,065
Balance with the sum of identified LDCs	R. −1,144.0 $−1,877	−2,487,8 −3,458	−1,088.2 −1,498	−1,596.6 −2,149	−2,049.9 −2,513	−2,131.8 −2,546	− 717.8 −1,007

Source: Calculated from Vneshniaia Torgovlia SSSR v…g., various years and Vneshniaia Torgovlia, No. 12, 1986

Soviet Financial Policy vis-à-vis the West

Guenter Boehr

What are the future possibilities for the Soviets to get credit from the West; how will the Soviets approach Western financial markets; what will be the amounts, the terms and conditions of future USSR-lending? Let me try to give some very personal answers to these questions.

Like most banks the Westdeutsche Landesbank has a ranking system for the country-risk of international borrowers: the best risk is A 1, the worst is C 3. The Economic Department of the Westdeutsche Landesbank has classified the USSR as « B 2 + keine wesentlichen Bedenken ». In other words, our analysts do see some critical aspects in the foreseeable future of the USSR, but they don't feel these aspects are essential ones. I think this ranking by Westdeutsche Landesbank fits well in the analyses which have been published by qualified institutions in the West.

The right or wrong of such a classification can be disputed. I am not, of course, an economic analyst but a banker, doing day-to-day business with foreign countries and especially with the USSR. Therefore, I would like not to deepen the analysis of the economic development of the USSR, but to draw your attention to some aspects of the international financial markets which will substantially influence possibilities and limits of the Soviet financial policy vis-à-vis the West.

As to these markets let me ask: how does the international banking community act vis-à-vis the USSR now, what are the reasons, and is this likely to change?

At the present time international banks busily cater for all kinds of business with the USSR, pay many visits and accept terms and conditions which are excellent for the USSR (long life-time of the loans, minimum margins for the banks), etc. In brief, the international banking community treats the USSR as a first class customer with a rating of A1 instead of a middle class customer with a rating of B 2.

These bankers do not do so because they think that the analyses of their economic departments are wrong. No, it was and it is the market which dictates strategy and actions of the banks. Let me explain that in more detail.

(a) The international operating banks have lost many potential customers: Latin-America is not creditworthy any more, some of the Far-East countries are in economic difficulties, the OPEC countries suffer under the fall of the oil prices, etc. There remain — in comparison with the past — only a few internationally acceptable borrowers. One of them, perhaps even the Number One of them, is the USSR. As a result of this situation, the market position of the borrower — USSR — has become better than it was before, in spite of the fact that its economic situation has not ameliorated.

(b) Many Western banks, traditionally only domestically active, have become international in the past few years, because of the slow pace of the traditional domestic markets. This has led to enforced competition in the international banking community. In other words: the market for the internationally active banks became smaller, the number of international banks become greater. As a result, the relative market position of the USSR became better.

(c) Western banks have lost a lot of money in the past few years both domestically and internationally. On the one hand they would now like to be very cautious, but on the other hand they need assets and have, in order to get business, to accept more risks than they like. As a result, the risk-policy of the banks of today is not very strict.

(d) This development was accelerated by another very important aspect: banks tend to exaggerate! To put it bluntly: if banks feel a risk is an acceptable one they all cater for it. But we know if the ram of a flock of sheep turns around, then the rest of the sheep will turn around too. I don't say banks are sheep, but the behaviour of banks sometimes reminds me of the behaviour of a flock of sheep. You doubt this? Well, look for example at Brazil, at Argentina. A couple of years ago, the banks proudly published lists of who arranged what Jumbo-Euro-Loan, bond issue, private placement, etc. for these countries. Now the same banks would be happy if at that time they had not been so successful in approaching these countries.

These are some essential aspects of the present situation, which is comfortable for those borrowing countries which represent an acceptable credit risk and uncomfortable for the international operating banks which urgently look for business opportunities.

What about the future? In my very personal opinion, the following developments are more likely than unlikely:

(a) Latin-America will — sooner or later — come back as an internationally acceptable borrower; those Far-East countries which presently are in economic difficulties will recover; even the OPEC countries will reappear as borrowers in the market. Consequently the present narrow market will broaden.

(b) The domestic banking business — today very calm — will revitalize. Those banks traditionally active only domestically and only recently active internationally will withdraw from the international banking scene (where in the meantime they have learned how difficult it is to make money in the international banking business and how easy to lose money). Consequently, international competition among banks will relax somewhat.

(c) This enables the banks to pay more attention to the credit risk than they do now. Consequently the relative market situation of the USSR will become weaker than it is now, and that without any change in the economic situation of the USSR itself.

(d) If such a change in market conditions occurs this will be enforced and accelerated by the above mentioned shepherding effect: all banks suddenly may say: «Oh, I had better stop for a while the grant of loans to the USSR».

One might argue that the USSR traditionally practices correctly a cautious policy in international borrowing and that they pay a lot of attention not to become financially dependent on anybody. But I doubt whether the USSR really looks enough to these market mechanisms which I talked about. They might look too much to ratios of international debt, to international earnings, etc., just as economic analysts all over the world do. Indeed, it is very difficult for Soviet leaders to understand that without any change in their «objective credit worthiness» the market may look to them one day much more critically than it does now.

Such a possible development might be even more accelerated by Mr. Gorbachev's modernization policy. If the Soviet economy is reformed, then decentralization and liberalisation might be accompanied by disorder, exaggeration etc., and there are few things bankers dislike more than disorder in the economic situation of their borrowers. And if Gorbachev cannot realise his reform plans? I am afraid the banks then might change to a more critical attitude towards the USSR than they have now. Maybe such reactions of banks are not logical, but they are reasonable and — more important — likely.

If such an abrupt change in the attitude of the international banks vis-à-vis the USSR occurs, what will happen then? Has the USSR more or less to face an impossibility of getting credits from the West? Do I even see a danger of a collapse of the international financial system? Not at all! Western governments will interfere and grant public cover for loans agreed upon by international banks to the USSR. The Western governments will do so in order:

— to avoid international tension between the West and the East;
— to avoid any danger of a collapse of the international banking system;
— to support their national exports to the USSR.

But for the USSR the situation will then be completely different from today's situation:

— the volumes of credits available will be limited;

— the Western governments may use their risk-cover (via Hermes, Coface, ECGD, etc.) for political purposes, a possibility the USSR dislikes very much;

— the terms and conditions of these credits will be less favourable for the USSR than they are now.

Now, to what degree is it likely that such a development might occur? Principally, I feel it is more likely than unlikely. But the more such a development is discussed and foreseen by the participants in the market, the less it becomes likely. As to the timetable, I expect such a development, if it occurs, not soon, but in the medium future, let me say 5 to 10 years.

These have been some remarks on the possibilities and limits which Soviet financial policy might face in the next five to ten years. Let me now switch to the question, what will be the attitude of the USSR in the near future vis-à-vis the financial institutions of the West?

In the past the USSR has been conservative:

— interest rates preferably fixed, not floating, to avoid risks of rising interest in the market;

— life-time of the credits as long as possible, to avoid lack of liquidity in hard currencies;

— tailor-made financing for each project to assure a project-related administrative handling of hard currency debts and of hard currency debt service;

— loans instead of public bonds, private placements or other international capital market instruments;

— bilateral instead of multilateral agreements.

This is not a strict rule but it has clearly been the overwhelming policy.

In the meantime, Western banks have developed a wide variety of new financial instruments: Swaps, Caps, Rifs, Snifs and so on. The Soviets are very interested in these new instruments, they ask for explanations, they occasionally even accept one of these offers but will they use these instruments to a degree which fits their importance as a market-partner? I doubt this for the following reasons:

(a) There are only a few people in the USSR who have the professional banking skill and experience for these complicated new instruments. There are enough people to try these instruments, but not enough to use them more extensively. This can be changed by training, but decentralization already demands so much training of financial managers outside of Moscow that the managerial shortage will probably continue to be an important obstacle.

(b) The USSR dislikes another element of these new financial instruments: many of them combine elements of fixed and floating rate, of short and long term markets, of different currencies, etc. I'm not going to bother you with banking techniques but, believe me, to combine all these elements in an optimal way in order to have a better result than using just the one or the other element does demand not only an understanding of the Western financial market, but also — and even more important — a confidence in the Western financial market, in its mechanisms and its participants. I have certain doubts whether many Soviet financial managers understand this market, but I have even more doubts whether they have the confidence and truth which is necessary to take part in this market.

(c) And if Soviet financial managers have — or will have — the professional know-how and the confidence in this market? Even then they remain part of an economic system which now, and at least for the nearer future, is more characterised by administration than by management, by regulations than by delegation. In such a system it is not very advisable for a single person to make decisions the results of which depend on Western markets and can be measured and judged only later. In other words, these instruments can only be managed by persons with broad individual responsibility, but to offer such working conditions to any substantial extent is still a long way off for Mr. Gorbachev and his reform-followers.

In summary, the USSR will use all the new financial instruments that Western banks have recently developed. But the USSR will use these instruments to only a minor extent and will stick mainly to the conservative attitude they have shown in the past.

The General Secretary as Peter the Great

Overall Comment by Peter Wiles

1. *Introduction*

A fair summary of a good conference is not possible. There are always too many good papers, already desperately compressed. How can they be re-compressed into the Black Hole of 35 minutes? So, the speaker warned our hosts, this presentation will scandalously neglect all contributions not directly about reform, and extrapolate from, not summarize, even those. Yet it owes nearly everything to what was said at the conference or on its periphery, and reflect, I believe, a consensus (with some exceptions) newly formed within the past few days.

2. *Not « Hungarian » but Piecemeal*

The Soviet reform has been the opposite of the Hungarian: not once for all on a date, but gradual and tentative. Indeed it has at times, until Brezhnev died, reminded one of Polish reform before Jaruzelski. This was described by Leon Smolinksi thus: the Polish reforms are like an opera chorus on the stage: they sing, with every sign of determination, Andiamo, andiamo, for several minutes, yet when the curtain falls they are still on stage. And yet again as in Poland, small measures were taken which conflicted with the main part of the structure left standing, and in a few years for lack of political will it was the small measures that disappeared, by a process of « tissue rejection ». This is Gertrude Schroeder's « Treadmill of Reform ».

This reform is different. So radical in its promises yet so hesitant in its implementation, indeed so devoid of a proper general concept, it can only have originated in a muddle. Yet « it », whatever « it » exactly is, has already passed into many draft laws unlikely to be amended, and into severe bureaucratic restructurings in foreign trade and agriculture. It is extremely serious, not in the sense that it has all been put into practice (little has), or that it is technically irreversible (whatever that means), but because the ruler has publicly staked his career upon it. If he falls — and he easily may — it falls too. If he stays, it goes through. None of us experts thought it would happen on anything like this scale. We have been surprised. This is because Nietzsche was right: great men (well, big men) make history (well, a lot of history). The reform is due to Gorbachev almost alone. *Its progress can mainly be recounted as the succession of Gorbachev's states of mind.*

First Andropov appointed him to the Politburo. Already, as a good Andropovian, he believed in discipline, and he had introduced normless links in the state and collective farms of Stavropol krai. These links were, as in the minds of most[1] people they still are, mechanisms not of liberation but of mutual supervision, i.e. a sort of discipline. Under Chernenko, or what one might call the Bourbon Restoration, he chaired the special 1984 meeting of experts in Moscow to which Zaslavskaya read her celebrated document[2] demanding more economic freedom for the individual, and prophesying systematic opposition to it by «certain social groups». When she finished speaking all eyes turned to him. He said «But what can I do alone?». I find this statement highly significant, for 1984 and for 1987 too.

His promotion to General Secretary was clearly due to his youth and to dissociation from Brezhnev. The succession of dotards had brought the USSR into ridicule and even danger; and Romanov was not personally acceptable. It is likely that his colleagues even felt personally guilty about the economic stagnation, and the three dotards in a row; they must have charged him to «get the show on the road again», and given him a fairly free hand. If they had known what he really wanted they would surely not have promoted him. But this multifaceted character did not himself know what he wanted. He learns while in power.

After he reached power he seemed at first to abandon agriculture, his one field of expert knowledge, but continued to press the «large-scale experiment» in industrial decentralization, left over from Andropov and Chernenko. This is what Aganbegyan has apparently called the first stage. It was combined in Gorbachev's mind with more discipline and less vodka. In other words he was an Andropovian decentralizer; the combination of discipline and the market being of course entirely feasible, though Andropov himself had reacted instinctively against it, and manifestly did not understand the issues. Gorbachev also then favoured more investment and better technology over decentralization, price reform and incentives: in the age-old Communist battle between technocrats and reformers he was a technocrat.[3]

Taking one thing with another, it was still possible for me to write, in a note of August 1985, «Gorbachev is a conservative Deng Hsiaoping». But I was out of date, for already in June 1985[4] he was asking for further decentralization and using words that clearly implied the firing of bureaucrats. Then came, in November 1985, a return to agriculture, with the Gosagroprom, the super-ministry that suppressed indeed the jobs of many bureaucrats. But it was not until the Party Congress that Gorbachev really made himself clear (26th February 1986), with his «we need a radical reform». Few supported him wholeheartedly at the Congress, and the general resistance was vast, taking the directions predicted by Zaslavskaya. And so began Aganbegyan's stage two, when Gorbachev demands «Full Khozraschet», admits to himself the political and sociological resistance to it, and becomes himself political about it. Superfluous bureaucrats are given unemployment pay (the first such pay since 1932), secret ballots and multiple candidates are introduced at Party meetings (plenum of February 1987). Also the new enterprise statute is published as a draft law (Pravda, November 1986), with revolutionary provisions for the enterprise to sue its own ministry and a regular and predictable profits tax to replace the automatic clawback of the whole profit residual.

Nothing less Hungarian, nothing more untidy and gradual can be imagined. Not Kádár and Nyers, but Peter the Great should be our paradigm: modernization as the Tsar understands it day by day, not for the sake of the people but for that of the Empire. «Without this reform», said a Soviet colleague to me recently, «we shall cease to be a superpower». That is one Petrine factor; here is another. Gorbachev himself said (Khabarovsk, 31st July 1986): «No-one has any ready made recipes ... we should learn as we go along ... we must not be afraid of advancing boldly, of doing things on the march». This is of course the exact opposite of what Kádár and Nyers did in 1967. It is *process not blueprint*. The Hungarian doctrine, that you must leap from one comprehensive blueprint to the other, has been too long tamely accepted. Nyers' secret committee with its formal blueprint was an unrepeatable miracle; other countries — China too — have been compelled by their internal politics to go about it piecemeal. Gorbachev's «muddle» is partly caused by resistance within the Politburo. There was none in Hungary.

3. *Spirit not Mechanism*

Indeed that same Soviet colleague, no doubt under the partial influence of Russian nationalism, denied that the reforms resembled the Hungarian one or even the East German one more than superficially[5]; nor even were they like that of Kosygin in 1965; because all these were differently motivated. The present reforms begin at the bottom and at the top simultaneously, he said (which is of course quite untrue). They are *dukhovni,* he insisted many times. The dictionaries translate this word as «spiritual». But in atheistic USSR this is not right: it means «pertaining to our basic morality, morale and *Weltanschauung*», it means indeed *geistig* (and so also not *spirituel*!). Pravda confirms him: «to shape the consciousness of millions of workers; to change their psychology and thinking in the spirit of perestroika (reconstruction), is one of the key tasks of ideological activity».[6]

So Gorbachev's mind is not concentrated on a new *mechanism*. That word too is Hungarian and quite insufficiently *dukhovni*. For him reform is not only a process (that may never stop) but also the building of a new Russia — I say Russia advisedly, because his minority policy seems very Russophile.[7] *This,* not «plan vs market», is his obsession. So since the old Russia was bureaucratic and bureaucracy is bad, the new Russia *may well, presumably,* have to adopt many elements of the market. The market is a mere instrument, if another one looked better it would certainly be abandoned. No wonder there is no cut-and-dried reform concept.

If the reforms go through, and growth is not accelerated, Gorbachev will of course have to go. If they are rejected he has said he will choose to go and it is very probable he will be thrown out in the process of rejection. But as we see below growth is quite possible without reform; moreover a politician is a politician, and he may choose shamefacedly to survive on a compromise, claiming that higher growth has resulted from the application of partial changes. So important is growth and so little popular or Party demand is there for the anti-Marxist, inconvenient and personally risky market!

4. *The Market and Growth*

The main purely economic question is, if the reforms go through — and I think they will — will this of itself accelerate growth? This is too quickly assumed. The guide-lines for answering this question have long been laid down in Sovietology, and are not specially pro-market:

(i) The increased adaptation of the goods profile to cost and consumer demand (more optimal resource allocation) is a once-for-all effect. We benefit, *in a manner undetectable by any statistic,* from the market-induced improvement when it happens. But thereafter it has happened, and that is that. Our welfare has been permanently raised, but its rate of growth depends, before and after the event, only on the growth of outputs as normally measured.

(ii) Then there is the smoother flow of supplies to factories and farms, and the cessation of planner's tension. This is not the same thing as incorrect proportions between final goods, and the neo-classical micro-economics does not observe it from its lofty cloud. The factory manager's supply problem would be solved by free wholesale trade and the abolition of the Gossnab. This is perhaps the greatest of all the inefficiencies of the Soviet system. But its abolition too would be a once-for-all gain, however great.

(iii) The same must be said of greater labour discipline. «Our» welfare — i.e. as consumers — is raised by the greater output when discipline improves, but that is that, this too is a once-for-all effect. Growth thereafter will start from this higher base, and be no easier than before. Then too labour discipline imposes costs on workers, which they may or may not consider to be outweighed by their greater welfare. They will surely not do so in the short run, and that is one of Gorbachev's troubles. Another is that it is human nature to succumb to backsliding in matters of discipline. Some of the gain will be lost.[8]

(iv) More important are those changes that are not once-for-all: an increase in the volume of investment, for instance. If a population becomes richer for any reason, whether once-for-all or otherwise, it is able to invest more each year thereafter, and so to raise the growth rate of its income. We have to admit that all three of our once-for-all effects can be converted in this way into permanent accelerations.

(v) The other, very similar, application of increased saving is to R and D. An increase in this, above all, has a permanent effect on growth, and it is fairly easy to switch money to it out of investment.

These five points may be summed up thus: investment and inventions are by far the main sources of growth. The only *permanent* contribution to be made by more efficiency (the first three points) is the extent to which they improve the efficiency of workers in investment and invention, or the amount of resources assigned to them.

These considerations explain how it is that the rates of growth of market economies do not as a whole differ from those of command economies. The special factors, that affect one type or the other type or both, are overwhelmingly more important; the achieved technological level, the natural resource endowment, the defence burden, the idiotic monetary policy of a particular market economy, the idiotic investment choices in a particular centrally planned one — all these and many more easily outweigh the mere fact that we have or haven't a market in itself.

5. *Inflation*

A lacuna on our agenda: Soviet inflation is of course repressed, not open. It is due to the fact that the population sees very few satisfactory assets which it prefers to cash or near-cash: books, dachas, ikons, gold, convertible currency (the last two illegal). So it adds to its footloose cash enormous (but unknown) sums every year, and stands in long *queues,* which in 1974 wasted perhaps 5.5[9] hours of a woman's week over and above « standard » shopping time, and 1.8 hours of a man's.[10] Thus incorrect monetary policy has lengthened the working week, for queues are work, by 4.3 hours or about 10 %.[11] Moreover queuing time seems to have increased by 2 % per annum in 1974-83.[12]

All data on queues are of course very bad, not least because of their political sensitivity. Definitions, too, are hard to find: what of the shortage of space inside shops? Did the observers count queuing within the shop at the cashier's desk?

If retail price fixing is decentralized prices will be bid up very quickly indeed and there will be very serious rioting. The poor, after all, would rather spend their time than their money. There have already been such riots, above all in Poland but sufficiently in the USSR. Many amateur enquiries reveal to me no shortening of the queues under Gorbachev, so no less reason than ever before to diminish the money supply.

This is of capital importance. Reforms in the retail sector must be very slow, simply for this reason. East and West, far too little attention is paid to it.

It was also pointed out that wholesale prices need to be reformed to rationalize foreign trade decisions. This is a very old point, always valid. It does seem likely that foreign influence will, as in Poland and Hungary, exceed domestic influence on wholesale prices. After all foreign trade has been partly decentralized already: it is ahead of domestic reform. But no reform of relative prices can, granted ordinary human laxity, sufficiently lower some prices in absolute terms to keep the average constant. Price reforms are inflationary.

6. *The Military-Industrial Complex and the Reform*

Readers will naturally not expect defence numbers from this conference. It is our hosts that generate them! But how do, and how should, the military regard these reforms? We may be sure that old Ustinov would have been horrified: he wanted a tightly planned system in which he wrote his own plan; so that if anything was in short supply he, with his priority, could just take it.[13] Whatever their disagreements may have been, I suppose Romanov took the same attitude. It is to this attitude of an influential power block that B.P. Kurashvili[14] tailored his extraordinary reform scheme, with the military-industrial system as a command economy sitting in the middle like a foreign country: reform elsewhere had to be made palatable to it.

Now we have it from the late Thorolf Rafto, of Bergen, that it was stated at his seminar on good authority that Ogarkov, the foremost military intellectual as well as a formidable practitioner, took the opposite view. He wants, it seems, an efficient and flexible economy which could make him sophisticated weapons and above all prototypes (the Soviet-type economy is very bad with prototypes). He also opposed the diversion of the Siberian rivers. True, the military require the water for some of their plants in Central Asia, but (perhaps) they fear that the huge capital cost will crowd out general defence expenditure. A similar snippet of evidence is the article in the Political Commissars' main journal *Kommunist Vooruzhennykh Sil*, 1973. The pseudonymous «Taras Bulba, Ph.D.» distinctly advocates a return to Kosygin's reforms, which Brezhnev has just reversed! He is, we must infer, prepared to forgo the privilege of just taking things, and will just wait or pay higher prices on the spot.

All this is extremely speculative, and includes my own imaginative input. But it does appear that *some* military men are not opposed. Of the present Minister and Chief of Staff I cannot speak. It should be possible for Gorbachev to use arguments like those above effectively. In addition there is the fact of the mixture of civilian and military production in each weapons factory: a thing very unpopular when Malenkov imposed it, but now widespread and seemingly accepted. Can one director work two systems? Kurashvili's proposal is somewhat unrealistic, but it seems that something like it operates in Hungary, as it does for enterprises exporting to the CMEA.

All in all the military are likely to suffer much more from the generally more peaceful and open-minded attitudes accompanying the reform, and from the changes in foreign policy, than from the reform itself. But they may not think so.

7. *Reform is not Necessarily a Primrose Path*

But will the system, in reforming itself in this way, destroy itself? The main problem is the unexplained empirical correlation between freer markets and freer thought. We can easily imagine a total disconnection between these spheres of human life: in Chile there is even monetarism and tyranny — or there was: the weaker partner has bowed out. But under Communism, which as a form of Marxism is opposed in principle to the market, its admission by any particular country is very unlikely except if the government is Revisionist, and therefore *independently* in favour of freer thought. Even under Communism however, greater decentralization and greater tyranny have occasionally gone together: under the Red Guards in China, for short intervals in Yugoslavia, and during the first Soviet Five-Year Plan. That is, cultural and economic policies were alike tough and alike decentralized in their implementation.

Let us now examine very briefly some historical examples.

(i) Yugoslavia, successfully weathering a far greater liberation of intellectual life, the arts and the press, has not on this account destroyed itself. Nor has the market destroyed it either. The Leninist form of government (we can hardly call Marxist a society resting on self-management in a market) is still there. The organs of repression, if not those of day-to-day administration, have hung together. But there are severe ethnic problems — see (iv) below.

(ii) USSR itself did not fly apart during the NEP, which was a market economy with *predominant* private ownership. The nationalities were not provoked in the way Stalin provoked them. The intellectuals were mildly persecuted, but that had happened before and there was indeed a Silver Age of all the arts. Controversy within the Party was public, sharp and open, more so than in any other ruling Party since. Some members feared the political effects of the weight of private capital within the economy, but they were wrong. Indeed nothing threatened Soviet power.

(iii) Then there is Hungary. Certainly here if anywhere the truth holds that if you introduce free wholesale trade between enterprises in January there will be sexual intercourse on the stage in July. And so there is: cultural decentralization has matched economic decentralization, and Hungary has reached « uncontainability at 40% » (below). The question, how is the uncontainable contained, is easily answered: she has been invaded by Soviet troops and is now occupied by them. In addition she has no ethnic problems that are territorially based.

(iv) The result is much greater stability than in Yugoslavia. But Yugoslavia suffers another vast disadvantage: its *ethnic* divisions which are surely the deepest in the world. The ethnicities are territorially based, and the spirit of decentralization has been seized and distorted by the governmental and Party machines in each republic or autonomous province. The situation is now so bad that the state and economy are in chaos, and we have to deal with a confederation, no longer a federation, of eight quasi-sovereign units. One, Bosnia, has retained many features of the command economy. But every such unit grossly interferes in the market. The dinar is not always valid tender in inter-republican trade. Kosovo is in open political revolt. All this is a sad accompaniment — and an irrelevant one — to self-management.

The lessons of these four points are, first, that the USSR is indeed unlike Hungary in not being occupied by the troops of a more orthodox power (say Albania?!); the well-known argument against Soviet imitation of Hungary, *quis custodiet,* is valid. But Yugoslav ethnicity is much more important. Alma Ata reminds us how similar is the USSR. Each major ethnicity possesses an embryo state machine, and could turn itself into a Soviet Bosnia. One thinks particularly, after Alma Ata, of Kiev, whose satrap appears to be irremovable. The Ukraine is a chained, but scarcely a sleeping, giant. His colleagues will surely not forgive Gorbachev a big riot in Kiev; still less an independent Ukrainian investment policy.

The Chinese lesson is more favourable to reform. A strong government with virtually no ethnic problems has raised output enormously, and slapped down with ease the inconvenient cultural and intellectual accompaniments (we must not say consequences) of the market. But this slap-down was not achieved without a change of government (Hu Yao-bang).

The obvious conclusion remains: no Marxist-Leninist regime yet actually fell because of the long-run indirect political effects of introducing the market. Only three such régimes ever did fall: GDR 1953, Hungary 1956, Czechoslovakia 1968. The first two had quite other causes. The Czechs were about to introduce a market, but first they took over their own Communist Party and democratized it. So the Party was not Leninist any more and the régime had indeed «fallen», for reasons far more important than economic. *This* was why the country was invaded. We must not exaggerate the causal importance of economic institutions.

Just as terror proved itself dispensable when Stalin died, so too can intellectual and artistic life, *and* internal Party discipline, be run on a looser snaffle without damaging externalities. More importantly, natural scientists and even technicians and bureaucrats are «intellectuals», whatever that precisely means: or at least demi-intellectuals. They have always had much more professional freedom than, say, economists or poets; but never enough. Where the latter gain a lot from the indirect «accompaniments» of reform, the former gain only a little, having less left to gain. But their gain helps R and D, which do at present greatly suffer from Stalinist habits of control.

All in all, the reform will be very substantial indeed if Gorbachev lasts. But what is substantial? Let us sum it in abstract and indeed indefinable terms. A 5 % economic reform will be like Kosygin in 1965 or Poland until Jaruzelski: there will be «tissue rejection». A 20 % economic reform will stick and be socio-politically stable, as in Bulgaria and the GDR today. But a 40 % economic reform will be uncontainable, and at this level we are out of economics into political economy. In technical economic/administrative/legal terms such a reform presents no insoluble problems of self-consistency, workability or inadequate performance[15], as Hungary shows. But it will infect the whole «superstructure»: ideology, Party control, Party life, literature, the arts, the press, the law, civil rights, everything. It will put and end, in a decade or so, to Soviet power (bear in mind the ethnic complication and the absence of an «Albanian» occupying force).

Therefore, whatever Gorbachev thinks or wants, there should in the end be only a 20 % economic reform. So probably that is what there will be: and the fact of a slightly more open society and a slightly more efficient economy will not hurt the original Leninist grand design.

Notes

1. In his Tallinn walkabout, report on TV only (18th Feburary 1987; cf. BBC Summary of World Broadcasts SU/8947/C/13 of 20th February) he seemed to support family links, or even just families. It cannot be said how he thought about that when he was in Stavropol. He certainly said (*Kommunist*, 2/1976, p. 36) nothing about it at the time.

2. Leaked to the West by Aganbegyan himself, it is said, for which Chernenko mildly punished him - and certainly he was temporarily moved to an institute of textile research. My story of Gorbachev's words is from two Hungarian sources. For Zaslavskaya's text see *Survey,* London, Spring, 1984.

3. Cf. Thane Gustafson and Dawn Mann's excellent «Gorbachev's First Year» in *Problems of Communism,* June 1986.

4. *Pravda,* 13th June 1985.

4a. This foolish proposal has been dropped from the actual regulations.

5. But Alan Smith (London University) told us that the joint venture law is a virtual translation of the Romanian one.

6. Leader of 15th April 1987, on the Central Committee's draft on «The Reconstruction of the System of Political and Economic Education of the Toilers».

7. Cf. his many speeches on his Baltic tour in *Pravda,* Feb. 1987, summarized and analysed in Radio Free Europe, *Baltic Area/2,* 20th March 1987.

8. There is a sectoral guesstimate of the effects of better discipline in Kontorovich, «Discipline and Growth in the Soviet Economy» in *Problems of Communism,* December 1985.

9. S. Pravdin, *Razvitie Neproizvodstvennoi Sfery...,* Moscow 1976, p. 110; I have deducted arbitrarily 2 hours as an *international* standard from Pravdin's 7.5 for «normal» shopping and queuing time, and assumed a six-day shopping week. Hedrick Smith, *The Russians,* London, Times Books, 1976, p. 87, puts 12 hours.

10. The male-female ratio is from Alexander Szalai, *The Use of Time,* The Hague 1972, the section on Pskov. His total for women is about five hours shopping and queuing. In 1966 repressed inflation was lower, and there should have been at any rate some growth of queuing time by 1974.

11. Cf. P. Wiles in ed. Werner Gumpel, *Das Leben in den Kommunistischen Staaten,* Hanns-Martin Schleyer Stiftung, BRD 1985, p. 55.

12. Cf. Aage here: 30 bn. and 37 bn. hours p.a. for «shopping» (the search for what is required and queuing) for the whole population — E. Novikova, *Pravda,* 9th June 1984, p. 3, col. 7; she says «in the last ten years».

13. Alexander Yanov, *Détente After Brezhnev,* University of California, Berkeley, 1977, pp. 22-30, is particularly graphic.

14. In *Sovetskoye Gosudarstvo i Pravo,* 6/1982 and many subsequent places.

15. But there has been no growth in Hungary since 1978, by official figures. The comparative failure of the only thorough reform in a Soviet-type economy cannot be too often insisted upon.

The Soviet Economy– A New Course?

Summing Up*

Reiner Weichhardt

Having dealt with East European problems in 1986, the NATO Economics Colloquium turned this year to economic developments in the Soviet Union. Since coming to power, the new Soviet leadership has announced a large number of measures designed to improve the functioning of the Soviet economic system. Major programmes, such as the 12th Five-Year Plan (1986-1990) and the development plan to the year 2000, have been adopted.

The Soviet leadership is pursuing a two-step strategy to revitalise the Soviet economy: in the short-term, « hidden productivity reserves » are to be mobilized (e.g. by increasing labour discipline and streamlining bureaucracy) and, in the long term, economic growth is to be accelerated through the application of modern technology. This leads, however, to several questions, e.g.:

— Is Gorbachev willing (and able) to introduce sufficiently far-reaching economic reforms to provide an adequate framework for better economic performance?

— Is the Soviet leadership prepared to follow a strategy of balanced growth, and satisfy simultaneously the demands of the major claimants for economic resources (consumption, civil investment, defence)?

— Will the Soviet economy be sufficiently flexible to react to external disturbances, such as low world market prices for fuels (reducing hard currency earnings)?

It would have been naïve to expect simple answers to these questions during the Colloquium which was held at NATO's Brussels headquarters last April. What could have been expected, and what was in fact fulfilled to a remarkable extent, was the presentation of a great number of theoretical insights and empirical observations which reduce the degree of uncertainty with regard to Gorbachev's economic strategy.

This article tries to provide short summaries of the presentations and to single out some salient points brought up during the discussions, as well as by Peter Wiles in his stimulating general comments on some major issues raised during the Colloquium.

Overall Economic Developments and Constraints
The general framework for Soviet economic development by 1990, as set out in the 12th Five-Year Plan (1986-90), was analysed by Philip Hanson. He underlined that the current Five-Year Plan is a crucial

* Based on an article first published in the NATO-Review, No. 3, June 1987.

element in Gorbachev's programme of economic acceleration and technological modernization. In favouring civil investment at the expense of consumption, and possibly also defence, the Plan includes a marked shift away from the economic priorities in the Brezhnev era. The continuing campaign to enhance discipline and the changes in personnel, together with reasonable luck in the weather, might yield some further improvement in Soviet economic performance but the productivity gains necessary to reach the ambitious Five-Year Plan targets are unlikely to be met. There is no doubt that the Soviet system is less able than Western market economies to introduce and diffuse new technological products and processes. Under the pressure of unrealistically high Plan targets, the element of hidden inflation (in particular in Soviet machinery output) is likely to increase thus disguising to some extent future failures in Plan fulfilment. Hanson argued that the « naïve observer » sometimes wonders whether Gorbachev is not pursuing his new course of modernization and economic acceleration at the expense of his own security of tenure as leader.

An important element of the new economic strategy is a better social policy, including incentives for higher labour productivity, which takes into account the country's main trends and problems in population, manpower, health and education.

Addressing these issues, Murray Feshbach pointed out that Gorbachev has called for a different approach to social issues. Health problems, including alcohol and drug abuse, have become an urgent topic, and at the 27th Party Congress in March 1986 serious attention was paid to population issues. Manpower will become a significant constraint for Soviet economic growth: from 1986 to the year 2000 the working population is expected to increase by only six million, most of whom will live in the « Muslim republics » of the southern tier. However, the industrial plant and the military-industrial complex are located in the north, especially in the Moscow and Leningrad areas. If the additional labour force is unwilling to migrate from the traditional locations, then the need to increase labour productivity in the highly industrialised northern regions will intensify considerably. In order to reduce regional imbalances, the reallocation of investment to southern republics might also become more urgent.

As shown by Silvana Malle, the Soviet leadership has recognised the general need to use labour more efficiently: a number of incentives for increased productivity have been introduced, such as new plan indicators, technologically substantiated production norms and wage reforms.

Despite quite impressive Five-Year Plan targets, Soviet consumption is given relatively low priority in the period 1986-90. Hans Aage argued that — beside housing — the main problems which the Soviet consumer is facing are poor quality goods, and shortages — due to low prices, rather than absolute scarcity. Shopping therefore continues to entail a considerable amount of queuing with a consequent loss of time. Of course, the larger share of investment in national income, which is envisaged by the plans, will limit consumption and, if the ambitious Five-Year Plan for overall economic growth falls short of the targets, the most likely claimant to suffer will be the consumer. This qualifies the large number of official declarations which stress the importance of higher living standards in order to improve family life, to dry up « speculation and uneasing incomes » and, most important, to provide incentives for increasing labour productivity. Although some recent reform measures, such as the new quality control system and the new law which permits certain limited individual activities such as taxi services, hairdressing, shoe and clothing repairs, may have a certain impact on consumer welfare, the main determinant will remain overall economic performance.

Environmental problems, addressed by Craig ZumBrunnen, are creating significant challenges to the Soviet economic and fiscal system. While some improvements were made in the past, major long-term problems persist and it will be very difficult to solve them in an ecologically meaningful way. Included among these chronic problems are water quality and quantity, deforestation, soil erosion, wildlife, habitat protection, and air pollution. Clearly, these issues are causing concern to the Soviet leadership, but the great number of decrees, resolutions and publications calling for more efforts in the area of environmental protection are not matched by adequate investment expenditure. Due to the general scarcity of investment resources, a significant increase in environmental activities is considered rather unlikely.

Energy

The session devoted to energy focused on three themes: the Soviet oil sector, treated by Serge Copelman; the gas sector, analysed by Helge Ole Bergesen and Arild Moe; and other forms of energy dealt with by Jochen Bethkenhagen. Overall, it was pointed out that availability of energy supplies is not likely to prove an obstacle to economic growth during the 12th Five-Year Plan (1986-90).

With regard to the oil sector, the present difficult situation is likely to persist: production from traditional oil fields has passed its peak, due also to outdated production techniques; new fields are far away from consumption centres in climatically unfavourable regions; no major oil field has recently been discovered, and current increments to output mainly depend on smaller fields with low productivity.

The main objectives of the Soviet oil industry will be the rapid development of oil fields in Western Siberia, Kazakhstan and the northern region of the European part of the Soviet Union, and the modernization of the existing installations by introducing both new Soviet equipment and technologically advanced equipment imported from the West. The situation of off-shore exploration is not very promising. The projects so far announced, such as those in the Barents Sea, off Sakhalin, and in the Caspian Sea, have been practically abandoned, due to technical problems and the high costs of exploration.

As far as the Soviet gas industry is concerned, however, the last few years have been something of a success story, with rapid expansion and a marked over-fulfilment of the Plan targets. However, the question is whether this can be kept up during the next decade. The bulk of any increased production must come from Western Siberia — mainly from the fields of Urengoy and Yamburg — but the gas industry may have trouble obtaining sufficient investment capital, unless total energy investment is increased. Because of low oil prices, there will be a growing focus on gas exports. The Soviet leadership gives very high importance to preserving the country's image as a reliable gas supplier and it tries to increase its market share as well as seeking new markets.

Apparently, the Chernobyl accident has not affected Soviet plans for an extension of nuclear power. This situation can be explained by three factors: firstly, nuclear power stations can be constructed in the immediate vicinity of consumption centres which helps to avoid high transport cost; secondly, it is considered to be nuclear energy which can safeguard the Soviet Union's self-sufficiency in the long run; and thirdly, there is a close interdependence between the military and civil use of atomic energy. Nevertheless, the construction plan for nuclear power stations has little chance of being realised because the need to improve safety equipment will lead to substantial production delays.

According to the long-term Soviet energy programme, coal is once again considered an important component. Substantial increases in coal production during the 12th Five-Year Plan are to come mainly from the Eastern parts of the country, which rely substantially on relatively cheap open-cast mining. On the other hand, considerable transport problems are likely to emerge.

In general, it can be assumed that the Soviet Union will continue to put the emphasis in its energy policy on supply. This is surprising because it has often been stressed that energy conservation measures cost far less than new energy production. If there has been no change towards a demand-oriented energy policy, this may be ascribed especially to the following factors: energy saving measures require a multitude of decentralised decisions concerning research, development, investment and organisation — a policy for which the practical instruments are still lacking; energy saving can only be achieved if the Soviet leadership can make up its mind to increase energy prices drastically — another pre-requisite for a new course which is still missing in Soviet energy policy.

Agriculture

Gorbachev, who has been confronted with agricultural problems throughout his career, is indisputably competent in this field, and as Chantal Beaucourt argued, one of his main concerns is the increasing inability of the Soviet system to satisfy the country's need for foodstuffs, mainly due, Gorbachev seems to believe, to the inefficient use of available resources. The agricultural burden on the Soviet economy is best illustrated by the fact that subsidies in foodstuffs constitute 15 % of the whole state budget. Gorbachev's agricultural reform, which — according to the influential Soviet sociologist Tatjana Zaslavskaya — should be a test case for the overall economic reforms, is to be based on three pillars: the enforcement of scientific-technical measures (such as protection of soil fertility, more economical use of water for irrigation and better seed techniques); the improvement of management, in particular by enhancing the autonomy of enterprises; and lastly, policy is to take into account the « human factor » in agriculture, i.e. remuneration in accordance with working results and more flexible organisation of work. Nevertheless, the official attitude towards private activities in agriculture remains ambiguous.

Industry

In a rather critical assessment of the civilian side of Soviet industry, Boris Rumer pointed out that Gorbachev's modernisation programme focuses on the reconstruction of industrial plant, rather than on its expansion. Old equipment is to be replaced with the most modern machinery designed to meet the highest technological standards, but leading Soviet economists see little chance of achieving the planned renovation targets by 1990. The industrial modernization strategy emphasizes the leading role of the machine-building branch with the focus here on advanced technology. Though some dependence on Western imports will persist, the envisaged large-scale programme must primarily rely on the domestic machine-building base, which implies a highly unbalanced investment policy at the expense of other vital sectors of the Soviet economy.

The Soviet leadership has taken a number of steps in order to reorganise the entire system of research and development, one of the most important being an attempt to break departmental barriers which inhibit integrated research. New Interbranch Scientific Technological Complexes have been established encompassing the entire research and development process from basic research to testing new products. In practice, however, there is still a remarkable lack of coordination in the work of the different bodies responsible for developing, financing and implementing technological progress.

Richard Kaufman examined the interactions between the civilian and the military side of the Soviet economy. The Soviet defence burden (defence as a share of GNP) in current prices is estimated to have risen from 12-14% in 1970 to 15-17% in 1982. Such a rising defence burden could cause increasing concern to the leadership, in particular with regard to the diversion of economic resources to the military that could be used for more productive civilian purposes.

A major question concerning the modernization programme is whether the high level of defence spending contributes to the retardation of industrial development and technology. There is some evidence that defence crowded out the civilian industrial component of investment between 1965 and 1985. Soviet weapons procurement absorbs about one-third of the output of the machine-building sector and, in general, there is little doubt that defence receives a disproportionally large share of industrial and high-technology production.

At present, Soviet military support for the modernization programme might be based on the conviction that, if it is successful, the defence sector will be the ultimate beneficiary. According to this view, the military believe that improvements will ease resource constraints and set the stage for more rapid military modernization, particularly as the new weapons of the 1990's are expected to require more sophisticated guidance, sensor, computer and communication systems. The expansion and upgrading of defence plants, which has taken place during the past decade, means that most of the production capacity to support military procurement in the coming years is already in place. Many western experts see the longer term as the real test of Gorbachev's programme. The Soviets will have to tool up for the next generations of weapons in the late 1980's or early 1990's. The demand for new investment for defence plant and equipment will thus rise in this period and is likely to lead to sharpening conflicts over resource allocation between civilian and military industries. As a result, the modernization programme could come to a halt or be drastically scaled back.

External Economic Relations

Soviet economic relations with the CMEA countries were analysed by Fredrik Pitzner-Jørgenson, who argued that these relations are still based on such traditional instruments, as plan coordination and specialisation programmes. As a result, the basic obstacles to intra-CMEA trade (bureaucratic procedures, lack of efficient division of labour) persist. Looking for the «cooperation of the future», the importance of «direct links» between producing enterprises in different CMEA countries was stressed. However, a pre-condition for this is full autonomy for enterprises regarding choice of production, partners, prices and markets. Obviously, there are many obstacles along this road and it is debatable whether the Soviet Union will succeed in overcoming them.

As concerns Soviet foreign trade with the industrialised West, Daniel Franklin focused on the effect on Soviet hard currency earnings of the decline in oil prices, and on the introduction of foreign-trade reforms.

He pointed out that, in the short term, the Soviet Union can survive the «reverse oil shock» without too much disruption, through a combination of increased borrowing, import restructuring (lower grain imports, fewer expensive «megaprojects», priority to modern, resource-saving machinery) and pressure on Eastern Europe to supply some products previously bought in the West. In the longer term, unless the oil price rises sharply again, the loss of hard currency from oil might become a far more serious problem. The Soviet Union will try to diversify its hard currency exports but in its attemps to enter new markets it will come up against Western protectionism, which partly explains recent Soviet overtures to the European Community and to GATT.

But the main question is whether the Soviet foreign trade reforms — devolution of trading rights to selected ministries and enterprises, as well as legislation on joint ventures — will really improve Soviet economic performance and help industry to compete effectively on the Western markets. As far as joint ventures are concerned, Western companies are showing considerable interest, but rather more scepticism mainly because of a lack of clarity in the legislation. The foreign trade reforms alone will not be enough to change the situation thus Soviet competitiveness is likely to depend, above all, on the extent of reform in the economy as a whole.

Soviet financial relations with the West were dealt with by Guenter Boehr who suggested making a distinction between the objective and subjective credit-worthiness of the Soviet Union. He stressed that the objective credit-worthiness is modest and even declining, due, in the main, to the deterioration of the Soviet terms of trade with the West caused by falling oil prices. From a subjective point of view, however, Soviet credit-worthiness is still good, because for the time being, the opportunities for Western banks to invest in other regions have worsened. However, the Soviet Union will remain cautious in accepting offers of Western credit. A particular problem is that there are only a

337

few people in the USSR who have enough professional banking skill and experience to deal with new and complicated financial instruments developed by Western banks. In the long run, the Soviet Union will increase its imports from the West, mainly from those countries which manage their foreign trade on a bilateral state-to-state basis thus attenuating future financial constraints.

Giovanni Graziani underlined that the sluggishness of Soviet foreign trade with the non-socialist less developed countries (LDCs) in recent years is a matter of growing concern to the Soviet leadership. The problem is the one-sided trade structure. The Soviet Union has always seen the LDCs as a source of food and raw materials and as an outlet for its manufactures (including arms). However, new approaches are discernible. Soviet specialists are speaking more and more openly about the possibility of a « redeployment » of some production lines from the Soviet Union to the LDCs, particularly concerning industrial consumer goods. On the export side, the new boost given to domestic production in the Soviet machine-building sector might provide a better potential for the delivery of machinery and equipment to the LDCs. Moreover, there are two additional forms of cooperation which could promote Soviet machinery exports. The first is tripartite industrial cooperation where a Western partner provides advanced technology, the Soviet Union the basic and intermediate equipment, and the recipient LDC, the labour and other resources. The second form is large-scale and project-oriented cooperation in third countries with the most advanced LDCs as partners.

Economic Reforms under Gorbachev: Scope and Constraints

Reviewing the changes in the Soviet economy since Gorbachev came to power, Hans Höhmann — mainly referring to domestic issues — argued that the measures introduced so far are more or less traditional. Gorbachev's strategy of « restructuring » the Soviet economy is essentially based on streamlining central decision-making, combined with certain liberal reform measures in the politically less critical consumer branches.

Though official Soviet declarations show clearly that economic reforms have not come to an end, their intended scope remains unclear. It can be assumed that particular importance will be attached to reforming the price policy, the supply system and the interaction between the planning authorities and the production units. The problem is that an operational theoretical basis which takes account of these aspects, is still lacking. Moreover, as resistance to change has appeared at all levels of the population and among the top leadership, Gorbachev has no ally of his stature and determination.

The future of «radical reforms», therefore, depends to some extent on Gorbachev's ability to obtain adequate support from society. Höhmann concluded that, in general, Gorbachev's strategy of restructuring is not only an economic issue but part of a broader socio-political programme based on a comprehensive revitalisation of socialism in the Soviet Union in accordance with Leninist principles.

Biographies of speakers

Name:	**Hans AAGE**
Current position:	Lecturer (associate professor), Institute of Economics, University of Copenhagen.
Main field of work:	Comparative economics, Soviet and East European economies, wages and income distribution.

Publications during last two years:

«Economic Problems and Reforms: Andropov's 15 Months». *Nordic Journal of Soviet and East European Studies.* Vol. 1, No. 2, pp. 3-43, 1985.

«Economic Inequality and Its Ideological Legitimation in the Soviet Union» (in Danish). Chap. 5, pp. 128-174, in S. Egsmose et al: *Sammenligningsundersøgelsen 2: Uligheden, politikerne og befolkningen.* Publikation nr. 139. København: Socialforskningsinstituttet 1985.

«The State and the Kolkhoznik». *Economic Analysis and Workers' Management.* Vol. 19, no. 2, pp. 131-146, 1985.

«Labour Incentives and Decision Making in Soviet Agriculture». Paper presented at the III World Congress for Soviet and East European Studies, Washington, D.C., October 30-November 4, 1985.

«Revenue Sharing in Different Economic Systems». Paper presented at the workshop on Wage and Payment Systems and Their Socio-Economic Environment. The Vienna Centre and the Hungarian Institute of Labour Research. Siófok, September 13-16, 1986.

«Unemployment: Lessons from the Socialist Countries». *Nordic Journal of Soviet and East European Studies 1986* (forthcoming).

«Labour Incentives and Collective Wage Systems in Soviet Industry», in S. Hedlund (ed.): *Incentives and Economic Systems.* London: Croom Helm 1987 (forthcoming).

Name: **Chantal BEAUCOURT**

Current position: Chargée de mission, CEPII, Paris

Main field of work: Energie, agriculture, emploi en URSS et dans les pays Est-Européens.

Publications during last two years:

«L'arme alimentaire», in *La drôle de crise: de Kaboul à Genève 1979-1985,* ed. Fayard, Paris 1985.

Cultivar, spécial céréales, juillet/août 1986.

Le Monde Diplomatique, novembre 1986, in *dossier céréales,* «La guerre du blé», «L'URSS - l'ombre de l'autosuffisance».

«Les contrats céréaliers occidentaux avec l'URSS ont-ils un avenir?» *Economie prospective internationale,* 1985, n° 22, présenté au colloque des économistes de langue française - Budapest.

«Les perspectives des achats céréaliers de l'URSS, après le 27ᵉ congrès du CCPC» — *Economie rurale,* août 1986, présenté au colloque «La société française d'économie rurale».

«La Hongrie et la Tchécoslovaquie entre l'Est et l'Ouest» (à paraître).

Name: **Helge Ole BERGESEN**

Current position: Research Fellow, Fridtjof Nansen Institute, 1324 Lysaker, Norway

Main field of work: International energy studies

Publications during last two years:

«Soviet Oil and Security Interests in the Barents Sea». London, Frances Pinter (Publishers), 1987 (with A. Moe and Willy Østreng).

Name: **Jochen BETHKENHAGEN**

Current position: Senior Researcher, German Institute for Economic Research, Berlin (West).

Main field of work: Energy in the CMEA region, East-West trade.

342

Publications during last two years: « Die sowjetische Energie- und Rohstoffwirtschaft in den 80er Jahren » (with Hermann Clement). München, Wien 1985.

« Trade ». In: R. Rode and H.-D. Jacobsen (ed.): *Economic Warfare or Détente,* Boulder and London 1985.

« Soviet - West German Economic Relations ». In: A. Stent (ed.): *Economic Relations with the Soviet Union.* Boulder and London 1985.

« Soviet Energy Supplies as a Factor in East-West Relations ». In: B. Csikos-Nagy and D.G. Young (ed.): *East-West Economic Relations in the Changing Global Environment.* London 1986.

Economic Bulletin of the DIW, London: Sept. 1985: « Soviet energy: oil exports stabilise thanks to increased natural gas production »; July 1986: « Oil price collapse causes problems for Soviet foreign trade »; Nov. 1986: « Nuclear energy policy in the USSR and Eastern Europe ».

Name: **Guenter BOEHR**

Current position: Senior Vice President — Head of Foreign Commercial Banking, Westdeutsche Landesbank, Düsseldorf.

Main field of work: Financing of German exports.

Name: **Serge COPELMAN**

Current position: Conseiller du Commerce Extérieur de la France, Directeur Zone Europe - TOTAL Cie Française des Pétroles, Paris.

Main field of work: Coopération industrielle avec les Pays de l'Est dans le domaine de l'énergie.

Publications during last two years: Conférences dans le cadre de:
— L'Association des Economistes de Langue Française.

343

— L'Association Internationale de Droit Econo-
mique.
— Conseil International de Vienne.
— Club de « Hongrie » du CNRS.

Name: **Murray FESHBACH**

Current position: Sovietologist-in-Residence, Office of the Secretary
General, NATO HQ, Brussels (until spring 1987).

Main field of work: Demography, economics of the USSR.

*Publications during
last two years:*

« Soviet Population, Labor Force and Health ».
Written testimony for the Joint Hearings of the
House Committee on Foreign Affairs and Joint
Economic Committe, *The Political Economy of
the Soviet Union,* 98th Congress, 1st Session, Washington DC, Government Printing Office, July 26
and September 29, 1983, pp. 91-138 (published in
1984).

« The Age Structure of Soviet Population: Preliminary Analysis of Unpublished Data », *Soviet
Economy,* Vol. 1, No. 2, 1985, pp. 177-193.

« Health in the USSR: Organization, Trends and
Ethics », paper prepared for International Collo-
quium « Health Care Systems. Moral Issues and
Public Policy », July 23-26, 1985, Bad Homburg,
Federal Republic of Germany. To be published by
D. Reidel and Co., Dordrecht, The Netherlands,
1988. Edited by Robert U. Massey and Hans-
Martin Sass.

« Population Policy-Making in the USSR: Actors
and Issues », RAND Corporation, Spring 1987
(forthcoming) ca. 100 pp.

« Soviet Military Health Issues », submitted to the
Joint Economic Committee, Congress of the United States. Volume on the Soviet Economy, 1987,
33 pp.

Name:	**Daniel FRANKLIN**
Current position:	Europe Editor, The Economist, London.
Main field of work:	European politics and economics, especially developments in Eastern Europe and East-West trade.
Publications during last two years:	« The Prospects for East-West Trade », *Economist Intelligence Unit Special Report,* October 1984.
	« Inside COMECON », Survey in *The Economist,* April 1985.
	Numerous articles on Eastern Europe and East-West trade.

Name:	**Giovanni GRAZIANI**
Current position:	Associate Professor of Economics, Department of Industrial Organization, Faculty of Engineering, University of Padua.
Main field of work:	International economics, with special reference to the foreign economic relations of Eastern countries.
Publications during last two years:	« Contrainte extérieure et politique d'adaptation dans les économies planifiées du centre », in M. Lavigne, W. Andreff, eds., *La réalité socialiste. Crise, adaptation, progrès.* Paris, Economica, 1985 (co-author W. Andreff).
	« Complementarities in foreign trade between EEC and CMEA countries ». International colloquium on East-West trade and financial relations, E.U.I., Florence, 4-6 June 1985.
	« The non-European members of Comecon: a model for developing countries? », Third World Congress on Soviet and East European Studies, Washington, D.C., 30 Oct.-4 Nov. 1985 (forthcoming in Cambridge University Press, R. Kanet, ed.).
	« Capital movements within the CMEA » in *Soviet and Eastern European Foreign Trade,* Spring 1986, Vol. XXII, No. 1.

«Energy in Soviet-West European Relations», International Colloquium on «Les marchés internationaux de l'énergie», Grenoble, 4-6 March, 1986 (forthcoming in Presses Universitaires de Grenoble).

«Commercial relations between LDCs and the USSR», forthcoming in *Cambridge Journal of Economics.*

«Price policy in Soviet trade with the Third World», Annual Scientific Meeting of the Italian Association for the Study of Comparative Economic Systems, Siena, 17-18 October, 1986.

Name:	**Philip HANSON**
Current position:	Professor of Soviet Economics, CREES, University of Birmingham, England (during 1986/87: Senior Mellon Fellow Harvard University, Russian Research Center).
Main field of work:	Soviet economy.
Publications during last two years:	

«Western Economic Sanctions Against the USSR: Their Nature and Effectiveness», in *External Economic Relations of CMEA Countries,* NATO, 1984.

«The Novosibirsk Report: Comment», *Survey,* Vol. 28, No. 1 (Spring 1984).

«The CIA, the TSSU and the Real Growth of the Soviet Investment», *Soviet Studies,* Vol. 36, No. 4 (October 1984).

«Economic Aspects of Helsinki», *International Affairs,* Vol. 61, No. 4 (Autumn 1985), pp. 619-631.

«Soviet Foreign Trade and Europe in the late 1980s», *The World Today,* Vol. 42, Nos. 8-9 (August/September 1986), pp. 144-147.

«The Soviet Economic Stake in European Detente», in H. Gelman (ed.), *The Future of Soviet Policy Toward Western Europe,* Santa Monica: RAND, 1985, pp. 29-51.

«Reforming the Soviet Foreign Trade System»,
Plan Econ. Report, Vol. II, No. 35, (August
1986).

«Soviet Foreign Trade Policies in the 1980s»; *Berichte des Bundesinstituts für ostwissenschaftliche
und internationale Studien,* No. 41, 1986.

Name:	**Hans-Hermann HÖHMANN**
Current position:	Research Director, Head of the Economic Department, Federal Institute for Soviet, East-European and International Studies, Cologne.
Main field of work:	Economic development and systems in the USSR and Eastern Europe, economic reforms, comparative economic systems.
Publications during last two years:	

«Wirtschaftsreformen in Osteuropa: Was ist neu
an neuen Entwicklungen?», in: *Berichte des Bundesinstituts,* 41-1985.

«Sozialistische Wirtschaftsplanung: Grundlagen,
Probleme, Reformperspektiven», in: *Berichte des
Bundesinstituts,* 45-1985.

«Strukturen, Probleme und Perspektiven sowje-
tischer Wirtschafspolitik nach dem XXVII. Par-
teitag der KPdSU», *Berichte des Bundesinstituts,*
22-1986.

«Wirtschaftsreformen in anderen sozialistischen
Ländern: Modell oder Herausforderung für die
Sowjetunion?», in: *Aus Politik und Zeitge-
schichte,* 3/1987.

«Veränderungen der sowjetischen Wirtschaft:
System, Struktur, Leistung», in: G. Simon
(Hrsg.), *Weltmacht Sowjetunion — Umbrüche,
Kontinuitäten, Perspektiven,* Köln 1987.

«The Place of Economic Policy Objectives on the
List of Soviet Policy Priorities», in: H.-H.
Höhmann, A. Nove, H. Vogel (eds.), *Economics
and Politics in the USSR — Problems of Interdependence,* Boulder Co., 1986.

Name:	**Richard F. KAUFMAN**
Current position:	General Counsel, Joint Economic Committee, United States Congress, Washington D.C.
Main field of work:	National security economics and centrally planned economies.

Publications during last two years:

«Navy Shipbuilding at General Dynamics: The SSN 688 Class Submarine Program, Flights I and II», Staff Study, Joint Economic Committee, April 2, 1985.

«Causes of the Slowdown in Soviet Defense», *Soviet Economy,* January-March 1985.

«The Bishops, The Bomb, and Reykjavik», *Kosmos,* March/April 1987.

Name:	**Silvana MALLE**
Current position:	Associate Professor in Comparative Economic Systems - Facoltà di Economia e Commercio - Università degli Studi di Verona.
Main field of work:	Soviet studies - Soviet type planning.

Publications during last two years:

«The Economic Organization of War Communism, 1918-1921», Cambridge University Press, 1985.

«Heterogeneity of the Soviet Labour Market as a Limit to a More Efficient Utilization of Manpower», in D. Lane ed., *Labour and Employment in the USSR,* Wheatsheaf Books Ltd., 1986.

«Planned and Unplanned Mobility in the Soviet Union under the Threat of Labour Shortage», *Soviet Studies,* No. 3, 1987.

«Capacity Utilization and the Shift Coefficient in Soviet Planning», forthcoming *Economics of Planning,* 1987.

Biographies

Name: **Arild MOE**

Current position: Research Fellow, Fridtjof Nansen Institute, 1324 Lysaker, Norway.

Main field of work: Soviet energy policy.

Publications during last two years: Soviet Oil and Security Interests in the Barents Sea. London, Frances Pinter (Publishers), 1987 (with H. O. Bergesen and Willy Østreng).

Name: **Fredrik PITZNER-JØRGENSEN**

Current position: Assistant Professor, Institute of International Economics and Business Administration, Copenhagen School of Economics and Business Administration.

Main field of work: The economics of the planned economies of Eastern Europe and the Soviet Union. East-West trade and cooperation. Intra-CMEA trade and cooperation.

Publications during last two years: (Selected)

« Siberia - Foreign Investment and Trade, a Comparison of Recent Experiences (after 1950) of the CMEA and Western Countries », *Cultures et sociétés de l'Est 3, Sibérie I,* Institut d'Etudes slaves, Paris, 1985, pp. 355-372.

« Comecon », contribution to a special issue of the Danish Slavonic periodical *Svantevit,* titled *Osteuropa 40 ar efter* (Eastern Europe - 40 years after), Copenhagen 1986, pp. 78-91 (in Danish).

« Danmarks varehandel med Øst-landene » (Denmark's Trade with the East European Countries), « Danmarks position i verdensøkonomiens liga », *Management,* Copenhagen 1986, pp. 54-62 and 101-108 (in Danish).

« The Scope for a Policy of Technological Development in the CMEA », contribution to a workshop on Technological Development in Comecon,

Aalborg University Center 1986 (to be published), 25 pages.

« The Comecon Cooperation - Models for Practical Planning for a System of Economies » (Ph.D. Dissertation), Institute of Economics, University of Copenhagen 1986 (in Danish), 227 pages.

Name:	**Boris RUMER**
Current position:	Research Associate, Harvard University, Russian Research Center.
Main field of work:	Soviet economy.

Publications during the last two years:

« Realities of Gorbachev's Economic Program, *Problems of Communism,* 1986, Wash., D.C.

« Soviet Economy: Structural Imbalance », *Problems of Communism,* 1984, Wash., D.C.

« Investment and Reindustrialization in Soviet Economy », Westview Press, 1984.

« Independent Investment Behavior in Soviet Industry », *Soviet Studies,* January 1987, Glasgow.

A series of analyses published in *The Christian Science Monitor* in 1985-1986:
« Reviving the Soviet Economic Engine », 10/7, 1985.
« Soviet Reform: So Far, Mostly Talk », 2/4/1986.
« Soviets' Secret Industrial Might », 9/23/86.
« Soviet Military Spending », 9/23/86.

Name:	**Peter John de la Fosse WILES**
Current Position:	Emeritus Professor, University of London.
Main field of work:	The Soviet economy.

Publications during last two years:

Soviet Military Finance, « ICERD » at the London School of Economics.

« What Became of the Merchants of Death? » in

Millennium, London School of Economics, Autumn, 1986.

Name:	**Craig ZUMBRUNNEN**
Current position:	Associate Professor, Department of Geography and Jackson School of International Studies, University of Washington, Seattle.
Main field of work:	Geography: Soviet environmental, water, mineral, and energy resource problems; mathematical programming and computer simulation modeling.
Publications during last two years:	With Jeffrey Osleeb, «The Soviet Iron and Steel Industry» (Totowa, NJ: Rowman & Allanheld, 1986).

«LP ///: An Interactive and Batch-Mode Linear Programming Package for Apple /// Microcomputers, *Modeling and Simulation on Microcomputers:* 1985, edited by R. Greer Lavery (La Jolla, The Society for Computer Simulation, 1985), pp. 114-117.

«A Review of Soviet Water Quality Management: Theory and Practice», Chapter 13 in *Geographical Studies on the Soviet Union: Essays in Honor of Chauncy D. Harris,* edited by Roland Fuchs and George Demko (Chicago: The University of Chicago, Dept. of Geography, Research Paper No. 211, 1984), pp. 257-294.

«Soviet Ferrous Metallurgy with Special Reference to Policies and Trends within the Iron-Ore Sector», in *Geographic Issues in Mineral Resource Development,* edited by Harley E. Johansen, Olen P. Matthews, and Gundars Rudzitis (Boulder, CO: Westview Press, forthcoming 1987).

«SUMGIS: A Microcomputer Geographic Information System of the USSR», *Proceedings of the International Symposium on Spatial Data Handling, Vol. II,* edited by Duane Marble, Kurt Brassel, Donna Peuquet and Haruko Kishimoto (Zürich: Geographisches Institut, Abteilung

Kartographie/EDV, Universität Zürich-Irchel, 1984), pp. 449-464.

With Marjorie Risman, « A Cursory Review of American Water Quality Planning and Conservation Literature: 1974-1983 », (forthcoming late 1986 or early 1987 in Russian by Akademiya Nauk SSR, Institut geografii).

Impression Malvaux, Bruxelles